Where the Negroes Are Masters

Where the Negroes Are Masters

An African Port in the Era of the Slave Trade

Randy J. Sparks

Harvard University Press

Cambridge, Massachusetts, and London, England

2014

Library of Congress Cataloging-in-Publication Data

Sparks, Randy J.
Where the Negroes are masters : an African port in the era of the slave trade /
Randy J. Sparks.
p.   cm.
Includes bibliographical references and index.
ISBN 978-0-674-72487-7 (alk. paper)
1. Anomabu (Ghana)—History—18th century.   2. Slave trade—Africa, West—History—
18th century.   3. Atlantic Ocean Region—Commerce—History—18th century.   4. Slave
trade—Economic aspects—Africa, West.   5. Africa, West—Economic conditions—
18th century.   I. Title.
DT512.9.A56S63 2014
966.701—dc23   2013012275

For James L. Meadows III

Contents

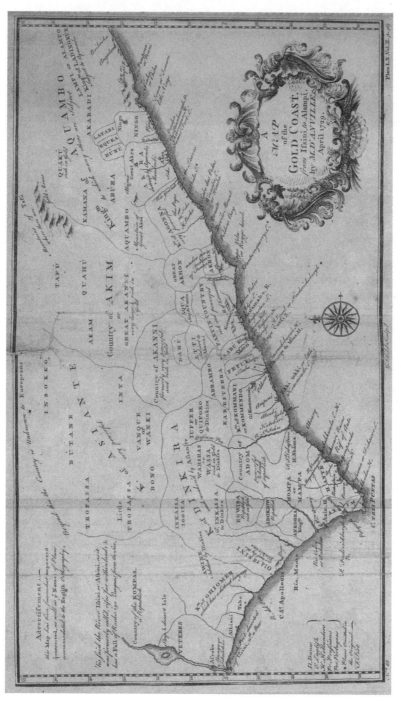

"A Map of the Gold Coast from Issini to Alampi, by M. D'Anville. April 1729." Thomas Astley, ed., *A new general collection of voyages and travels: consisting of the most esteemed relations, which have been hitherto published in any language; comprehending everything remarkable in its kind, in Europe, Asia, Africa, and America* (London, 1745–1747), vol. 2 (A 1745 .N49 v.2). Library Company of Philadelphia.

Map of eighteenth-century West Africa and some of the major European forts along the Gold Coast. Map by Richard Campanella.

The World is at present so over-stock'd with Books, that 'tis almost impossible to bring any new thing to Light, unless another new World were discovered; the Countries and People in all Parts of the World, being already described by various Authors. But 'twas an ancient Saying among the Romans, That Africa always produces something New; and to this Day the Saying is very just.

—*William Bosman (1705)*

He is a good workman and does very well to repair the forts, but is not fit to go where the Negroes are Masters.

—*Thomas Melville (1753)*

Introduction

The young Prince William stood at the ship's prow, watching anxiously as his hometown came into view. He was elaborately dressed in the latest style befitting his station—his rich scarlet coat was trimmed in gold lace, and its buttons, set with diamonds, flashed in the sun while the white feather in his point d'Espagne hat fluttered in the breeze. He had been away for many years, had seen many adventures, and had even been rumored to have died abroad, so his homecoming was to be an especially joyous one to his father, who waited impatiently on the shore, equally anxious to see his beloved son once more.

The prince set sail in 1750 from London, where he had been the toast of the town. He had been presented at court and attended a session of Parliament when King George II addressed that assembly. He had been invited everywhere, to grand entertainments like the lavish garden party thrown by the Duke of Richmond at Richmond House in May 1749 to celebrate the end of the War of the Austrian Succession. Everyone of fashion attended that event, including the Duke of Cumberland (the son of George II), the Duke of Modena, and Horace Walpole, while the king and Princess Emily watched from their elegant barge docked at the terrace and other fine barges crowded the river. Handel wrote "Music for the Royal Fireworks" for the occasion. A contemporary etching shows the elaborate fireworks launched from barges in the river and fireworks wheels spinning along the terrace. Walpole reported that all the ladies there knew the prince's romantic story, and many knew considerably more since the tale had been richly embroidered in the telling. Society artist Gabriel Mathias, the son of Huguenot refugees who administered the king's subsidies to the Royal Academy, painted the prince's portrait, showing him dressed in his rich silks and satins, and the popular *Gentleman's Magazine* reproduced it in mezzotint for its interested readers.

The emotional high point of the prince's stay in London came when he attended a performance of *Oroonoko,* the stage version of Aphra Behn's celebrated tale of an African prince enslaved in Surinam. Adapted for the stage by Thomas Southerne, the play was among the most popular of the day. It tells the story of an African prince named Oroonoko, who has been kidnapped by the unscrupulous captain of a slave ship and brought to Surinam, then under British control. In the play, one character is incredulous: "What, steal a prince out of his own country! Impossible!" But the captain describes how he lured the prince and his companions on board his ship, plied them with alcohol, clapped them in chains when they were too intoxicated to resist, and sailed away with them. The captain had planned to carry Oroonoko to England to put him on display there, but the prince was too troublesome, so he sold him into slavery instead. Oroonoko found a good master, helped save the colony from an Indian attack, and then found his wife, Imoinda, who had also been captured and sold into slavery. As the play reached its emotional climax, where Oroonoko is forced to take Imoinda's life, the prince was overcome with emotion and fled from the theater. The audience watched the prince as intently as the actors on stage, and when he ran from the theater in tears, there was not a dry eye in the house.

Why was the prince so moved by this implausible tale? Because in many ways, the story mirrored his own. The prince was William Ansah Sessarakoo, whose father, John Corrantee, was the chief caboceer, or magistrate, of Annamaboe, the principal slave-trading depot on the Gold Coast. In 1747 Corrantee decided to send his son to London to be educated. He had previously sent another son to Paris, where he had been proclaimed Prince de Corrantryn, and since the English and French were vying for Corrantee's support, he used his sons as his eyes and ears in London and Paris. Corrantee entrusted his son to the captain of a British slave ship, who was to take William Ansah to London after selling his slave cargo in Barbados. But rather than deliver William Ansah safely to London, he sold him into slavery and reported that he had died on the Middle Passage. The captain himself died a short time later, and William Ansah's fate was unknown to his father until several years later, when an African sailor from Annamaboe saw William Ansah in Barbados and reported that he was alive and well. The British, eager to win Corrantee's favor and restore the damage the loss of his son had done to relations between them, rescued William Ansah and carried him to London, where they treated him royally as the prince of Annamaboe. After that stay in London, he returned to his home and to the warm embrace of his father, who carried his son ashore through the rough surf to the beach. Days of celebration followed in Annamaboe as John Corrantee and the entire town rejoiced at William Ansah's safe return.[1]

In order to fully understand how this African prince found himself on board this English naval vessel, it is necessary to explain the rise of Annamaboe as an important Atlantic port. Annamaboe, as it was known across the early modern British Atlantic World, is located on the Gold Coast of West Africa and known today as Anomabu, Ghana.[2] Even a focus on a relatively small port like Annamaboe reveals a vast and complex world in motion. Almost no aspect of life in the town escaped the influence exerted by the confluence of Africa, Europe, and the Americas—agriculture, settlement, warfare, economic life, family relationships, goods, trade, and culture were all impacted as Annamaboe and the Gold Coast were drawn into the Atlantic World. Best known as a slave-trading port, it was actually much more than that. It funneled a great variety of goods from Europe and the Americas into the Gold Coast and farther into the interior, and it sent out cargoes of goods and men that found their way around the Atlantic World. By the 1750s the African Committee regarded Annamaboe as "the Key to the Whole Trade of the Gold Coast," and it was described in 1773 as "the Mart for Trade" on the entire coast.[3]

The successful, capable, and wily merchants of Annamaboe were as integral to Atlantic commerce as those of Liverpool, London, Cádiz, Nantes, Charleston, New York, or Kingston. The residents of Annamaboe were traders down to their fingertips. People and their cultural possessions traveled the vast Atlantic World, and many of those travelers found their way to Annamaboe—sailors, captains, soldiers, administrators, and

missionaries all converged on the town. Their cultural baggage varied
enormously, but they all contributed to the town's social, cultural, and
economic life, and the town's "history is the keyboard on which these
individual notes are sounded."[4] This book listens to those individual
notes and seeks to understand the history of Annamaboe by focusing on
the people from Africa and from around the Atlantic World who lived,
worked, and traded there. The concept of Atlantic history has its detrac-
tors, and the Atlantic World has little meaning unless we can see it reflected
in the lives of individuals. Whenever possible, this study emphasizes the
lives of men and women whose collective experience shaped Annamaboe's position in the Atlantic World.

Since Annamaboe was the most important port on the Gold Coast in
the eighteenth century, the Royal African Company (RAC) (known after
1750 as the Company of Merchants Trading to Africa [CMTA]) maintained
a fort there for parts of the seventeenth and eighteenth centuries. In the
seventeenth century, Annamaboe traded primarily in gold and grain, but
by the turn of the eighteenth century it was moving aggressively into the
rapidly expanding slave trade. The Fante first allowed the Dutch to establish a trade factory in their town, and then encouraged the English to
build a larger fort there. The fort looked impressive, but the Fante remained in full control of their town and usually won out over the English
in the many disputes that arose between the two parties. The growth in
trade and the increasingly intimate relationships between the townspeople and the Englishmen in the forts gradually influenced the town's
economic and cultural life.

The RAC lost its monopoly on the African trade in 1698, and that
loss, combined with the continual troubles with the Fante, encouraged it
to abandon its fort in 1730. Annamaboe's capable leaders traded with all
comers as they expanded their trade and influence during the early decades of the eighteenth century. The Fante and Asante wars of expansion brought a steady supply of slaves to Annamaboe, and European
powers, especially the French, began to negotiate with the town's chief
caboceer, John Corrantee, to rebuild the town's fort. Corrantee skillfully
played the French and British off each other before allowing the CMTA
to reestablish its presence in the town. The fort once again brought British administrators, soldiers, and traders to Annamaboe; they and the

Fante traded together, slept together, fought one another, and together shaped a creolized society deeply embedded in the Atlantic World. One of the British chiefs of the fort, Richard Brew, left the CMTA to establish himself as an independent trader in Annamaboe. He became one of the principal slave traders on the Gold Coast, integrated himself into the local society, and became a well-known figure throughout the Atlantic World. New England traders known as Rum Men were major players in the Annamaboe trade after 1750, and it is possible to follow the export of enslaved Africans from the inland markets, to Annamaboe, onto the ships, and across the Atlantic to ports like Charleston where Gold Coast slaves were in high demand.

Individuals from Annamaboe traveled the Atlantic World. Some of them were the sons of the ruling elite who were sent to Britain or North America to be educated. Others were the sons of African or mixed-race women and British men who were sent by their fathers to Britain to be educated before they returned to the Gold Coast. Still others were Fante linguists or sailors who found employment on the European ships that frequented their hometown. While these individuals left voluntarily, many others were kidnapped by unscrupulous slavers and sold into slavery in the Americas. In such cases, their families and their entire community fought to have them returned, and in a surprising number of cases, they succeeded. The residents of Annamaboe were major players in the eighteenth-century Atlantic World, eager to travel, to learn, and to engage with their counterparts in Europe and America and as much architects of that world as any of its other actors.

In the early nineteenth century, Annamaboe's fortunes fell. In 1807 the Fante's traditional enemy, the Asante, virtually destroyed Annamaboe and, with the connivance of the British, enslaved and sold many of the residents that survived the war. The following year the British abolished the African slave trade on which the town's economy relied. The British forts like Annamaboe's that had long sheltered and nurtured the slave trade were turned against it. These were body blows from which the town never recovered; its economy collapsed, its population shrank, and it was no longer a major Atlantic port.

Despite Africa's centrality to the early modern Atlantic World—far more Africans moved across the Atlantic than Europeans during that era—historians have paid less attention to the African Atlantic than to other parts of the Atlantic World. This work is inspired in part by the pathbreaking scholarship of John Thornton, who has done more than any other historian to give Africans the attention they deserve as actors in the Atlantic World. One frequently aimed criticism of the Atlantic World paradigm is that it has largely been framed as a story of European expansionism, the old wine of imperial history in a new bottle, often focused on the British North Atlantic. But that Euro-Atlantic worldview has been under steady assault since Paul Gilroy first proposed the concept of a "black Atlantic" where the Atlantic basin would be treated as a single unit and where blacks would be "perceived as agents" as much as whites.[5] Much of the study of the black Atlantic has focused understandably on the slave trade and its millions of victims, but less attention has been paid to the African merchant elites who facilitated that trade and were as essential to the Atlantic economy as the merchants of Liverpool, Nantes, or Middelburg. A biographical approach can bring these merchants into sharper focus, and allow us to reimagine how they negotiated their complex role as mediators between Africa's interior slave trade and the European slavers and the crucial role that a town like Annamaboe played in the Atlantic economy.

1

Annamaboe Joins the Atlantic World

A NNAMABOE WAS A relatively sleepy fishing village at the opening of the eighteenth century, but within a short time it had become a thriving Atlantic hub. It was the center of shipping and trade for the Gold Coast and one of the largest exporters of enslaved Africans along the West Coast of Africa. That remarkable transformation was driven by Annamaboe's entry into the Atlantic World and by its expansion within the Fante confederacy. The Dutch established a trading lodge there in 1638, but they were displaced by the English, who built a fort in the town in 1679. At that stage, Annamaboe was not an important port for the slave trade but rather a convenient place for slave-trading ships to stock up on provisions before embarking on the Middle Passage. The Asante wars of expansion that began in the 1680s brought a steady flow of slaves to the town and made it a major slave-trading port. Annamaboe's links to the rapidly expanding Atlantic commercial system transformed its culture, economy, and society. The town's capable leaders worked to capitalize on those changes, and they quickly learned to exploit every advantage presented to them. The English expected to monopolize trade there, but they were forced to negotiate the terms of their relationship with the Fante, who operated from a position of strength. The English and Fante sometimes cooperated and compromised, but more often they engaged in conflict and chicanery as each tested the other. While the English chiefs and the caboceers sparred, the townspeople and the soldiers in the fort worked out their own relationships with one another.

Annamaboe was founded before the end of the fifteenth century as the Fante moved from the interior down to the coast, but that date is highly speculative. Its name, meaning "bird rocks," derived from the jagged stones that jutted out of the sea just off the beach and were considered sacred. The countryside was hilly and fertile, especially in the valleys. The coast was rocky and often dangerous to approach by sea due to heavy currents and pounding surf. The history of the town comes into sharper focus with the arrival of the Europeans, though even that early history is somewhat murky. The Gold Coast got its name from the Portuguese, who began inching their way down the African coast in the 1430s, and their rights to the region were recognized in 1455 by Pope Nicholas V, who issued a papal bull declaring the "coast of Guinea . . . the sovereign property" of Portugal. African resistance compelled the Portuguese to rely on diplomacy rather than force. They sent peaceful missions to the states of West Africa and even brought African princes to study in Portugal. In 1482 they loaded a prefabricated castle onto their ships and sailed to the coast of Guinea in search of a location to erect it. They negotiated with a local ruler for a spot on the coast of modern Ghana, where they unloaded their numbered stones and built the imposing medieval-style Castle of S. Jorge da Mina, usually called Elmina, the first of what would become a string of European forts along the Gold Coast. The very name of the castle indicates that the Portuguese were primarily in search of gold, and it was the European lust for that precious metal more than for slaves that drove the fierce competition among the Portuguese, the Dutch, the Danes, the English, the Brandenburgers, and the French for forts there before the eighteenth century. From the perspective of the Portuguese crown, the most important object at Elmina was the giant *arca com tres chaves* (chest with three keys) which held all the gold acquired by the fort and could be opened only by using three separate keys in the hands of three separate individuals. During the last twenty years of the fifteenth century, gold from Elmina nearly doubled the crown's total revenues and by 1506 made up about one-quarter of the crown's income.[1]

Fortunately for the Portuguese, the other major European nations were focused on the riches of the Americas, in the case of Spain, or pre-occupied with internal troubles, in the cases of England and France. The French sometimes preyed on the treasure ships, but from 1480 until 1580 no European power directly challenged Portugal's claims on the Gold Coast. In 1580 Portugal was conquered by Philip II of Spain, and Spain's rebellious Dutch provinces began to prey on Spanish posses-sions around the Atlantic World. Gold shipments from Elmina steadily declined, and in 1598 the Dutch established posts at Mouree, Cormantine, and Commenda, hemming in the Portuguese at Elmina. The rapidly ex-panding plantation system in the Americas also meant a rising demand for slaves, and the trade networks that shaped the Atlantic World began to emerge. The rising demand for slaves in England's American colonies led to the creation of the Company of Adventurers Trading to Africa in 1618, but it failed. In 1629 the Dutch West India Company began its operations in West Africa, and the English reorganized their African company in 1631, setting up a rivalry between those states on the African coast. A 1625 Dutch attack on Elmina failed, but in 1637 they succeeded in taking that prize, and by 1642 the Portuguese had given up their set-tlements on the Gold Coast. The Portuguese left an important legacy, including such cultural changes as the introduction of Christianity and the trade languages that emerged to facilitate commerce. They also in-troduced citrus fruits, rice, and sugarcane from their possessions in the Far East, and maize, tobacco, pineapple, cassava, and other fruits and plants from the Americas. The Dutch tried to establish their own mo-nopoly over the Gold Coast but failed in that attempt, and soon a race for Africa was under way as the Dutch, the English, the Danes, the Swedes, and the Brandenburgers vied for position. They built, abandoned, attacked, captured, sold, and exchanged forts in thirty-five towns and villages along the Gold Coast in a dizzying game of thrones that continued throughout the seventeenth and eighteenth centuries.[2]

The emergence of Annamaboe as an Atlantic port played itself out against this background. One of the Portuguese commanders at Elmina, Duarte Pacheco Pereira, left the earliest recorded mention of the Fante in European documents in the sixteenth century when he referred to fishing

Print depicting eleven of the European forts along the Gold Coast. Annamaboe Fort is third from the left in the second row. This image represents the first fort built there. National Maritime Museum, Greenwich, London.

villages called "Fante the Great" and "Fante the Small." It is unclear whether either of these were in Annamaboe, but they were located in that region. In 1624 the Fante signed an exclusive trade agreement with the Dutch, who built a lodge or trading establishment in Annamaboe in 1638. It was occupied at various times by the English and the Swedes, and in 1679 the English took advantage of Dutch preoccupations in Europe to construct Charles Fort at Annamaboe, making them the major players there for the remainder of the slave-trading era and beyond. For most of the seventeenth century the place was known as a supplier of provisions, especially maize, for slave ships and as a market for gold, though its gold was "accounted the worst, and most mix'd with brass, of any in Guinea." The late seventeenth century was a period of transformation in Annamaboe as trade expanded there. Before this period, the inland Fante towns were larger, more prosperous, and more powerful than the coastal towns like Annamaboe, which had an estimated 6,000–7,000 residents by 1680. Its rapid growth can be determined in part from the number of soldiers in its militia; in 1681 the town could muster about 500 soldiers, but by 1700 that number had grown to 2,000. An early Dutch account described the interior towns as "richer in goods and gold" than those on the coast, and described the inland towns as having "more houses" and being "more populous." They were also centers of trade, and according to the Dutch "they also have wealthier merchants who conduct more trade than those in the coastal towns."[3]

The change in Annamaboe's fortunes was tied directly to the emergence of the slave trade. So long as the economy of the Gold Coast relied on the production and trade of that ore, then the inland towns enjoyed the advantage. Up until the end of the seventeenth century, gold was the region's most valuable export, and the Gold Coast was a net *importer* of slaves, who were needed in the mines and as agricultural laborers. But the Asante wars of expansion, which began in the 1680s and continued into the next century, brought a steady stream of slaves to the coast. Evidence suggests that by the first decade of the eighteenth century, the value of the slave trade was over twice that of the gold trade, at least for the Dutch and probably for other European traders as well. The expansion of overseas trade fueled a different sort of domestic economic growth. The value of the gold trade declined gradually toward the end of the seventeenth century and began to fall more dramatically as the slave trade increased. In part, the decline in the export of gold resulted from the fact that the Fante traders increasingly demanded payment in gold. As the Gold Coast became a net exporter of slaves, it became a net importer of gold. One RAC official on the coast reported in 1773 that gold was essential for the purchase of slaves; "he who has got the Gold is sure to make the quickest dispatch—what the natives do with such immense quantities of that commodity, I know not, nor do I think the most experienced man in the trade can devise or find out." The fast-growing plantation economies in the Americas produced a demand for enslaved labor more profitable even than gold.[4] Annamaboe was poised to capitalize on that shift.

In 1689 Annamaboe was described as "the principal granary" for the Gold Coast. Behind the town's export of maize, a commerce that continued throughout the slave-trade era, lies a major Atlantic agricultural revolution. In his landmark study of the exchange of plants and animals in the wake of Columbus's voyages to America, Alfred W. Crosby Jr. explored the impact of the introduction of Old World plants and animals to the New World. He observed that "the successful exploitation of the New World" by European conquerors and settlers "depended on their ability to 'Europeanize' the flora and fauna of the New World." He focused on the best-known crops—rice, wheat, sugar—but he paid much less attention to the "Africanization" of New World plants that offers an important qualifier to his thesis. Maize came to the Gold Coast with the Portuguese, and mentions of the crop appear in the historical record in the sixteenth and seventeenth centuries. It began to supplement millet and sorghum, the traditional grain crops in the region, and by the eighteenth century it had become the chief grain crop on the coast. On the Gold Coast maize was called *burro* or *aburro*, both derived from *milho zaburro*, the Portuguese name for the grain. The Fante and other Akan speakers along the Gold Coast even described overseas countries as *aburokyire*, countries "where maize comes from." There are five major types of maize (sweet, pop, floury, dent, and flint), and all of them made their way to Africa by different routes. Flint maizes came from the Caribbean and are characterized by a high starch content, early maturation, and brightly colored grains. The Spanish brought this variety back to Seville with their early voyages, and from there it spread to places like Venice and Egypt, and from Egypt along the caravan routes into the African interior. Along the Gold Coast farmers preferred floury maize, which they treated as a grain—drying it and grinding it—rather than as a vegetable to be eaten fresh, as was the case on other parts of the coast, especially the rice coast, where the growing season of the flint variety complemented the rice cycle. Maize could be interplanted with other crops like cowpeas. Combined with New World root crops like yams and cassava, maize provided the carbohydrates necessary to support a growing population and helps explain the rapid population growth among the Fante during the seventeenth century, which would not otherwise have been possible. Henry Meredith, an RAC officer on the coast in the late eighteenth century, commented on the centrality of maize: "Maize, or Indian corn, is the staple commodity of the country, and . . . much attention is paid to the cultivation of it."[5]

Before the introduction of maize, Gold Coast residents faced a shortage of carbohydrates. African grains like sorghum and millet were slow growing and needed ample sunlight and a long dry season. Yams, one available source of carbohydrates, were well adapted to the region's forest soils but were also slow growing and labor intensive. One key to the growth of maize was clearing tropical forests, back-breaking labor that must in part explain why the Gold Coast continued to import slaves in the seventeenth century along with the need for more agricultural workers. The by-product of forest clearing, wood, was also exported from Annamaboe; in 1691, for example, John Gregory sent a canoe "loaden with wood from thence." The scale of that labor may also be reflected in the tons of iron bars that were a staple of the goods sent from Europe to the Gold Coast. In 1680, one English ship carried 32,000 bars to Cape Coast Castle, and between 1673 and 1704 the RAC shipped over 5,000 tons, or more than 400,000 bars, there. African smiths then crafted farm implements like hoes, axes, and saws for clearing forests from the iron bars. Knives were also sent out by the millions, almost 1.5 million from 1673 to 1704, and one important use for them was harvesting maize. Cutlasses were another common trade item; some cutlasses were used as weapons, but others, including machetes, billhooks, and chopping knives, were used to clear farmland. Another important feature of maize was

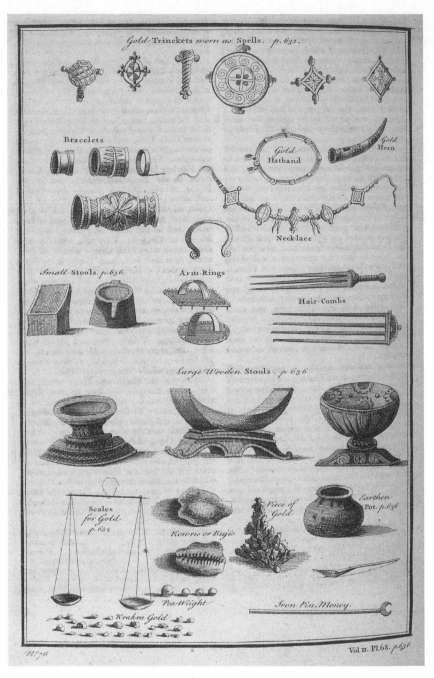

Engraving of items from the Gold Coast. Note particularly the scales used by the gold-takers in the lower left and the cracra (krakra) gold. Thomas Astley, ed., *A new general collection of voyages and travels: consisting of the most esteemed relations, which have been hitherto published in any language; comprehending everything remarkable in its kind, in Europe, Asia, Africa, and America* (London, 1745–1747), vol. 2 (A 1745 .N49 v.2). Library Company of Philadelphia.

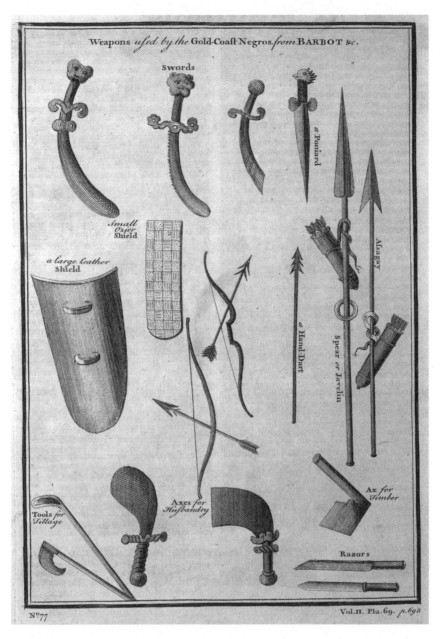

Engraving of Gold Coast weapons and implements, almost all of native manufacture from imported iron. Note the "Tools for Tillage" and the axes along the
bottom row, which would have been used in clearing fields and growing and
harvesting corn. Thomas Astley, ed., *A new general collection of voyages and travels:
consisting of the most esteemed relations, which have been hitherto published in any
language; comprehending everything remarkable in its kind, in Europe, Asia, Africa, and
America* (A 1745 .N49 v.2). Library Company of Philadelphia.

that two crops could be grown in a single season, adding enormously to the food supply. Records from Charles Fort demonstrate how the rhythms of the clearing, planting, and harvesting of corn governed the life of the town. Even major Fante holidays were tied to it.[6]

Annamaboe's growth, the introduction of New World crops, the expansion of the Fante state, and the rise in the slave trade were interlocking processes that revolutionized the town during the seventeenth and early eighteenth centuries. These factors were not only interconnected; they fueled one another. The rising food production encouraged a larger population, which in turn enabled Annamaboe to mount a larger army. That army was able to conquer more territory, which gave them more land, which led to more food production. That cycle continued so long as Annamaboe and the Fante were victorious over their rivals, as they were from the late seventeenth century through much of the eighteenth century. Maize even provided an ideal food to feed an army on the move— nutritious, easily prepared, easily transported, and nonperishable. The growth in population, territory, and military might have necessitated a more centralized and powerful state. The agricultural expansion also increased the demand for enslaved laborers, and the Fante victories allowed them to enslave their defeated enemies. It was safer and more profitable to sell off their enemies to Europeans and acquire slaves at lower cost from the interior for their own needs. Their growing power enabled them to keep trade paths open and to maintain a steady supply of enslaved laborers from the interior. It is important to note that this process was under way all over the Gold Coast and into the interior, where even larger and more powerful states like the Asante were undergoing a similar transformation. These wars were not exactly fueled by the slave trade or provoked by Europeans, as has sometimes been alleged, though they were not unrelated to the trade. Europeans did arm their African allies and sometimes participate in these conflicts in a very limited way, but they did not play a central role in them. In 1686, for example, the Fante came to Ralph Hassell, chief of Charles Fort, asking for lead and gunpowder to fight the Akyem and Agona, which he supplied. He noted that the conflict had shut down trade, and only the fishermen, women, and children remained in the town, but he added, "We hope it will be a good time shortly for slaves." The Fante were victorious over their enemies and reported that they had taken many slaves, fulfilling Hassell's hopes. The growth in agriculture and the expanding slave trade meant more wealth. The Fante and others could use that wealth to buy more European goods, and they could afford to hoard gold rather than sell it to Europeans.[7]

The Fante in the late seventeenth and the eighteenth centuries were growing in number, wealth, power, and prestige, expanding their territory and building a more efficient government. The Fante needed the Europeans as trading partners—their wealth depended in part on that relationship—but the Fante operated from a position of growing power and confidence that explains much of their attitude toward Europeans on the coast. In the Atlantic World, the presence of a European fort usually indicated military might; in the Americas forts were a base from which European states expanded their colonial enterprises and allowed them to control territory. It would be a mistake to view European forts along the Gold Coast in that context. The forts were primarily trade establishments, housing only a handful of men, and aimed more at their European rivals than the Africans. The forts belonged to the Royal African Company, and the soldiers were hired by the company on five-year contracts. As the mulatto population grew up around the forts, they were employed as soldiers to supplement the small number of Englishmen on the coast. The forts also housed a number of enslaved African men and women who cooked, cleaned, and provided for the needs of the officers and soldiers. Europeans paid ground rent for the forts, and it was clear that they were there at the Africans' pleasure. The forts were conduits through which European goods arrived on the coast and through which enslaved Africans left it. The presence of a fort also encouraged private traders to trade there. In addition, the forts were themselves a source of wealth for the Annamaboe elites—steady financial payments and gifts, known as customs and dashes, flowed into the pockets of the ruling elite and the townspeople in general.

The physical layout of Annamaboe reflected its origins and growth, and its thriving economy fitted its station as the most important Fante town on the coast. It was divided into what was known as the Fishing Town and the Pynin Town, also known as the Upper and Lower Towns. The Fishing Town reflected the old economy of the town, which relied on fishing, although supplying the growing town and the fort with fish continued to be a profitable enterprise. The fishermen used their canoes and their understanding of the sea to carve out an important niche for themselves in the slave trade. They ferried goods to and from European ships and moved goods and people up and down the coast and from fort to fort. Almost everyone in the town engaged in an occupation tied to trade: linguists, gold-takers, farmers, market sellers, slave traders, bomboys, canoemen, craftsmen, artisans, and laborers all found steady employment related to the town's growing commercial activity.

The Annamaboe government was in the hands of the commercial elite, whose influence increased with the rise in trade. Through the seventeenth century, Annamaboe was politically dependent on inland towns and played no important political role. The Dutch signed their treaty of 1624 with someone they identified as the "King of Fante," but in fact the Fante were not a monarchy but a confederation, and their highest government official was known as the Obrafo or Braffo to Europeans. The Europeans paid the ground rent for their forts to the Obrafo, but he exercised little power over the independent Fante states. William Bosman, writing around 1700, described the Fante government as having "no King, the Government being in the Hands of a Chief Commander; whom they call their Braffo, a Word importing Leader. He is a sort of Chief Governour, and has the greatest Power of any in the whole Land, but is somewhat closely restrained by the old Men, who are a sort of National Councellors, not unlike some European Parliament . . . every part of Fantyn hath also its particular Chief, who will sometimes scarce own himself Subject to the Braffo." Independent Fante towns had their own "stool," the seat of authority occupied by the leader of their state. Just when Annamaboe made the transition from a dependent to an independent Fante state is unclear, though it was probably in the 1680s. In 1688, Eggin, who was a leader of Annamaboe, became Obrafo, another important signal of the growing power and political and economic clout of his town. One of the leading men of Annamaboe explained to the Englishmen there that "whenever a man is made Braffo he cannot see the salt water," which may hark back to the Fante nation's traditional focus on the interior. In 1697 both the Dutch and the English paid hefty bribes to the Fante to garner their support; the pro-Dutch Obrafo was overthrown and killed by a pro-English faction, which ended Dutch hopes of winning over the Fante.[8]

Below the Braffo were other officials who governed the independent towns. Records from Annamaboe in the late sixteenth and early seventeenth centuries often mention curranteers and cabushiers (later caboceers appear more often). Historian Robin Law defines a curranteer as a ruler of an individual town and cabushiers as chiefs, but the duties of these individuals are unclear, and the confusion is compounded by the fact that both terms are used in the plural in the records from Annamaboe in the early period. In 1686, for example, James Nightingale, chief of Annamaboe Fort, reported to his superiors at Cape Coast Castle that "our Cabusheers of Annamaboe gives your Worship hearty thanks for their yearly customes, also the Braffo and Curranteer." These yearly payments were made to these officials to ensure their support of English interests. But when Nightingale's successor Ralph Hassell reported similar payments in 1686, he referred to "the Capushers of Annamaboe" and "the Braffo and Quareenterrs [Curranteers]." Hassell might have referred to payments to curranteers outside Annamaboe, but that is not clear from the record. The English also referred to captains who were appointed to "look after the white men" in Annamaboe. These men may have gotten their titles from serving as captains of the local militia companies, called *bendefoes*. At the end of the seventeenth century, one of the caboceers of Annamaboe, Bonnishee, seemed to exercise more authority than the others. In 1695, for example, William Ronan, chief of Charles Fort, referred to "Old Bonnyshee, on whom depends the whole management of this country." By the eighteenth century, the records regularly refer to the town's chief caboceer, and the title of curranteer largely disappears from the records, as do references to captains.[9] This change could reflect the growing independence and power of the town and a decline in the authority of the Braffo over its affairs, and/or the growing authority of the caboceers over the town.

The Fante welcomed European traders, and even though they allowed and encouraged the English to build a fort at Annamaboe, they were not subject to them in any way. Europeans often bristled at their inferior status and at the Fante's assertion of their power and authority, and the seventeenth-century records show the English and the Fante working out their relationship day by day. William Bosman described the Fante territory as "so populous, it is very rich in Gold, Slaves, and all sorts of Necessaries of Life; but more especially in Corn, which they sell in large Quantities to the *English* ships: This great Opulency has rendered them so Arrogant and Haughty, that an European who would traffic with 'em is obliged to stand bare to them." He reported that the English at Annamaboe were "horribly plagued by the *Fantynean Negroes.*" That was the European view of the Fante determination to maintain their independence. Disputes often occurred over the payments the Fante expected to receive from the fort, over their right to trade with all comers rather than give the English the monopoly on trade at Annamaboe, and over specific transactions. James Nightingale, chief of the fort in the late 1680s, argued with the Fante caboceers over their annual custom and dashes. In 1686 he informed the RAC that the Annamaboe caboceers would not accept the payments he offered, claiming that the RAC "promised to be larger to them this Christmas, as per your letter in February last; but they plainly tell me, they will not loose their old customs, which have been paid them by the Royall Company." The RAC agreed to the larger payments, and the caboceers promised to serve the RAC "with their lives and their ffortunes," and to "procure slaves and corne." Nightingale assured the RAC that he tried to "keep these people under and not to be ffooled by them." He invited the caboceers to dine with him at the fort as a part of his attempt to maintain good relations with them.[10]

Despite those efforts, Nightingale's relationship with the caboceers steadily deteriorated. In May 1686, they revived an old dispute involving another RAC official at Annamaboe; he had a "long palaver" with them which forced him to give them large quantities of brandy, and he forwarded their demands for payment in cloth and brandy to the RAC. He remarked that he was "much troubled with them." A palaver was a formal means of settling disputes all along the West Coast of Africa, and has been described as "the art of settling matters through talk." Palavers brought together the parties involved in a dispute, such as members of the same household or extended family, members of a community, African nations, and Europeans and Africans at every level. Europeans complained of the long, drawn-out nature of these discussions, and all trade often

Engraving showing the original Fort Charles at Annamaboe before it was abandoned by the British in 1730 and destroyed by the Fante. Note the Bird Rocks in front of the fort and the Fishing and Pynins Towns separated by the fort. Thomas Astley, ed., *A new general collection of voyages and travels: consisting of the most esteemed relations, which have been hitherto published in any language; comprehending everything remarkable in its kind, in Europe, Asia, Africa, and America* (A 1745 . N49 v.2). Library Company of Philadelphia.

stopped during the palaver, but all disputes on the coast were settled through this means, or violence often resulted. Annamaboe, like most towns on the Gold Coast, had a Palaver House, essentially a court of justice presided over by elders, which as a part of its jurisdiction served to oversee credit, debt, and the protection of pawns. Cases between English and African traders often came before it. On May 13, Nightingale notified the RAC that the caboceers "for some time shut up my gates" and allowed no one in or out of the fort. He did not report the cause of the palaver, but another official reported that it was settled on May 18. Troubled also brewed inside the fort, and on June 3 he sent three soldiers who he claimed were "very turbulent and [re]fractory" from the fort to Cape Coast Castle for punishment or reassignment. He noted that one of them, Jeremiah Mitchell, "has made many of the Capushers his friends, who desires when your Worship has ordered such punishment as your great prudence shall think fit, that he may be returned." Mitchell also begged to be allowed to come back to Annamaboe because he "has a child who he pleads will be ruin'd, if he not return againe."[11]

Mitchell's friendship with the local caboceers and his affection for his mixed-race child illustrate the complex relationships that emerged as the Fante and English lived side by side in Annamaboe. Englishmen and other Europeans who lived on the coast often entered into relationships with African or mulatto women known as "country marriages," and their relationships usually lasted as long as the men remained there. The men supported the women and their children during the time they were together and sometimes afterward. Some Englishmen had their children baptized, some sent them to England to be educated, and the grown children often found employment in the forts as soldiers, writers, or accountants. Ludewig Ferdinand Rømer wrote that European men often took native women as brides, and he noted that "under our fort, as well as the forts of the other nations, we have many children begotten of such a . . . marriage. They are neither white nor black, but yellow, and are called Mulattos." These country marriages were regulated under the Danes but more informal among other nations.[12]

Thomas Phillips, captain of an English slaver that visited the Gold Coast in 1694, witnessed a ceremony celebrating a country marriage between a gunner at Cape Coast Castle and the daughter of a caboceer named Amo, a girl Phillips estimated to be about twelve years old. Henry Meredith noted that the "change from adolescence to puberty, in this country, . . . is very rapid; girls become women at the early age of ten years, and boys men at twelve." Meredith further indicated that "on the first indication of the flow of the menses, a female is obliged to walk abroad, habited in a peculiar manner; thus publishing her attainment of womanhood" and her marriageability. Early marriages were common on the Gold Coast; William Bosman observed, for example, that young people were "frequently married before they become acquainted with the distinction of Sexes." The marriage ceremony followed local African customs, and according to Phillips "the wedding being concluded with only giving a treat to the castle officers, and some of her jetty relations, and a cloth to herself, they were man and wife." Typically, the groom also paid a symbolic bride price to the girl's family, a payment that included gold, brandy, and cloth and depended on the status of the bride's family.[13]

These unions had many advantages for both parties. The wife's family and her children often gained access to employment, education, and financial rewards, and these families often became prominent in trade with Europeans. Men gained not only sexual partners but providers. Their wives maintained a house for the family, nursed their husbands during times of sickness, and had access to cheaper food. Given the unhealthiness of Europeans on the coast, care during illness was a major concern, and among the Fante, women were generally the ones to "perform the office of Surgeon, as well as of the Physician . . . Their manner of selecting different roots and herbs, and their choice of them, discover no mean knowledge in botany; there is scarcely a plant without its peculiar virtue among them." Europeans like the gunner at Cape Coast Castle sometimes married the daughters of prominent African traders and thereby gained advantages in the trade. Their children carried the father's name but were reared in their mother's household. They were African creoles, their identities shaped by their European and African inheritances, and they often moved between both worlds. One European on the coast, Mrs. R. Lee, described the racial classifications that emerged from these relationships: the child of a black person and a white person was known as a mulatto, the child of a mulatto and a white person was called a mustee, and the child of a mustee and a white person was called a mustafee. She reported that "after this the children are supposed to be white."[14]

Mitchell's problems did not end with his punishment. He returned to Annamaboe as he requested, but by February of the following year the new chief of the fort, Ralph Hassell, sent him away again complaining that he was "ill humourd," but more significantly that "there is nothing said nor acted but what he relates to the Blacks." By September he was back, but again in hot water. This time the chief complained that he was a "very drunken ffelow" who could not be trusted, and was spending time on a Dutch interloper "on board which all Cabushiers and traders resort." Once again, his friendship with the caboceers seemed to be the real cause of complaint against him. This time, the RAC moved him to another fort. The problem of soldiers from the fort colluding with people in the town was a recurring one. In 1699 Gerrard Gore, chief of the fort, faced a mutiny from a number of soldiers who he caught buying goods from interlopers, hiding them among their friends in the town, and selling them at prices lower than the fort's.[15]

Isolated in a foreign land, eager to learn, to survive, and, with luck, to prosper, Europeans had little choice but to reach out to the townspeople. Simply staying alive was a struggle for the soldiers. Thomas Phillips was captain of a ship that brought thirty soldiers to Cape Coast Castle in 1694; all were in perfect health when they landed, but by the time Philips left two months later, over half of them were dead, and the survivors were so ill that they were "scarce . . . able to carry their fellows to their graves." These men needed the townspeople for their very survival. Rømer explained how European men on the coast found their footing. He noted that at first, a man was shy and unsure of how to act or how to manage his salary. For a time, the old hands in the fort assisted him, but eventually, he had to learn to manage for himself. The first step was to learn at least a little of the local trade language so that he could communicate with the townspeople. Next, he became "acquainted with a Black in the town, who becomes his friend and gives him advice for his benefit." The European's new friend might even lend him a bit of gold to purchase alcohol or tobacco from one of the ships in the Annamaboe Road; his "Black friend smuggles it in to land for him; and the White hucksters it." With those profits he could buy parrots, parakeets, and monkeys, which were in high demand on the ships. By these means, he could increase his salary by 100 percent. If he earned enough, his Fante friend would arrange to buy a slave for him from the inland markets. If the broker who agreed to make that purchase absconded with the funds or if the slave died, then he had to start all over again. But Rømer observed that once "a European has come that far . . . then he can survive." He became accustomed to the native food, and soon he wanted "to have one of the daughters of the country, or keep a black mistress. . . . When the White's Negress has borne him a couple of Mulatto children he cares as much for her and his children as a man does who had his true wife and children in Europe. Some among the Europeans do not wish to leave their family on the Coast even if they know they could live better in Europe."[16] Clearly, Mitchell and the other men from the fort were deeply engaged in just these clandestine economic pursuits, and Mitchell's concern for his mixed-race son perfectly mirrors Rømer's generalized example. While the Fante caboceers and English chiefs of the fort sparred and argued, the men in the forts and the townspeople were building very different relationships, and in so doing, were reshaping the culture and society of the town.

Nightingale's problems with the caboceers continued to fester. In September 1686 he notified his superiors that he and they "were at variance through their insolences," and he warned that he would "no longer suffer the daily affronts as fformerly." A few days later he wrote, "All differences are ended between self and Capushers," but that pronouncement proved to be premature. Later in that same month he reported "several gross abuses per the natives, not sufferable to be borne." He pleaded for "a sufficient supply to suppress their insolencies, and without that the Royall Company intrest and servants will be dayly abus'd." These disputes ended with Nightingale being stripped naked, beaten, and driven from the fort. He was replaced as chief of the fort at the insistence of the caboceers. James Walker, who replaced him temporarily, reported in October that he was "endeavouring to live peaceably and quietly with the natives, but it is not my will but theirs must be done. Their good success in their rogeries has brought them to such a hight that they esteem and vallue a white man as nought, and as for the Castle, they say can distroy it at pleasure. Likewise say no man shall live their as Chiefe but whome they approve of." When Ralph Hassell arrived as the new chief of the fort, he paid out large sums in customs and dashes to the caboceers and curranteers to meet their demands and to restore good relations.[17]

The Fante continued to challenge the English at every turn, eager to establish their dominance over them. By December, Hassell had problems of his own. The caboceers demanded their Christmas custom, and Hassell asked them to wait until he could find out how much they were to be given; "they answerd they would not be delayd." He tried, to no avail, to have them reduce their demands since the RAC had spent additional funds in replacing Nightingale. They were adamant, and Hassell complained that their "insolence is in reality so great that it is not sufferable." In January 1687 the Fante went to war with several of the neighboring nations, and they needed weapons and supplies from the fort. Hassell initially provided them with what they needed, but a month later denied them additional supplies. The Braffo and caboceers then called on their priests to hang "a fittish on the gate that no man should come to trade to sell any corn or any other thing." Fetish, from the Portuguese *feitiço,* or "agent," embraced a complex set of religious beliefs and practices. To make fetish was to perform worship or cast a spell, to take fetish was to swear an oath, to drink or eat fetish was to drink water or swallow a substance made sacred by a priest that was believed to bring death to anyone who swore a falsehood during the ritual, and anything made in honor of a god was a fetish. Disputes were often resolved by eating or drinking fetish, and the method was used to judge guilt or innocence in trials. Evidence indicates that the English merged these legal practices into their own. In 1780 the Cape Coast Castle Council resolved that "the Oath or Fetish of a Native (unless descended from White Parents) shall not be allowed or accepted by us as evidence . . . relative to . . . a European . . . but the Council will allow the Black or Mulatto People's Oath or Fetish according to the Custom of the Country in all Disputes . . . they have with each other."[18]

Every Fante town had its own gods who resided in sacred spaces; those of Annamaboe inhabited the Bird Rocks and a sacred grove known as Nananom Mpow, located about two miles from the beach in the hills behind the town. As the power of Annamaboe grew, so too did the power of its oracle, which came to be revered across the Gold Coast. The fetish or god spoke through an oracle, and priests or priestesses, known as fetish men and women, were often consulted about major events like wars or more daily concerns like when to travel or make a bargain. In the disagreement between the Fante and Hassell, the priests ritually barred anyone from entering Charles Fort. They did so by hanging a fetish on the door of the fort; Thomas Thompson, an eighteenth-century missionary to the Gold Coast, described a fetish as "Pieces of Gold, single Beads, little Shells, and the Teeth of some Animal" that were tied in a bag. While some Europeans on the coast laughed at the practice, others were "much afraid of them."[19]

Hassell knew that the fort could not survive without supplies from Annamaboe and therefore had to make concessions to have the fetish removed. He wrote the RAC that he "was forced to give the Braffo and Cabushers to take it down againe 2 lead barrs and ½ barrel of powder and a pintadoe [an East Indian batik cloth] that we might not be debard the liberty of people to bring refreshments to sustain us, which is granted, and people have the liberty of free egress and regress." Like Nightingale, he argued when the caboceers demanded their "usuall custom . . . at their putting their corne in the grounde," but because of their "hideous taunts" he gave in to their demands. When the RAC questioned that payment, the Fante instructed them to look in the original contract for the fort where it had been specified. Within a week the Corranteers were demanding similar payments and threatened to expel Hassell if he did not pay them. The following month they again threatened to take their trade elsewhere because he refused to accept their cracra money. Cracra money was small bits of adulterated gold, widely circulated on the coast. The Fante warned Hassell that "no English men should tarry here." On July 27, 1687, the caboceers ordered the Annamaboe bendefoes, the militia, to bar Hassell from entering the fort unless he paid three cases of spirits and half a barrel of powder, and later that month they demanded dashes for cutting their sorghum and millet, known as small corn. Hassell replied that he knew of no precedent for such a payment and refused. They suggested that he contact the RAC to request the gift, and if the RAC refused then they would pay for it. With that agreement he gave them a case of rum and they left the fort. A short time later, they sent messages of thanks and invited him to join them for a celebratory drink "as it was their new year all Chiefs did use to drink with them." He accepted their invitation.[20]

Once he stepped outside the gate, the bendefoes moved in between him and the fort's entrance. He found the caboceers sitting underneath the fort's wall a short distance away—where they knew no gun from the fort could reach them—and they asked him to sit and talk with them. They began what he called their "long storyes," a series of complaints about his conduct as chief of the fort.[21] Their long stories offer insights into the conduct of the trade at Annamaboe and their expectations. First, they complained that he would "take no pawns, nor trust them," a complaint that referred to the widespread credit system that supported the slave trade on the Gold Coast and all along the West African coast.

James Arnold, who practiced as a surgeon on several slave ships, explained how the system worked:[22]

> It was useful in those Parts . . . to trust such of the principal Traders as were People of Character with Goods from the Ship. . . . But though . . . we intrust the Traders with Goods, with which they go to the Fairs, yet we expect that they should leave us something as a Pledge for their Return. To satisfy us in this Particular, they leave their Children and Relations in our Custody, whom we distinguish by the Name of Pawns. As the traders bring us Slaves, or, in other Words, as they pay their Debts, so these are released. But if they are unable to discharge them at an appointed Day (which Day is fixed for the sailing of the Ship), they are taken to the West Indies and sold.[22]

Pawning is another example of how indigenous African systems were adapted to facilitate trade. European traders held the children of Fante merchants either in the forts or on board their ships as collateral for the trade goods they advanced to them, and the individuals held as pawns were typically the sons of the African traders. Fante merchants took the goods that had been secured by the pawns—the cloth, liquors, metal wares, beads, weapons, and other goods—and carried them to the inland slave markets, where they exchanged them for slaves. Their children were essentially held as hostages to insure that the Fante traders would return with the required number of slaves within a specified time. If they failed to live up to the terms of the contract, the pawns were considered slaves and could be sold off the coast. This practice contributed to more personal relationships between the European and Fante traders that endured over time. Pawns might spend weeks or months living with the Europeans on the ships or in the fort, and as a result they learned English and gained insights into European culture and trade that benefited their fathers and contributed to their own educations, which helped them when they entered the trade themselves.[23]

The Fante's complaint suggested that Hassell was not extending sufficient credit to conduct the trade. He admitted as much in his response to them; "I told them . . . that I could not take pawns, knowing that they do not care to redeem them, and that for severall years Mr. Thelwall [chief of Annamaboe factory from 1681–1685] had pawnes from severall of them and that time the Royall Companyes money lay dead, and so they would do again if I took any pawns, and as for trusting of them I had to my losse done to much." It may be that the slave trade and the commercial systems that supported it were not yet fully formed. It might also be that so long as their relatives were not in immediate danger of being sold, the merchants were willing to continue using that credit. But if Hassell refused to either take pawns or trust the merchants with goods, then the trade could not expand. The situation was far different at Annamaboe by 1715, when Captain Peter Holt reported that "there is no factory on ye Coast that Can live without it [pawning] or differ with their best Traders, I have many times since my coming here taken half ye Goods given for a Slave (after they have been Carryed out into ye town & brought back) & given money for them to oblige ye traders for ye Owners of ye Slaves that bring them out of the Country seldom Come into the Castles themselves, the Waterside People not Suffering them, & when ye Goods are Carried into Town, the Owner wanting some other Goods than the Trader has got from him, to Oblige them such things must be done." Clearly, Holt was accepting pawns, trusting the traders with goods, and doing all he could to meet Fante demands and to expand the credit system at Annamaboe to encourage the growth of the slave trade there.[24]

The caboceers also raised another issue related to the commercial side of the trade, complaining that Hassell would not accept their cracra money. Annamaboe was notorious for circulating the worst gold on the Gold Coast, but if the English refused this widely accepted medium of exchange, then trade would suffer. Hassell countered that if he accepted their bad money it would only encourage them to bring more and that he had to make up any deficit. The caboceers also suggested that the Dutch gave them more favorable terms than the English did, and that the English showed greater favoritism to the Fetu, their enemies who resided closer to Cape Coast Castle. These claims are difficult to judge, but the Dutch were certainly eager to woo the Fante away from the English and did all they could to undermine them. Hassell's peevish response was that the Fante were "less treacherous" to the Dutch and the Fetu were more "faithful" to the English. Dissatisfied with his responses, they ordered him to go to Cape Coast immediately without even returning to the fort. Furthermore, they demanded that he immediately send for an anker of rum (which contained ten and a half gallons) or they threatened to "strip me naked and beat me as they had Mr. Nightingale." They agreed to allow him to go into the castle only if he left his fellow RAC employee James Walker behind as a pawn and if several of them accompanied him. He wisely left for Cape Coast Castle.[25] Clearly outmanned and outgunned, he pleaded with his superiors to remove him "from these diabolicall evill people."[26]

Three days later the RAC sent him back, even though he had pledged "never to return to Annamaboe," and they sent James Nightingale with him to try to reach an understanding. The caboceers were out of town on a palaver, but when they returned on August 7, a two-hour meeting ensued in which they reiterated their complaints. They charged him with "having spoiled the country," they refused to accept his oversight of the fort, and they demanded that he and Nightingale depart. They had no choice but to comply, and they requested a canoe from Cape Coast Castle. The caboceers insisted that they would accept anyone else the RAC chose to send. Hassell warned that the fort was in a bad state of repair, which contributed to the problem, and he asserted that the caboceers had "growne to such a height that unless speedily suppression this place will not be long tenable." Despite their orders to stay put, Nightingale left the following morning, and Hassell reported that "since the departure of Mr. Nightingale all the Cabusheers of this place have been with a full cry, why did I not goe with him as I came with him. I told them he went contrary to your orders," but they would not allow him to remain until a canoe arrived, so he was "forced to foot it all the way." Once he was gone, James Walker was left in charge. He reported that the caboceers were "impatient for a new chief . . . they offer no abuse, but continue their visitts every morning." In the end, they once again accepted James Nightingale, and gave him a "civill reception" when he returned on September 9, 1687.[27] Walker understood clearly that "it is not my will but theirs must be done. . . . As for the Castle, they say can distroy [sic] it at pleasure."[28]

These sorts of disputes between the chief of the fort and the caboceers continued to occur periodically, each of them a test of the relative strength of each party and each helping to define the terms of their relationship. In June 1691 John Gregory became chief at Annamaboe and immediately found himself embroiled in a dispute with Bonnishee, the chief caboceer. The month before Gregory's arrival Bonnishee and the previous chief, John Bloome, had differed over the price of maize, and Bonnishee notified Bloome that no maize would be sold unless they met the price he demanded. Gregory held palavers with Bonnishee and the other caboceers in an effort to lower prices and acquire maize, but they were steadfast. The RAC also remained adamant that Gregory pay less. The caboceers also demanded that he pay the Settling custom, a payment made on the arrival of a new chief of the fort. In addition, the Fante were about to go to war again, and they wanted powder and other supplies, which Gregory was reluctant to advance.[29]

On a Tuesday evening, Christmas Eve in 1691, Bonnishee knocked at the castle gate. The sergeant on duty went to ask Gregory if the gates should be opened to the chief caboceer, who apparently felt insulted that the gates were not opened immediately, walked away, and refused to return when the sergeant opened the gates for him. Later that night, he sent a messenger to ask Gregory why the gates had not been opened for him immediately. Gregory responded that Bonnishee could either come when the gates were open or he could wait until they were opened, an arrogant response that further angered the caboceer, who responded by panyarring slaves en route to the castle, beating them, and barring anyone from entering or leaving the castle. Panyarring was a widespread practice on the coast whereby persons seized goods or people and held them until a dispute was resolved or payment was made. It could be used as a means of forcing a palaver, as it was in this case. It differed from pawning in that this was not a mutual agreement, but a seizure of goods by a creditor or by the aggrieved party in a dispute, and it was employed by both Africans and Europeans. Gregory asked his superiors at Cape Coast Castle if they intended to protect him or not, and he expressed his fears that had he gone out of the castle for a walk, as he often did, then they would have seized him "and served me as they did Nightingale." On December 29 a delegation visited Gregory from the town and offered to settle the palaver for a payment in rum and cloth, but the chief was not in a mood to compromise. Instead, he chose to force a showdown with

Bonnishee, expressing his determination to "make the Cabbosheers pay as well as Bonnishee, who I believe [I] shall get from this towne. I shall keep the gates shut. . . . I shall have satisfaction and Bonnishee to goe from this towne." It is unclear how long he kept the gates closed, but by the end of January trade had resumed. The dispute was not yet over, and matters came to a head in April when Gregory decided to take Bonnishee and four other prominent caboceers prisoner (the others were Eggin, Humphrey, Finny, and Peter Quashi). He claimed he did so because they were trading with interlopers, some English captains who violated the RAC's monopoly, and he complained that one of those interlopers, Captain Parish, was "keeping a white man in Bonnishees house with goods." But he also reported that he had taken the prisoners because he had received so many "unsufferable abuses from Bonnishee and several others belonging to this town," and to preserve "the intrest and honour of the Company."[30]

The results, predictably, were disastrous. Spoiling for a fight, Gregory wrote to Cape Coast Castle reporting that he had provisions to last a month, requested that about a dozen female slaves and their children belonging to the fort be moved to Cape Coast to relieve him of their support, and asked for more gunpowder and "hand granadoes." What happened next is unclear from the records. Gregory claimed that he ordered the Fante who had surrounded the fort to disperse, but "instead of goeing they turned their backsides to it, a thing we think not to be taken lightly by any [that] has command of a Fort, especially knowing how sufficiently we have been abused." The men of Annamaboe were clearly taunting Gregory, and they refused to allow any white man into the town. Gregory reported that his sentinels had been struck and had "hats stole of[f] their heads." The men of Annamaboe threatened to put Gregory in irons if they could take him, and Bonnishee boasted that "the Fort and all that belonged to it was his and he would sell or do with it as he pleased." There is no indication in the record of who fired the first shot, but violence erupted. Gregory turned the fort's guns on the town, and "the great part of it burnt togither with the peoples goods." In addition to the destruction, Bonnishee informed the English "that 6 men were killed and dead of their wounds and 6 more lay so that they thought they would not recover." The fact that Gregory was immediately removed from this post may indicate who the guilty party was. His replacement,

William Cross, found the "place much altered since I was here last." Whites were too afraid to leave the fort, and the thatched roofs of the corn room and other parts of the fort had been burned and would soon wash down if not repaired. Bonnishee and other caboceers called on Cross, who tried to heal the dispute. He "told them that I was come to make peace and recompose all the differences, and for the future no man whatsoever under my command should wrong or abuse any of the Blacks." The caboceers demanded their Settling custom and brought palavers for the damages; Bonnishee helped smooth over the differences so that life could return to normal.[31]

Disputes between the caboceers and chiefs over matters of trade and custom were ongoing. In 1693, Edward Searle, chief of the fort, pan-yarred one of Bonnishee's slaves because the caboceer traded with an interloper from Barbados, and Bonnishee sent word that "he would doe any such thing in spite of me." The people of Annamaboe refused to recognize the RAC's trade monopoly and were determined to trade with all comers. The RAC interpreted its ground rent for the fort as giving them a monopoly on trade at Annamaboe. In 1696, John Rootsey, chief of the fort, locked horns with Bonnishee over a trade dispute, and after the two men argued, Bonnishee said "he will not come againe into the Castle and if he be good as his word it will be both for the good of the Company and our selves that live here. Our white men and the Company's slaves had been abused and beaten by the blacks severall times." In July 1704, for instance, the Annamaboe people seized Mr. Chaignoan, chief of the fort, as he returned from the English fort at Agah. They carried him back to Agah and refused to allow him to return to Annamaboe because, they said, he had not paid "Setling customs nor their dancing Customs." The dancing custom referred to the Dancing Time, a festival of commemoration for the dead that took place in June or July, and the chief of Annamaboe Fort had traditionally paid a custom for it. Eggin, a longtime leader in Annamaboe, traveled to Cape Coast Castle to explain the dispute to Chaignoan's superiors there. The RAC officials at Cape Coast sent Jo Brown to Annamaboe to negotiate with the caboceers, and he was able to bring Chaignoan into the castle and end the palaver.[32]

Out of these many confrontations, the English and the Fante worked out the terms of their relationship, and on almost every count, the English were forced to bend to Fante demands. Whether the issue was the payment of dashes and customs, the right of the Fante to trade with whoever they chose, their right to set the price for their goods, the necessity of the English accepting cracra money and being more liberal with credit through pawning, the Fante won concessions. The Fante used every means at their disposal to force the English to accede to their demands—they shut down trade, they blocked the fort, and they humiliated the chiefs and forced them out of Annamaboe.

These continual palavers and disputes eventually exhausted the patience of the English, who abandoned Charles Fort in 1730. Ludewig Ferdinand Rømer wrote that the English "were so plagued by the Negroes at that place [Annamaboe] that they thanked God to be able to get away. The Negroes then tore the fort down completely and negotiated directly with the ships." He added that the Fante at Annamaboe "have not cared to have [resident] any Europeans." The English decision to abandon the fort may also have been encouraged by 1698 changes to the RAC that allowed any Englishman to trade in Africa upon payment of a 10 percent duty on imports and exports, which gave these traders the name Ten Percent Men. Without a monopoly to protect, and with the trade at Annamaboe open to all comers, the RAC retrenched, but the English slave trade continued to expand, fueled by the booming plantation economy in America and by the Treaty of Utrecht (1713) allowing the English to export slaves into Spain's American colonies. It was only after 1700 that the Gold Coast became a major player in the slave trade; the region saw a "massive increase in slaving" encouraged by strong demand for slaves from the Caribbean and Brazil, though many Gold Coast slaves also went to mainland North America. The best estimates are that 883,100 enslaved Africans left the Gold Coast from 1701 to 1800, and more of those men, women, and children left from Annamaboe than anywhere else.[33] That massive increase in slaving meant a similar increase in Annamaboe's links to the Atlantic World—the routes grew more numerous and well traveled, more goods flowed in and out, more residents of Annamaboe took to the seas, more and more Europeans arrived at Annamaboe, and the wary English and Fante merchants began to consider again the advantages of a closer working relationship.

2

John Corrantee and Slave-Trade Diplomacy at Annamaboe

A MILITARY COMMANDER, a skillful political leader, and a successful trader and diplomat, John Corrantee was the most important caboceer in eighteenth-century Annamaboe. The town's growth and increased importance in the middle of the century owes much to his remarkable leadership. He appears in the records as early as 1734 and is described as "Captain" at Annamaboe beginning in 1747.[1] His name also appears as Currantee, Corrantrin, Corrantryn, Koranting, and Kurantsi in various European sources, and his African name was Eno Baisee (Ano Bassi) Kurentsi. Along with his diplomatic duties, he was also "a very considerable Trader himself in Gold, [and] Slaves."[2] It is important to note that Corrantee was not simply a slave trader, but rather a merchant involved in trading European goods to the interior and slaves from the interior to the coast, and someone with important political duties as well. Thomas Melville, governor of Cape Coast Castle, noted in 1751, "I was taught in England that John Corrantee was absolute master at Annamaboe," and Melville saw firsthand that this was indeed the case.[3] Richard Stockwell, governor of Cape Coast Castle, described Corrantee to the Board of Trade in 1751: "Indeed John Corrantee deserves the name of Caboceer," he wrote, "and a very great one he is, [he] can command a great number of men in Arms whenever he thinks proper, and none of his subjects, if I may so call them, dare disobey him, such is his Power."[4] The British were not alone in recognizing Corrantee's authority and influence; the French were also courting his favor as a part of their goal to expand into Annamaboe. The French also "took extraordinary Pains to gain the good-will of the *Caboceir John*. . . . Neither will it appear at all strange or unbecoming in him, that he accepted . . . these Addresses, or entered into a Correspondence with them; for the *Fantinians* [*Fantees*] were never under any kind of subjection to the [Royal African] Company, even in its most prosperous Condition, but held themselves at full liberty to deal with whom they pleased, and to vend their Commodities how, when, where, and to whom they thought proper."[5] An intense rivalry among the European nations along the Gold Coast continued throughout the eighteenth century, a rivalry that Corrantee often used to his benefit.[6] While it has been assumed that African merchants were the least informed of those involved in the Atlantic trade network, they were eager to learn as much about their fellow traders and the European nations as they could, and prepared to use that knowledge to their advantage.[7]

The exact date of Corrantee's birth is uncertain, though the Reverend Thomas Thompson, who came to the coast in 1751 or 1752, described him as about eighty years old, which would put his birth in the early 1670s.[8] While information on Corrantee's early life is scant, he claimed that it was his father who allowed the British to build their fort at Annamaboe, an important indication that he may have inherited the position of chief caboceer. Exactly how he came to that position is unclear, however. According to Fante oral tradition, the previous chief caboceer died without an heir, and Corrantee was elected to the position because of his wealth and the respect he had earned among his peers. Succession for positions like caboceer on the Gold Coast was usually matrilineal. The heir apparent would not normally be the eldest son but rather the caboceer's nephew, his sister's son. It may be that Corrantee's father had no heirs along the female line of succession, which opened the door to his son. Corrantee is sometimes identified as "John Bannishee Corrantee," and he had a son named Bonnishee, which indicates a family tie with the prominent caboceer of the late seventeenth century of the same name, who was likely Corrantee's father or uncle. A second important insight into Corrantee's youth was his report that "his Father delivered him into the Englishman's hands when he was very young."[9] This information is crucial in understanding Corrantee and his relationship with the British on the coast. The British took the sons of men of prominence into their forts for several reasons. They recognized the value of having their African associates learn the British language and British customs. As one British official pointed out to the Royal African Company, it would be useful to have Africans learn to write and "to Speak English . . . & to become familiar with People."[10] John Roberts, writing from the British factory at Dixcove in 1750, told his superiors that a local chief, "one Tom Coffee who I knew in England Informs me he will . . . send two of his favorite Sons to live with me to learn Trade & English."[11]

Corrantee might have come into the British fort at the time of its construction in the 1680s as a pawn to guarantee his father's support for the fort's new occupants, who would have been busy consolidating their position. Corrantee also indicated that he spent time in Cape Coast Castle as a boy, and he could have been held there as a pawn to guarantee the good behavior of the people of Annamaboe. When Anglican missionary Thomas Thompson met Corrantee in 1752, he informed the caboceer that he had opened a school in the castle; Corrantee responded by repeating "some Letters in the Alphabet, telling me that he had been a Scholar there."[12] Ralph Hassell, an RAC official at Annamaboe in 1686–1687 noted that "4 of the Cabushers [caboceer's] sonns [sons] were sent to me" with requests from their fathers, indicating that the caboceers were employing their sons to interact with the English.[13] It is likely that Corrantee was one of these youngsters.

What did African elites gain from placing their sons in the British forts? While the stated purpose behind the pawning of relatives was to secure the trade, there were other factors at work. Men like Corrantee's father clearly saw the advantages of having their own eyes and ears inside the European forts where they might remain for long periods. One Danish official observed that the children sometimes remained so long that "we have fed their children until they became fully grown." That practice echoed in a song popular along the Gold Coast that said in part, "A little boy lives in this house, but when he grows up, what will become of the entire world?"[14] As Corrantee suggested, African traders and rulers saw the value in having their heirs learn as much as possible about the British and the other Europeans on the coast—their language, their customs, and their culture. Out of necessity, these African coastal elites sought to better understand the larger world that the Atlantic commerce opened to them. The European forts were their windows into that world. Corrantee's remarkable career is an indication of just how important that education could be, and he carried it even further by ensuring that his own sons saw even more of the Atlantic World than he had.

When Corrantee stepped into his position of caboceer, probably in the 1730s or 1740s, he was well prepared for the complex role he inherited as leading caboceer, merchant, military captain, and chief magistrate.[15] While his relationships with the British are better documented, his roles as ruler of Annamaboe and mediator between the Fante interior and the Europeans on the coast, and his position as a successful trader, are equally important aspects of his life story. One of his many wives was reported to be a woman named Eukobah (also Ekua), the daughter of Ansah Sessarakoo (Ansa Sasraku), king of Aquamboo (Akwamu), and niece of the king of Akron. Such a marriage would have been a strategic one in forging alliances with other African coastal elites. The Aquamboo kingdom was located farthest to the east on the Gold Coast, stretched along the coast from Accra to the Volta River, and extended about twenty-five miles into the interior. The kings of Aquamboo came to control trade and the trade routes to the coast when the slave trade with the Europeans expanded and they defeated and annexed Accra. The British, the Danes, and the Dutch had forts there. Ansah Sessarakoo was the Aquamboo king who defeated Accra and brought it into his kingdom in 1677. He died in 1689, but subsequent rulers took his name.[16] One of Corrantee's sons, William Ansah Sessarakoo, carried the king's name, lending credence to the marriage. That union suggests how Corrantee allied himself with other African elites similarly involved in trade with the Europeans.

Thomas Thompson reported that Corrantee "had been a noted Warrior, and kept all those Parts in Subjection to him by the Terror of his Sword."[17] His duties included the command of the bendefoes, the Annamaboe militia, which would have made him an important figure in any Fante military campaign since by this time Annamaboe was the largest town in the Fante confederacy with the biggest fighting force. That militia could be called up to join Fante wars, but the caboceers also employed them against the forts when necessary. These militias far outnumbered the handful of Europeans in the forts, and gave the Fante the clear advantage. The British needed them, however, in their conflicts with other European and African states on the coast, and so had no choice but to arm them. In 1687, for example, James Nightingale, commander of Annamaboe fort, used the bendefoes against the French, and the CMTA once presented Corrantee with a broad sword as a token of thanks for his "late gallant Behaviour" in their conflict with the French and expressed their hope "that he will always be ready to use it in the service of the British Nation."[18]

An important aspect of Corrantee's position was keeping the vital trade paths between Annamaboe and the interior open. To keep a path open meant literally to keep it cleared of the fast-growing tropical plants that would otherwise obstruct it, and also to negotiate successfully with the nations through which it passed. The dramatic expansion of the Fante in the beginning of the eighteenth century owed a great deal to the British, since they relied on the Fante to move trade from the interior to the coastal forts.[19] The Fante acknowledged in 1753 that the British "furnished Arms Ammunition & money not only to take possession of the lands now inhabited by us, but likewise to conquer all those little states around us at present Subject to our Dominion."[20] One motivation for their expansion was to cut off the Asante from direct access to the European forts so that they could control the trade.[21] Competition between the Fante and others could close the paths and cripple or disrupt coastal commerce. For example, when the Wasa blocked the paths through their territory in the 1750s in an effort to stop their Asante enemies from acquiring arms from the coastal trade, the British turned to Corrantee for help. Officials in London instructed Thomas Melville, governor of Cape Coast Castle, "to cultivate a good Correspondence and Harmony with the Fanteens, particularly with John Currantee and in the Prosecution of your Attempt to open the Ashiantee Paths we recommend you most carefully to avoid any Thing that may give the least Distrust or Suspicion of a Design to prejudice the Trade of his Town."[22]

William Bosman, who traded on the Gold Coast in the late seventeenth century, described a caboceer as a "Civil Father" whose principal duty was to "take care of the Welfare of the City or Village, and to appease any Tumult."[23] Certainly, these duties occupied a great deal of Corrantee's time and attention. When Thomas Thompson visited him at Annamaboe he found him "employed in making Peace among his own People, who were every Day coming to him with their *Pallavers*," that is with their disputes and discussions. According to Thompson, Corrantee began hearing their complaints before 9:00 a.m., joined by the town's other caboceers, who helped decide the cases. These disputes were "sometimes very long, and clamorous," which may explain why Corrantee heard them while soaking in his "Bathing-tub" with a flask of rum by his side, smoking a traditional long pipe, "the Head of which reasted upon the Ground."[24]

Annamaboe was the major supplier of slaves on the Gold Coast during this period; in fact, the period of Corrantee's rule marked the high point of that trade and speaks to his ability to keep the paths open and to keep the trade running smoothly. The traders at Annamaboe were widely regarded as shrewd, a description that often took on more negative connotations from the Europeans who were often bested by them. The same was true for Corrantee himself. British officials and traders described the residents of Annamaboe as "insolent," "insufferable," "unruly, and "avaricious," and the adjectives often applied to Corrantee were no more flattering.[25] One British official described him as "a creature in whom no confidence is to be put."[26] When Thomas Thompson set out to visit Corrantee in Annamaboe, Thomas Melville commented drily that "if he can put old John's morals to rights he will perform a miracle."[27] And another official contemptuously portrayed an African trader "to be as great a Villain as even Old John Currantee (at Annamaboe) possibly could be."[28]

Europeans recorded instances of Corrantee's supposed treachery, and these episodes, no matter how prejudiced they may be, offer some insight into his successful ploys. The first example comes not from the British but from the Dutch sources, and supposedly recounts the caboceer's underhanded dealings in the slave trade. Corrantee was said to have had two of the Annamaboe townsmen kidnapped and sold to a slaver whose ship was sailing that same night to the Slave Coast. But friends of the two men managed to foil the scheme by sailing in their canoe to Accra, where the ship stopped after leaving Annamaboe, and offering to exchange four slaves for the two freemen, a bargain that the captain was only too happy to take. Here was indisputable evidence that Corrantee was guilty—the victims recounted spending eight days locked in Corrantee's slave dungeon, they identified which of Corrantee's men had kidnapped them, and they fingered a different set of the caboceer's men who had taken them on board the slave ship at night. They reported that Corrantee himself had been on board at the time, that he had received goods for their purchase, and that they had heard him ask the captain to hide these stolen men. The two men belonged to the family of another Annamaboe caboceer, and, according to the Dutch, "everyone thought if the insulted caboceer did not kill Corrantryn, he would at least take from him everything he had in the world." Everyone expected Corrantee to be ruined since the case implicated him not just in this case, but in a long string of such disappearances where "people had gone missing every week, . . . and no one knew what had become of them." British traders testified that kidnapping was widespread at Annamaboe. One trader reported that he often bought slaves who were brought on board his ship during the night, "every one of them taken in the neighborhood of Annamaboe." He also reported having many boys and girls on board his ship, and "many of them told him they had been kidnapped in the neighborhood of Annamaboe." The British trader noted that these slaves often were not paid for until the ship was ready to sail in case their sale was disputed.[29]

Determined to see Corrantee punished, the offended caboceer sent a messenger with gifts to all the Fante "Big Men" asking them to come to Annamaboe to hear the case and pass judgment on Corrantee. The Big Men arrived on the scheduled day, and first heard the testimony from the angry caboceer and the kidnapped men. Corrantee had to either successfully defend himself on the second day or suffer punishment. Corrantee came before the men and claimed that the charges were entirely false, and as proof of his innocence he offered to "cut the throat of his dearest son." Corrantee seized the boy, who was about twelve years old, pulled his dagger, and prepared to kill him. Horrified, the Big Men and others present rushed to stop him, and "since that time this case is neither thought of or spoken of any more." The Dutch official who recorded the story, Ludewig Ferdinand Rømer, compared Corrantee to Nanni (Anase or Anansi), the spider who figures so prominently in trickster tales from the region, and other stories of Corrantee's escapades confirm that association.[30]

According to one source, Corrantee lavishly entertained the captains of European slavers in his compound, invited them to stay overnight, and provided them with sexual partners he knew to be infected with a venereal disease—he was said to be "tremendously pleased" to learn that the Europeans had been infected.[31] It is difficult to say how often Englishmen were provided with African women. Certainly, some men expected to be. CMTA agents at James Fort on the Gold Coast had difficulties with an Englishman who "because he could not be accommodated with Black Girls . . . treated us in terms very disrespectful."[32] The captain of a Liverpool ship trading to Sierra Leone obtained a girl from King Tom, the ruler of the country, "to use as a mistress for the time being." He was to return her before he sailed, as was "usually done," but instead he "took her away with him." When George Young arrived there a short time later on a navy vessel, "the king . . . complained . . . to me very heavily, and begged me to apply to his brother George (meaning our king) to get her restored to him." The records do not reveal whether or not she returned.[33]

Corrantee the trickster showed himself again in 1762 when he sent messengers to Charles Bell, governor of Cape Coast Castle, complaining that Richard Brew, a former CMTA official and a private trader at Annamaboe, "had used him very ill, & even beat him, & desired I wou'd give him satisfaction." Before Corrantee's messengers could finish their "second Harange," Coffee Aboe, the linguister from Annamaboe Fort, arrived with a letter from Brew in which he discounted Corrantee's allegations and convinced Bell that the charges against Brew were "entirely false." Bell sent word back to Corrantee by his messengers that Brew "had only been too much his Friend, & that I looked upon as most ungrateful for sending me a false accusation against him, & I advised him to make up all Differences, which he accordingly did as he found he wou'd have no Encouragement from me in his Roguery. This only show you what a Man he is, which indeed, I think you must have known long ago."[34] Whatever transpired between Corrantee and Brew, the caboceer attempted to use Bell to gain some advantage over his rival, and while he might have failed in this attempt, his ability to play his opponents off one another to his advantage was more often successful.

Coffee Aboe's involvement in that episode may help explain why Corrantee brought a palaver against him later in 1762. Charles Bell reported that "Old John Currantee" and his son were engaged in "a most Villi-nous Palavar" against Coffee Aboe.[35] It is also likely that Corrantee and Coffee Aboe had come into conflict before, given the important position of linguist in the European forts. The linguist acted as interpreter, but also as a middleman in all negotiations between Europeans and Afri-cans, and a linguist's skills could mean the difference between winning and losing, profits or losses. One English RAC official, who was setting up the factory at Dixcove in 1693, wrote of his need for a linguist "who may be serviceable in procureing trade," a request he repeated in his next letter, noting that "such a person will bee absolutely necessary, upon any palaver whereby the Company interest may bee concerned."[36] The linguist's official duties ranged from semidiplomatic negotiations on the part of the governor of the fort to acting as mediator in matters of trade or in palavers, and the job also gave him ample opportunities to engage in private trade.[37] While the exact nature of Corrantee's dispute with Coffee Aboe is unclear from the records, it is easy to see how the two might have come into conflict over matters of trade and diplomacy. The linguist was in an ideal position to know most of what was going on, and Bell reported that Corrantee and his son "owe his Man a spite, be-cause he tells Truth (a thing very disagreeable to them) to the Chief, & to the White Men in general."[38]

These negative stories, filtered through European pens, probably say more about Corrantee's skills as a trader and wily diplomat than about his true character, whatever that may have been. It is clear that Corran-tee the spider wove a large and complex web designed to ensnare his many rivals and opponents. Over time, that web grew increasingly large and complex, and reached not only up and down the Gold Coast and inland, but all the way to Paris and London. Nowhere were Corrantee's skills more on view than in his long-running game of playing the British against the French at Annamaboe.

The French had established themselves in the area around the Sene-gal River in Upper Guinea beginning in the 1630s, but the trade there was not profitable, and the Senegambian region could not meet the French demand for slaves. For this reason, the French tried to gain a foothold on the Gold Coast, and Annamaboe presented an attractive op-portunity.[39] Why Annamaboe? First, it exported more slaves than any other town on the Gold Coast during the mid-eighteenth century, and its ability to provision ships was an added bonus. Since the British fort had been demolished there the traders of Annamaboe had welcomed all comers, and while the British continued to pay tribute, Corrantee and the other caboceers saw this tribute as "a Customary Duty paid by all Europeans . . . for the leave of Trading," not as some monopoly on their trade.[40] The British saw things differently, and warned the French that "all the Trade on that Part of the Coast in the undoubted Right of the Royal African Company."[41] Corrantee was just as determined to keep Annamaboe open to trade. He "insisted on his own Independancy, & on the Freedom of the Fantins [Fante], who acknowledged neither the English, nor any others, for their Soverigns, & who had always traded, & wd [would] continue to do so, with all Nations that came, & particularly with the French."[42] Why particularly with the French? According to Dutch sources, the French paid higher prices for slaves and provisions, and Corrantee himself received more payments in custom (or duties) from them.[43]

The French courted Corrantee, denigrated the British, and "boasted mightily of the great Power of their King, the Magnificence of his Court, the Extent of his Dominions, the Number, Wealth, and Politeness of his Subjects."[44] In order to demonstrate that superiority, they urged Corrantee to send one of his sons to France to see for himself and report back to the caboceer.[45] For Corrantee, the benefits of sending one of his sons to France to gain firsthand intelligence about the European nation was obvious. In the early 1740s a French captain took one of the caboceer's sons, Bassi, on board his ship bound for France. He began tutoring Bassi in proper etiquette, showed him "great respect" on board, and called him "Monsieur le Prince." Once they arrived in France, the captain took Bassi to court, introduced him to the ministers, and promoted the benefits that the French could gain from the connection. He was enrolled in Lycée Louis-le-Grand, an elite Jesuit school in Paris, where he learned to speak and read French. The French treated him royally, and Bassi "played his role excellently." He was given four lackeys and a chamberlain. When he was christened "Louis Bassi, Prince de Corrantryn" by the Archbishop of Paris, King Louis XV acted as his godfather.[46] A newspaper in Bristol, which was deeply invested in the slave trade, reported that "the son of the King of Annamabo came to take a

View of the Castle and Grounds of Versailles. As the Reception of a Negro Youth Shews the French Court have views upon this Place [Annamabo]; which belonged to the Royal African Company of England, whose Fort there lies in ruin. Orders no Doubt are already given to rebuild and put it in a state of Defence."[47]

Bassi "was sent home in one of the Company's Ships, in a very handsome Manner, and with fine laced Cloaths to dazzle the Eyes of the Negroes, and to draw the Father over entirely to the *French* Interest."[48] Corrantee celebrated his son's return and made offerings to the powerful Nananom Mpow oracle in gratitude, though he offered only a goat rather than any share of the lavish trade goods he had gained from the French. The French government also sent Monsieur de la Cour, formerly governor of the French fort at Whydah, to Annamaboe with Bassi. De la Cour carried with him a cargo valued at 100,000 livres intended to fund the construction of a fort. Until the fort could be built, de la Cour stored the goods with his new ally, Corrantee. The British had no intention of allowing the French to build a fort there. When England and France went to war during the War of the Austrian Succession (1740–1748), British warships forced Corrantee to abandon the French by actually shelling Annamaboe. Without French naval support, de la Cour was compelled to leave Annamaboe for Whydah while Corrantee made off with the French goods stored with him.[49]

Corrantee learned a great deal from his son's stay in France, and it had also sent fear through the British ranks. They invited Corrantee to send a second son to England, an offer he accepted in order to gain further insight into the relative strength of the two nations, and to continue the diplomatic game he was playing. Bassi was the child of one of his enslaved women and, as such, was not of equal rank to a son born of a free wife. According to the British, the son he chose to send to England, William Ansah Sessarakoo

was his greatest Favourite; his Mother was not only a free Woman and his chief Wife, but also the Daughter of one of the principal Persons in the Country. The Youth had been always distinguished by the . . . Affability of his Behaviour, as well as by a graceful Deportment. . . . He had lived for a Time . . . in the Fort with one of the *African* Company's principal

Officers, where he had learned to speak *English,* and had acquired a great Confidence in as well as a sincere Affection for the Nation.[50]

In 1747, William Ansah and his father happily accepted the invitation of the captain of the British slaver *Lady Carolina,* David Bruce Crichton, to take the boy with him to England after he delivered his slave cargo to Barbados. Apparently, Crichton died around the time the ship arrived in Barbados. When the ship arrived at that island, William Ansah got into a boat that he thought was transferring him to a ship for England, but in reality, he was sold into slavery. Corrantee, ignorant of his son's fate, nonetheless blamed the British for his loss and began to favor the French cause.[51] Cases of Europeans kidnapping African elites go back to the earliest arrival of the Portuguese along the West African coast, and posed a serious threat to the trade since Africans often stopped the trade or captured or even killed Europeans in retaliation. Those interested in the smooth conduct of the slave trade were eager to prevent kidnapping and the threat it posed to the trade. Among the Acts of Parliament for Regulating the Slave Trade passed in 1750 was a provision that stipulated that "no commander or master of any ship trading to Africa shall by fraud, force or violence or by any indirect practice whatsoever take on board or carry away from the coast of Africa any negro or native of the said country or commit or suffer to be committed any violence to the natives to the prejudice of the trade."[52]

Corrantee eventually learned that his son had been kidnapped, and he pleaded with British officers on the coast to redeem him. John Roberts reported that when he "left the Coast of Africa in the month of Octr. 1747 John Corrantee followed the Rippon Man of War four Leagues to sea in order to beg of me to redeem his son who had been sold at Barbadoes for a Slave in case of the Death of Mr. Crichton and assured me that he would pay me any Cost I was at in Redeeming him as he sd [said] he was very desirous to see him and . . . I think the said Redemption most Expedient and Necessary and may be of great Service is Consistent with the Character of the British Nation on the Gold Coast."[53] Corrantee made it clear to the British that he could not commit himself to them after the loss of his favorite son, and the CMTA agents on the coast promised to locate William Ansah and return him to his father. One of their agents sailed from Cape Coast Castle to Barbados, carrying a young man from Annamaboe to be a companion to William Ansah, who was quickly located in Barbados. The CMTA paid the man who had purchased him, and they transported William Ansah and his escort to England.[54]

Once he arrived in London, the British showered William Ansah with attention, and the plight of the prince of Annamaboe, as he became known, garnered widespread sympathy and notoriety. The most dramatic moment of his stay in London came when he and his companion attended a performance of *Oroonoko; or the History of the Royal Slave,* based on Aphra Behn's sensational 1688 story of an African slave-trading prince who was captured and sold into slavery in Surinam. The story, adapted for the stage by Thomas Southerne and widely translated, became one of the most popular stories of the day and an important source for the image of the noble African slave. Life and art met at the 1749 performance of the play at Covent Garden when William Ansah—bewigged, powdered, and dressed in his finery—walked into the theater to a standing ovation. The audience watched the prince more closely than the actors on the stage, and when he broke into tears during the performance and ran out of the theater, the audience wept with him. The entire scene was reported in the press.[55]

The prince caused a sensation in London. A contemporary magazine reported that "the young Black Prince of Annamaboe, and several other persons of distinction, were in the gallery of the House of Lords" for a speech by King George II.[56] Horace Walpole observed that "there are two black Princes of Annamaboe here, who are in fashion at all the assemblies, of whom I scarcely know any particulars, though their story is very like Ornoonoko's: all the women know it—and ten times more than belong to it."[57] He also described an elaborate event given by the Duke of Richmond which included a concert and fireworks display; "you can't conceive a prettier sight," he wrote, "the garden filled with everybody of fashion, the Duke [of Cumberland], the Duke of Modena and the two black Princes. The King and Princess Emily were in their barge under the terrace."[58] William Ansah's portrait was painted, showing him in his finery, and an etching based on it appeared in the *Gentleman's Magazine.*[59] Along with his busy social calendar, William Ansah also received religious instruction. Bishop Thomas Sherlock appointed Mr. Terret

Gabriel Mathais's elegant 1749 portrait of William Ansah Sessarakoo. The Menil Collection, Houston, Texas.

(Territ), reader of the Temple (one of two clergymen serving the Temple Church in London), "to instruct the young Prince of Anamaboe . . . in the principles of the Christian Religion."[60] Those lessons went so well that he was baptized in London on November 30, 1749.[61]

The prince's dramatic life story was celebrated in drama, poetry, and in a popular biography. By the 1770s and 1780s, many of Britain's most famous Romantic writers, including William Blake, Robert Burns, Sam-

The etching of the prince of Annamaboe from the *Gentleman's Magazine* (1750) based on Mathais' portrait. Another version of the engraving was also published in separate sheets and sold at 1 shilling, 6 pence each. University of Virginia Library.

uel Taylor Coleridge, and William Wordsworth, had taken up the plight of the noble African slave. The British showed little sympathy for the millions of Africans enslaved in the Americas or for the impoverished Africans in England, but a kidnapped and enslaved prince was another matter.[62] While one should not overestimate the importance of the trope of the noble savage or the enslaved prince in changing popular sentiments, such literary conventions, did, in the view of David Brion Davis, "modify Europe's arrogant ethnocentrism and provide expression for at least a momentary ambivalence toward the human costs of modern civilization."[63]

At the same time William Ansah was being feted in London, Corrantee was eagerly trading with the French, despite the assurances from the CMTA officers that his son was being treated like a prince and the offer of financial rewards. John Roberts, governor of Cape Coast Castle, complained that "the generosities to his Boy in England are of little concern to him and no Avail to us at all." Roberts also warned that they might have been misled about William Ansah's parentage by his trickster father. He had been informed that William Ansah was not Corrantee's son at all, but the son of one of Corrantee's enslaved women and was an infant when he came into Corrantee's household.[64] Englishmen at Annamaboe complained loudly that Corrantee continued to allow the French to trade there while William Ansah was being treated royally in London. They expected that "he will concert proper Measures . . . to prevent their Trading . . . if he does not do we will write home to the K[ing], our Master & Lord Halifax that he does not act for the Service of the English in the Manner he ought and is expected from the honourable Treatment his Son meets with in England." The British officer at Annamaboe reported that Corrantee would not "assist to drive them [the French] away but will & does trade with them & encourage the natives to do the same . . . I might sit down & suck my Fingers for w[ha]t assistance I was to expect from him."[65]

After making their mark in London, William Ansah and his companion set sail for Annamaboe in 1750. The noted slave trader John Newton met William Ansah on his return voyage. He wrote, "William Ansah Setarookoo [sic], one of the African princes, as they were stiled in England, who is on his passage to Anamaboo in the *Surprize,* came on board with me, and spent the evening with me very much to my satisfaction, being master of a great deal of solid sense and a politeness of behavior I seldom meet with in any of our own complexion hereabouts."[66] He arrived back home in a state befitting a prince. A sailor on board the *Surprize* recorded the prince's return to Annamaboe and his reunion with his father:

His Majesty the King received us with all possible kindness and dignity. We delivered to him his son . . . magnificently equipped in a full-dress scarlet suit, with gold lace a la Bourgogne, point d'Espagne hat, handsome white feather, diamond solitaire buttons, & c. The King bore no other mark of Royal dignity than a piece of broadcloth thrown over his shoulders. He carried his son on shore in full dress, under a Royal Salute from our man of war, and the moment he landed stripped the poor Prince, giving him no other mark of distinction . . . than that borne by himself. Great fetes were subsequently held in Anamaboo . . . and one is not surprised to learn that the distressed and humiliated prince did not appear again on board the ship in his undress uniform.[67]

While the sailor assumed that William Ansah's literal dressing-down was shameful, but it was more likely a mark of reintegration into Annamaboe society. Along with the celebration that marked his return, William Ansah reported that his father gave him slaves as a gift, and he probably sacrificed to the oracle, as he had for Bassi. Corrantee's humble attire had long been traditional among caboceers. In the late seventeenth century, William Bosman observed that "the *Cabocero's* or chief People are as meanly and plainly Habited, choosing rather to pass for poor than rich Men. They wear only a good Paan, a Cap made of Harts Skin upon their Heads, and a Staff in their Hands . . . and a String or Chain of Coral about their Heads: And this is the Dress they daily appear in."[68] Corrantee sent his expressions of gratitude for his son's treatment directly to London: "Was read before the board of admiralty a letter, sent by captain Jasper, from the prince of Annamaboe, in which he expressed his gratitude for the civilities shewn his son while he was at our court, and offered the assistance of 20,000 men to build a fort on the coast of Africa, in case of threats from the French."[69]

When Thomas Melville arrived at Cape Coast Castle to take up the duties of governor in 1751, he was surprised to find the former celebrity prince of Annamaboe working as a writer at the castle. As charmed by William Ansah as others had been, Melville described him as "a very honest, modest and a Sensible Lad . . . who I believe deserves Encouragement." He found that the young man enjoyed the respect of his countrymen and the doting attentions of his father. Melville hoped to use those things to his advantage by rebuilding the fort at Annamaboe, and by sending "down William and some white man to live there, and hoist English Colours."[70]

The British found, however, that Corrantee was a clever politician indeed, and he used both his British and French sons, as he referred to them, to play off the ongoing French-British rivalry on the coast. The British debated building a fort at Annamaboe as early as 1750; one argument in favor of the project was to provide "a more certain means of securing the Government of Corranteee's family."[71] When the French came courting Corrantee in 1752, he was once again eager to hear their entreaties. While he may have been sympathetic to the British, he recognized the advantages of keeping both nations on the coast. Not only did it ensure the arrival of more slave ships and therefore higher prices, but it kept him in the strongest possible position as he worked both sides to his greater advantage. He also used his sons in that complex diplomatic game. Corrantee apparently promised the French that he would allow them to build a factory at Annamaboe, a move he knew would provoke a strong reaction from the British. First, he had William Ansah write a letter to Melville notifying him that the French wanted to build a fort "if his Father & the People would give them leave."[72] Two days later the young man sent another letter to Melville by messenger saying that "the English need fear nothing while he was at Annamaboe."[73]

The continued French interest in Annamaboe made it more important for the British to complete work on the fort and reestablish their presence there.[74] The competition between the British and the French at Annamaboe came at the moment the old Royal African Company was being disbanded and the African trade was being put on a new footing. The old monopoly system that justified companies like the RAC, the East India Company, and the South Sea Company faced growing opposition in the 1740s; these companies could not keep up with the expansion of trade, and private traders protested loudly against the monopolies. In 1747, the RAC requested additional funds for the support of its forts, but Parliament denied that request, setting off a debate over the future of the company. In 1749, a group of Bristol and Liverpool merchants presented a proposal to Parliament that called for freedom of trade to Africa, the maintenance of secure forts there, the separation of trade and defense, and an open company without a monopoly.[75]

As a result of the newly proposed bill, the Lords Commissioners of Trade and Plantations reviewed the entire African trade and the supply and demand for slaves to the plantation colonies in the Americas. In part, the discussions revolved around competing proposals from the merchants of London on the one hand, and those from Liverpool and Bristol on the other. London merchants spoke in favor of the creation of a joint stock company to conduct the African trade, while the merchants from the provincial ports favored an open and unrestricted trade. The Gold Coast figured prominently in these discussions. The commissioners learned, for example, that more British manufactures were sold on the Gold Coast and Whydah than in all the rest of the African coast combined. Given the importance of that inland trade and the nature of the trade on the Gold Coast, it was necessary to have large quantities of trade goods on the coast rather than relying on the irregular supply directly from slave ships. Those goods could be best housed and protected in forts. They also heard from "gentlemen interested in the Sugar Colonies" who reported that more slaves were carried from Annamaboe than all other parts of the Gold Coast combined. Those planters complained that "plantations were now distressed for Gold Coast negroes" and that the supply of slaves from that coast had been declining for twenty years. Planters alleged that many slave traders who claimed to have Gold Coast slaves did not, and that they would pay twice as much for Gold Coast slaves as those from other regions. Mr. Sharpe, for example, a slave trader on the Gold Coast since 1716, told the commissioners that slaves were brought down to the coast from 400 to 500 miles in the interior at "different and uncertain times," and if the African traders could not get the British goods they wanted immediately, then they traded with other European nations. He further reported that the RAC's forts "were of great utility, and never obstructed him, but on the contrary saved an protected his goods." After a week of testimony, the commissioners agreed that the trade to the Gold Coast and Whydah was the most valuable of the African trade. Furthermore, they agreed that the trade required some government support. Since the French were trying to take control of the Gold Coast trade, they agreed that forts should be maintained and used to protect the trade for all British merchants, and that the trade should be supervised by a company.[76] The result was the African Trade Act of 1750, which represented a victory for private traders and for the Fante, who had long advocated free trade. The new law opened the trade to all British subjects, and those who traded on the African coast between Cape Blanco and the Cape of Good Hope would form a corporation called the Company of Merchants Trading to Africa. A committee of nine men known as the African Committee (AC) managed its affairs. Merchants paid forty shillings in annual dues to join the company. The RAC's forts became part of this corporation, and would be used to protect, encourage, and defend the trade. The new Company of Merchants could not trade on its own behalf but would instead promote private trade.[77]

The commissioners began to receive reports of greater French activity on the African coast. In September 1750 a letter arrived from James Fort in Gambia with the news that the French were attempting to establish a settlement at Albreda in the Gambia River, and similar reports filtered in. In January 1751 the commissioners met with the African Committee to discuss the construction of a fort at Annamaboe. The directors argued in favor of the fort, which they saw as necessary to protect the trade, and they identified Annamaboe "as a key to the whole trade of the Gold Coast." Another motivating factor was that John Corrantee "was now very old," and "they apprehended that his view in proposing the building of a fort at Annamaboe was to secure to his family his riches and possessions, and that if his offer was not accepted, there was reason to believe he might apply to the French." In addition, the commissioners were swayed by Corrantee's offer to provide 20,000 men to help build the fort.[78] A month later, the commissioners expressed their displeasure with Melville, the governor of Cape Coast Castle, in part because "he was not on good terms with John Corrantee," and they directed him "for the future upon all occasions to cultivate and improve a good understanding with the Fanteens [Fante] and particularly with John Corrantee and his son William who has been very serviceable to the English interest and has done all that lay in his power to promote and secure it."[79]

In January 1752 French warships arrived in Annamaboe. Bassi "instantly went on Board them . . . and gladly Received them & welcomed them." The commander informed Bassi that he had a message from the king of France for his father, and Corrantee agreed to receive the French the following day. A lieutenant and a messenger met with the caboceer and told him that they had "considerable Presents for him from the French King who desired to know whether the whole Coast & Kingdom of the Phantees was the Property of the English?" Corrantee answered that "they were not Slaves to the English but that . . . his Fore-fathers and his present Generation were English," and that the British paid ground rent and made other payments to the town. Corrantee ordered that the men be entertained by Bassi for three days in the palace. The French asked Corrantee to call together all the leading men of the town, which he agreed to do, and the French divided among them sixty ankers of brandy (each containing fourteen gallons). They also gave rich presents to Corrantee including "4 very Rich Pieces of Brocade (viz) one Red & two Green trim'd with Gold & Lace each containing about 18 yards in Length & ¾ in Bredth; and likewise with a brace of Pistols Richly mounted with Gold and Silver, two Rich Gold Lac'd Hats with a fine feather in each, & two Rich Scarlett Cloakes embroder'd with Gold." When the caboceers assembled, forty or fifty in number, the French handed out another forty ankers of brandy and gave each of them "a lac'd Hatt & a feather (some Lace being Gold & some Silver) & with a Piece of thick Brocade (some of Red, and some of Green & others of a Pink Colour) each embroidered either with Silver or Gold" and canes mounted in gold. Though these presents "were not so Rich as those presented" to Corrantee, they were clearly intended to dazzle the caboceers with the wealth of France. They surprised Corrantee by asking the assembled caboceers for the privilege of building a fort there, which the elders agreed to do if the French paid a sufficient amount of money.[80]

Corrantee asked the caboceers why they were willing to go over to the French. They replied that the British had not built their fort as promised, and that they did not give presents to them as they once had. They also complained that the British did not encourage their ships to come to Annamaboe, but rather to Cape Coast instead. Since that trade was "the Support of our Kingdom & by which we Ship off our Gold, Elphant's Teeth & Poor People's Wood, Yams, Corn which ws the only Support & Maintenance of us," they were ready to change their allegiance or at least allow both nations to build forts there. They also complained that the British governor at Cape Coast had ignored them on these matters, and that he gave them only four gallons of brandy and told them "to go plant cotton trees." Highly insulted, the Fante caboceers replied, "We never yet Planted Cotton but have always had cloth & all other Necessaries by our trading with them in Slaves, Gold & Elephants teeth & likewise told the Governor that from hence forward they would never come to Cape Coast more, nor accept of any favours from them whilst they Live'd, for that they was Considerable men and had Money & Slaves to Trade with other Nations which would maintain them." In fact, Governor Melville's pet project was to encourage "the Natives to plant Indigo Gum & Cotton Trees," a scheme that the Board of Trade found "very commendable," but which the Fante clearly had no interest in pursuing.[81]

Corrantee reportedly told the caboceers that he had been served well by the British; they had educated William Ansah in England and showed him "great respect," and he refused to allow the French "to hoist flag or lay foundations until William had written to England." Here William Ansah's connections at the highest levels in England came into play, and Corrantee used those connections to full effect. Corrantee had his son write a long letter to Lord Halifax laying out the details of the negotiations with the French and Melville's many failings. He reported that the French intended to return in sixteen months to begin construction of their fort, and he asked that the British send naval ships in the interval. He also reported that he had worked hard to prevent the Fante from going over to the French, but that he had gotten no support from Melville. He wrote Melville requesting presents to counter the lavish gifts the French were handing out, but he got only "a Bottle of Brandy containing about Three Gallons which was too Little to gain the Affections of the People . . . and at which my Father and Self was Surpriz'd at and he ordered it to be sent back again . . . & to tell the Governor that it was a Shame to use the English Nation so." To counter the French, William claimed that he sold two of the slaves his father had given him on his return to Captain Shields of the *Angola* from Newfoundland so that he could purchase 228 gallons of brandy to give to the caboceers on behalf of the British. He even claimed that his exertions on behalf of the British caused him to fall ill with a "violent Feavor." When the French tried to give him rich gifts of gold-laced clothes and hats, he refused them; "their Bribes shall never Blind me," he wrote, "tho all the Phantees call me a great Fool for not accepting the Presents." The French had given his brother "a Scarlet Coastt trim'd with Gold, and a Brown Silk Coat & Waistcoat Trim'd with Silver, a Gold Lac'd Hatt & Feather, with a Sword Silver mounted & Gold Belt & likewise several Shirts, Handkerchiefs, and Pairs of Shoes all very Rich," and the captain had promised to bring him more rich gifts on his next trip.[82]

Records from the French officers on the scene paint a somewhat different portrait of Corrantee's meetings with them. They reported that the French had a "long Conference" with the chief caboceer, "which turned chiefly upon the Pretensions of the English to the Sovereignty at Anamaboe [sic]." Corrantee acknowledged "his Desire of cultivating the Friendship of the English, but insisted on his own Independency, & on the Freedom of the Fantins, who acknowledged neither the English, nor any others, for their Soverigns, & who had always traded, & wd continue to do so, with all Nations that came, & particularly with the French." He told the French that his father had allowed the British to build their first fort there, but that it had been razed because the townspeople saw it "as a Check upon Them and their Trade, & that it had not been rebuilt, tho' The English had continued the Payment of their Tribute: That however the Fort, if it really existed, could give no right of Dominion or exclusive Trade, & that The French mght erect likewise a Fort in the same Manner, if they please." Corrantee concluded by emphasizing his resolve "to preserve the Liberty He had of admitting every Nation to trade there; . . . this was the Language not only of the Cabaicher, but of all the Fantins . . . that the Tribute paid by them (the English) to the Chief of the Fantins, is a customary Duty paid by all Europeans to the Negroes for Leave of Trading."[83]

At this critical moment, a British squadron arrived on the scene, a show of power accompanied by well-timed "gifts from the King himself to him [Corrantee] & other Cabbonceers [sic] of Fantee." William Ansah reported that he was "greatly Overjoyed" to see them, and that he had been "very well entertained on Board." Then the captains of the warships, Melville, and other British CMTA officials met with the caboceers in a palaver to ask why they were about to sell British forts to the French. The Fante denied that charge but responded by accusing a British captain of stealing their pawns and driving them into the open arms of the French. It also appeared that Corrantee had given one of his sons as a pawn to the French to guarantee them the right to build a fort at Annamaboe. Corrantee tried to dismiss that by claiming that the boy was merely the son of a slave, though Melville believed that "in reality he is his Son." The matter was tricky, and Melville did not blame Corrantee for playing the British and French off each other. "And how can it be otherwise?" he asked, in an unusually candid moment. "The nature of the Trade excludes what we call affection." He rightly observed, "The Negroes know we would buy every one of them if we could sell them again, and reckon it as fair Trade to sell our Interest as we do to Sell their persons."[84]

How much of William Ansah's reports of his father's loyalty to the French and his own efforts to win the caboceers over is true and how much was a tale woven by his father to spur the British into action is impossible to say, but negotiations between Corrantee and the French were still under way, as William Ansah knew quite well. When Melville later confronted him and asked how he could have pulled such a ruse, "when he then knew, and now owned that every man in Fantee except himself were for allowing the French to settle," he replied: "his Father Desired him to send it. At that time the French Brother was in Fashion for John's two son's like Castor & Pollox are never seen in splendor at the same time."[85]

William Owen, a midshipman on board one of the British warships, recorded just how close Corrantee came to siding with the French. In mid-February 1753 the British squadron arrived at Annamaboe to find a French man-of-war, Le Proteè, with sixty-four guns; a frigate called La Syrene with twenty-six guns; and two French storeships anchored there. Owen reported that "upon our arrival at Annamaboe we found two contending parties formed, and by the influence of French brandy, and a superior force, the English interest the weakest, & things in great forwardness for building a French fort." The British show of force was perfectly timed. Owen wrote, "The scale soon turned, Prince William [Ansah] all bedaubed with lace and transported with joy came on board as soon as we arrived, several messages passed between the commandants of the two nations but our orders being peremptory, the French agreed to depart when they had filled some water & taken in a few refreshments for their sick, who were very numerous." Within two days British storeships arrived "with an engineer, artificers & materials for building a fort." A few days later "three French ships came into the road all of whom saluted their commodore, and next morning before day, the men-of-war & all the merchantmen of that nation weighed & steered to the SE." Their departure marked the end of the French attempt to build the French fort.[86]

Melville also began to understand that William Ansah was playing his own game. Melville gave him a supply of brandy that he was supposed to distribute among the caboceers at Annamaboe, but they reported "that he had never given them one drop." Since brandy was a very valuable trade item on the coast, William Ansah was likely using it for his own profit. He also complained that the Fante were not allowed to trade with whoever they chose, and in Melville's view, "he exclaims as loudly against us as any Man at Annamaboe." He gave everyone to understand that he and his father "have great controlling Powers promised them from home by Letters. I hope he's no Foundation for this," though if Melville himself thought it possible, others on the coast must have found it easy to believe given the close ties father and son had long maintained with England. Corrantee was, in fact, better informed than Melville of just where the commissioners' confidence resided.[87]

Corrantee then sent word to Melville that he could not rest easy until the British took his "French Son" into service. Accordingly, when he was next at Annamaboe, Melville met with the young man and asked him if he would accept employment from the British. Melville warned that "if he once took our pay and went back to the French, I would certainly make him repent it." Faced with that threat, Bassi asked for time to think about the offer. He came afterward to Cape Coast Castle with William Ansah and declined, explaining quite honestly that "if the French did not return, he would be very glad of our pay, but if they did, he would serve them." Melville wrote, "Indeed I could not blame him. . . . When his consequence ceases, as it must do . . . for he is only John's Slave, and has wanted a cloth to cover his nakedness since he made such a brilliant figure in France, when I call him John's Slave I do not deny he is his Son, but he is so by one of John's Slaves, which makes him Slave to John's heir." Ludewig Ferdinand Rømer claimed that Bassi so infuriated his father by continuing to advocate for the French and by refusing the British that Corrantee banished him from Annamaboe. Rømer employed him in the Danish fort at Christiansborg. He wrote that he employed Bassi "in order to retain Corrantryn's friendship with the Danes, not only for the sake of the trading ships but also for the safety of our Company slaves, who, at that time, had to fetch provisions for us from Fante," which meant passing through Corrantee's territory.[88]

The commissioners, in fact, had no idea just how far Melville had gone to try to win Corrantee and the Fante over from the French. While negotiations were under way at Annamaboe, Melville decided to try to influence those talks by gaining the support of Fante priests who spoke for the Fante's powerful oracle. Melville sent a secret messenger to the priests offering twenty ounces of gold for them "to make their God declare in our favour." But once again, the trickster was one step ahead of him. Imagine Melville's "great Mortification" when his messenger returned to inform him that "John Corrantee has offered 60 to speak for the French."[89]

In May 1752, the African Committee met again with the commissioners and read several letters from Annamaboe, one of them Willam Ansah's brilliant letter to the Earl of Halifax. These letters convinced them "that unless a fort was begun to be built as soon as possible not only that place would be lost, but with it the whole British interest upon that coast."[90] They once again lambasted Melville for his poor handling of the situation and for all he had done to alienate the affections of the Fante at Annamaboe, just the outcome Corrantee sought. The directors requested a copy of William Ansah's letter, which was provided to them. When the directors and commissioners met later that month they reviewed letters from Melville defending his conduct, but with regard to Annamaboe, they found his conduct "inconsistent with the principles which ought to be observed by the Company's agents." They concluded that he was "a very improper person to carry on so great and important a work as that of building a fort at Annamaboe."[91] The commissioners came very close to firing Melville but yielded to the entreaties of the African Committee, who asked to keep him on and proposed sending an agent to oversee the construction of the fort. The commissioners warned, however, that "if the French should get possession, the [African] Committee must take the blame upon themselves."[92]

In 1753 the British prepared to rebuild the Annamaboe fort at a cost of over £6,000, but problems arose immediately. When the surveyors laid out plans for a much larger fort, the people of the town complained, in part because they feared being overawed by it and because the new construction would require the desecration of burial sites that were sacred to them. The British relied on Corrantee's "mediation" to acquire the land, but the townspeople expected the French to arrive at any time, and since they had promised to pay £40,000 for land on which to build a fort, the townspeople were "very insolent" toward the handful of Englishmen at work on the fort.[93] The townspeople even came in the night and filled in the foundations as fast as the workmen could dig them, so that the surveyor complained that he had dig the foundation for the third time. When Melville complained to Corrantee about it, he said that "he is our Friend, but he is sick and they do not obey him." When he went to William Ansah, he replied that "he is but a Boy & has no power."[94] It is impossible to say with certainty whether or not the trickster was behind such tactics, but it seems likely, especially given his and William Ansah's false pleas of weakness, and the upshot was that the family had outmaneuvered Melville again.

Corrantee continued his clever diplomacy as the British worked hard to get the Fante to agree to a law excluding the French from trading among them. As Melville pushed the Fante caboceers to sign such a law, Corrantee refused to go against the long-standing Fante determination to trade with all comers. He wrote that Corrantee claimed that "he was an Englishman" based on the time he spent in the English fort as a youth, "but that those who had given the Sons to the French could not come up to Cape Coast to sign any agreement to exclude 'em." William Ansah also sent a message claiming that "his father was an Englishman (the common preface)." However, Melville knew that Corrantee held out against the law since he clearly saw the advantages of having both nations on the coast. Other Fante told Melville that Corrantee "was the 1st Fantee who had ever sent a Son to France, that their Father's always serv'd the English . . . that he [Corrantee] had lately sent another son to France, and had taken an Oath to be true to the French." Senior caboceers told Melville that both Corrantee and another caboceer named Coffee Yango had given the French their sons for pawns, and that they would have to be returned before any firm agreement could be signed.[95] In the midst of these discussions, Cudjo, the caboceer at Cape Coast Castle, resorted to casting spells against Corrantee. Melville reported, "The priests of Bura Bura Wergan (i.e. the Father of Fantee) have sent here to make a Fetiche in the following manner. To write on a p[iece]. of paper in the English Language these Words, 'the practices & designs of the French & Jn Corrantee are bad.' then the Messenger was order'd to carry the paper to the Water side, there to tear it & throw it into the Water. I took this for a Joke, but Cudjo (who is a firm believer in these matters, tho' he does not chuse to have it thought so) assured me it was not so meant, & therefore takes care to have it performed according to their directions."[96]

Melville doubted that Corrantee and his sons could be trusted. He complained that "the kind civilities & genteel treatment of his boy in England was then of no concern to John and no avail to us."[97] Melville conveniently forgot that the genteel treatment of William Ansah was preceded by his enslavement in Barbados. He complained that "the making use of Wm to transmit Falsehoods against me was extremely cruel in respect to himself and very bold." He now regretted that he had trusted William Ansah with trade goods to launch him as an independent trader, which he saw as a continuation of "the same plan that had been begun in England to bring John Corrantee to our Interest by every Act of Kindness."[98]

Despite the many delays, construction on the fort got under way under the supervision of John Apperley, chief engineer. Melville report that "the Annamaboe People are different every Day; now they will give us Ground enough for our Fort, tomorrow they will not, & must have more Dashees to stand to the Agreement of the Day before. John [Corrantee] they now do not obey. However we rub on by sometimes bribing; sometimes threatening to leave them; declare War and drive away Ships of all Nations which Mr. Apperley finds the most effectual method of bringing them to Reason, and if they thought we had the Power they durst not use us as they do, but some good People have now informed them that only the King can declare War. Apperley tells them the Men of War can do it as well as the King so they fear to offend too much."[99] The Fante saw the huge construction project as an opportunity to squeeze funds out of the British; they even told the British, "Now is our time to eat when we are going to Build our Fort."[100]

Corrantee, of course, was first in line when it came to profiting from the fort's construction. The workmen who came from England lived with Corrantee in his palace, an impressive, fortresslike, two-story building constructed by the Dutch in the first half of the seventeenth century, and they paid handsomely for the privilege. Along with rent, the boarders paid for their own food. They could have bought food more cheaply directly from the local farmers, but Corrantee forced them to go through

him instead. They complained, "We are hard set to get Provision to support us without paying an exhorbitant price, for Johns Boys who command all below Stairs, stop the Bush people from bringing us Fowls & c,
& buy them at their owne price & make us pay double for them, or
Starve."[101] Corrantee was not alone in getting as much profit as possible
during the fort's construction; canoemen who carried goods and materials from the ships to shore struck for higher wages.[102]

Before the fort could be completed, the Seven Years' War renewed hostilities between Britain and France, and in 1757 French warships appeared off the Gold Coast, captured a number of British trading ships,
and prepared to attack Cape Coast Castle. Letters published in London
from merchants familiar with the Gold Coast observed that the forts could
not defend themselves against the French squadron and predicted that
eight French ships "could drive all the *English* from *Africa*."[103] No one
knew better than the Africans around the forts how poorly defended
they actually were, and everyone expected a quick French victory.
When the French squadron appeared off Annamaboe, Corrantee assumed
that the French would succeed, and he "sent some of his dependents, with
a present . . . for their Commodore," but Richard Brew, commander of
the fort, prevented the party from leaving the shore. Corrantee then prepared to send a delegation by land to Cape Coast Castle to be the first to
compliment the French on their victory, but when the French attack failed,
he sent the same delegation to compliment the British instead.[104] The
outbreak of hostilities prompted the commissioners of the Board of Trade
to insist that "speedy measures . . . [be] taken to compleat the fort building there, the workmen of which were entirely at a stand for want of materials, and the chief [engineer] there is in so bad a state of health that his life is
despaired of."[105] As the work dragged on Apperley fell dangerously ill; as
Melville reported, he "is so ill that I am afraid we shall lose him." Feverish
and delirious, Apperley believed himself to have been poisoned, and as
Melville predicted, he died without living to see the fort completed.[106]

Apperley's death slowed construction of the fort even further, and replacing him was no easy matter. The only other person with any engi-
neering or construction experience on the Gold Coast was John Slater,
engineer and surveyor at Cape Coast Castle. But, as Melville informed
his superiors in London, he could not send Slater to Annamaboe. He

described Slater as a drunkard who would "quarrel with every Negro which came into his way." While he described him as a "good workman," he fully expected that if he sent him to Annamaboe, "his Brains would be beat out in less than a week." He concluded that "he is not fit to go where the Negroes are Masters." With all these complications, it was not until 1759 that the fort could be described as "near being finished."[107]

Even before the fort was finished, it fulfilled Corrantee's goals of attracting more trade to Annamaboe, providing a regular income for the townspeople, and contributing to the power and influence of himself and his family. The fort's account books reveal the quantities of goods that went into the town every month as payments to Corrantee's family and to the townspeople for a range of goods and services. Dashes or gifts went to Corrantee's three wives and to his sons George Banishee and Quasah. Dashes might be given on almost any imaginable occasion, or for no apparent reason at all. The British dashed George Banishee because he was paying a visit to Cape Coast and to allow him to entertain a visiting "Mulatto Relation." Both William Ansah and Quasah received gifts for building new houses. Corrantee received gifts "on coming home from Braffo Town & his wife who attended him on going." Corrantee received a gallon of rum because he was "Complaining of its being a Cold Day," a half gallon of rum because he wanted to "wash himself," and more rum and brandy for the New Yam harvest festival. From November to December 1755, for example, Corrantee received nineteen gallons of rum in dashes. The entire town received rum for the New Yam Festival, "a great day with them." They dashed George Banishee's wife because she was "with child & Longing for it." The pynins of the Upper Town and those of the Lower Town were also paid.[108]

During the negotiations with the Asante in 1768, the British made payments to pynins from other towns who came to Annamaboe to discuss those issues, and to the "principal men among soldiers" in the town "to induce them to settle the Ashante Business." They gave dashes to the "Townspeople for clearing the paths above the Town (as usual)," and to "a Mulattoe for making a New Flagg" for the fort. Dashes went to Corrantee's Chicko (or Chickee, a messenger identified as his "public cryer") and to his "Wenches." In July and August 1768, for example, the fort made sixty-four payments to Corrantee's "favorite wives."[109]

When Richard Brew became chief of the Annamaboe fort in 1756, he tried to reduce the payments and dashes. The result was a palaver where he was charged with not paying "proper Respect to the Caboceers and Pynins." In effect, the Fante repeated the same tactics they had used so successfully against the chiefs of the earlier fort. They threatened "to tye him & the rest of the white people there & send them in a canoe to Cape Coast [Castle], whereupon Richard Brew laid his case before Charles Bell [governor at Cape Coast Castle] who agreed to Stop their Mouths" by paying them in tobacco and rum.[110] Brew learned his lesson, and he became much more liberal with the townspeople. Twice in 1763 he rewarded them for capturing sailors who attempted to run away from British ships. He even had to pay a Fante man in the town "whose Wench was debauched by a Co. slave," and he sent four gallons of rum to the townspeople to "save the life of a man they were about to put to death." The Christmas holiday brought generous dashes to the entire town, and special gifts went to the "Mulattoes of the town."[111]

William Ansah's position of privilege continued at Annamaboe, while his relationship with the British at Cape Coast Castle deteriorated to the point that he came to blows with William Mutter, governor of the castle, in 1761. William Ansah learned that he had been paid in watered brandy, as other Africans were, but the brandy paid to white traders was not watered. He was loudly arguing this point with a white trader in the castle when Mutter walked by, heard raised voices, and went into the room. When he ordered William Ansah to lower his voice, their argument turned violent. Mutter hit him with his fist, then beat him with his cane and drove him from the castle.[112] Mutter said that William Ansah "is not a person of Consequence in this Country."[113] Gilbert Petrie, who was in the room at the time, wrote that William Ansah's conduct "was intolerably provoking from a black to any Gentleman."[114]

William Ansah was no longer a prince or even a gentleman in the eyes of the men at Cape Coast Castle. In fact, it must have become clear to Mutter and the others at the castle that William Ansah was not, in fact, John Corrantee's heir, a discovery that no doubt helps account for Mutter's fury against him. Corrantee had duped them into spending a small fortune on his son and presumed heir and won a steady income for him, but his true heir was George Quasah. As early as 1752, Melville wrote,

"As John Begins to think himself not far from the grave, it behooves us to get him a Successor who is in our Indent. By the custom of the country George Banishee, his eldest Son, ought to succedd as Capt [Captain] but without our aid he will not be able to bear the Expense."[115] By 1761 the British were already dealing with Quasah, whom they referred to as "My Lord."[116] In part because, as Melville explained, "this Lad went to England very early and stayed there and on Board an English ship 8 or 9 years and has ever since he came home behaved to the Satisfaction of his Masters he is the Man we ought to support."[117] This may be the same son often referred to in British sources from Annamaboe as "My Lord" who sometimes used the name "My Lord Augustus FitzRoy," which probably refers to the Captain in the British navy by that name who died in 1741, and suggests that this son may have served on board one of FitzRoy's ships.[118] It was clearly important for a European on the coast to have as complete an understanding of African family structures as possible given their importance in diplomacy, but in fact they often misread the complex family relationships among the Fante. Melville understood that John's eldest son, George Quasah, by tradition should follow his father as commander of the bendefoe companies, and later payments to him suggest that he did. He did not inherit the position of chief caboceer. The British had considered Corrantee to be advanced in years as early as the 1750s, and his death in 1764 could not have come as a surprise.[119] Richard Brew reported that an outbreak of smallpox had killed many people along the coast, "amongst them your old friend . . . John Corrantee, he has died worth a great deal of money, and is a great loss to this Town."[120]

Corrantee founded a dynasty that ruled Annamaboe during its subsequent history as an independent polity, and his descendants hold the Annamaboe stool down to the present day. He was succeeded not by one of his sons, but by Amoony Coomah, a relative whose exact relationship to Corrantee is unclear but almost certainly followed the matrilineal line. Quasah, identified by the British as Corrantee's heir, may have inherited his fortune, but not the position of caboceer.[121] The British reported that "the Post of Capt. Of Annamaboe is elective and in all Probablity without our Assistance will go into another Family."[122] Amoony Coomah was initially called "Principal Caboceer," but eventually called "King of Fantee" and acknowledged to hold considerable authority along the coast.

He died in 1801, though another John Corrantee became principal caboceer in 1804, further evidence that old Corrantee's line continued.[123]

Corrantee's skillful diplomacy kept both the British and French ensnared in his webs throughout his long life, and he manipulated the European presence on the coast to build his own power base in Annamaboe. Through his skillful diplomacy and military prowess, he played a major role in securing Annamaboe's place as the primary state in the Fante confederacy and as the major slave-trading depot on the Gold Coast. As historian David Northrup has observed, "African slave traders are usually cast in the role of victims . . . naïve persons caught up in the vicious machinery of a larger economy they could not begin to comprehend," a view that badly misrepresents men like Corrantee who helped to shape the eighteenth-century Atlantic World. Corrantee and other figures like him among the African merchant elite were an essential link in the Atlantic slave trade, the middlemen between the Europeans on the coast and the African traders from the interior. As middlemen, they maintained ties with both European and African traders, and Corrantee's case demonstrates how they built those relationships with the Europeans and inserted themselves into the eighteenth-century Atlantic economy. Corrantee lived among the British in his youth; allied himself through marriage to other major players on the Coast; used his own sons to foster close ties with the British, French, and Dutch; and then made those sons his own eyes and ears in Paris, London, and throughout the Atlantic World, as far afield as the plantations of Barbados. He was even able to rescue one son from plantation slavery in the Americas, a feat accomplished by only a tiny handful of Africans. But it is important to remember that while he rescued his own son, he helped enslave tens of thousands of others. As accomplished international merchants, local rulers, and diplomats, Corrantee and his fellow caboceers should occupy a central place in the historiography of the slave trade. These African merchants were as fully engaged in the Atlantic economy as their European counterparts, equally citizens of the Atlantic World, to paraphrase David Hancock, and deeply engaged in trading networks that extended deep into the African continent and across the Atlantic.[124]

3

Richard Brew and the World of an African-Atlantic Merchant

O THER THAN JOHN CORRANTEE, the most visible figure in An-namaboe during the eighteenth century was Richard Brew, a na-tive of Ireland, an RAC official, and a private merchant. Brew was one of the very few British merchants who settled permanently on the Gold Coast. For capable, ambitious, and adventurous men like Brew, the At-lantic World opened up opportunities for advancement, travel, and profit. The slave trade was a very risky enterprise; slave trader John Newton wrote that "there were some gainful voyages, but the losing voy-ages were thought more numerous; it was generally considered as a sort of lottery in which every adventurer hoped to gain a prize."[1] Brew was the biggest player in this lottery on the Gold Coast. Like Corrantee, he made the most of the opportunities presented to him. From Annama-boe, his trade connections stretched along the African coast and around the British Atlantic World, and his well-published views on the African trade influenced policy makers in London. His aspirations were re-flected in Castle Brew, the fine house he built in Annamaboe, and his marriage to John Corrantee's daughter allied him with Annamaboe's ruler and gave rise to an Atlantic Creole family of great distinction in the history of Ghana. Through that marriage, Brew integrated himself into Annamaboe's ruling family, and through the marriages of his mixed-race children, he allied himself with other prominent Atlantic Creole families on the Gold Coast. He understood Fante politics and culture as few other Europeans did, and he used that knowledge to make himself the most important private merchant on the Gold Coast and a major player in its political affairs. Brew's remarkable career demonstrates just how important Annamaboe was as a trade hub, how deeply entwined it was in the Atlantic World, and how transformative the Atlantic experience could be for everyone caught up in it.

Brew's early life is as murky as Corrantee's. Historical and genealogical research suggests that the family originated on the Isle of Man before moving to county Clare in Ireland where Richard Brew, probably his father, appears as a vintner and brewer. If this identification is correct, then he would have been born around 1725. The elder Richard was also identified as a gentleman, which would account for the younger Richard's high level of education and his lifelong taste for history, poetry, and literature. But the records also show that the elder Richard had financial difficulties, which may have prompted his son to seek his fortunes abroad. He was also probably related to William Brew, a slave-ship captain who sailed in 1725 from Boston to Bilbao, Jamaica, Saint John's, and Leghorn.[2] That connection could explain the younger Richard's involvement in the slave trade.

Brew entered into the employ of the Royal African Company and arrived on the Gold Coast in 1745, though his role there is unclear until 1750, when he appears in the records as registrar at Cape Coast Castle and began a quick rise up the ranks. A short time later he was appointed chief factor of the fort at Tantumquerry. First occupied by the English in 1662, that fort had fallen into disuse until Fante chiefs approached Sir Dalby Thomas in 1709 to reopen the factory there, offering to provide labor and materials for the building and to allow the British one-fifth of all catches of fish. The fort was built close to the sea with four flankers and twelve mounted guns. In 1730, the fort's small staff included one corporal, five soldiers, twenty castle slaves, and five canoemen, the smallest installation of the nine British forts on the Gold Coast. Like Annamaboe, Tantumquerry was a Fante town that had benefited from the expansion of that nation along the coast. Like Annamaboe, Tantumquerry had militias, markets, and attached hinterland villages, but it was mostly important for keeping the lines of communication open to Accra.[3] Such an appointment was a relatively minor one but an important step toward the governorship of a major fort. He remained in that position for over two years, including a brief stint in command of the fort at Dixcove and a short appearance in the records as a factor at Cape Coast Castle.[4] It is also likely that he began to make his own important trade connections with Fante merchants during this period.

RAC officials were prohibited from trading on their own account, but when the RAC was disbanded and its holdings and employees transferred to the CMTA in 1750, the rules changed. Officials in Africa were permitted to trade on their own accounts, a change that quickly produced an outcry from British merchants and brought Brew his first taste of controversy. The British merchants charged that officials on the coast had gone well beyond private trading and had cooperated with one another to give themselves a monopoly on the trade. Instead of assisting the British merchants as required by law, they used their connections on the ground to keep others out of the trade, and even denied British traders canoes, canoemen, wood, and water. Initial complaints fell on deaf ears, but eventually the Board of Trade ruled that officers should not trade for slaves in amounts higher than their salaries, but that stipulation was not enforced, and the British merchants continued to suffer. They alleged that Thomas Melville and Charles Bell, governors of Cape Coast Castle, continued to invest heavily in the trade and sent shipments of slaves on their own accounts to the Americas.[5]

Brew was implicated in the scheme. Private traders alleged that Brew had visited the slave market at Lagu, near Tantumquerry, and offered to pay forty shillings more than private traders paid as part of the effort to cut them out of the trade. William Brown, master of the slave ship *Bristol,* appeared before the African Committee and testified that when he visited Tantumquerry, Brew informed him that he; Withers, the chief of the fort at Winnebah; Melville; Young; and other officers at Cape Coast Castle had formed a partnership. Brew reported that they were expecting a ship from Holland with a cargo of Dutch goods, the same ship they had earlier sent to Jamaica—the prime destination for British ships from the Gold Coast—with a cargo of slaves. Brown reported that he could not buy slaves from the fort because they were priced higher than those sold by African traders outside the forts. He "found the Negroe traders under said forts, cautious and fearful of trading with him, lest the chiefs

[Brew and his compatriots] should know thereof." He also noted that the men were using the forts to house their own slaves for market.[6]

Ship captains alleged that Brew was doing all he could to cut them out of the trade. James Hamilton, chief mate of the slaver *Polly* of Bristol, found Brew determined to monopolize trade. Hamilton hired a factor at Logoe and tried to purchase slaves, but Brew sent African traders with trade goods there to cut him out. Brew told Hamilton that he could not match his selection of trade goods, and that if Hamilton offered eight ounces of gold for prime slaves then he would pay eight and one-half. Furthermore, he threatened to send castle slaves up the trade paths to prevent slaves from being sent down, and he carried out that threat by sending his men to the traders coming from the interior with liquor and payments to divert them to his fort. Brew refused to sell Hamilton slaves at any price, claiming that he was acting on Melville's instructions. The governors at the other forts who were in on the arrangement also refused to sell him slaves, provide water, or allow canoemen to serve his ship.[7]

The committee examined the charges against Brew, and determined that he was a part of the effort to fix prices and cut out the private traders. In November 1753, the committee found that "Mr. Brew's conduct at Tantumquerry has been very blameable." They ordered Melville to suspend Brew for his conduct, and if he could not prove his innocence, he would be dismissed. Though evidence strongly indicated that many other governors of forts were involved, including Melville himself, only Brew was suspended. Rather than fight the charges, Brew resigned and opened shop as a private trader at Mumford, a small factory near Tantumquerry where his ties with local traders facilitated his business endeavors.[8]

His partnerships with current and former committee officials continued once he left the committee's service. For example, in 1756 Charles Bell and Brew traded with William Vernon and Jonas and William Redwood of Rhode Island for 4,350 gallons of rum to be exchanged for "good Men and Women at *Vizt* Men at One hundred and fifteen Gallons each or Women at Ninety five Gallons each" to be loaded on the *Cassada Garden* lying at Annamaboe. Brew and Bell also purchased the sloop *Titbitt* from Captain Thomas Tickell Taylor of the *Cassada Garden*.[9]

Brew had his defenders, who published their arguments in his favor. John Hippisley, a company official and one of Brew's compatriots in the trade, defended the right of the heads of forts to engage in the slave trade. He argued that the company could not pay salaries high enough to lure men to the African coast. Furthermore, he reasoned that most of the governor's influence came from his involvement in the slave trade. "It is this," Hippisley wrote, "that gives weight to his interpositions in the affairs of the coast; it is this that obliges him to make himself of consequence; as the increase in his trade depends very much upon his figure in the country." If a governor lived upon his salary, he would have no cause to strive for popularity among the African traders, and he could watch while ships passed the English forts for the Dutch without much concern. Governors of forts who depended upon the success of the trade for their own profit "must become masters of every thing relative to the coast, . . . capable of being active and useful in the general trade, and watchful against the encroachment of foreigners." He also defended Brew (though not by name) by condemning the company for dismissing "the chief of Tantumquerry for *saying* he would give more for slaves than the captains of ships . . . notwithstanding their long service." And he complained that they suspended the governor of Annamaboe Fort "merely *because he carried on too much trade*" when Parliament had declared the trade free and open. When the company could not legally prevent this "enterprising man from forming and executing what legal plans he thought proper for his advantage," Hippisley complained, he was suspended. He also devoted an appendix to a further defense of Brew, and though he still did not name him, the identity of the suspended governor of Annamaboe would have been well-known to anyone engaged in the African trade.[10]

Despite those charges and the cloud hanging over Brew, his close ties with and intimate knowledge of the Fante made him valuable to the committee as they worked to appease the Fante and keep them from going over to the French. The French presence on the coast aroused fears around the British Atlantic World. In 1760, for example, newspapers in the American colonies raised the alarm that a French squadron had left Dunkerque with 1,500 soldiers on board headed for some part of Africa.[11] In 1765 the *Georgia Gazette* warned that the French and Spanish had signed a commercial treaty that allowed the French to furnish the Spanish colonies in the Americas with 40,000 slaves annually, "which naturally accounts for their extraordinary solicitude to extend their settlements on the coast of Guinea."[12] The Board of Trade launched an investigation into the strength of the British forts and possessions on the West Coast, and recommended that the Senegal and Gambia regions be transferred from the committee to the Crown due to the French threat.[13] With the competition heating up between the French and the British at Annamaboe and the ongoing problems with the construction of the fort there, the committee needed someone who could match wits with John Corrantee. As Charles Bell, governor of Cape Coast Castle, wrote to the committee in 1756, the Annamaboe governor needed "a thorough Acquaintance with the Temper and manners of the natives and no small Interest with the ruling men." Most importantly, Bell notified the committee that Brew had a "remarkable ascendant" sway over Corrantee—given how much time and money the CMAT and the committee had expended on Corrantee and the fort, this piece of information must have been crucial.[14] Certainly the company concluded that Brew was their best hope to bring peace to Annamaboe and to finish the fort, and he was appointed governor there in 1756. Like the two governors before him, Brew moved into Corrantee's palace since the fort was not yet habitable.[15] For Corrantee, these prominent guests were one more source of revenue, and having them under his roof, of course, gave him some measure of control, or at least influence, over them.

Brew's governorship began at the moment when tensions between the French and the British were rising, and when Corrantee was playing the two great powers off each other over the construction of the Annamaboe fort. The fact that Corrantee did not go over to the French can be credited in part to Brew's carrot-and-stick approach. First, he laid out "extraordinary expenses" in presents and the many traditional payments intended to buy the loyalty of the Annamaboe caboceers. Brew paid regular allowances to Corrantee and made other payments and gifts of rum, tobacco, chintz, and other luxury goods to Corrantee's favorite wives, to William Ansah, Quasah, and Corrantee's other sons, and to other Fante elders and caboceers.[16] But the arrival of the French on the coast in 1757 with a superior force convinced Corrantee that the balance of power had shifted in their favor. When the French squadron appeared at Annamaboe, Corrantee prepared to send "a present of refreshments for their Commodore." Brew responded by blowing the canoe to pieces from the unfinished fort before it could be launched, and he threatened to level the entire town of Annamaboe before allowing it to fall into French hands. He also gave liberal gifts to three bendefoe companies from the town "for their good behavior when the French Man of War came into the Road." He also made payments to the caboceers, pynins, soldiers, and townspeople "in order to strengthen the English interests and to Encourage them to stand by us." Combined with the quick thinking of Charles Bell at Cape Coast Castle, who also mounted a strong defense, the French threat evaporated and the fleet sailed for the West Indies instead.[17] From Cape Coast Castle, Charles Bell notified the committee in London that thanks to Brew's skills, Corrantee and the Fante had been "sometimes foiled . . . at their own weapons."[18] At last the British had found someone who could spar successfully with Corrantee.

Despite that success, Brew faced growing criticism during the next three years of his governorship. Problems began when Brew's supporter and trading partner Charles Bell was replaced at Cape Coast Castle by Nassau Senior, and the two men were soon at loggerheads. Both men sent a growing list of complaints against the other to London, and their relationship became so acrimonious that the committee considered sending Bell back to restore order. By August 1758, Senior expressed his conviction that Brew would "be under no authority" and should be removed, though even he admitted that this could not happen until someone could be found who could keep the fort supplied, which only Brew had been able to do. In that same month, Brew informed the committee that he was considering leaving Africa after thirteen years on the coast, expressing his desire to visit his "native country."[19] He did not say so, but he must also have been weary of the constant battles with Senior, and he may also have been intent on going back into private trading.

Whatever his motivations, by January 1760 Brew was ready to depart. Senior came down from Cape Coast Castle, no doubt pleased to see his foe off, and a grand procession of soldiers accompanied by drums and flutes escorted Brew to the canoe that took him to the *Chesterfield* bound for London. Brew visited Ireland and he spent time in London meeting with Samuel Smith, a merchant and member of the African Committee who became Brew's business partner, an indication that the lure of private trading took him back to Britain. Still, the committee relied on Brew's expertise; they sought his advice while he was visiting Dublin, and when he returned to London in February 1761 he met personally with the committee. Clearly, Smith was laying the groundwork for Brew's reentry into service. A petition in support of him came to the committee in March, and with Smith's backing, the committee voted to reinstate him as governor of Annamaboe Fort.[20]

He was appointed governor at Annamaboe for the second time in March 1761. Brew arrived in Annamaboe in September, with marks of high favor from the company. As a result of some uncertainty about the chain of command on the coast, the company made it clear that Brew was third in the rankings. He was also authorized to lay out a garden near the fort to supply it with fresh produce, and a gardener was sent out from London to maintain it. He brought with him a lavish blue velvet umbrella with rich gold fringe as a gift for Corrantee from the company. When the chief caboceer arrived to pay his formal respects to the new governor, he was greeted with an eleven-gun salute. Corrantee and Brew continued to spar, and competition between the French and the British at Annamaboe continued to dominate politics there. Despite Brew's success in that arena, the old charges of private trading continued to haunt him as merchants in Bristol and Liverpool complained about his activities. They leveled specific charges against Brew, allegations that give insight into his already extensive trade operations. In 1761, Brew, then in England, fitted out two ships, one called the *Brew* at Liverpool and another in the river Thames. The *Brew* carried a large cargo to Africa to trade for slaves while the other went to Holland to take on a cargo of trade goods also aimed at the African market. That ship returned to Plymouth in July 1761, and Brew went on board with two of his partners, Thomas Westgate and John Fleming, both of whom had been CMTA officials in Africa. According to the charge, the ships traveled to Annamaboe and stored the goods in the fort, bought slaves with the cargoes, and shipped them to Jamaica. Samuel Smith, Brew's partner and chief supporter, acted as agent for the men in London. Smith had fitted out another large ship with a huge cargo also intended for Annamaboe on the account of Brew and his partners. They charged that some goods had been paid for using committee funds, and that committee memberships were rigged among the same small group of traders working for their own benefit. "The committee's servants, having such advantages, can it be supposed any private trader can stand a chance in with them," they asked, "as said trader must settle in a negroe town, in a mud house covered with thatch, there being no other fort or dwelling to be got."[21]

Those allegations, widely circulated at the time, also came as the Seven Years' War ended in 1763, and tensions between the French and British diminished, perhaps making Brew less indispensable. In December 1763 the committee suspended him, though they allowed him to keep an apartment and storage space in the fort for a period of six months, later extended to a year. Rather than fight those charges, Brew resigned his post in April 1764 to expand his business as a private trader. The scale of his ambitions was reflected in the house he began constructing for himself right outside the fort, which he styled Castle Brew, a combination of a counting house and a fortified residence, with large warehouses and holding rooms for slaves awaiting sale and guns mounted on its high roof. He took advantage of the 1750 act replacing the Royal African Company with the Company of Merchants Trading to Africa, which included a provision making it lawful "for any of his Majesty's Subjects trading to Africa, for the Security of their Goods or Slaves, to Erect Houses and Warehouses, under the Protection of the said Forts . . . for the better carrying on of his or their Trade there; which Houses and Warehouses shall be the Property of the Person or Persons who shall build the same."[22]

He began building Castle Brew at the same time as he supervised construction of the fort, and the castle was built by the same European and Fante craftsmen who built the fort. One of Brew's rivals informed the AC that Brew's "great House was built at least the exterior part of it, while he had the Command of the Fort himself, and a considerable number of your Slaves were employed several years in that Service." And William Mutter, governor of Cape Coast Castle, wrote the AC that "his (Mr. Brew's) house in Town [is] taking up all his attention. The Fort is neglected; the ordnance in particular . . . & many other repairs that I can mention. The Garden is going to destruction the Gardener being wholly employed about his (Mr. Brew's) house. He (the Gardener) & the rest of the Company's Slaves, have been . . . cutting timber for him." The temptation to use the company's slaves and employees may have been too great to resist, particularly given the time and expense involved in building an English mansion on the African coast. An impressive structure, Castle Brew stood at the fort's northwestern corner and was clearly intended to awe the Fante, the British inside the fort, and European traders who came there to do business. The Georgian British Palladian building, constructed of brick and stone, boasted arches, arcades, and an elegant black-and-white marble walk leading from the rear courtyard. A double staircase led up to the veranda and the entrance that most visitors would have used to reach the elegant reception hall. One departure from the Palladian style was an exterior staircase leading to the second story, the one concession to local building styles and one of several construction details the castle shared with the neighboring fort.[23]

Castle Brew offered a comfortable stopping place for weary ship captains, and Brew's lavish hospitality encouraged them to do business with him. The luxurious surroundings also gave some assurances that Brew was a man to be trusted with goods and credit. An inventory taken at the time of Brew's death reveals the elegant furnishings that graced the castle. He furnished the reception hall with two settees, twenty-three Windsor chairs, four tables, two bureaus and bookcases, and a sideboard, all made of mahogany. That elegant furniture was itself a product of the Atlantic World. Mahogany was a tropical hardwood from the Americas and the prized wood for fine eighteenth-century furniture. The first mention of mahogany furniture in England comes in Bramston's satirical *Man of Taste*, published in 1733, in which the author asks, "Say thou that dost thy father's table praise/Was there *Mahogena* in former days."[24] The origin of the tree's name is obscure, but one suggestion is that it is derived from *m'oganwo*, the name used by the Yoruba and Ibo for a related species native to West Africa. The taste for mahogany furniture was an Atlantic phenomenon, and there were links between the slave trade and the production of mahogany furniture. Rich planters from the West Indies, where the trees were plentiful, helped make the wood a popular status symbol, so popular that British scholars have dubbed the eighteenth century the "age of mahogany." Rhode Island and South Carolina slave traders often traded in mahogany furniture as well, and the furnishings of Castle Brew mirrored those of West Indian and South Carolinian slave trading merchants and planters.[25] The furniture that graced the halls of Castle Brew could have been made in London, or it could have come from Rhode Island, where furniture made up a part of the cargo of ships bound for West Africa and where Brew had close trading partners. Nicholas Owen, who sailed on a voyage from Rhode Island to West Africa in this period, recorded that the ship's cargo included "rum, tobacco, sugar, chocolate, snuff, and houshould [sic] furniture." Perhaps the most unexpected piece of furniture was an organ, no doubt one of the only such instruments on the African coast. The hall was lit with a crystal chandelier and decorated with four mirrors and "66 pictures of different sizes." Brew was prepared to entertain in lavish style. Silver candlesticks lit the dinner table, there was a choice of twenty-six tablecloths, food and drink could be served from a silver salver, the table could be laid with silver dinnerware, and up to five dozen china plates, some of them Wedgwood, were ready for use. Special decanters were available for wine, punch, and water, along with the appropriate glassware. Guest could play games of cards or backgammon.[26] It is hardly surprising that Castle Brew attracted many visitors.

Much of the furnishings of Castle Brew would have been found in the counting house of a successful London merchant, but the most elegant (and expensive) articles found there were marks of a higher and more formal style. The quantity of silver and china on display, the crystal chandelier, the mirrors, and the organ were more luxurious than the furnishings typically found in the London merchant houses of the day. These items were not intended for comfort, but to display fashion, elegance, and gentility. The two bureaus mentioned in the inventory are reminders that Castle Brew was a place of business as well as a residence; the merchant's bureau was an essential piece of furniture for a merchant like Brew. Typically these large "double desks" were outfitted with drawers, shelves, pigeonholes, and boxes to keep track of correspondence, accounts, bills, and other important documents.[27]

Brew's library, impressive by the standards of the day, illustrates the reach of the Atlantic intellectual and commercial world, and the role books and publications played in the structure of that world. It included multivolume works by such writers as Shakespeare, Addison, Swift, and Pope (the latter alone in twenty volumes); novels including *Tom Jones* and *Don Quixote;* several dictionaries; historical works including sixteen volumes of Rollin's Roman history, a three-volume history of Ireland, military and naval histories, and a history of Guinea; and long runs of periodicals like the *Spectator.* He often petitioned his correspondents on the Gold Coast and in England to send him reading material. In 1774, for example, he wrote Thomas Eagles, "A cargo of Newspapers & Magazines, some New publications, and a map of Liverpool upon the largest scale will be very acceptable." Keeping abreast of current events and remaining involved in the world of letters was clearly important to Brew and many of his friends and associates on the Gold Coast whose standards of civility necessitated such involvement, and the regular flow of books and periodicals from home helped ease the isolation they felt. The scope of Brew's collection suggests his efforts to remain connected to Britain's secular national literature, to its national canon. The "reach of the book trade extended through merchants" in the eighteenth century, and Brew's library is evidence of just how far that reach extended. His interest in keeping abreast of the latest news, his eagerness to have the most current newspapers and periodicals, also had a utilitarian function for someone engaged in international commerce. Success or failure in an Atlantic trade often depended on the most up-to-date information on politics, diplomacy, and commerce, all of which directly impacted trade to and from the Gold Coast. So too did laws and treaties, and debates about the future of the Royal African Company and its successor, the Company of Merchants Trading to Africa, were widely reported in the press and of great interest to Brew and every other British trader and official on the coast.[28]

The importance of Annamaboe as an Atlantic trade hub attracted ambitious young men on the make for whom employment in Africa or the Americas could be an important stepping stone toward a career in a large metropolitan concern. Brew's business operation was too extensive for him to operate alone, and he employed clerks to assist him, as would have been typical in a London counting house. Clerks were often seen as potential future partners and were often relatives of the merchants. That probably explains the presence of Brew's young relative, identified by his surname, Reddan, who is mentioned as residing at Castle Brew in the 1760s and 1770s. Reddan, however, turned out to be a disappointment for Brew. Brew's friend Thomas Westgate wrote to console him: "I am very sorry that any Relation of yours should turn out a Rascal in which case I think the sooner my friend Reddan decamps the better."[29] Brew also employed William Grant, a native of Rhode Island who sailed to Annamaboe on board the *Friendship* from Newport in 1762. Grant planned to set up in business for himself in Annamaboe, but on his arrival he found "the times very indifferent," and rather than striking out on his own, he went to work for Brew, probably as a clerk, at wages of £60 annually, but three months later he was dead.[30] Brew also hired capable men out from under the CMTA. William Webster resigned his post as chief of Commenda Fort in 1763 for "a much more advantageous offer from Mr. Brew." Webster's superior, Charles Bell, noted to the AC that "the advantages Mr. Webster expects from his having a share in the Trade & Capital with Mr. Brew is infinitely more than any of your Servants who have the best forts can expect." In 1769 Francis Cahuace left his post as secretary at Cape Coast Castle to work for Brew.[31]

Castle Brew was more than a counting house; it was also home to Brew's family, and it is that family life that most evidently marks Brew as a member of the African Atlantic World. Brew's wife and the mother of two of his four children was John Corrantee's daughter Effua Ansah. It is unclear when their relationship began; it may be that Brew's most significant personal relationship began during his residence under Corrantee's roof during the construction of Annamaboe Fort. Relationships between European men and African women were common in the coastal communities where Europeans set up residence, but since most Europeans remained on the coast for a relatively short time, their relationships were usually brief and ended once the European left. For that reason, they were usually referred to as "country marriages," emphasizing that they were expected to last only so long as the European man lived on the coast. Anglican missionary Reverend Philip Quaque, Thomas Thompson's protégé and the first African to serve as a missionary, became chaplain at Cape Coast Castle in 1766 regularly baptized the infants of these country marriages all along the Gold Coast. A number of the chiefs of the British forts also sent their mulatto sons to study with him before

A French engraving of a mulatto woman on the Gold Coast. Her dress mingles Fante and European clothing, and she carries an umbrella of European manufacture. Thomas Edward Bowdich, *Voyage dans le pays d'Aschantie, ou, Relation de l'ambassade envoyée dans ce royaume par les anglais: avec des détails sur les moeurs, les usages, les lois et le gouvernement de ce pays, des notices géographiques sur d'autres contrées situées dans l'intérieur de l'Afrique, et la traduction d'un manuscrit arabe ou se trouve décrite la mort de Mungo Park* (DT507 .H9815 1823). Special Collections, University of Virginia Library.

they sent them on to English boarding schools, and his classes in the fort at Cape Coast Castle also included mixed-race girls. Quaque noted that Gilbert Petrie, governor of Cape Coast Castle, had four mixed-race children of his own. Relationships between British men and African women were so common that Quaque regarded them as the "prevailing Vice" on the Gold Coast. When Captain Thomas Phillips visited the Gold Coast forts at Cape Coast Castle and Annamaboe and the lodge at Agah, he found that the governor of Cape Coast, the chief at Annamaboe, and the factor at Agah all had country wives, local mulatto women who they referred to as their wives and who joined the men at dinner. Phillips reported that he was given a "cordial reception" by Mr. Cooper, the Agah factor, "having the company of his wife (as he call'd her) to dine with us." Phillips regarded this as "a very pleasant way of marrying, for they can turn them off and take others at pleasure; which makes them very careful to humour their husbands in washing their linen, cleaning their chambers & c. and the charge of keeping them is little or nothing."[32] Whether or not his views on the casual nature of these relationships reflects those of the RAC officials is unclear, though his remarks do suggest many of the advantages white men found in their country marriages. The efforts the British governors, chiefs of forts, soldiers, and traders made to educate their children, often in England, and to find them employment in the forts is also testimony to the obligations these marriages imposed.

Most of the British officials and soldiers were only on the coast for a few years and their country marriages were relatively short-lived, but Brew's relationship with Effua Ansah was lifelong, and she bore him two daughters, Eleanor and Amba. It is highly significant that, if Brew's family history is accurate, Eleanor was his mother's name, and the choice of one African name and one English name for the daughters reflects their mixed heritage. These country marriages conformed at least in part to African practices and conventions. Among the Fante, marriages were often an important means of forming desirable alliances between families—a union between Brew and Corrantee held obvious advantages for both. Historian David Northrup has suggested these relationships might best be termed "commercial marriages" since they were tied to Atlantic trade and to furthering those relationships on both sides. According to Fante custom, everyone in the community belonged to some family, and strangers belonged to the families of their landlords, an understanding that could have further encouraged the match. A man was required to ask a woman's father for his permission for marriage, and he was expected to pay a symbolic bride price including rum and gold, depending on his and the family's wealth and status.[33] It is probable given Corrantee's high position that Brew met these expectations. In keeping with the practice among Europeans on the coast, he referred to Effua Ansah as his "Wench," as he did when he took on the responsibility of acquiring the necessaries to bury her mother, an act that a Fante husband would be expected to perform for his wife.[34]

The term *wench*, which the Englishmen on the Gold Coast used routinely to refer to their country wives, is jarring to modern sensibilities, and it is difficult to judge precisely how it would have sounded to eighteenth-century ears. Samuel Johnson, in his eighteenth-century dictionary, defines a wench as "a young woman," the original meaning of the term, followed by "a strumpet," suggesting that the word could have either meaning. Linguists have found that the term lost its pejorative meaning in the sixteenth century and after—a process they refer to as amelioration—when it became a term of endearment used by husbands toward wives and parents toward daughters. A writer in the *Gentleman's Magazine* claimed that the term was applied to young women "without any offensive meaning" in some parts of England in the early decades of the nineteenth century. In English-speaking slave societies in the Americas, the term was routinely applied to enslaved women. Noah Webster identified this meaning in his 1828 dictionary: "In America, a black or colored female servant; a negress." An aphorism reportedly from Jamaica in 1745 said that someone was almost as kind "as a Jamaica Merchant is of his Mulatto Wench." The term as it was used in Anglo-America could be sexualized, as in the Jamaica example, though it was commonly used without that implication when applied to enslaved women. Whether or not the term was sexualized, it was certainly racialized and must be read in that context in the Gold Coast as it was in the Americas.[35]

It would be a mistake to think that we can comprehend the range of commitment, love, and exploitation expressed in the relationships between European men and African and mixed-race women on the Gold Coast from the use of this word alone. While Brew referred to Effua

Ansah as his wench in this letter, he spent his entire life on the Gold Coast with her, recognized his children with her, and provided for her and their children (and not his sons by a previous country wife) to the best of his abilities in his will. While we know how Brew referred to his wife in his correspondence with other white men on the coast, where he conformed to the conventions of his time and place, we do not know how he spoke to her in the privacy of Castle Brew. There is only one hint of that household setting in the correspondence, when Thomas Westgate in a letter to Brew sent his compliments "to all the family," which suggests that he had spent pleasant time with the all the members of the Brew household.[36]

Certainly many of the Europeans on the Gold Coast had real affection for their country wives and their children, and these relationships mirror Brew's country marriage. Richard Miles, who spent over eighteen years on the coast and served as chief of several out forts, as the smaller forts along the coast were known, and as governor of Cape Coast Castle, educated his mixed-race son at a boarding school in Hillingdon where members of his family studied. He also expressed his desire to take his country wife, Sal, back to England with him. He asked one of his friends on the coast after his arrival in England to tell Sal "as I am not yet settled I let her remain. Should I go to the Coast next year I can bring her of[f] with me."[37] A similar case involved James Phipps, who began his career in 1703 as a writer at Cape Coast and later chief at Accra. He served as the highest official at Cape Coast Castle from 1711 to 1722, and he had a long-lasting country marriage with a woman who was the mulatto daughter of a Dutch soldier at Elmina. The couple had four daughters and a son. Phipps sent at least three of the daughters to England to be educated and planned to send his son as well, though he may have died before that took place. He provided for his country wife in his will. John Atkins, a slave ship captain who knew Phipps in Africa, reported that Phipps "dotes on this Woman." Atkins noted that he persuaded her to accompany him to worship services in the chapel, but that she maintained her faith in her own religious beliefs and her traditional dress. Atkins also criticized Phipps for sharing her belief in fetish and for "wearing them on his Wrists and Neck," an indication of the cultural exchange that occurred in these relationships. According to Atkins,

Phipps had tried to persuade his wife to return to England with him, but she refused for fear that she would not fit in there.[38]

Brew's lifelong devotion to Effua Ansah and his mixed-race children fits into this well-established pattern. Brew also had two sons from a previous country marriage, perhaps from his time at Tantumquerry. One son, probably the eldest, was named for his father; the second, Henry, was known as Harry. These young men were genuine Atlantic Creoles, and like some other Englishmen on the coast, Brew sent his sons to England to be educated.[39] Richard worked as a clerk in his father's business after the brothers returned to the coast in 1768. The busy Brew household also included a cook, a servant, and house slaves.[40]

Along with entertaining the ship captains in lavish style, Brew also paid host to the Reverend Quaque in 1766. In January 1767 Quaque spent a week as a guest in the Brew household on the "kind Recommendation" of Brew's partner in the slave trade, Samuel Smith, who Quaque must have met through the African Committee in London. Quaque conducted services in Castle Brew's "most noble Hall" before a large audience composed of "both White and Black." He baptized Eleanor and Amba Brew and three other mixed-race children belonging to a ship captain and to CMTA officials. Quaque observed that Brew behaved toward him "in the most polite manner imaginable," but those good relations cooled. Perhaps Quaque's sermons hit too close to home, for Brew later informed the governor of Cape Coast Castle that he would not come to the castle "to be Subservient to and to sit under the Nose of a Black Boy to hear Him pointing or laying out their faults before them."[41]

Quaque criticized the Englishmen for "consorting" with local women, and he antagonized the "gentlemen" at Cape Coast Castle by endeavoring to convince local women not to become their "wenches." It is easy to imagine that Quaque's attacks on country marriages could have provoked Brew's outburst. Quaque also believed that no people were "more vicious, villainous, revengeful, malicious, and none more brutal and obdurate in their disposition, than the natives of Annamaboe," a harsh judgment unlikely to endear him to Brew.[42] Over time, however, their relationship improved to the point that Brew's son Harry married Abba Kaybah, who was related to Quaque along the female line, and the Brew family considered Quaque to be their uncle.[43] Quaque was also related to Cudjoe Caboceer, the most powerful figure at Cape Coast Castle and Corrantee's counterpart there, and so the union between Quaque's family and Brew's son also united those powerful African families as well. Certainly the two families had some similarities; Quaque married his first wife, who was white, in England, and educated his sons in England as Brew did. These families belonged to the Atlantic Creole elite on the Gold Coast. Quaque also became involved in the administration of the slave trade, and a connection with Annamaboe's chief slave trader would have benefited him in that business. Quaque became a writer at Cape Coast Castle, and in 1775 he served as temporary governor of three of the smaller English forts, a job his father-in-law once held.[44]

From the time of his marriage around 1770, Harry Brew disappeared from the records, but it is likely that he worked in his father's business as a clerk. After his father's death, Harry moved to Cape Coast Castle and secured a position as a linguist and writer there beginning in 1792. He did so well in that position that within a few years' time the Englishmen regarded him as "the best Interpreter" on the coast. He was an especially important link between Cape Coast Castle and Amoony Coomah, chief caboceer at Annamaboe. Harry died in a smallpox epidemic in March 1796. He had his entire family inoculated, but could not bring himself to take that step.[45] The mixed-race sons of other former CMTA employees found employment in the forts, but there were limits on how far they could hope to advance. In 1794, former official Robert Collins tried to use his influence to get his mulatto son, then completing in education in England, in line to become a commander of a fort, but the African Committee informed him that "no mulatto, or Person of Color, can hold a seat in Council in this Service upon the Coast, consequently the Committee regrets they cannot comply with the request you make . . . in behalf of your Son, which otherwise it would have afforded their pleasure to grant." He appealed again to the committee, who agreed that since he was "an old Servant" they would appoint his son as an assistant clerk at the salary of £60 annually.[46]

Richard Brew Jr. also entered his father's business as a clerk after his return from England in 1768, but he was a troubled young man. Brew was forced to disown his son and namesake after he "gave himself up so entirely to all Kinds of Debauchery, that his Father was under the necessity of turning him out of Doors, after which he lived like a Vagabond amongst the Natives." He learned enough about the slave trade from his father to work with Mr. Butler, an English trader at the small town of Amanda on the Gold Coast. In August 1773 he was visiting and drinking with William Spooner, a fellow trader at nearby Lagoe. The men argued after dinner, an argument so serious that it led Spooner to put two pistols down on the table and challenge Brew to take one, if he was a man. Brew refused and said that "he would put his Life on par with a Highwayman." With that, Spooner picked up one of the pistols, put it to his own chest, and fired. Brew fled the scene, and Spooner died a few days later. Brew was not accused of any crime—the case was clearly suicide—but trouble seemed to follow him. After some years Richard managed to pull himself together sufficiently to be employed as a gunner at Annamaboe Fort, and he did well enough there to be promoted from that position to the job of a writer at Cape Coast Castle, where his superiors praised his abilities as an accountant. By 1780 he was serving as Cape Coast governor John Roberts's private secretary; one of Roberts's enemies described Brew as "a vile chap, a Mulatto in Collage with the Natives, to whom no doubt he tells everything." But his troubles hounded him; he lost that position, and Dutch officials at Elmina reported the death of the "English deserter Richard Broüw" in June 1782.[47] It would be easy to see him as a figure caught between two worlds, as someone without a clearly defined sense of identity whose inner contradictions led him to a life of failure. But we are seeing him through European eyes, and it is equally possible that he moved easily between these worlds and was as at home among his mother's people as his father's. Europeans on the coast were often extremely critical of the Afro-Europeans, and particularly of those who chose native ways over European ones. In a typical description, William Bosman described the mulattoes on the Gold Coast as a "bastard Strain . . . made up of a parcel of profligate Villains, neither true to the *Negroes* not us . . . I can hardly give them a Character so bad as they deserve. I can only tell you whatever is in its own Nature worst in the *Europeans* and *Negroes* united in them; so that they are the sink of both."[48] The European view of Richard Brew Jr. was colored in some measure by these prejudices.

From Castle Brew, Brew presided over his family and his extensive business operations. His long residence on the coast enabled him to build close relationships with the slave traders, particularly with the New England merchants known as the Rum Men who he traded with for over twenty years. Those relationships will be traced more fully in the following chapter, but Brew's name appear frequently in their accounts and their letters from Annamaboe, where they were frequent quests at the castle. Two of the most important merchants in Newport, the brothers Samuel and William Vernon, recommended Brew to their associate, John Thornton, of Fredericksburg, Virginia. They referred to Brew as "our Friend," and they reported that he "perhaps ships more slaves than any one man in the Kingdom." Brew employed another Rhode Islander, William Green, on board his sloop *Triton* to move goods up and down the Gold Coast. Green won a judgment against Brew in the Rhode Island for nonpayment of wages, a dispute that arose when Brew accused Green of embezzling a cargo and fired him. One of the Rum Men reported in 1775 that he had taken on a crewman who was returning to Rhode Island after having "been in Mr. Brews Sarvis [Service]."[49]

There is every indication that Brew's business thrived in the 1760s, and building the largest private trading firm on the Gold Coast involved Brew in a complex commercial enterprise. His partnership with Samuel Smith provided Brew with the credit he needed to purchase the trade goods he used to barter for slaves with the African traders. Entire shiploads of trade goods came from London and Liverpool on his account, laden with the textiles, metal wares, gunpowder, and other goods necessary for the trade. Brew had to know exactly what goods were in most demand on the coast at any given time, down to the color of the fabrics. Smith's firm, Barton and Smith, acted as Brew's agent and underwrote the bills of exchange he used to buy goods from ships on the coast, especially rum and tobacco necessary for trade, and to handle his financial needs in the Caribbean and North America. He set up factories at other posts along the Gold Coast, but more importantly, he established a string of factories on the Slave Coast in Whydah and Popo, at Lagos and Benin, and at Cape Lopez. Staffed by a single European factor and a number of Africans, these were lonely and isolated outposts. One factor noted that his factory employed six hammock men, two factory men, an interpreter, a washerwoman, a cook, and several porters. In 1763 he purchased a brig that arrived on the coast filled with rum, a brig he used "to bring up Slaves which his Factors" at Whydah and Popo purchased for him. By 1766 he owned two ships he "sent to different parts of the Coast for Slaves," part of a small fleet of schooners, brigs, and sloops that plied the waters between Annamaboe and the outposts carrying trade goods from Castle Brew and returning with slaves. In June 1770, for example, he wrote that one schooner he had sent to the River Del Rey the preceding August had returned with one hundred slaves, and he expected a second schooner to arrive in another month from Old Calabar with eighty slaves.[50]

Brew also employed his ships in carrying cargoes of slaves directly from Africa to the Caribbean. In 1776, for example, he sent his schooner *Jenny* to Cape Lopez where Jonathan Helbrand, his factor there, purchased 120 slaves to be loaded onto the ship and sent directly to the West Indies, where Brew planned to sell the slaves and the schooner. He laid out the details of the voyage in a letter insuring the ship. He informed them that once he received the proceeds from that voyage that he intended to send another of his schooners, the *Lively,* to Cape Lopez to take on 130–140 slaves and sail them to Granada. A part of the proceeds would go to his London agents, and the rest he would send with the *Lively* to Rhode Island to purchase a cargo of rum. In addition, the ship needed repairs, and he planned to install a new deck and new upper works, the sort of repairs that could not be made on the African coast. He further explained that if the conflict then beginning between Britain and her North American colonies interfered with that plan, then the ship would return from Granada with a cargo of West Indian rum.[51] This example gives an indication of just how far Brew's trade networks reached, from Africa to the West Indies to Rhode Island, and how complex every single voyage could be.

Gilbert Petrie, governor of Cape Coast Castle, reported to the AC that there were three ships currently at Annamaboe: "Two of them, Mr. Brew has contracted for their whole Cargoes . . . Mr. Brew has the most flourishing trade ever known at Annamaboe." When he contracted for entire cargoes he could either pay the captains with bills of exchange drawn on London or he could barter for slaves, tobacco, or other goods stored at

Castle Brew. In most cases, he exchanged slaves for trade goods. Brew did not just trade with British or American ships, though they were his primary trading partners, but also with the Dutch, the Portuguese, and the French. Brew controlled so much of the market for slaves at Annamaboe that Petrie worked with him on a plan to force the price of slaves down, but competition from the Dutch foiled that scheme. Another AC officer remarked on Brew's dominance of the trade at Annamaboe; he observed that of the 440–450 slaves then held for sale in the crowded pens in the fort there, all but fifty or sixty belonged to Brew and half of the warehouses in the fort were filled with his trade goods. He also complained that those pens had been built to accommodate no more than 150 slaves, and that conditions were very bad; "the place is more disagreeable and unhealthy," he wrote, "than any Goal in Europe."[52]

Brew's influence was so great at Annamaboe that he continued to play a major role in diplomacy along the coast, and those efforts reveal how far his influence extended into the African interior and how his close ties with the Fante caboceers gave him greater insight into African affairs than the CMTA officials with whom he was often at odds. In 1767 CMTA officials reported "a most unlucky quarrel between the soldiers of the Fort & the Blacks" at Annamaboe "is likely to produce very serious Consequences." The dispute began when "a Black Man from the Town, standing on the Draw Bridge at Sally port where the Centry [Sentry] is always posted, attempted with the utmost effrontery to make water where he stood, and did not even scruple to bespreach [?] the Soldiers Legs." The soldiers, "enraged by a piece of indecency unheard of at any other Fort," pushed the man down the steps, "but he, not deterred by that Correction, jumpt up & attacked the Centenil on his post." The man fled into town, and the governor of the fort "sent the rest of the Soldiers to seize & bring him in." The townspeople, however, refused to allow him to be captured; "a Mob was instantly assembled and who not only opposed the Soldiers but attacked & beat them & wounded one with a Knife & beat them back into the Fort." John Grosle, chief of the fort, fired a cannon into the mob in an attempt to disperse it, "but that so far from having the desired effect only excited them to greater insults. They presented their posteriors to Grosle in contempt of his power, and then to convince him of theirs they repaired to his Garden, where they burned the Houses of his Gardener and Compny's slaves & carried off the former a prisoner." The mob then attacked the fort; "they fired briskly at the Fort," until fire from the bastions drove them into the town and "set fire to that part of Town to which they belonged." The battle ended only as night fell. Officials in the fort sent to Cape Coast Castle for assistance, and the next morning thirty marines attempted to reinforce the fort, "but they were no sooner Landed than the Blacks rushed out of their Houses and fired upon them which frightened the Canoemen & prevented the landing of the rest of the Marines." Twenty marines fought their way into the Fort, and once inside they fired on the town and burned the remaining houses belonging to the rebels. One townsman lay dead, many others on both sides were wounded, and half the town was a smoldering ruin.[53]

Brew attempted to resolve the dispute. He invited the governor of Cape Coast Castle to join Grosle and Annamaboe's caboceers to meet in a "neutral place"—Castle Brew—to negotiate a settlement, but the CMTA officials were too angry to consider negotiating in the "House of a Private Trader" rather than "in the Nation's Fort." Trade stopped at Annamaboe; the blacks seized canoemen and planned to prevent the fort from being resupplied. Brew knew that the Africans could carry out their threat, and he was eager to reopen trade and bring the unfortunate conflict, which had clearly blown far out of proportion to the original incident, to an end. The CMAT officials, however, stubbornly refused to budge. Brew cleverly found a way to bring them to the table. He warned that if the fighting resumed, as it would unless some resolution could be found, that his house's proximity to the fort meant that it could be used to shelter hundreds of townspeople in an attack on the fort and that it would be burned to ashes in the fighting. He reminded the officials that the fort existed in part to protect private traders, and he threatened that if the men refused to settle the dispute, he would sue them individually and personally for the loss of Castle Brew and its contents, which now could not be moved to the safety of the fort. That threat badly frightened the men, who estimated the castle and its contents to be worth £6,000–7,000; as the governor of Cape Coast Castle realized, "the value of this House is more than I am worth." Suddenly eager to settle the palaver, the governor offered twenty ounces "in Trade to be given away amongst the Town's People." The governor complained bitterly to the AC about the entire matter and the need to protect Castle Brew: "To fulfill that National purpose; with a View of preserving that House, at least from a fear of being ruined with it, is this Palaver settled."[54]

The matter was not quite over, however. Samuel Smith, Brew's business associate and a member of the African Committee, sent Brew a copy of Petrie's letter to the AC justifying his actions in the dispute and criticizing Brew. Petrie was furious at Smith, but since Smith was one of the directors of the CMTA and Brew one of its freeholders, Petrie had to admit that Brew had a right to see any committee correspondence. Brew was outraged, not only at Petrie's petulant attitude, but also at what he considered Petrie's attempt to mislead the committee about the settlement of the palaver. According to Brew, the governor paid far more than twenty ounces of trade goods to settle the bloody affair. Given that one man was killed and so much damage done to the town—and all as a result of where a man chose relieve himself—makes it almost certain that the blacks demanded more than a token payment. Brew had the caboceers and pynins of Annamaboe sign their marks to a document stating as much. He sent other documents attempting to establish that the palaver was a far more important matter than Petrie had led the AC to believe, one that hurt the trade at Annamaboe and would have done far greater damage had it not been settled quickly, thanks to Brew's intervention.[55]

Brew's influence was not limited to Annamaboe but extended into the African interior. His effort to lengthen his reach beyond the coast is best illustrated by his involvement in negotiations between the Fante and the Asante. Most of the slaves sold at Annamaboe came from the Asante who brought slaves to the interior markets where Fante traders came and purchased slaves to sell to Europeans. The Fante acted as intermediaries between the Asante and the Europeans on the coast, but the two nations were traditional enemies, and conflicts between them often cut off the supply of slaves entirely. The Europeans were eager to keep those supplies flowing, and they hoped to either see the Asante and the Fante at peace or to have the Asante open paths directly to the coast, something the Fante, of course, were eager to prevent. William Mutter, governor of Cape Coast Castle, took an interest in opening a direct path to the

Asante. The first Asante to visit any European fort since 1740 came to Cape Coast in 1764 thanks to Mutter's efforts to lure them there rather than see them go to Elmina, where the Dutch were courting them as well. Their arrival suggested that they had a path opened, but Mutter reported that it lay perilously close to the Fante, who would plunder any Asante traders who used the path.[56]

Brew undertook to act as mediator between the Asante and the Fante, a mission that involved him with the French and that put him at odds with both the Dutch and the English officials in the forts. If he could win that role, then he could become the conduit for the flow of slaves from the Asante to Annamaboe. The Fante had sold captured Asante as slaves, and one of those men was a chichee, or messenger, belonging to the king of Asante, a member of the king's personal staff whose value Brew immediately recognized. He was entertaining the captain of the French ship at Castle Brew when he learned about the captive, and he redeemed the king's messenger, a transaction for which he received a receipt from the French captain. At the same time Brew and the Frenchmen were enjoying food and drink at the castle, the Dutch chief of Axim went on board the French ship; he, too, knew the value of the enslaved chichee and saw a chance to win favor with the Asante. He redeemed the slave from the ship's chief mate and took him into the Dutch fort, promising to pay a slave in return. The French captain endorsed Brew's claim and did not accept the pawn from the Dutch, but he had no power to secure the man for Brew. The Dutch simply refused to put the man in Brew's hands. Brew wrote Mutter asking him to intervene to regain his property being held by the Dutch. Mutter wrote the Dutch governor Jan Pieter Theodoor Huydecoper on Brew's behalf, but he simply refused to acknowledge Brew's claim. Letters flew between the parties, and Brew warned that returning the chichee "may prevent some disagreeable consequences which may probably attend refusing immediately to deliver the Chichee," and he warned Mutter that he was "determined if it costs . . . £10,000 to have him." Good to his word, Brew saw a chance to gain the upper hand. A messenger from Huydecoper stopped at Annamaboe, and Brew immediately captured the man and clamped him in double irons. Brew continued to demand that Mutter have the chichee returned, Mutter complained, "as if it could be done with the stroke of the Pen," even though he knew he could not compel the Dutch governor to do so. Brew's request was a ploy intended, Mutter claimed, "to embroil us from one end of the Coast to the other after all not be able to extricate myself with any sort of Credit," and should that happen, he knew that Brew would be "the first to have censured me for my rash and precipitous conduct." Aware of the corner Brew had backed him into, he lashed out at him for his "degree of Arrogance extremely disagreeable. He has become the Object of everyone's aversion . . . [he] seems to respect no Laws of his own Country, nor Customs of this . . . Shamefully abusive in his Language, Domineering in his Conduct & behavior, Implacable in his hatreds."[57]

Brew also knew that Huydecoper would lose face by surrendering the chichee, one reason he was so eager to make it happen. Though no longer a CMTA official, Brew relished a chance to get the best of the Dutch. Brew told Mutter that the Dutch governor "is extremely Sensible of the Importance of his acquisition, as he knows perfectly, if he is obliged to deliver up this man he must Cut a very poor figure as a mediator between the Ashantee & Fantees."[58] He warned Mutter, correctly no doubt, that the Dutchman wanted to prevent "any Englishman from having any hand in it, if it was in his power, but we hope to Convince him that as inconsiderable as he takes us to be, our influence in this Country is far superior to his own, and let the palaver [between the Asante and the Fantees] be settled when it will, we shall have as great a share in that Transaction as himself."[59]

The relations between Brew and Mutter only grew worse as Brew continued to insist that Mutter recognize the Dutchman's intentions and assist in "protecting the property of British free traders." Messengers went back and forth every day as the men fired off letter after letter. Mutter responded by denying that Huydecoper wanted to cut the British out of negotiations with the Asante, questioning Brew's claim to the man and criticizing him for holding the messenger hostage and for selling slaves to the French. Brew continued to repeat his claim, called on Mutter to do his job, and criticized Mutter for trading with the Dutch and the Danes in violation of CMTA regulations while reminding him that he was a free trader and could trade with whoever he chose.[60] Mutter convinced the entire council to formally condemn Brew's seizure of the messenger.

Brew responded that their opinions on the matter were "no manner of Consequence."[61] Mutter confessed to the AC that neither he nor Huydecoper "have hither to advance one single Step towards settling the matter between the Fantees and the Ashantees . . . we have done all we can," he claimed, "but unfortunately have no reason to boast of our Success."[62]

While clearing enjoying goading Mutter and encouraged by the lack of any progress on the part of the British or the Dutch, Brew was working on other fronts. Brew's connections to the Fante and his grasp of the intricacies African politics gave him a decided advantage over his rivals. The king of the Asante, the Asantehene, had given one of his relatives and others as pawns to the Fante to insure that he had no hostile intentions against them. The caboceer of Murram, a principal Fante town in the interior, first held them, but since the town was close to Asante territory, he feared they would escape, so they were sent to Annamaboe and put under the watchful eye of Quasah, John Corrantee's heir and the brother of Brew's wife, who grew tired of maintaining them. Brew convinced him to allow him to take the Asante pawns under his supervision at Castle Brew, thereby giving him a valuable card to play with the Asante, and he beat out both Huydecoper and Mutter, who had tried to get the men housed with them.[63] Those pawns gave Brew an opening to negotiate directly with the Asantehene.

Brew sent messengers from Annamaboe to the Asantehene "in a *clandestine manner*," along with some of the Asante pawns who had been held in Castle Brew as a testament of his good faith and a demonstration of his own capabilities. It was a bold stroke, one he took without the knowledge or approval of the Fante caboceers "except for one or two who were bribed for conniving at it in the absence of the rest."[64] Brew's efforts came as a surprise both to the Fante and to all Europeans along the coast. Mutter was skeptical, of course, and informed the AC that Brew would spend a lot of money for nothing and that the Fante were playing their own game. He also complained of Brew's "effrontery" for claiming that he had made "great Strides towards settling affairs & are prodigiously angry that I don't throw away great sums of money in presents."[65] When the entire body of Fante caboceers learned of Brew's maneuver, they ordered the men to be retaken dead or alive, but they were too late to catch the men who made it safely back to Asante territory.[66]

Brew's clever move worked, and the Asante were willing to negotiate with the British acting as intermediaries between them and the Fante, but who would spearhead the British effort? Brew had cast himself in that role, but Gilbert Petrie, governor of Cape Coast Castle, deeply resented what he saw as a clear usurpation of his role, and he refused to work with Brew as an equal. Petrie initially told Brew that he would join the negotiations, and he reported to the AC that "Mr. Brew received the proposal with joy, upon a supposition that he and I were to act jointly & on terms of equality in every Respect; a plan which was inconsistent with my Duty to you, and with the Regard I owed to my own character considering my Station as that of the first officer of the publick establishment in this Country." He wrote Brew to clarify that he would work with him "on so important an affair" so long as Brew agreed to conditions consistent with the proud Petrie's "station." But Brew held a trump card—two of them, actually—two Asante hostages. While Brew had sent some of the Asante prisoners home, he kept two behind to force the Asante to the table, to *his* table. Petrie insisted that any messages or proposals to the Asantehene should be delivered by his messengers, not Brew's, and that should hostages be returned, they would be returned by Petrie's delegates rather than by Brew's men. In return, Petrie promised to help Brew get reimbursed for the expenses he had incurred in the negotiations, particularly for the lodging and support of the hostages. Brew's reaction came as no surprise to Petrie, who wrote, "Any one acquainted with that Gentleman will conceive how he treated the offer of such conditions; that he rejected it with the utmost disdain declaring he would never agree to act in a *Subaltern character to the Committee* or any of their servants . . . and he would not continue to act as a principal when joined with me." Clear about his own position, Brew told Petrie that "he was resolved to persevere in the affair himself." Brew communicated that resolution to the Fante caboceers who had assembled to discuss the entire matter, and Petrie also notified them his "reason for not chusing [choosing] to sacrifice the dignity of my Station . . . to gratify the Vanity & extravagance, the affected self-importance of an individual like Mr. Brew." The Fante demanded dashes, trade goods, from both men "to be

given to the priest before he declares the Sentiments of the Fantee Deity."
The Fante routinely consulted their oracle before making such major decisions, and no doubt they intended the size of those gifts to measure the
relative strength of the two men. Petrie sent £20 in trade goods, but
Brew, the son-in-law of John Corrantee who learned much from the great
caboceer, far outmatched that paltry showing by sending "fine Silk &
chintz cloths together with Liquour amounting on the whole to upwards
of thirty ounces, to be distributed amongst the Cabboceers, Priests, and
Curranteers." Recognizing that he had been outdone, Petrie lamented
"what a diminutive appearance much be my little dashee . . . when compared to all that!"[67]

Apparently Brew's superior gifts won the day, and negotiations continued with him as intermediary, much to the consternation of the CMTA
officials. In the course of those talks, Brew allowed one of the hostages to
return, trusting him with trade goods, but the man escaped on the way
with those goods. The Asante threatened to attack unless the other hostage Brew held was also returned, which Brew agreed to once the Fante
pledged thirty slaves to allow the transfer to go forward and to cover
Brew's expenses.[68] But even the CMTA officials had to admit that the
while no formal agreement had been reached between the Fante and Asante, there was "very little fear of further disturbances," and that peaceful
situation continued for many years. Despite that success, CMTA officials
continued to resent Brew's involvement, and when the Fante refused to
give Brew the thirty slaves they had pledged, the CMTA officials also
refused to reimburse him. David Mill, governor of Cape Coast Castle,
like several of his predecessors, opposed paying Brew not because his
important diplomatic efforts had failed but because that expense "was in
great measure incurred to gratify his [Brew's] pride by endeavoring to
acquire popularity & to establish an Opinion among the Blacks, he was
superior in Wealth and importance to the Committee."[69]

Brew's career reached its high point during the 1760s, when he was the
largest exporter of slaves on the Gold Coast, when his business prospered,
and when his diplomatic efforts brought peace to two of the bitterest enemies along the coast. By the 1770s, however, he was facing financial difficulties, which he blamed in large part on the illegal trade activities pursued by the CMTA officials on the coast. In the 1770s Brew launched a

high-profile campaign against the African Committee and the conduct of its officers on the Gold Coast. His published attack on the committee offers insight into his own business dealings during the period and
his often hostile relationships with other Englishmen on the coast. In 1772
John Peter Demarin, former collector of customs at Senegambia, published a defense of slavery and the African slave trade entitled *A Treatise
Upon the Trade from Great-Britain to Africa Humbly Recommended to
the Attention of Government,* and letters from Brew account for about
thirty of the publication's 124 pages.[70] The conclusion noted that the entire treatise "is not the reverie of any one single person, but the joint
sentiments of the best writers upon the trade, and the result of the united
opinions of the most capital merchants to Africa, drawn from their long
experiences and perfect knowledge of the subject."[71] After twenty years'
residence on the Gold Coast, longer than any other British man, Brew
was certainly in a good position to review the conduct of the slave trade.

Brew's relationship with many of the CMTA officials had always been
strained, but his attempts to discredit them brought those relationships
to a low point, and company officials used Brew's worsening financial
difficulties against him. During one argument between in 1771 between
Brew and Charles Bell, governor of Cape Coast Castle, Brew heaped
abuse on Bell, who he called a "Wretch of Wretches," whose "Wretched-
ness, Rapacity, and Parsimony are become proverbial."[72] The argument
began when Bell took in a crewman from one of Brew's ships who Brew
claimed owed him a considerable amount of money. Bell refused to surrender the man, who he claimed had suffered physical abuse.[73] Bell returned his "Compliments to the Bankrupt Brew," promised to settle the
matter in person, and apologized that he could not respond in Brew's
cutting tone, claiming "not to be sufficiently Conversant in the Billingsgate Stile for that Task."[74] Billingsgate was London's notorious fish market, and its fishmongers, particularly the women, were known for their
vulgar language. The two barely avoided a duel. In 1774 Bell criticized
Brew for being late on payments to David Mill and hinted at his money
problems, and Brew lambasted Bell for his "rascally Impertinent Insinu-
ation which no Gentlemen would have made." Brew ended by calling
him a "Villainous Scoundrel."[75] When Brew told Mill about the insult-
ing note, he said that it was "couched in the Most Insolent affronting

terms of any I have Rec'd from any human being." He charged that Bell could "not Exist if he is not Ridiculing or Slandering Somebody and he thinks his Station & fortune will Screen him from Resentment." Brew warned that such insults "will bring a horsewhip over his shoulders." He went on to paraphrase Jonathan Swift: "of how Small Estimation is Wealth in the sight of God by his bestowing it on the most unworthy of Mortals," a quote that suggests Brew turned to his books for consolation during these troubled times.[76]

What is perhaps most interesting about Brew's sustained attack on the African Committee and its representatives on the Gold Coast is that much of what he condemned in them was precisely what he had himself been accused of as governor of Tantumquerry and Annamaboe. Brew's most serious charge was that the officers of the CMTA were dealing in slaves on their own account in violation of company rules—the very offense that got him dismissed from his positions. He made several specific and damaging accusations: first, that all the governors of Cape Coast Castle from 1763 to the present time (except one) had shipped large numbers of slaves on their own accounts; second, that other company employees at the forts acted as traders on behalf of the governors; third, that the governors sold slaves to the Dutch contrary to law; fourth, that the governors operated "floating factories," ships that they could move from one trading post to another; and fifth, that the governors traded with one another.[77]

Brew laid out many specific examples of the governors trading in slaves on their own accounts. He alleged, for example, that one of the New England traders known as Rum Men, David Dunn of Boston, arrived in Annamaboe in 1770 and told him that one-third of his ship and its cargo was owned by John Grosle, governor of Cape Coast Castle, who had just died. Dunn disposed of his rum quickly to the new governor and his men; loaded his ship with dry goods, which he claimed to have bartered for rum; and then sailed down to the fort at Mumford, where he was loaded with slaves in preference to other traders there. Brew also charged Mill and Bell, governors of Cape Coast and Annamaboe, with purchasing the cargo of a Rhode Island ship on five months' credit, with the proviso that they would use that vessel during that time to trade jointly with its captain along the coast. Brew named a long list of merchants from

London and Bristol who had brought out large shipments of goods for Mill and Bell. There can be little doubt that Brew's charges were legitimate. Surviving accounts from the Rum Men clearly show these sorts of dealings. For instance, Captain Peleg Clarke reported that he had sold rum to Mill and Bell on three months' credit. In 1775 Clarke reported that he "brougt [sic] Off the Coast 100 Slave Freight for Mr. Bell at 5 Sterling per head and have Delivered them all in good Order."[78] Another of the Rum Men, Robert Champlin, wrote to his brother, Christopher, from the Gold Coast, "Mr. Mill and I Is on Good Tarmns [terms]. He ofered [offered] To Take all my Carg[o] if I would Land It at widough [Whydah]."[79] The following year Clarke noted that "if Mr. Mill Complies with his promise have 20 More [slaves] from him."[80] Brew had complained of exactly that sort of arrangement between Thomas Trinder, the CMTA factor at Winnebah, and one of the Rum Men.

Another reason that Brew knew that the CMTA officials engaged in private trade was that he had dealt with them himself in clear violation of the regulations. In 1769, for example, one of Brew's ships bound for Lagoe stopped at Whydah and offered its cargo to Archibald Dalziel, chief of that fort, if he would pay all expenses involved in the deal. Dalziel agreed, paid the custom fees, and slaved the ship. He confessed his transgression to the AC, explaining that since trade so was slow at that time, he made the private trade only as "a Service to the Nation."[81]

Brew also pointed out that David Mill, governor of Cape Coast Castle and the highest CMTA official on the coast, was the brother of James Mill of the prominent London-based slave-trading firm of Ross & Mill, and another brother was Hercules Mill, the captain of slavers bound for the Gold Coast. Both James Mill and Gilbert Ross served as representatives for London on the African Committee at various times, and they were accused of conspiring to control the elections of London's representatives to maintain their positions of influence on the committee. In one of his letters Brew wrote, "Before this reaches you, a brother of Mr. Mil's [Hercules] will be sailed from England for this Coast; whether he brings out the Ruby of four or five hundred tons, in which he sailed from here last March full of slaves . . . he is certainly to be out here shortly with a large quantity of goods, and to carry off a cargoe of slaves. I cannot positively say, if his brother here is concerned with him, but it is more than probable he is; at any rate he can ship as many slaves as he pleases on freight without fear of discovery." Ross & Mill dealt heavily in slaves from the Gold Coast to South Carolina and to Jamaica. Brew complained that although the trade was terribly slow and that several vessels had been at Annamaboe for many months and were still not half slaved, Hercules Mill's ship and others sent by the firm of Mill & Ross were quickly loaded with their full cargoes of slaves within a relatively short stay at Cape Coast Castle.[82]

‹ Brew alleged that the commanders essentially turned the forts into their own private trading houses. He described the melancholy situation of Robert Johnston, a former CMTA official in Senegal and on the Gold Coast who turned private trader at Winnebah, whose house and all his goods were lost in a fire in October 1770. Brew argued that Johnston's losses would not have been so great had he been allowed to store his goods in the fort, which stood forty feet from his house. Such a loss hurt not only Johnston but the British slave traders who placed their trade goods in his hands while bargaining for slaves. Brew reported that he was forced to build his own slave pens and storage facilities at Castle Brew because he could not rely on the forts to provide those services and because gunpowder he stored in the fort was used by the commander without reimbursement. Johnston also complained that his house was burned by one of his own African servants, who was caught plundering the house during the fire. The chief of Winnebah fort, Thomas Trinder, along with the caboceers of the town, advised Johnston to capture the man, who was taken into the fort in chains. In order to determine the man's guilt, Johnston did not rely on a trial in the British custom, but rather "at his own request administered fetish to him," as Africans on the Gold Coast did to determine someone's guilt or innocence, and "by which fetish he was condemned."[83]

Despite having followed the "laws and customs of the country," Johnston's actions against his servant provoked controversy. When Johnston visited Annamaboe in December 1770 to conduct business with Brew, he faced the wrath of the town's soldiers, who surrounded Castle Brew carrying "drums, musquets, and other weapons; all of whom threatned [sic], if I did not send down to Winnebah for the aforementioned servant, who is an Annamaboe man, and deliver him up to them, they would not suffer me to go off the beach, and would carry me into the bush." Johnston appealed to Charles Bell, commander of Annamaboe Fort, and "claimed the protection and assistance of the fort." To his surprise, Bell replied that "it was not in his power to render me the smallest assistance" and "that he would not involve the committee in any dispute with the natives upon any account whatsoever; also that he would not fire a gun in my defence [sic]." Without any hope of assistance from the fort, Johnston had little choice but to give in to their demands. Brew agreed to act as his security, and he "was obliged to give up a man who had not only plundered me, but in all probability set fire to my house, by which my loss amounted to upwards of six hundred pounds sterling." He further alleged that the soldiers, slaves, and other servants of Winnebah Fort who helped to carry what goods he salvaged from the flames into the fort "were as industrious in plundering me as the town's people."[84] Brew charged that the governors of the forts were so dependent on their own good trading relationships with the townspeople that their personal interests blinded them to the needs of private traders like Johnston, and, even more than that, weakened them to the point where they could not effectively challenge the townspeople.

Brew supported his charge that the other company employees at the forts acted as traders on behalf of the governors with testimony from Isaac Garrick, who was employed by David Mill for three years on the coast. He worked as a factor at a trading post called Shadoe, near Winnebah. He reported that a private trader, John Hyde, attempted to settle at Shadoe, but that Mill ordered him "turned out of the town if possible, or trade in such a manner that it would be impossible for him to continue there without a very great loss." Garrick soon succeeded in having Hyde driven out of town.[85] Brew gave many instances of the committee's officials undermining the private traders, just as Brew himself was alleged to have done at Tantumquerry. Captain John Ritchie of Liverpool reported that he sent his mate to trade for gold at Fort Apollonia, but once the mate arrived there, Richard Miles, chief of the post, sent his servant to the town with his scales and weights, and the servant offered to sell his goods at as low a price as the mate and, moreover, to give them a gallon of rum for every ounce of gold they brought him. The ploy worked; the servant took in at least forty ounces of gold the next day, while the mate could get less than five ounces. Brew and others blamed the trading activities of the company officials for driving up the price of slaves and for encouraging the African slave dealers to trade slaves for gold rather than for trade goods, a practice that greatly diminished the amount of gold sent off the coast to Britain.[86]

Brew's charges that the CMTA officials traded with the Dutch also seem certain. Brew alleged that the officers traded slaves for Portuguese (actually Brazilian) tobacco, which was popular among the Africans on the Gold Coast, particularly Mill and Bell, who sold "great numbers" of slaves to the general of the Dutch fort of Elmina for tobacco. The officials claimed that they needed the tobacco to pay the natives for various expenses related to the forts, but Brew claimed that only a tiny fraction went for that purpose—the officials used most of it to purchase slaves.[87]

CMTA officials resorted to clever accounting strategies to increase their incomes. The governors of the forts were responsible for furnishing the forts—that is, they advanced goods of their own or on their own accounts to pay the garrison for repairs of the forts and other charges. They paid these expenses with trade goods—rum, tobacco, and inexpensive cloth—that they bought cheaply from the slavers. They marked these goods up, however, and repaid themselves with the very best trade goods sent out by the company in its annual supply ship, so they paid in coarse cloth, for example, but took repayment in India silks. The governors paid the garrison with rum; they bought it for slightly over one shilling per gallon from the Rum Men but billed the company six shillings per gallon. Through these sleights of hand, they managed to always be in arrears in their pay and ready to claim the choicest trade goods to double their salaries at CMTA expense. Brew also noted that if he could attend the auditing of the accounts of the forts, "I dare say, I could unravel many iniquitous scenes, which you are and must remain ignorant of," a claim that certainly rings true.[88]

Brew's charges were highly specific; indeed, he seemed surprisingly well-informed about the inside affairs of all the company's officials on the coast. It appears that along with the general flow of rumors among Europeans there, Brew had informants on the inside. He and Thomas Westgate kept up a regular correspondence in which Westgate, who felt slighted by the other company officials, fed Brew a steady stream of damning information. On one occasion, he wrote Brew a hurried letter at 9:00 p.m. on a visit to Cape Coast Castle. He threw the letter out of his window in the fort "to one of Abbah's people," who delivered it to Brew. Abbah was Westgate's country wife, and it was her relatives who he trusted to carry his letter to Brew. After Brew's death, Westgate's letters showing that he sympathized with many of Brew's criticisms of the CMTA officials and that he was the source of much of Brew's inside information fell into the hands of the company through Brew's executors. Westgate defended himself by saying that he was dependent on Brew, and therefore no one should be "surprised that I should flatter him a little upon his favourite plan." Brew had often tried to hire him away from the CMTA, but he refused, and he claimed that he advised Brew to "lay down his pen," not because what he wrote was untrue, but because "I was sure nothing he could say would answer his purpose and that Things would certainly go on in the old Way." Because of those damning letters the company held a hearing on Westgate's conduct, labeled him an "Enemy to the Service," and dismissed him. In addition to Westgate, William Lacy, the accountant at Cape Coast Castle, was another of Brew's inside contacts.[89]

Brew's criticisms of the CMTA, sent to the African Committee itself, to private traders in England, and published in book form, hit their mark. The African Committee complained loudly about Brew's "*voluminous production,*" as they referred to his letters. Not surprisingly, they attempted to discredit Brew's charges by attacking him personally. Brew, they argued, still harbored resentments over his dismissal from the service years earlier. They described him as "a disappointed peevish man," to which he replied that if he was disappointed and peevish, "their ignorance and folly, and the scandalous behavior of their servants, has helped greatly to make me so."[90] But Brew was joined by influential merchants in Liverpool, particularly Miles Barber, who began gathering information and talking to influential politicians. Barber reported that Brew's letters "are highly applauded by the Gentlemen in this Port & Town far exceeding anything of the kind I ever perused. . . . The Spirit of this Town," he assured Brew, "is heartily & firmly embarked in the cause."[91] Barber and a group of merchants wrote the AC in support of his accusations. They informed the AC, "We are convinced the foundations of those complaints is just and not exaggerated having long experienced the shameful modes of operation practiced against the fair adventurer." They added, "We are much obliged to Mr. Brew joining his endeavors to put the Trade on the Gold Coast upon the most eligible footing, and very much admire his remarks."[92]

If there were any doubt that at least some of Brew's most serious charges were true, a smoking gun lies in the papers of Richard Miles in the form of a letter to him from Gilbert Petrie, former governor of Cape Coast Castle. When Miles took over as chief of Annamaboe Fort, Petrie wrote him with advice on how to circumvent the restrictions against trading in slaves. Petrie wrote:

> The clause in the act of Parliament concerning shipping slaves in an absolute one and a total prohibition of remittance in Slaves. The Co. may wink at a breach of that clause, but they cannot approve of it. However, when you have a safe method of doing a thing, you will do wrong to run any risk.

He referred Miles to the firm of Ross & Mill, with whom he had communicated in order to facilitate Miles' trade in slaves. The firm would advance Miles the funds to engage in the trade. Miles was to ship the slaves in Petrie's name, consign them to selected slave dealers in Grenada, and "direct the person who sells the slaves to remitt the Proceeds on good Bills of exchange at the shortest date to Mess. Ross & Mill on account of G. P."[93]

As Brew's letters had their effect and as Barber and the other merchants from Liverpool entered into the fray, Petrie wrote Miles

> to warn you of the danger which indiscretion seem to have drawn you into. The Committee has received from Liverpool complaints of many of their officers, transmitted by Mr. Brew, and some of them said to be attested to by Masters and Mates of ships. . . . What notice the Committee have taken of that affair I know not, but certain I am, that if the Fact be proved, allthough it might not induce them to suspend you the will only of committing a crime, not the crime itself appearing yet, yet it would . . . affect your character as to prevent your promotion and add great weight

to any complaints which might appear in future be lodged against you. The Committee are now hampered by the constituents at Liverpool, and their officers so narrowly watched by Spies in Africa, that it is scarcely possible for you to escape detection wherever you are, and it is not in the Power of your Masters to pardon any offence committed by you when it shall be already proven . . . conduct yourself in word and deed, in every thing you say and do, with utmost circumspection.[94]

Petrie clearly understood many of these allegations to be true, and in times past, he also made clear, the CMTA would have turned a blind eye. Despite all the scrutiny, company officials on the coast remained sanguine, and business proceeded as usual. David Mill, governor of Cape Coast Castle and therefore Miles's superior on the coast, assured him, "I see no danger of your being turned out till your story is heard, and then I dare say no harm will come."[95]

Mill was correct that the charges against Miles had no immediate effects, and he was reconfirmed as chief of the fort at Tantumquerry with no complaints. Mill also reported, however, that ship captains and mates had gone before the lord mayor and sworn out complaints against him that could get him dismissed, though again, he did not think that would happen. A number of captains alleged that Miles prohibited them from trading for tobacco, prevented them from trading with a Portuguese ship, and threatened the African traders and barred them from trading with the ships. He warned Miles that their complaints "will make much Disturbance" and added that he had just purchased "a few prime slaves" to sell.[96] Since Miles was now under scrutiny, Mill informed him that a Captain Cummings was sailing to Tantumquerry; "he wants you to barter for 30 slaves, if I was in your place . . . I would not take on slave goods for anybody. You can however promise Cummings but more than that you should not do." He urged Miles: "Keep up your Spirits be not sick it will answer no end and will just give the Brew Party reason to crow if they hear you are frightened."[97]

Once the entire matter was laid before Parliament, which only happened many years after Brew's letters first appeared, Miles once again faced scrutiny. Richard Camplin, a committee member, wrote Miles a very direct and knowing letter. He advised Miles to pay very close attention to the investigation, and he warned that Parliament would look for examples of CMTA officials on the coast conducting private trade "in conjunction with persons at home." He suggested that they were mostly concerned about his predecessors at the moment, but he added a pointed reference that clearly indicates he was aware of Miles's arrangement with Petrie; he wrote, "If you have already unwarrily commenced an improper connection of that Sort either with the Same Persons or under the artful Covert of another Name, let me advise you to drop it immediately." He warned that there was evidence to support these charges, and advised Miles to "be wary & circumspect that the answers you send are founded in truth & justice and supported likewise by evidence."[98] This damning correspondence leaves no doubt that many of Brew's most serious charges were accurate.

What motivated Brew to undertake such a public campaign against the CMTA and its officers on the Gold Coast? Was he simply seeking revenge for his own treatment at the committee's hands and for his disputes with the governors of the forts? Was he embittered, or did he have other motives for launching his broadside against the company? While Brew's business dealings are impossible to reconstruct fully, there are indications that these years were difficult ones for him financially, and it is likely that he laid part of the blame on the abuses of the CMTA officials on the coast. Such a ploy might have been part of a larger game to win favor with the merchants of Liverpool and Bristol and to salvage his own reputation, which was the coin of the Atlantic realm for merchants like Brew. As one South Carolina writer explained in 1732, "The most unhappy of all Men, and the most exposed to the Malignity or Wantonness of the common Voice, is the Trader. Credit is undone in Whispers."[99] Gossip was a favorite pastime for the Europeans on the coast; as Thomas Westgate told Brew in 1770, "The Conversation of this place seldom turns upon any thing other than Scandal." By the 1770s, those whispers about Brew's financial situation were making the rounds among the merchants with whom he did business. In 1771, Brew's nemesis, Charles Bell, governor of Annamaboe Fort, referred to Brew as "the Bankrupt Brew," and in 1774 Bell's negative remarks about Brew's solvency to slavers on the coast almost resulted in a duel between the two men. Bell complained that he saw Brew shake his cane toward him as he walked along the fort, and he demanded an explanation from Brew. Brew responded by lambasting Bell for "Wantonly & Inhumanely" attacking his "Character & Credit." Brew asked, "Do you Imagine that all the Misfortunes or Afflictions which ever befall a man Could make me Bear such Infamous Treatment Tamely? No, Sir, . . . my cane to day which was most Certainly Shook at you Must Convince you how deeply you have Wounded me, and that I am determined to lay hold of the first Opportunity to Revenge your most scandalous treatment, but it will Sir give me Infinitely Greater pleasure to meet you as a Gentleman, time and Weapons to be at your Own Choice provided the Affair is decided in the Garden without any attendants than Each a Black boy and in the most private manner as you know perfectly well if our affair is once made publick Means will be sought to prevent our Deciding the Matter as we ought. Nothing, sir, but your Asking my pardon from under your hand for the Injury you have done me can possibly . . . put an End to the affair." Probably realizing how a duel with Brew would play in London, Bell apologized for "the offense I gave you in mentioning so abruptly the state of your Credit with Vessels in a letter I wrote to you Some time ago, I cannot help blaming myself . . . I am realy ashamed of, & sorry for, my conduct."[100]

Unfortunately for Brew, negative reports about his financial troubles were circulating around the Atlantic World. Peatt and Westmorland, a slave-trading firm in Kingston, Jamaica, complained in 1775 that slaves acquired from Brew "turnd out mere Rubbish." Captain Peleg Clarke, in his reply to them, noted, "I was much Surprised when I arrived on the Coast to find Stockford [another slave ship captain] had Trusted Brew knowing that times wass [sic] much altered with him for the worse which he certainly wass told before he let him have the 20 Hogsd. Rum, As I was informed by Mr. Hill."[101] Trusting referred to the common practice of allowing merchants on the African coast to take goods on credit in order for them to use those goods to acquire slaves.

Company officials suggested that Brew's goal was to have the factories maintained along the coast by the CMTA officials closed so that he could take them over himself. John Grosle, governor of Cape Coast Castle, reported that Brew had done just that to a man named David Dunn who was working as a private trader "settled in a Negro Town" near Brew's old post at Tantumquerry. According to Grosle, about two years before Brew had bribed the Fante there "at very great expense" to drive Dunn out of the town and quickly replaced him with one of his own employees.[102] That charge could well be true; bribery was certainly one of Brew's chief methods of winning favor among the Fante, and he was trying desperately to improve his financial circumstances.

The biggest crisis facing Brew was that his London partner, Samuel Smith, had deepening financial problems beginning in the late 1760s that led to his bankruptcy in 1775. As early as 1767 Brew's friend Thomas Westgate, then in London, warned Brew to *"beware of Smith,* by God you are deceived and grossly imposed upon . . . there does not exist a more plausible deceitful fellow." The partnership between Smith and Brew was so complex and intertwined that the property held by Smith and Brew in Annamaboe, including Castle Brew itself, were included in Smith's estate. Richard Miles, governor of Annamaboe Fort and one of Brew's chief targets, was appointed attorney to represent the creditors on the coast. He was to confiscate Castle Brew, sell it, and send the proceeds back to London to help settle the outstanding debt. Brew was released from any further claims on the condition that he pay £6,000 sterling. In the end, the assignees agreed to sell the castle to Brew for an additional £1,000, provided that the larger sum was paid by April 1777. It is inconceivable that all Brew's financial difficulties resulted from the trading activities of the CMTA officials, though in a tough financial climate, such unfair competition might have made the difference between a profit and a loss. As John Newton pointed out, the slave trade was a risky business by any measure, and the trade from the Gold Coast fluctuated wildly in the 1770s, but it was the fallout from Smith's financial troubles more than anything else that led to Brew's financial woes.[103]

His financial embarrassment also led him into a humiliating fight with Samuel Smith's cousin, Horatio Smith, a young man in Brew's employ with whom he had been very close. Because of his financial difficulties, Brew had been unable to pay Smith, who became increasingly resentful and demanding. During one of their arguments, Brew assured Smith that he had slaves in the Road and payments due him that would enable him to pay Smith's back wages, but the young man insisted that Brew had lied to him many times before. Brew tried to convince him, but

Smith again called his employer a liar and added "a good deal of Morti-fying language all of which," Brew later wrote, "worked me up to such height of passion that I sayed if he told that I had falsified my word to him or any man I could not answer for the Consequences." Smith, to Brew's outrage, "repeated his words twice more upon which I struck him and a scuffle ensued between us." It was a sad end to a long friendship, and Brew claimed, "I was and have been since Extremely sorry that any thing he had to say should provoke me to lift my hand to him." Brew lamented that he and Smith "had lived together from his first coming out . . . about 6 years in the utmost friendship & harmony." Miles and others had tried to reconcile them, to no effect, partly because they differed over just how much Smith was owed. An agreement between Brew and Samuel Smith's trustees gave Smith's cousin certain privileges, including being lodged and fed at Castle Brew. After the argument, Smith began to stay out late enough to disturb Brew's sleep. As Brew explained, his "hour of going to Rest" was from 8:30 to 9:00 p.m., when he locked all the gates and doors of Castle Brew and put the keys under the head of his bed, because, he explained, he could not trust the black servants with the keys. That meant when Smith came in later in the evening, Brew had to wake up and give the keys to a servant to let him in. Despite Brew's com-plaints, Smith refused to change his hours. Brew felt wounded that Smith had not shown "some little Regard . . . to my age & Misfortunes of which Mr. Smith must be too Sensible."[104]

By 1775 Brew's relationship with Mill and Miles had greatly improved. Brew said that he had given up his battle against the company officials and pledged "never to write a syllable more about them." It may be that Miles's handling of the complications for Brew surrounding Smith's bankruptcy and his efforts to help Brew hold on to his castle had helped heal their breach, and if Brew was to maintain any sort of reputation on the coast, he had to work with these powerful men with whom he now claimed to be "upon very decent terms."[105] Perhaps the men recognized that they could benefit one another in tough economic times. Early in 1776, a captain reported that Mill, Miles, and Brew had "taken up" the entire cargo of rum from a Caribbean slaver in trade for slaves. Brew even appointed Miles as one of two executors of his will in that same year.[106]

It took time, but Brew's criticisms of the CMTA officials and the effects their trading practices had on the fair conduct of the trade, boosted by similar protests from slavers and merchants in Liverpool and Bristol who complained loudly about the efforts of London merchants to dominate the CMTA, prompted an investigation. Just as Demarin and Brew had hoped, their document reached the "attention of Government." Parliament instructed the Lords Commissioners of Trade and Plantations to investigate the company's activities, and early in 1777 the commissioners summoned the African Committee members to appear before them and ordered them to prepare a full report "upon the general state of the trade to Africa, as shall be requisite to evince the truth or fallacy of the complaints therein contained."[107]

The commissioners launched their "Enquiry into the Administration of the West African Trade" in February 1777. They ordered the CMTA to deliver its voluminous records for their inspection—seventy-five journals and ledgers bound in vellum, seven unbound, five letterbooks, account books, and papers belonging to the out forts. They also began to interview witnesses, and very quickly Brew's many charges began to be confirmed. The first witness they called was Charles Miles (brother to Richard Miles), who had appeared in Brew's letters. Miles had been one of the accountants at Cape Coast Castle in 1775 when the company's annual supply ship arrived. The commissioners asked how the goods on the ship were distributed to the several forts, and Miles reported that the entire cargo went to pay advances made by the governors of the forts, and even then, it fell short of the debt. He also acknowledged that the goods advanced by the governors were "of an inferior quality passed at the same nominal price," and that the governors used the whole cargo to support their own private trade. He reported that when a new governor came in, the other governors advanced him the goods he needed to begin supplying his fort. When Governor David Mill resigned from Cape Coast Castle, for example, Miles's brother Richard replaced him and paid Mill the amount he was in arrears and transferred that debt to his account.[108]

The commissioners then called in a number of the captains of slave ships with long experience in the trade. Once again, they confirmed

Brew's account of the state of the trade. David Dunn, who had traded on the Gold Coast since 1763, reported that the trade had "suffered greatly" in recent years. Slaves were in short supply and could be purchased only with gold, when they were formerly paid for with merchandise, and it was difficult for free traders to obtain that gold. Prices had gone up dramatically; measured in gold, the price of male slaves stood at eight ounces for men and six for women in 1763, but now stood at eleven and a half for men and nine and a half for women. He confirmed that the CMTA officials carried on their private trade from the forts to the detriment of the free traders, as those outside the employ of the company were called. The governors had the advantage of storing their goods and their slaves in the forts, had better connections to the African traders, and, since they bartered with the natives on a daily basis, had more opportunity to acquire gold. Dunn reported that he himself had carried out goods consigned to the governors of the forts from the London firm of Ross & Mill when Mill was a member of the AC and his brother was governor of Cape Coast Castle. In return for those goods he was quickly supplied with slaves from the forts, including 220 prime slaves from the Dutch, a deal that "the Dutch General and Governor Mills [Mill] concerted . . . between themselves."[109]

William Chalmers, another captain with eleven years' experience in the trade to the Gold Coast, confirmed Dunn's account and elaborated on aspects of it. He reported that gold had been plentiful on the coast, and that "considerable quantities were exported from the Coast and brought home."[110] In a mercantilist system, companies like the East India Company and the Royal African Company were thought to be essential to regulate trade and compete against the country's rivals, and the flow of gold into Britain was considered to be of vital importance. By the 1770s, however, the critics of the company argued that it was free trade rather than a government monopoly that promoted the positive flow of specie into Great Britain and promoted trade.[111] He explained that the change in the gold market was due "wholly to the interference of trade carried on at the forts by the Committee's servants." He reported that the governors collected all the available gold by trading alcohol for small quantities of it daily, and their profits were huge since spirits bought at two pence per gallon were sold at five shillings per gallon. Free traders, on the other hand, bought gold at a loss, when they could find it at all. The governors competed with the free traders in other ways as well. They sold slaves from the forts at about an ounce and a half above what the black traders charged, and Chalmers believed that this increased the price of slaves and lowered the supply since African traders could make the same income on smaller numbers. British slavers were willing to pay the higher price because of the long delay involved in buying slaves in small lots from the African dealers, and even so the average length of a stay on the coast had gone up by an average of three months. Trading only with the African dealers could add months onto the length of a voyage, and such delays added to the costs of the voyage and to the death rate among the slaves. All of these changes in the trade had contributed to a decline in the number of ships trading on the Gold Coast, and in the numbers of slaves exported from the region. Chalmers observed that when he first went to the coast he found twenty-four other ships there, but in the previous year only fifteen. His personal observation is borne out by the data, which shows that the volume of the slave trade from the Gold Coast declined from the 1750s to the 1770s.[112]

He summed up the many advantages that the governors had over the free traders: they had goods sent out in CMTA ships free of any freight changes; they were able to lodge their slaves in the forts; they made use of the company's craft on the coast for their private trade; they had the first chance at buying slaves since they lived permanently on the coast; they were able to collect gold; and they could channel trade from the interior to their forts. Trade was carried on at all the forts, he noted, and the governors of the out forts were "no more than factors" to the governor of Cape Coast Castle. He further charged that the forts did not act to protect the private traders. He reported seeing the captain of one slave ship "taken into a black town and flogged" in the past year, and the governor knew about it but did nothing. In a reference to Brew's disastrous battle with the Annamaboe gold-takers, he also reported that "Mr. Brew and his servants were fired at by the blacks, and one of his slaves killed thereby. The Governors of the forts have so much concern in trade with the blacks, that they will not fall out with them."[113] Another captain reported that he had been fined by the natives for not hoisting his colors, and they stopped his trade after he sold them beef they did not like. He did not ask the governor for assistance, knowing that they would not quarrel with the Africans.[114]

All the traders and other witnesses that came before the commissioners echoed these observations, and added even more damning evidence. Thomas Bennett, who had been trading on the Gold Coast since 1748, echoed all the evidence provided by Dunn and Chalmers, and added that the governors traded with the Dutch. He reported that a ship owned by Archibald Dalziel, at that time governor of Whydah, took on part of her cargo in Holland, and the *Peggy,* owned by Ross & Mill, also traded there en route to the Gold Coast. It is worth noting that not only the governors were implicated in trading with the Dutch; Chalmers confessed that the year before he sailed from London to Rotterdam, where he took on goods for Africa for Brew (Brew had been accused of doing the same thing earlier in his career). Bennett also noted that the governors had no incentive to open the paths to the interior and increase the supply of slaves, since most of that increase would go to the private traders through the African traders rather than through the forts.[115]

When the commissioners had their own accountant review the books sent from the forts, he found that their bookkeeping was "vague and indeterminate, the books being kept in three different rates of exchange," and this despite a 1773 order to keep all the accounts in one rate of exchange. When he reconciled those accounts he found "that near 20 percent, or one fifth part of the whole money annually sent to Africa, for the support and maintenance of the forts and settlements, is by one stroke of policy, transferred into the Governor's own pockets." Another fraud in the accounts inflated the number of Gold Coast slaves traded off the coast. Captain Chalmers reported that small boats were sent from Annamaboe to bring slaves from other parts of Africa, from Lagos, Gabon, Benin, and Calabar, to make up for the shortfall of Gold Coast slaves. Brew was said to monopolize this underhanded business, which turned a good profit since Gold Coast slaves sold for higher prices than those from the other regions. Experienced captains could distinguish Gold Coast slaves from those brought from other regions, he claimed, but inexperienced captains could not, and they were called Gold Coast slaves when they were sold in the Americas. John Roberts, who held many positions on the coast from 1744 to 1752, reported that about 800 slaves annually came from Lagos, Benin, Gabon, and Calabar; about 1,000 from the Windward Coast; and about 1,500 from the Dutch and Danish forts. When they compared records kept at the forts with records from Liverpool, for example, they found repeated instances where the Gold Coast records showed that ships carried more slaves than they actually did. These numbers were damning because it appeared that the governors were inflating the number of slaves exported from the Gold Coast. Furthermore, the books showed that the goods sent out in the annual store ship were not used as intended, and the accountant found that "most of the salutary orders made by the Committee, were either evaded or disobeyed by their servants in Africa."[116]

The commissioners' report, conveyed to Parliament on April 30, 1777, set off a heated debate in that body. The report was a scathing denouncement of the CMTA and upheld Brew's damning allegations:

> It appears, so far from this trade having been carried on in a free and open manner, for the benefit of the public, according to the intention of this honourable House . . . that a private trade, directly tending to a monopoly, hath been set up and established by the governors and chiefs of the forts in Africa; and this private trade, so injurious to the interests of the public, hath been carried on by them in conjunction with persons at home, some one or more of whom have at the same time been members of the committee.

CMTA officials on the coast like Richard Miles complained about the "Sad Noise" and "clamour" against them. Not surprisingly, CMAT members, one of whom sat in the House of Commons, vehemently denied the charges, and Edmund Burke, among others, rose to defend the AC, but other members condemned the committee in no uncertain terms. The report was referred to a House committee, which the following month brought forward two rather lukewarm resolutions, one absolving current members of the AC from any charges of wrongdoing, and the second stating that the abuses in the trade might be taken up by Parliament in the future.[117] The Lords Commissioners of Trade and Plantations, however, continued their investigations and put the CMTA under a microscope. While charges against the officials were eventually dropped, the efforts of Brew and others to eliminate abuses in the trade brought results and ensured that company officials could no longer monopolize the trade, an outcome protested by the CMTA officials on the coast, who complained that "such Hardships and Restrictions were never before laid on the Servants of any public company whatsoever."[118]

Brew, however, did not live to see this outcome. Thomas Westgate expressed his concern that he must be ill, or "you would not appear so emaciated." His health began to decline late in 1775, though his curious mind remained alert; he wrote to Richard Miles saying, "For God's sake bring down a Cargo of News Papers. I am 50 pcent better this Day than I have been yet thanks to God."[119] But he did not fully recover, and he fell seriously ill in May 1776. He complained that "the fever has not left me for two hours together." His attempts to treat his condition had no effect, though he had not lost his sense of humor; "I have taken 2 doses Physick . . . none of which ever operated . . . I have this moment swallow'd a Hell of a dose of Castor oil and if that does not open a passage, I believe I . . . must go to work to piss up the whole altogether." He signed off uncharacteristically by wishing Miles "all Earthly Blessings," perhaps a realization that his own time was slipping away, and it was certainly a mark of how the two men had put aside their differences.[120] By August 2 his condition was so serious that Miles was called back to Annamaboe by a ship's captain. David Mill also wrote from Cape Coast Castle urging Miles to return to Annamaboe Fort "without delay." Mill warned that Brew had been ill for so long that there was little chance of his recovery, and that he would have to save Brew's property "from the Plunder the Blacks will make." Mill believed that "there ought to be a very large Property in his House to answer all the Demands which are both due to Residents on the Coast, Masters of Ships, also due to his Trustees in England." Mill feared that the situation could turn violent, but he warned Miles that he did "not think it would be prudent in you to fire on the Blacks without a majority of the Captns in Annamaboe Road should petition you in writing to do so—if no other method can be got to prevent the Blacks plundering his House."[121]

By August 4 Brew was unconscious, tended by two doctors and nine or ten captains from slave ships lying in the Road. He died on August 5, 1776, at about 1:00 a.m., and he was buried later that same day in a coffin made by a carpenter off the slave ship *Constantine*.[122] The furor Brew's death caused at Annamaboe reflected the complicated life that Brew had carved out for himself there. As he grew weaker and his death seemed imminent, the ships' captains who had trusted him with their trade goods, no doubt those nine or ten who stood at his bedside, demanded that their goods be returned to them. As one of those captains, Peleg Clarke, wrote, "He Died much in Debt in the roade to the Shiping and they are in alikely [sic] way of being grate [great] Sufferers, it is the On-ley [sic] troble [sic] that has been going that we have Steard [sic] clear off, and the Capt'ns he ow'd mony [sic] to *viz* Capt. Leads a rumman 110 Slaves, Capt. Eagles, 56, and Capt Robe 52, and in Shortt all the Road more or less."[123] Miles was reluctant to allow the goods to be returned without Brew's permission, but he was unconscious and unable to give his assent. Miles was "amazed" and the captains stood "thunderstruck" when Brew's clerk reported that there were not enough goods remaining in Castle Brew's warehouses to pay one captain's debts (those goods may have been sent to Brew's trade depots along the coast, trusted to local African slave dealers, or perhaps taken as Brew lay ill, though the clerk seemed unable to account for them). Miles's troubles were just begin-ning—he reported his "utter astonishment" at being named as executor of Brew's estate, along with Jerome Bernard Weuves, a writer at the fort.[124] The small store of goods in Castle Brew is even more surprising given Mill's conviction that there were enough there to cover all Brew's debts. Brew's last surviving letter on his financial situation, admittedly written to his trustees in England and therefore intended to put a rosy view on things, certainly painted a different picture than the one Miles discovered. Writing in April 1776 shortly before he fell ill, he noted that in the previous year he had sold 780 slaves "as much as any Two Forts on the Coast, by which I have made a Considerable Sum of Money," he boasted. The rumors of financial ruin that had plagued him had passed, and "every body now are courting my favours in trade . . . Every thing I have taken in hand has thank God prospered with me."[125] But as Miles and Weuves quickly discovered, the facts now appeared very different, and Miles complained that "since I've known Africa, I have never under-taken so disagreeable a Piece of Business."[126] Brew's will stipulated that his creditors on the coast were to be paid first before his creditors in

England or elsewhere, a stipulation of doubtful legality that favored the creditors in Africa over those abroad. Miles's position was even further complicated when Samuel Smith's assignees, who had a firm claim on a very substantial sum, took legal action to prevent anyone else taking control of the estate, and they appointed Miles as their agent. The executors inventoried all the contents of Castle Brew and began going through Brew's accounts, which were in "terrible confusion." In fact, the accounts were so poorly kept that Miles complained, "His Books indeed don't deserve the name, except in Numbers, it's true there's plenty of them . . . but scarce an account appears to be properly settled."[127]

The other immediate problem was with the Fante residents of Annamaboe and the members of Brew's mixed-race family who were related to the town's ruling elite. Brew had often told the Fante that if he died on the coast, then they would inherit his property. How much property actually remained to him was unclear, but his will specified that his slaves and the proceeds of the sale of his expensive silver plate, the fine furniture, and clothing were left to his wife and John Corrantee's daughter, Effua Ansah, and to their daughters (his sons were not mentioned in the will). The house slaves fled immediately following Brew's death to avoid being sold off the coast. Miles knew that British law required that those slaves and the goods be considered a part of the estate and sold to satisfy Brew's many creditors, but he could not ignore the customs of Annamaboe without great risk to the fort and to British interests. He and Weuves recognized that Brew's wishes in regard to the slaves would have to be respected regardless of what the law might say. They reported that the house slaves simply could not be sold: "There is no shipping them off the Coast, to attempt it would be involving the Fort here in a very serious dispute with the whole Town . . . they have lived so long here, and have their children and other connections that they are in a manner incorporated with the Town."[128] Among the tragic consequences of the breakup of the Brew household was the fate of six "Old Slaves" who were considered so worthless that no one would bid on them at auction. Miles recorded that four of them were given to the townspeople, while the remainder died.[129]

In a further effort to pacify the townspeople, the executors paid the debts owed to Brew's African creditors in full before any funds were sent back to England—these included "unavoidable charges" to "John Currantee's people," and payments to house slaves, African sailors, and to suppliers of household goods like eggs, plantains, and wood. They paid Brew's "Black Cook" and Sam Suton, his "Mullattoe Taylor." They also gave out liberal gifts of rum, including four gallons to Effua Ansah and Brew's daughters, and they spent £87 on Brew's funeral, which was celebrated according to African customs with rum, gunpowder, cloth, and a cow. These items along with several other payments went to Amoony Coomah, John Corrantee's successor as chief caboceer, whose role as organizer of the funeral is testament to Brew's standing among the Fante and his connection to Amoony Coomah's family. Payments also had to be made to "the Principal Inhabitants of the Town at different times in order to induce them to lessen their demand for Custom." John Bosman described funeral customs on the Gold Coast in the late seventeenth century, which probably suggest what Brew's burial was like. He observed that the townspeople joined the family in grieving for the deceased and brought with them presents of gold, brandy, and cloth, and that the mourners drank brandy in the morning and palm wine in the afternoon. As the body was carried to the grave, "a parcel of young Soldiers go, or rather run, continually loading and discharging their Muskets, till the Deceased is laid in the Ground." Once the body was buried, most of the crowd went to "the House of Mourning, to drink and be merry, which lasts for several Days successively; so that this part of the Mourning looks more like a Wedding than a Funeral."[130]

The executors raised over £4,000 through the sale of the contents of Castle Brew and the goods retrieved from Brew's coastal factories, though even getting those goods from the factories required gifts like a set of a dozen silver tablespoons and liquor to local elites. The sale of slaves owned by Brew being held for shipment at the time of his death brought in another £4,000. Once payments, expenses, and executors' fees were subtracted, approximately £6,500 remained, less than the executors had hoped to realize and not nearly enough to cover Brew's debts, which Miles estimated at £20,000.[131] His creditors' problems were confounded when American privateers, now preying on British shipping during the American Revolution, captured the ships carrying Brew's property and requests for insurance.[132] Horatio Smith bought Castle

Brew from the assignees. One of Smith's first moves was to change the name of the castle to Smith House, a smart move, according to Richard Miles, who observed that "its late Incumbent paid for calling it a Castle." Miles managed to complete the settlement of the estate by the end of 1776, but it had been a very sticky business that left everyone dissatisfied. "The trouble I had with these *righteous Fantees* and abuse . . . from his Coast Creditors is incredible," he wrote. But still problems lingered; as late as 1779 Miles feared prosecution from some of Brew's creditors.[133]

Though the exact scale of Brew's trading activities cannot be fully reconstructed, there is little doubt that he was the most active British merchant on the Gold Coast from the 1750s to his death, and he probably sent more slaves off the coast than any other individual. For over twenty years, he imported huge amounts of trade goods—various cloths, cooking utensils, firearms, and luxury items that he used to barter for the hundreds of enslaved men, women, and children he sold annually. For decades, those goods flowed in and out of the storerooms of Castle Brew, itself a monument to the Atlantic World and Brew's place in it. In many respects, the Georgian mansion situated incongruously on the African coast was a microcosm of the African Atlantic World. Along with Brew himself, the castle sheltered his mixed-race African Creole family and connected him to John Corrantee, the most able political leader in Annamaboe's history. Perhaps because of his intimate knowledge of the town, Brew was the only CMTA official who was able to match wits with the wily Corrantee. Castle Brew also served as the hub of his business enterprise, which stretched up and down the coast, into the African interior, to England, to Holland, and to the British colonies in America from the sugar islands to South Carolina to Rhode Island. Its storerooms held goods from India, Africa, England, Holland, and America, along with the African slaves imprisoned in the castle's pens. His business employed men from Ireland, Britain, and the Americas, and local Africans also worked within the castle's walls. He entertained ship's captains from England and America, hosted religious services conducted by an African Gold Coast native who studied in England and who baptized his children, and even listened to musical performances on the hall's organ. He was well-known not only in Annamaboe and on the Gold Coast, but throughout the Atlantic World, where his name appeared in newspapers from Britain to America, where the letters of merchants commented on his business, and where his views of the African trade were widely published and influenced British policymakers in London. His position as a merchant in Annamaboe might seem to be an isolated one, far removed from the main currents of day, but his deep integration into the eighteenth-century Atlantic World emphasized the important position that Annamaboe played as one of the nodes of the great commercial, social, and cultural network that defined it. He was a man of contradictions, a characteristic he recognized in himself; in 1770 he wrote, "I am a friend to Liberty and . . . I Mortally hate logs & Chains, tho I live in the Midst of Slaves & Slavery."[134]

4

The Process of Enslavement
at Annamaboe

W HEN AFRICANS WERE SOLD and loaded onto the European ships
lying at anchor in Annamaboe Road, that sale marked the end of
an African process of enslavement, a process that often began months
before and hundreds of miles from Annamaboe. The town was the primary export center for enslaved Africans on the Gold Coast, and hundreds of thousands of captives left there during the eighteenth century.
Those numbers beg the question of where those men, women, and children came from; how they were enslaved; and how they were sold. The
answers to these questions are essential if we are to fully understand
the process of enslavement, a process that began long before the slaves
were actually purchased by a European captain. For the majority of captives sold at Annamaboe, their enslavement began as a result of their
capture in wars fought deep in the interior. Their enslavement was often
accompanied by the defeat of their nation and the destruction of their
homes and communities, and their shock and loss is evident in the descriptions captains left of them. These men, women, and children were
often ignorant of the fate that awaited them. A substantial portion of the
captives were residents of the coastal states who were convicted of a
crime or sold for debt. These individuals knew very well the fate that
awaited them in the plantations societies of the Americas. Others, especially children, were kidnapped, stolen, and spirited away before their
families even knew they were gone. These individuals found their way

to the Annamaboe market along different routes and illustrate how the experience of enslavement varied considerably for its victims.

It is also important to recognize that the process by which slaves were marketed varied considerably from one African nation to another. At Annamaboe, slaves were sold by the fort and by Fante merchants, by small-time bush traders with one slave to sell, by brokers from the interior with coffles of slaves, and by Fante merchants who bought them from inland markets. Criminals and debtors were sold after being convicted by the courts. The trade with Europeans was supported by the credit system of pawning, whereby merchants used their own children as collateral to access the credit they needed from their European trading partners to purchase slaves. In all cases, slave sales were supervised by gold-takers, who made up a substantial portion of the town's population and acted as agents and brokers for every sale. Their role in the process of enslavement at Annamaboe was a critical one. The other major players were, of course, the ship captains who brought the trade goods to exchange for the captives, and it was the captains who made the final decisions on which captives would embark on the Middle Passage.

While historians have debated where the slaves sold from the Gold Coast originated, contemporaries agreed that the great majority were war captives supplied by the Asante from the interior. In 1789 the British Parliament opened an investigation into the conduct of the slave trade, and that provides a rich means to examine the conduct of the slave trade at Annamaboe and on the Gold Coast. Among the captains and company officials who appeared before the committee was Richard Miles, the CMTA officer who lived on the Gold Coast from 1765 to 1784 and whose brothers were also engaged in the trade. No one understood its workings better than he did.[1] When asked where the supply of slaves came from, Miles reported that the "Fantees on the water-side provide near one-fourth of the slaves purchased by us on the Gold Coast; the other three-fourths from inland believes the whole from 7 to 8,000." His insight helps answer one of the most important questions surrounding the trade. Miles, like other Europeans on the Gold Coast, suggested that the major source of supply was trade with the interior, and other evidence supports his claim. CMTA officials on the coast along with captains of slave ships experienced in the trade agreed that the vast majority of slaves sold on the Gold Coast came from hundreds of miles inland and were drawn from many different nations. As Jerome Barnard Weuves, a company official on the coast, reported, "brokers go from 100 to 150 Miles up the Country to pursue them; from what further Distance they may be brought, it is impossible to say; but it is probable they come from very great Distance, and from different Countries, for they talk different Languages."[2]

Those contemporary sources also agree that most of the slaves sold on the Gold Coast were prisoners of war. The eighteenth century was a period of turmoil and almost continual conflict on the Gold Coast, and military incidents took place in at least forty-three of the sixty-five years between 1700 and 1765. In the early decades of the eighteenth century, a series of wars either between the Asante and coastal states or between coastal states provided most of the captives sold at Annamaboe. Between 1701 and 1721 the Asante fought wars with a number of smaller nations in the Gold Coast region: Assin, Dankera (Denkyira), Warsaw (Wasa), Cuffero (Twifo), Awomweye (Aowin), and Amanahia. While wars often interrupted the trade during the conflict itself, the end of the war usually brought a flood of war captives onto the slave market. Sometimes the connection between inland wars and the increased supply of slaves to the European forts is clear and compelling. In December 1721, for example, RAC officials observed that "slaves are likely to come down to the Coast in plenty, from the Battle said to be lately fought by the Ashantees in which They have got the victory." Slave exports indeed rose from an estimated 450 in 1721 to an estimated 1,180 the following year, when the Asante were coming often to the coast to trade, an increase that can be attributed to that conflict.[3] There were big spikes in the trade from Annamaboe from 1730 to 1732 when Aquamboo (Akwamu) was defeated by Akim (Akyem), a supply of slaves so great that Europeans claimed they could "buy a slave for a bottle of brandy."[4] The 1740s and 1750s saw another spike in the trade from Annamaboe, which corresponded with a major Asante campaigns against Akyem, Aquamboo, Gonja, and Dagomba. Even after these nations were conquered, it often took far longer to actually subdue them. In some cases guerilla wars continued for some time, and raiders preyed on merchants traveling along the paths and roads. For this reason, the victors in these wars often pre-

An image from the log of the *Sandown,* a slave ship that sailed from London in April 1793 and arrived at the Isles De Los off West Africa in June. Its captain, Samuel Gamble, stopped at the Rio Nunez in Sierra Leone to buy slaves. Gamble traveled inland and illustrated his log with a series of color sketches, one of which shows African slaves being brought to the coast at Sierra Leone by the Fulani people. After leaving Africa, Gamble sailed to Jamaica with a cargo of Africans. National Maritime Museum, Greenwich, London.

A coffle of enslaved men and women, and a child, being marched from the interior to the coast. They are bound at their necks so that they can walk more easily.
A. [Abel] Hugo, *France pittoresque ou description pittoresque, topographique et statistique des départments et colonies de là France* (Paris, 1835), vol. 3, facing p. 270 (bottom). Copy in Library Company of Philadelphia.

vented their opponents from regrouping by enslaving and selling off as much of the population as possible, a practice known as "eating the country."[5]

But it was wars fought by the Asante along their interior borders during their great expansion in the eighteenth century that kept the supply of slaves flowing to Annamaboe. These interior wars were longer and generally spread over a larger area than those along the coast itself. This long series of wars was not driven by the slave trade per se, though the two were closely intertwined. The Asante sold slaves in part to replenish their supplies of guns, powder, and shot, which could be acquired only from Europeans on the coast. The accessibility of guns for the nations on or near the coast is one reason that the Asante had a more difficult time subduing those states as opposed to those nations on their interior

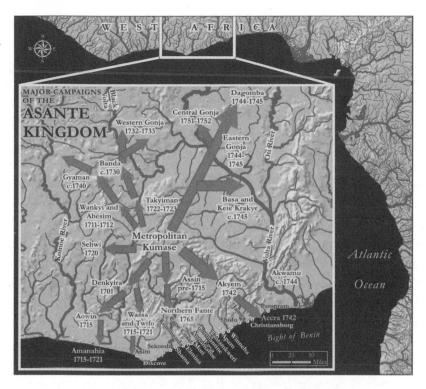

Major military campaigns of the Asante kingdom in the eighteenth century.
Map by Richard Campanella based on campaign information from Wilks (1975).

borders. The Asante were able to prevent those interior nations from acquiring weapons from the coast and thereby gained a great advantage. The slave trade, in effect, made it possible for the Asante to carry out their conquests, and the "gunpowder revolution," as historian John Thornton calls it, played a major role in those conflicts.[6]

The northern provinces were more easily integrated into the Asante kingdom than those to the south where instability continued throughout the eighteenth century, instability that both fueled and interrupted trade. The Asante determination to keep trade open to the coast, by force if necessary, resulted in an agreement between the Wasa, Twifo, Denkyira, and Akyem Abuakwa to make peace with the Asante and to keep the paths open. In 1753 representatives of these states traveled to Kumase and swore to such an agreement. The results were dramatic, as the number of slaves sold at Annamaboe jumped from an estimated

1,768 in 1752 to 4,208 in 1753 and 4,483 in 1754.[7] But these coastal nations chafed under Asante rule and periodically challenged their over-
lords. As a result of this continued resistance, the Asante prepared to
launch a major expedition against the Wasa and Akyem in 1764, news
that was warmly greeted from London to Newport to Boston since the
Atlantic slave traders knew that the result would be a rise in the supply
and a drop in the price for slaves.[8]

Knowing that the war would bring a flood of slaves to their markets,
the Fante agreed in 1765 to allow Osei Kwadwo, the Asantehene, to establish a military base in their territory from which to launch renewed
attacks against both the Wasa and the Akyem Abuakwa. William Mutter
wrote the African Committee in 1765 that the Asante were at war with
the Akyem, and had surrounded the Akyem army. He reported that the
Fante army was encamped nearby, intent on plundering the loser. The
Asante went on to defeat the Akyem and "got possession of their camp,
in which were all their women and children, and the greatest part of
their men, to the number of about 15 or 20,000 in all." At the same time,
"the worthy Fanties were very busy, pillaging and stealing the Akims,
who were so reduced by famine, that they gave themselves up in great
numbers to any body that would promise them victuals, so that slaves
became very plentiful among these gentry." In addition, the Fante had
captured between 1,200 and 1,500 Asante soldiers who were pillaging
the "Fanty Crooms (towns) and plantations." Mutter noted that the price
of slaves was dropping because of the influx of Akyem war captives,
news that spread around the Atlantic World. The Fante were holding on
to large numbers of the Akyem and Fante captives in hopes of forcing the
prices up. One unidentified slave ship captain reported that he purchased 300 of those Asante captives in eight or nine days from Richard
Brew, a report that was published in London and Newport. Brew knew
how to cover all his bases. John Marshall, who made about twenty voyages to the Gold Coast, reported that he was at Annamaboe when the
Asante and the Fante were at war. The conflict totally interrupted the
trade to the point that it took sixteen months to slave his ship, but the end
of that war brought a flood of captives. He reported that the Fante took
many Asante prisoners, most of whom would have been sold or executed
had Brew not intervened and proposed instead to the Asantehene "the

redemption of those prisoners, which he gladly acceded to." That move, of course, curried favor for Brew with the Asantehene, who was probably unaware that Brew was selling Asante prisoners at the same time. The result was very high exports from Annamaboe; in fact, 1767 marked the high point of the trade with an estimated 7,073 slaves sold from the port in that year.[9]

Company officials strove to keep the peace. John Grosle, chief of Annamaboe Fort, labored to improve the strained relations between the Fante and Asante nations; he sent presents to the Asantehene Osei Kwadwo (also known as Osei Kuma or Coomaha to the British), he gave gifts to the Ando pynins who were trying to negotiate between them, he gave out rum and tobacco to the Annamaboe soldiers "to induce them to settle the Ashantee business," and he sent messengers and goods to Abra to get the assistance of the leaders of that town to help the Asante and the Fante reach a settlement.[10] It is impossible to say what effect his efforts actually had, but in 1769 Grosle notified the African Committee that "a perfect tranquility seems now to Reign" between the Asante and the Fante, and as a result there were several years of very high exports from Annamaboe.[11] In 1774 David Mill reported to the AC that there was "but very little fear of further disturbances" between the Fante and Asante, and that trade remained open. A year later the paths were still open and Mill boasted that more slaves were exported in 1774 than in previous years, and estimates show that he was correct; an estimated 2,352 slaves left Annamaboe in 1773 and 6,221 in 1774.[12]

Ongoing resistance in the lands the Asante conquered meant that they continued to round up captives in these areas even after the wars were over. Before the British abolition of the slave trade in 1808 lowered prices and demand, the Asante generally insisted that tribute from the conquered territories be paid in the form of slaves, another source of the captives they sold on the Gold Coast. When disorders broke out in Dagomba, decades after its initial conquest, the Asante reoccupied the region and imposed an annual tribute of a thousand slaves. These payments may have encouraged tributary states located on the edges of the Asante Empire to mount raids against their neighbors to acquire the slaves rather than enslaving their own people.[13] Those tribute payments provided another steady stream of slaves to the coast.

Once the Asante captured and enslaved their enemies, they had to get them to market by marching them overland along the trade paths. Paths were literally footpaths connecting the towns and villages. The most efficient means of transportation was by water, but lacking an extensive river system, trade between the coast and the interior ran along these paths. Trade goods, those bulky and heavy bundles and boxes of fabrics, basins, lead bars, and guns, had to be transported by human effort since, as Jerome Barnard Weuves pointed out, "There are no cattle of burthen on the Gold Coast, and very few bulls and cows." Europeans and African elites preferred to travel by sea, and when they did use the paths, they were carried in hammocks by African porters. William Smith, an Englishman who visited the Gold Coast in the early decades of the eighteenth century, described this unusual mode of travel; he reported that people "are carried in a Network Hammock, fasten'd at each End to a Pole, call'd a Bamboe, about the thickness of a Man's Leg, which a couple of stout Negroes can easily carry with a white man in it . . . they always sit up in the Hammock, with their Legs and Feet hanging over one Side, and leaning their Breasts over the Bamboe, while the Slaves run along by their Hammocks holding Umbrella's over their Heads, to guard them from the sun."[14] Henry Meredith, a CMTA official on the coast in the early nineteenth century, noted that the cotton hammocks were imported from Brazil by the Portuguese, and that to travel a distance of twenty miles required six to eight bearers for each hammock. These men relieved one another without stopping, and another two or three men carried other goods, especially "a case of liquor for the people to drink; without which nothing is done in this country." When well supplied with rum, he estimated that they traveled about five miles an hour. He added that "two or three Europeans travelling in this way with the flag of their country carried before them, attended by a number of stout Black men, almost in a state of nature, singing and running, make a most whimsical procession." The men were paid in goods or gold to the value of about five shillings each for the trip.[15]

Perhaps the oldest of all Asante administrative agencies was one created in the mid-eighteenth century to send out inspectors to see that the roads and paths of the kingdom were kept open. The regularity of the slave trade along the Asante roads is further indicated by the fact that the king kept a

A French engraving showing the British officers leaving a Gold Coast fort being carried in their hammocks by African porters. Thomas Edward Bowdich, *Voyage dans le pays d'Aschantie, ou, Relation de l'ambassade envoyée dans ce royaume par les anglais: avec des détails sur les moeurs, les usages, les lois et le gouvernement de ce pays, des notices géographiques sur d'autres contrées situées dans l'intérieur de l'Afrique, et la traduction d'un manuscrit arabe ou se trouve décrite la mort de Mungo Park* (DT507 .H9815 1823). Special Collections, University of Virginia Library.

toll collector on the road to collect payments from "the black slave traders." One of the Asante "great roads" ran directly from the capital at Coomassie (Kumase) to Annamaboe, a route that required eleven stops to cover the 125 miles. The heavy traffic along that path indicated the importance of trade between the two, but the primary Fante foreign policy was to prevent the Asante from gaining direct access to the coast since that would cut them out as the middlemen in the traffic.[16]

In order to prevent that calamity, the Fante forged alliances with "all the nations lying between the coast and Assiante [Asante] . . . All the nations west of Fante joined this alliance." The Asante and other inland nations who wanted to sell slaves to the Europeans on the Gold Coast brought them to markets where Fante brokers acquired them for resale. William Mutter observed in 1764 that "regular markets have been settled on the Borders of the Fantee Country where the Warsaws, Akims, &

several others keep up a constant intercourse between the Ashantee &
Fante country."[17] Jerome Barnard Weuves noted that "the black brokers
told him [Weuves] that they go three, four, or five days journey to a market inland, to which slaves are brought, by more inland brokers, and so
from many more inland brokers." By this means, slaves from throughout
the Asante nation were funneled to these markets located on the border
with the Fante nation. He rightly "judges such slaves to be of various
tribes (from their different mode of marking their bodies, some filing
their teeth, above all their different languages . . .)." Weuves told the
committee that he had purchased "20, 30, or 40 who did not know each
other's language." Clearly, captives were drawn from far in the interior
and from scores of different national and ethnic groups. The vast majority would have been war captives, but Asante and other nations in the
interior also sold criminals into slavery.[18]

Tensions between the Fante and their neighbors sometimes closed
the paths, with devastating consequences for the trade, and CMTA officials used all their diplomatic skills to try to keep the paths open and to
give the Asante better access to the coastal forts. William Mutter, the
governor of Cape Coast Castle, wrote his superiors in London in 1764 to
report that he had sent two messengers to the Asante and those men returned four months later with about 200 Asante traders who brought
slaves and gold dust with them. Mutter doubted, however, that the paths
would remain open due to "the quarrels & disturbances which are continually happening in this Country," and he claimed that "the Greedy
Avaricious & Villainous disposition of the natives puts it out of every
White Mans power to keep up a free & uninterrupted intercourse with
the Inland Countries." Conflicts and disturbances among the Asante
and their neighbors, along with a conflict between the Wasa and the
Akyem, threatened to close the path again. He wanted the AC officials to
"see what an unsettled way of affairs are generally in, in this Country &
how little dependence there is either in opening the Paths or keeping
them so when they are opened." He also noted that the Fante would
plunder the Asante when they could, but Brew's skillful diplomacy
helped establish a peace that endured for many years.[19]

That peaceful interlude encouraged the Fante to allow the Asante to
travel through their territory to trade directly with the forts, something

the British encouraged. In 1775 David Mill, the governor of Cape Coast Castle, reported that the Asante "wanted to open a Market nearer the Watersisde than before, the Fantees have acquiesced," a move that he saw as being "very beneficial to the Trade in general." Mill intended to send the best presents he could find to the Asantehene to encourage the move, but he asked the African Committee to send more lavish gifts including "a large Umbrella of crimson Damask with gold Fringe, and Gilt Elephant on Top to spread 15 feet . . . a large silver basket Sword and a Gold headed Cane with the arms of the Company engraved." In 1775 messengers from the Asantehene received dashes or gifts including rum, beef, and tobacco from Annamaboe Fort when they came to negotiate with the Fante "concerning a free Passage for the former to the Waterside." The 1770s saw great fluctuations in the supply of slaves depending on the relations between the Fante, their coastal neighbors, and the Asante, and as Mutter suggested, the Europeans had little control over those affairs despite their efforts to act as mediators.[20]

The next step in the process of enslavement was to get those slaves from the inland markets to the coast. Slaves were brought to Annamaboe by traders from the interior, who acquired them at the inland markets and marched them to the coast, or by Annamaboe's brokers who traveled to those markets or, more often, sent their employees there. As Miles reported, brokers did not like to keep slaves on hand but preferred to sell them as quickly as possible to avoid the expense of feeding them and to cut down on the risk of mortality. It was not necessary to confine these men, women, and children; "being from inland, the black broker is not afraid of their deserting." Since they were obviously strangers, they could not mingle with the local population. These brokers were not just slave traders; they traded in other goods as well, especially ivory, and slaves marched to the coast frequently carried the heavy tusks on their heads. The inland brokers also acted as commission merchants, buying goods on the coast for people in the interior who could not reach the coast themselves.[21] Traders who brought slaves from inland returned with trade goods to the interior. As Captain John Fountain reported, the "commodities received by the natives in exchange for slaves, they carry away made up in small bundles, upon their heads."[22] Jerome Barnard Weuves reported that brokers were

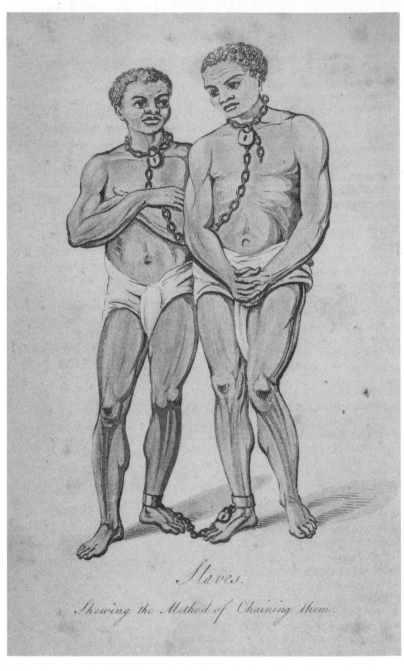

Slaves.

Shewing the Method of Chaining them.

Male slaves on the Gold Coast chained together by their ankles and necks.
Francis B. Spilsbury, *Account of a voyage to the western coast of Africa; performed by His Majesty's sloop Favourite, in the year 1805. Being a Journal of the Events which Happened to that Vessel* (G161 .P55 1st ser. 1805 vol. 6 no. 5). Special Collections, University of Virginia Library.

"obliged to bring down a number of people to carry back the goods so purchased."[23]

Captives brought from far inland over long distances often suffered great hardships and often arrived on the coast in poor health. In 1715 Asante traders visited the English fort at Commenda to purchase guns and powder, but they brought only gold and ivory to trade, a disappointment to the slave traders there. The Asante reported that they had been recently victorious over Ginegbra, one of their inland enemies, and they had taken many captives they intended to sell into slavery, but their prisoners were still "so very Maugre [meager] & Lean" that they were "not Yet able to Undergo the fatigue of So farr a journey to be Vendeble when Come here."[24] John Fountain, who came to the Gold Coast in 1778 as a soldier and then rose through the ranks to become chief of several of the forts, reported that slaves brought long distances often arrived "in general poor in flesh; great eruptions over all their skin; very scorphulous, and frequently have bad ulcers."[25] John Adams, a slave trader on the Gold Coast in the late eighteenth century, described captives from Chamba, who were called Duncos by the Fante, and who made the long march from the north of the Asante Empire to be sold on the coast: "When they first arrive upon the sea-coast," he wrote, "they are very meagre in consequence of the fatigue experienced by them in their long journey from the interior; but their constitutions being excellent, they are soon restored to their natural vigour and plumpness by rest and plentiful dict."[26] Allowing these captives to remain outdoors to take some exercise rather than keeping them closely confined would have been beneficial to their health and probably explains that practice.

Richard Miles estimated that approximately three-fourths of the slaves sold at Annamaboe were purchased from the inland markets, while the remaining one-fourth were from the coast. Captain John Marshall estimated that "of the slaves bought on the Gold Coast, one third may be inhabitants of the coast, the rest are Ashantees and Duncoes, who both speak the Fantee language." There were several means by which the Fante and other coastal people were enslaved and sold off the coast. Some historians have suggested that kidnapping was the major source of captives for the Annamaboe trade. While it seems improbable that an unreliable source like kidnapping could have provided the thousands of captives often exported from Annamaboe during a single year, it was certainly an important source of supply of coastal captives. Even John Corrantee was accused of kidnapping and selling people from Annama-boe, but such a practice was a dangerous one that could bring severe punishments to anyone convicted of enslaving a free person. The British observed that "kidnapping is too dangerous a trade to be commonly followed." Captain James Luttrell suggested that it was usually the "poorer traders" who "take off private families by surprise." These were the men described as "bush traders" who preyed on children and adults who fell into their hands.[27]

An example of this form of capture is provided by Ottobah Cugoano, an important African abolitionist in late eighteenth-century Britain and a friend of Olaudah Equiano, author of the best-known slave narrative of the eighteenth century and the most famous black abolitionist of his day. In 1770 Cugoano, who was about thirteen years old at the time, was playing in the woods with a group of his friends, gathering fruit and catching birds. Cugoano was born in the coastal Fante village of Agimaque in about 1757, and he was visiting his uncle who lived inland from the coast. After a couple of hours engaged in their pastimes, "several great ruffians" suddenly confronted the boys. With cutlasses and pistols drawn, they demanded that the boys accompany them, allegedly to meet their overlord to answer for an offense against him. The terrified children were divided and marched through several towns during a journey of several days until they arrived at a town on the coast, where Cugoano saw his first white men and feared that they would eat him, as the tales he had heard as a child suggested. He was taken into the European castle that dominated the town, and although he did not know the name of the town, it could well have been Annamaboe. There he saw other Africans "chained two and two, some handcuffed, and some with their hands tied behind." He saw his captor take a gun, cloth, and lead in exchange for him, and he joined the prisoners. He was held there for three days until he and many others, including some of the boys who had been captured with him, were loaded onto a ship and taken to Cape Coast Castle, where they were transferred onto another ship, a slaver bound for Granada. He saw African merchants coming and going as the ship's hold filled with enslaved Africans, and after several days, the ship sailed out into the Atlantic.[28] So common was this practice that Thomas Trotter, a surgeon on a slaver in 1783, reported that on board his ship "during the passage, some of the boy (slaves) played a game, which they called slave-taking, or bush-fighting; shewing the different manoeuvers thereof in leaping, sallying, and retreating."[29]

It was necessary for bush traders to spirit their captives away from their homes as quickly as possible before they could be rescued and to transport them to a slave-trading port where few questions would be asked. The penalties for enslaving a free person were harsh among the Fante, and anyone convicted of that crime would either be put to death or sold into slavery themselves. As Captain John Fountain told the parliamentary committee investigating the slave trade, "A captain never asks a broker how a slave was obtained, because the native is aware, that if he is found to have come by the slave illegally, he and his family are liable to be sold for the offence." Similarly, Captain Thomas King reported that he had never "heard of the natives being stolen, except from slaves from the inland country. These have mentioned a few being stolen or carried away." Richard Miles agreed; he reported that he did "not know he ever heard the word kidnapping mentioned out of this country. It cannot be practiced to any extent, without certain detection; for the natives have one general language, and the brokers have daily intercourse with the shipping. Hence a kidnapped slave on board would tell his case to the brokers, who, from interest and regard to the laws, would find the offender."[30]

Thomas Trotter painted a somewhat darker picture of kidnapping on the coast that supports Cugoano's story. He testified that there were many enslaved boys and girls on his ship who had no relatives on board, and that many of them "had been kidnapped in the neighborhood of Annamaboe, particularly a girl of about 8 years, who said she had been carried off from her mother, by the man who sold her to the ship." He also observed that their gold-taker, Fat Sam, who was identified as a "person of consequence in this town" by CMTA officials, "very frequently sent slaves on board in the night," and Trotter learned that all of them had been kidnapped in the Annamaboe neighborhood. Captains refused to pay for slaves that were sold under these circumstances "till they had been some time on board" for fear that they would be reclaimed.

Trotter saw one boy, who told him that he had been kidnapped from his home in the Annamaboe vicinity, reclaimed by his family and rescued from the slave ship. He summed up the view of many slave ship captains when he remarked that the captain of his ship "urged his gold-takers daily, to get him slaves by any means." Other veterans of the trade suggested that the presence of the gold-takers on board the ships and their role as intermediaries in the trade served to prevent the kidnapping and sales of locals, but Trotter's testimony suggests otherwise. He pointed out that "all communication is prevented between the slaves on board and the traders; and canoemen who come to sell slaves; hence it could not be supposed that any of their connections were informed of their situation."[31]

"Panyarring" was probably a more common practice, and one that could provide larger numbers of captives. To panyar was to seize or capture an enemy by any means other than on the battlefield to obtain redress or restitution. It also meant to kidnap a debtor or his relations to force repayment, so if African traders did not return to redeem their pawns as agreed, European traders could seize any of their townspeople to cover the value of the debt, and then demand a palaver or trial to settle the matter. Raiders from states hostile to the Asante, for example, often panyarred Asante traders who came near them, captured the traders and their coffles of slaves, and sold all of them into slavery. John Atkins reported in 1735 that the Asante were buying up arms and ammunition in preparation for an attack on Appolonia, "provoked by the frequent Depredations and Panyarrs of the Appollonians" against the Asante traders. Atkins noted that the Fante were especially guilty of abusing this practice with their neighbors, to the point that they had made "perpetual enemies" of them. Panyarring was endemic along the coast, and its prevalence made it dangerous for traders and travelers who were alone or in small groups.[32]

Another source of slaves from the coastal region and inland were criminals who were enslaved rather than executed. Richard Miles noted that coastal people were "made slaves for theft, debt, adultery, and witchcraft." He believed that the trials were generally fair, that the judges gained nothing by convictions since convicts were "sold for the benefit of the injured," and that judges received a flat fee when suits were brought before them. He noted that he had "known thousands of debtors sold for the benefit of creditors." Trials were held in the town's Palaver House "or Court of Justice, where the judges or elders (few under the age of 60 or 70) hear the parties, openly, for theft and adultery." These respected elders, or pynins, could be identified by their broad-brimmed straw hats. Only witchcraft trials were held in secret, and in cases of convictions, witches were usually put to death and their entire families were sold into slavery. In cases other than witchcraft, a conviction did not automatically mean that a person would be sold off the coast. Miles observed that often a convict's family would redeem him with a slave before he was sold. He noted that "most people of consequence" owned some slaves from the "inland country," and they willingly exchanged those "foreigners" for their own family members. If they did not own slaves to exchange, then they purchased one, from the Europeans if necessary. He reported that a "towns-man on the coast" would go to great lengths "to redeem his son." On the coast, it was the poor, the isolated, and the most vulnerable who were in danger of enslavement and sale. The major traders like Brew and Corrantee had facilities to house slaves awaiting sale, and others were lodged in the fort. While the foreign slaves were not necessarily confined at all times, captives from the coast were; men, for example, had their wrists chained to a twenty-five- or thirty-pound log to prevent them from escaping. It was this image that haunted Brew when he said that he loved liberty but hated logs and chains.[33]

At any given time, Annamaboe would have been crowded with slaves and their brokers, but even so, there were seldom enough slaves on hand at any given moment to meet demand. The fort usually kept some slaves in its holds for immediate sale, and major traders like Brew and Corrantee sometimes did also, but there were never enough slaves to fully supply every ship immediately, which explains why it often took weeks or months to fill a ship's cargo. The next step in the process of enslavement was to sell the captives to the European slavers. Slave ships often crowded Annamaboe Road; when a slave ship arrived at the Road and cast anchor, it lay a mile or more from the coast. It was not uncommon to have a dozen to twenty ships all competing for slaves at the same time, a situation that drove prices up. The ship fired a salute to alert the Annamaboe

caboceers that it was ready to initiate trade. Before captains could engage in trade, the chief caboceer sent pynins or other trusted town elders
on board the ship to receive customs payments for himself and the other
caboceers. Given the importance of Annamaboe as a trading port, it
charged the highest customs on the coast; in 1781 every ship that traded
there paid £97 in trade goods or £48 sterling to the town. Those rates
were so high that some captains tried to avoid the town altogether. Once
those payments were made, the ship fired several salutes and hoisted its
ensign to show that it was prepared to trade. British merchant ships used
the "Red Ensign," a red flag with the Union flag in the canton, which
flew from the stern. Soon traders crowded on board, and "scarce a day
passes afterwards, but black brokers come and sleep on board, at pleasure, to see the trade properly carried on."[34]

Captains could get the lowest prices by buying directly from the Fante
traders. In 1774, for example, Christopher and George Champlin, prominent Newport, Rhode Island, traders, advised their brother Captain
Robert Champlin to "make what trade you can with the blacks . . . If
you find the black Trade brisk so that you may git of[f] in three or four
months, we advise that you finish your Trade with them." On the other
hand, there were times when buying slaves quickly from the fort was an
advantage. Two years before, the Champlin brothers instructed Captain
Samuel Tuell in their sloop *Adventure* to "sell all the rum you can to the
Castles on the best terms you can for prime Slaves, and make all dispatch."
They advised him that several other vessels were headed to the coast, "and
should you tarry 'till they get down the chaunce will be lost . . . to lay a
long time on the Coast to piddle with the blacks must be against the voyage." Despite those instructions the trade was slow, and Tuell wrote
Christopher Champlin from the comfort of Castle Brew to report that "I
should due very well if there was any black traid, but there is none."[35]
Like all the slave ship owners, the Champlins did their best to predict
what the trade conditions might be on the coast and instruct their captains accordingly, but since those conditions often changed, captains
had to exercise their own judgment once they arrived at Annamaboe.

Captains needed great skill and experience to carry out a successful
venture; they had to determine whether to buy from the forts or from the
traders or some combination of the two, along with assessing when,
where, and how to sell or trade their goods to the best advantage. And

Text within the illustration: P.16. · comme les Negres rament de bout · Coscou · Commerce des Esclaves

A European trader bargaining for slaves. The African trader is smoking a tobacco pipe, while an African woman pounds grain. The male slaves are bound at their ankles. In the background, canoes carry slaves to the ships anchored in the Road.

Plate in François Froger, *Relation d'un voyage fait en 1695, 1696 & 1697: aux côtes d'Afrique, détroit de Magellan, Brezil, Cayenne & isles Antilles, par une escadre des vaisseaux du roy, commandée par M. de Gennes* (Paris, 1698), p. 16. Library Company of Philadelphia.

any number of other challenges could arise on the coast. Captain Champlin reported in 1775 from Annamaboe that he could move his entire cargo of rum if he was prepared to pay the high prices the African traders were demanding, but he informed his employers that he was prepared to spend three months on the coast in order to get the best prices possible. It was those substantial differences in price that made trading with the Fante more advantageous, even if it was sometimes more time-consuming and difficult than buying directly from the forts. Rum Men like Peleg Clarke and Champlin also faced the danger of leakage from the rum casks. Clarke described the plight of the Rum Man Captain Stanton Hazard who "lost on[e] forth part of his Cargo" due to "Uncommon Leakage." Clarke complained that he was having trouble collecting payment from the Dutch at Christiansborg due to a troublesome palaver there, and a pawn he was holding had escaped. He mourned that "diasspointments, Crosses, and Losses has closely attended us in this Voyage."[36] Captains sometimes found that the demand for goods had changed since the time they had loaded their cargos. John Bell reported from Cape Coast in 1776 that the "most Commanding articles here at present is Rum and Tobacco." He observed that no Portuguese ship had arrived with tobacco for some time, so it was scarce and fetching high prices. He also noted that "powder is at present much wanted all along the Gold Coast, many of the beech towns being at Warr amongst themselves or with their Gov'rs."[37] Any of these factors could raise or lower demand and prices for particular goods and determine the success or failure of a voyage.

Letters went back and forth between the captains and their employers, keeping them abreast not only of the events related to their own voyage, but of the most current information about trade conditions on the coast. Merchants used that information to prepare for future voyages. In 1785, the owners of a Boston vessel, probably Joseph and Joshua Grafton, instructed their captain, "We shall expect to hear from you, by every opportunity, to Europe, the West Indies, or any of these United States; and let your letters particularly inform us, what you have done; what you are then doing; and what you expect to do. We could wish to have as particular information as can be obtained, respecting the trade in all its branches on the coast . . . You will be careful to get this information from gentlemen of veracity."[38] With that sort of detailed information in hand, merchants in places like Newport, Liverpool, and Bristol could plan their next trading ventures, and the more reliable and current that information, the higher the profits would be.

Like most every aspect of the trade, the transport of men and goods between the ships and the shore was monopolized by a part of the Annamaboe community. The busy traffic was in the hands of the canoemen, who formed "a class distinct from all others." Canoes, of local construction and measured by the number of rowers they held, ranged in size from a three-hand canoe up to the largest twenty-one-hand canoes used to move the largest and heaviest cargos. The smaller canoes were generally used by the Africans for fishing and other purposes, while Europeans generally employed those from seven to fifteen paddles. Larger canoes were more easily overturned than smaller ones, and the twenty-one-hand canoes were rare. The most elaborate canoes had a platform covered by an awning with curtains to protect the traveler from rain or the heat of the sun. Canoemen made their vessels from the local silk-cotton tree, which was soft and easily hollowed out with a simple iron chisel when green and hard but light as cork when dry. These men were extremely skilled at their trade, their rowing timed by their distinctive songs and chants, and only they could expertly navigate the pounding surf along the Gold Coast. Ludewig Ferdinand Rømer noted that the "waves come rolling in as high as bell towers. You can see when the wave will break, and the black boatmen must then see to it that the canoes ride on top of the wave before it breaks; or, in all haste, row their vessel back, letting the wave break first. Should it happen that a wave breaks over the canoe, the vessel will be broken into small pieces, the goods will be lost, and the people, if they cannot swim, will be drowned." Leaving shore with a loaded canoe was far more hazardous than landing. The canoemen were known mischief makers who took "great delight in frightening all newly arrived persons," and they did "not hesitate upsetting a person against whom they have any spite; but they take great care that a ducking shall be the extent of the injury received. They right the canoe, place their victim in again, leap in themselves, and start once more with the most provoking composure."[39] The canoemen were another large segment of the town's population who had found a profitable niche

EMBARKING

Canoes of various sizes embarking for European ships at anchor in Annamaboe Road. From the *Illustrated London News* (1873).

Another image from the log of the *Sandown,* depicting canoemen rowing through the surf in a three-hand canoe. National Maritime Museum, Greenwich, London.

within the trade system, one that they monopolized, guarded, and used to demonstrate their independence, superior knowledge, and skill.

Before trade could begin, the captain had to employ a gold-taker, and his role in the process of enslavement was crucial. The gold-taker worked to bring brokers with slaves to sell to the ship and weighed and judged the quality of any gold that changed hands, taking a commission on every transaction. The gold-takers were highly skilled Atlantic traders; expert metallurgists and goldsmiths; fluent in the local languages, trade languages, and European languages; quick-witted and fast studies both of slaves and traders; and fiercely protective of their prerogatives and their crucial role in the lucrative trade. According to custom, the first gold-taker to board a ship was employed by that vessel, and he was to be employed by that captain on any future visit. Gold-takers received a payment of cloth, called their "sea-cloths," which they were given immediately when the ship arrived, and when the ship had loaded all its slaves, they were paid one ackey of gold (one-sixteenth of an ounce) for each captive sold at Annamaboe. Their assistants also received a monthly payment and subsistence while on board the ship. Either the gold-taker or his deputy stayed on board the ship during its time in the Road, acted

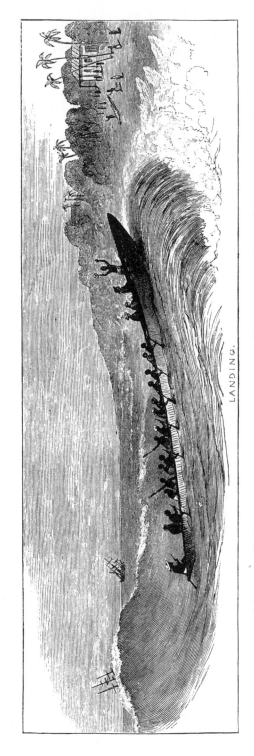

LANDING.

This image shows one of the unusually large seventeen-hand canoes in the Gold Coast's pounding surf. From the *Illustrated London News* (1873).

as a scouting agent to bring brokers and their slaves on board, judged the quality of any gold that changed hands during the transactions, and settled any disputes that might arise between the European and African traders. Like the canoemen, the gold-takers had carved out an important niche for themselves in the trade. The position was inherited and, as Richard Brew discovered, jealously guarded by the guild.[40]

In February 1776 Brew's gold-taker, Aggery, introduced him to a bush trader from the northern Fante state of Abra named Brinory who had one male slave to sell. In Brew's view, the slave was not worth buying. As Brew's employee, Aggery was not supposed to sell slaves on his own account to ships in the Road, but in this case, he asked "leave to carry the Slave into the Road to sell him," which Brew agreed he could do. But instead of carrying one slave, Aggery carried four. Customarily, Aggery would take a percentage of the value of a sale between Brew and Brinory, but in this transaction, he cut out his employer and took all the profits for himself. When the Abra trader came to Castle Brew for a customary dram without Aggery, Brew repaid Aggery's chicanery by offering to pay Brinory a higher price for slaves if the two dealt directly without giving a percentage to his gold-taker. Brinory reported Brew's proposal to Aggery, who quickly recognized the danger such a deal posed to the lucrative place he and other gold-takers had carved out for themselves. He called a meeting of all the gold-takers in Annamaboe, which Brew estimated as almost "half the inhabitants"—no doubt exaggerated, but with their families and dependents, they composed a large and influential segment of the population. Like Aggery, they all recognized the danger and "Immediately Resolved on making a palaver" on Brew.[41]

On the evening of February 20, 1776, an angry mob surrounded Castle Brew beating every drum in the town "which they continued to do for upwards of 3 hours without Intermission and Proclaimed to all the town that no person whatsoever should supply me with the smallest article of provision under penalty of being sold off the Coast." The next morning, men were back beating the drums around Castle Brew. They called a meeting of the entire town to discuss the palaver, and they sent delegates to demand rum from Brew to drink during their deliberations. Brew sent two gallons, which they refused as being too little. He sent two more, which they also rejected and demanded sixteen gallons instead. Brew refused to send that quantity unless they agreed to settle the palaver with it. Angered by Brew's attitude, he reported that they "immediately determined on Storming my house."[42]

About 1:00 that afternoon Brew was shocked by the sound of gunfire, which he took to be part of a burial ceremony until a shot came through his bedroom window. It hit the ceiling and fell beside his bed, followed by a volley of fire into his bedroom. Brew called together everyone in the house and tried to mount a defense, but to his dismay he could not find a single musket ball in the house. He set people to work making them from lead bars. While that work was under way the castle was surrounded by about a thousand men "who kept up a Continual fire upon us from Every Quarter and shot one of my people thro the body." They set fire to a part of his compound "which our women put out at the Greatest Risque Imaginable of their lives." Once the balls were made, Brew posted about a dozen men on the roof. They fired down into the crowd, which quickly dispersed. Brew was outraged by the "Hellish affair," carried out, he noted, within fifty yards "of the most Respectable Fort on the Coast & in the Noon day." Shaken by the attack, Brew wrote that "till this Blessed time I allways Imagined I had Liberty to dispose of my goods to who I thought proper, Town man or Bushman . . . I also thought I had Liberty of Speech & that I may tell a Trader the price . . . without bringing my life & property into Danger." He concluded that "tis high time for us to pack up our sails and be gone." Despite his protests, he was aware of his mistake in challenging the gold-takers, although he continued to criticize them for raising the price of slaves and then spending the profits on "dicipation [sic] and Drukenness at the Waterside."[43] Writing from the fort, Richard Miles said that he would have stepped in to settle the palaver had anyone notified him of it. He claimed that the mob dispersed once he sent messengers to demand an end to the attack. He guaranteed Brew that the attack would not be repeated, but he added, "I do not at all wonder at their asking satisfaction from you, as by your own confession, you have proclaimed them a Set of Thieves, without Provocation."[44]

This dispute between Brew and the gold-takers opens a window onto the conduct of the slave trade at Annamaboe and the crucial role the gold-takers played in that traffic. Every major slave trader at Annamaboe employed a gold-taker, just as Brew employed Aggery, who worked ex-clusively for him. They brought the brokers to the traders and took a percentage of the trade from both parties as a brokerage fee. If the inland trader sold ivory along with slaves, as they frequently did, then the gold-taker also took a hefty markup on that traffic. If the merchant sold goods to the inland traders—cloth, gunpowder, or weapons, as they usually did, then the gold-taker took a markup on those goods as well. The in-land traders lodged with the gold-takers. British officials alleged that the gold-takers watered down alcohol and diluted gunpowder before turning those goods over to the inland traders. The fort employed its own gold-taker, who performed the same services for the CMTA. Other gold-takers worked for the captains of the slave ships. But since they took a percentage on the sale and purchase of every slave that changed hands in Annamaboe, and a percentage of all the gold that exchanged hands there, it is easy to see how important and lucrative their profession could be.[45]

The prosperous gold-takers displayed their wealth and status when they approached the ships. They were described as being brought to the ships in five-hand canoes, accompanied by assistants who shielded them from the sun with handsome umbrellas. Their appearance was distinc-tive. Traditionally, their heads were shaved except for a small patch on one side "from which hung a handsome gold ornament . . . round their wrists were Aggry beads, mixed with string charmed by their Fetish man or priest; also heavy gold manillas in the form of snakes; round each ankle was a string of golden ornaments, made in the shape of little bells, stools, musical instruments, weapons, & c.; thick gold rings were upon their fingers, and their sandals were made of leather of various colours, beautifully worked in narrow strips, and the strap of which had a large tuft of many-coloured silks." They wore "an ample cotton cloth of native manufacture, striped blue, white, and red . . . wrapped around them like a Roman toga and this was decorated at the lower edge with a fringe of cowries, which rattled with the slightest motion." The aggery beads, gold ornaments, and cowries were all marks of wealth and status. When they met the captain, they lowered their wrap from one shoulder, and "snapped their fingers within his as a sign of friendship, and then followed him into the cabin." The captain showed the gold-takers his merchan-dise, and the two shared a few drams as they prepared to trade.[46]

Like all successful traders at Annamaboe, the gold-takers were some-times criticized by the European traders as being "cunning." The also accused them of preying especially on inexperienced captains. Henry Meredith, governor of Cape Coast Castle, noted that the gold-takers "were encouraged in proportion to their expertness and knowledge; and as they were rewarded in proportion to their success, they used much alertness in seeking for trade . . . and they took care to exact handsome sums for their trouble."[47] Thomas Melville, governor of Cape Coast Castle, reported to the African Committee in 1753 that "every black man Except the Gold takers of Annamaboe is happy, but these people say that if we trade we destroy their Business, and tho we buy their slaves, they are very angry when we sell them again."[48] In this case, the gold-takers com-plained about the fort's buying their slaves and reselling them to ships in the Road, which cut them out of a substantial portion of their commis-sions. Captains could get better prices from the black traders, but some inexperienced captains or those who needed slaves quickly often turned to the fort and paid the premium.

The ships became busy places as Fante merchants came on board to sell their slaves. A growing number of the sons of elite traders lived on board as pawns while their fathers carried out their business transac-tions. Sailors and the captain moved back and forth from the town to the ships and between ships. Peddlers from Annamaboe circled the ships in their small canoes selling fresh provisions including plantains, yams, limes, eggs, greens, ducks, poultry, and sheep to slavers. An unnamed writer in the *Gentleman's Magazine* noted that Annamaboe's traders and peddlers "give the preference of their trade to the shipping" rather than the fort, and "they will wait many days in the towns under the forts, if the sea happens to be rough, and at last run all risks rather than not let the captains have the refusal of their slaves . . . even in the article of provi-sion for the table . . . it has been the constant observation of every chief, and particularly at Annamaboe, that they hardly ever had a sheep, fowl or duck, offered them for sale, till it had been the whole round of ship-ping in the road, and brought back sea-sick, and half drowned with salt water." The writer noted that the ships brought the most recent and highest-quality goods, and that traders were often in debt to the forts and were therefore eager to trade with the ships rather than have their profits deducted from their debts.[49]

The captains sometimes trusted the gold-takers with goods that they sent with their assistants to the inland markets to acquire slaves on their behalf. Captains trusted the "best traders" who promised to make payment within a certain number of days, "when their servants or boys (as they call them tho they be sixty years old) return from the inland countries." They pawned "great collars of gold, and other large fatishes [sic] of exquisite workmanship, which their great men wear, and which they will be sure to redeem." If, however, they do not return with payment in the agreed time, the British traders panyarred or seized "as many of the negroes of that town where our debtor lives, as we can, or as will come to the value of the debt, which we secure aboard, and threaten to carry away with us if they be not redeemed." A palaver followed, and either the debtor was required to pay the debt or deliver himself up instead of the townspeople. Such palavers were common on the coast, but these disputes were usually resolved and seldom resulted in the townspeople actually being taken to the Americas.[50] Captains also trusted goods to the chief merchants of Annamaboe. One 1767 account book from an unidentified Newport captain contains, for example, these entries:

> Trusted my Lord Augustus Fitzroy five Ounces Gold and has put his Son on board as a pawn and is to pay me a fine young Woman and one Ounce gold.
>
> Sent Old Peter Qua 1 Oz gold and he is to put his Son on board as a pawn and is to pay me gold in One Weak Or a fine young Woman

The captain gave "My Lord Augustus Fitzroy"—who was John Corrantee's son, usually referred to in the records simply as "My Lord"—trade goods valued at five ounces of gold and held his son as a pawn for repayment either in gold or with a slave, a transaction he repeated with Old Peter.[51] Annamaboe traders relied on this type of credit to allow them to purchase slaves, even putting their children in the hands of the captains to guarantee the loans. Captains needed to be able to evaluate the reliability of the traders when making these advances, which gave experienced captains an advantage.

These transactions sometimes ended badly, and disputes could have serious consequences for the trade. It was in everyone's interest to prevent trade disputes from getting out of hand. CMTA officials and Fante caboceers attempted to negotiate peaceful resolutions to trade disputes according to mutually accepted rules governing the trade. In 1790 Aqua, the linguist at Tamtum, pawned a set of aggery beads to Captain Fountaine. Aggery beads were highly valued on the coast. They were "perforated, vitrified substances, of various colours, sizes, and shapes, which with gold, are found in the earth. . . . They mystery attending them has made them sacred . . . so that they are purchased for twice, thrice, or even four times their weight in gold . . . The possessor of a string of Aggry beads is reckoned a rich man."[52] In 1790 William Fielde and the Cape Coast Castle Council informed the African Committee of Fountaine's failure to return the aggery beads that had been pawned to him before he sailed. They warned that "the consequences will be very serious" if indeed Fountaine had "really carried them off the Coast." The caboceers at Tantum pressed for their return, and letters went back and forth between the officials and the AC. It was over two years before the AC was able to pay Fountaine what he demanded and return the beads to the coast, by which time Archibald Dalziel, governor of Cape Coast Castle, warned that "the settlement of his Affair will not be easily effected."[53]

Captains sometimes won these disputes, and that sense of fair play was necessary since so much of the trade relied on trust. In 1788 the Captain Lewis of the slave ship *Friends* claimed that while he lay at anchor in Annamaboe Road, a buoy was stolen for the lead it contained. That theft caused him to lose his anchor, and as a result he panyarred a slave. He remained there three days in an attempt to settle the affair, and when he could not, "by Advice of the Masters of Ships there, [he] carried off the Slave." The people of Annamaboe responded by closing the trade entirely until they were paid for the slave since no palaver had taken place. The masters of the ships in the Road agreed to pay for the slave to reopen the trade.[54] A year later, for example, a Mr. Fitzhenry, supercargo of a French ship at Cormantine caught two men from Annamaboe stealing his goods. He captured them and "declared he would keep [them], unless he got proper Satisfaction for the Theft." He made the mistake of leaving his ship and going on shore, and men from Annamaboe "beat and very ill used him, until he got the two People in Question on Shore, when they released him." CMTA officials on the coast called his beating "a most unprecedented Act of Insolence!" In the palaver that followed in Annamaboe, he got "The 2 Thieves and 2 oz of Gold, Gold . . . for sundrys stolen," trade goods, and four sheep "for the ill usage they gave him."[55] As these examples illustrate, it was in everyone's interests to keep the trade open and to give everyone involved a sense that it was being conducted fairly. In some cases the captains worked together to settle disputes; in others, the townspeople acknowledged their wrongdoing and made amends. In that sense, the Annamaboe and European traders operated in a shared legal community.

Captain John Adams described the gold-takers as "sagacious fellows, and keen observers, who soon find out the weak side of a man and treat him accordingly." They gave every European a nickname based on some personal characteristic or vice; so "one man they call *cheegwa,* or red head; another *pockum-pockum,* or long chin; a third, *amphiteshu,* or, don't spit upon deck; a fourth, *cocroco,* or big; and a tall thin man, *tsin tsin lan,* or long fellow; a hypocrite, *dada;* an avaricious man, *acacumma,* or a little more." Adams recalled that on one occasion an especially vain captain was putting on airs and verbally abusing his gold-taker, who Adams described as "a sly old fellow." The gold-taker somehow learned that despite his pretentions, the captain came from humble origins. The gold-taker looked at the captain "with the most ineffable contempt," and said, "with great emphasis—'Who you? Your father no make lead bar. You be big man? You no big! Your family nobody.' Then, snapping his fingers in his face, coolly marched over the ship's side into his canoe," to the delight of the crew, who were equally tired of the captain's boasts.[56]

Captain Adams left descriptions of two other prominent and "long established" gold-takers at Annamaboe, Yellow Joe and Tom Coffee. Yellow Joe, he said, looked like an Egyptian, of a lighter complexion than most of the Fante. He described him as having "a most penetrating eye, and much gravity in his demeanor, particularly when he is in the society of Europeans, with whom he is reserved and cautious, seldom smiling or saying much; although when he does speak, it is always to the purpose." He was reputed to be rich but lived simply, dressed in plain and inexpensive clothes, and never wore much gold, unlike many of his fellows. He entertained well but plainly at his "chief residence" in Annamaboe, "where he carries on his commercial pursuits and pays and receives visits of ceremony." His croom, or village, was at Annishan, about a mile away, where he was reputed to have a much finer residence where he could enjoy his wealth unobserved. Tom Coffee, on the other hand, Adams described as "portly" with "a hearty generosity" who was a "great favourite" of the Europeans traders and those African traders from inland who enjoyed his hospitality. Unlike Yellow Joe, Coffee liked to display his wealth. His house in Annamaboe was "splendidly furnished" with "many articles of European luxury," and had a "princely" retinue of servants and retainers. He and his wives dressed luxuriously, and he wore on his person "many pounds weight of pure rock gold." He was caught up in an expensive palaver and lost all his fortune, while the more cautious Yellow Joe was unmolested.[57]

Men like Yellow Joe and Tom Coffee were an important link in the long chain that brought enslaved Africans into the hands of the European traders on the coast. They facilitated almost all of the final transactions that transferred Africans to the slave ships, and they had as much contact with the European traders as any class on the Gold Coast. Men of talent, skill, and keen observation, they played a vital role in the process of enslavement. Their complex occupation required many skills, such as an understanding of metallurgy, languages, calculating the values of goods and men, maintaining connections with traders in the interior, and fostering good relations with the European traders while keeping their own profits high. This skill set enabled the best of them to live lives of wealth and comfort.

When the gold-takers brought brokers and slaves on board, captains carefully inspected slaves, and they could refuse to buy a slave for any reason. Traders tried to make their slaves look as healthy as possible by rubbing them with palm oil and shaving them closely to hide any gray hairs. Captains and ship's surgeons checked slaves' teeth and limbs, and examined their sexual organs for any evidence of venereal disease. Richard Miles reported that captains refused about one of every eight or ten slaves that he offered for sale. Miles along with some other ship captains reported that slaves who were refused were "importunate to be bought, and endeavouring to show himself as capable of labour as the rest."[58]

Captives were often desperate to remain with their families and friends rather than face the Middle Passage alone. Miles made the unlikely sounding claim that nine-tenths of the slaves he purchased "seemed pleased at exchanging Black for White masters . . . their joy arises from removing from a situation, where they think their lives in danger." Slaves had good reason to prefer being purchased to being refused, because a terrible fate could await those who could not be sold. Captain Fountain concluded that "slaves not saleable, are put to death, from an instance of an old woman at Cape Coast Castle, who, on being refused to be bought, to save her maintenance, was murdered."[59] African slave traders had no reason to pay the costs of feeding and maintaining an unmarketable slave. George Young reported that he purchased a "a beautiful infant boy, brought alongside the ship in a canoe . . . having been along-side all of the trading ships, and not being able to sell it there . . . and threatened to toss it overboard if no one purchased it; saying at the same time they panyarred that child, with many other people the night before." Traders sometimes abandoned infants since captains usually refused to buy them, and elderly or infirm captives who could not be sold might also suffer death or abuse.[60]

Captains carefully evaluated their human cargo, and they knew that slaves from inland nations reacted differently to their situation than those from the coastal states. Captives from the coast were not as traumatized as those brought from far inland; they could blend into the local population if they managed to escape, and they were more knowledgeable about the fate that awaited them. Captain Thomas King reported that slaves from some "nations have an idea, that the whites buy them to kill and eat them. They are sometimes a good while on board before they are quite reconciled." Dr. Thomas Trotter also reported that "slaves, on being brought on board, shew signs of extreme distress and despair, from . . . regret at being torn from friends and connections." He noted that "many retain those impressions for a long time; in proof of which, the slaves being often heard in the night, making an howling melancholy noise, expressive of extreme anguish." When he asked the woman who served as his interpreter to find the cause of their despair, "she discovered it to be owing to their having dreamed they were in their own country, and finding themselves when awake, in the hold of a slave ship."[61] In the bowels of a slave ship, the nightmares came during waking hours, and only dreams provided any escape. King understood that the slaves from the coastal states who were "sold for crimes from near the shore, are for a time discontented at separation from their friends and families; particularly while they lie near the shore."[62] Captains knew that the most dangerous time for slave uprisings were while their ships lay near the shore.

Captains evaluated the risk involved in determining which slaves needed to be restrained while the ship lay in the Road. Captain King reported that a "part of the men slaves only are fettered on board." He noted that of a representative cargo of 500 slaves purchased on the Gold Coast, about 120 or 125 would be women and girls—a figure that matches current estimates, which suggest that men made up about 64 percent of the slaves from Annamaboe—and that females were never fettered. Of the males, at least 100 or 125 were under the age of fifteen and would never be put in irons. Men from the "most interior parts of Africa, who are quiet, are never put in irons," he said, so that of a cargo of 500 only half or less would be in fetters at once. He observed, "They are generally chained two and two together, the right leg of the one to the left leg of the other." He added that some men judged to be most dangerous might also be shackled by the hand as well.[63] Captain Fountain agreed that the "manner in which slaves are confined to be take on board ship, depends upon the nation they belong to. Duncoes are never put in irons, they supply a great number of slaves. The Fantees always. The Ashantees and other nations, according to circumstances."[64] Leaving the slaves unchained and on deck could have disastrous consequences, as Captain Peleg Clarke found in 1776 when slaves rebelled on board his ship in Annamaboe Road. There were 160 slaves on the ship, and several of the crewmen were onshore when the men were released from the deck chains in order to wash themselves. With the ship poorly manned, the men saw their opportunity to revolt. They wounded one crewman, and for forty minutes tried to take the ship, but when that failed all of the Fante and most of the Accra male slaves jumped overboard. Thirty-two men and boys and two women escaped recapture. He confessed to the ship's owners that "the Insurrection on board happen'd not by Accident So much as through avery grate Neglect . . . in not Chaining the Slaves that day."[65]

In 1721 William Snelgrave, captain of the slaver *Henry* from London, purchased a cargo of slaves on the Gold Coast that included a number of Cormantines, also from the Gold Coast. He regarded them as "stout stubborn People . . . who are never to be made easy." They rebelled and attempted to take the ship. After he put down the revolt, he asked them through his linguist why they had rebelled. They said that he "was a great Rogue to buy them, in order to carry them away from their own Country, and that they were resolved to regain their Liberty if possible." Snelgrave replied "that they had forfeited their Freedom before I bought them, either by Crimes or by being taken in War, according to the Custom of their Country." He informed them that they were now his property, and that he "was resolved to let them feel my Resentment, if they abused my Kindness." He asked them if "they had been ill used by the white Men," and they replied that they had not. He warned them that even if they were able to "escape to the Shore, it would be no Advantage to them, because their Countrymen would catch them, and sell them to other ships." John Fountain accused unscrupulous canoemen of encouraging slaves to jump overboard or rebel so that they could recapture and resell them. Snelgrave claimed that this argument—which gives some insight into how slavers salved their own consciences—pacified the rebels. Whether or not that was true, he did use the customs of their own country against them, and he was no doubt correct that they would have been reenslaved had they escaped.[66]

While Snelgrave claimed that his arguments calmed the slaves and prevented any further trouble, it was more likely the brutal execution of the slave who killed the white crewman that convinced them that rebellion was useless. Once the revolt was put down, Snelgrave called together the captains of the other eights ships lying in the Road and informed them of the attempted uprising and the murder of the crewman. They unanimously advised him to execute the murderer, arguing "that Blood required Blood, and by all Laws both divine and Human." More importantly, they reasoned that a public execution would deter other uprisings since "the Negroes on board their Ships would see it; and as they were very much disposed to mutiny, it might prevent them from attempting it." When Snelgrave informed the man that he would be executed, he replied through the ship's linguist that "if I put him to death, I should lose all the Money I had paid for him." The captain had the interpreter reply that "he should find that I had no regard to my Profit in this re- spect; For as soon as an Hour-Glass, just then turned, was run out, he should be put to death." While the sands ran down, the other captains brought their slaves up on deck. As the hour approached, the sailors took the man to the forecastle where they tied a rope around his waist in order to hoist him up to the fore yardarm. His countrymen assured him that he was not about to be executed or the rope would be around his neck, but Snelgrave had other plans. Once the man was hoisted up, ten armed sailors placed on the quarterdeck fired their muskets and killed him instantly. They cut the body down, cut off the man's head, and threw it into the sea. Snelgrave reported that many the Africans believed that if they died during the Middle Passage they would return to their country, but not if they were dismembered. Snelgrave observed, however, that the Fante did not suffer from that illusion.[67] Snelgrave did not appeal to the chief of the fort or to the Fante in the case. Their authority stopped at the waterside, and the ships' captains did not answer to them for mat- ters that took place on board their ships.

Once the ship was slaved, the captain made preparations to leave An- namaboe Road. By custom, the ship did not just suddenly sail away, but rather gave ample warning of her intent to leave the coast so that all ac- counts could be settled in hopes of avoiding costly and time-consuming palavers. To signal its intent, the ship's crew would "loose the topsail, hoist the ensign, and fire a gun, often for three, four, or five weeks, as a signal for sailing, that such of them as have accounts to settle with the captain, may come on board; the usual time for getting under way, is with the land wind from two in the morning." That nighttime departure had the advantage of making it more difficult for the slaves to realize that they were finally being taken off the coast for good, for that realization often provoked rebellions like that on Snelgrave's ship. Settling accounts could be a time-consuming affair. For example, in 1777 Captain William Chambers prepared to leave Annamaboe, but his departure did not go as planned because he and the gold-takers disputed their payments. He

A painting of a Liverpool-based ship believed to be involved in the slave trade. Attributed to the artist William Jackson, ca. 1780. National Maritime Museum, Greenwich, London.

notified Richard Miles, chief of Annamaboe Fort, that he would leave the goods that the gold-takers demanded in the fort. He wanted to pay them in goods and pipes, "which they refused." Things apparently went more smoothly the following January when Chambers wrote Miles, "I intend Sending Abary and any other Goldtakers on Shore Tonight and Desire them to Come and take their Customs tomorrow morning" before his departure from Annamaboe.[68] Captain Peleg Clarke wrote that "in order to fill our Water, get our Wood and provisions, and . . . Collect our debts . . . at Annamaboe, to Compleat which it will take 6 or 8 Weaks."[69] After provisioning the ship, collecting debts, and settling accounts, the ship left the coast and the process of enslavement entered its Atlantic phase.

The African process of enslavement at Annamaboe involved moving thousands of captives over great distances to inland markets and then to the coast. Other captives were enslaved through panyarring, kidnapping, or through the courts. Asante enslaved their defeated enemies rather than kill them, their lives already forfeited in battle. To the Asante-hene his subjects were his property, body and soul, his to do with as he pleased. The Akans, the Akyem, and other nations on or near the coast enslaved enemies taken on the battlefield or panyarred on the paths, and sold their criminals into slavery. For desperate bush traders, who played the slave-catcher game in earnest, greed alone was justification enough. The Fante, like all the rest, panyarred their enemies, enslaved criminals and others they considered a danger to their society—a fate better than death, they reasoned—or purchased those foreigners already enslaved long before they ever reached the coast. Ludewig Ferdinand Rømer, who was employed on the Gold Coast by the Danish West Indian and Guinea Company from 1739 to 1749, recorded his discussions with the Fante on the topic of the slave trade. They told him, "'It is you, you Whites . . . who have brought all the evil among us. Indeed, would we have sold one another if you, as purchasers, had not come to us?'" In their view, the Europeans had helped create a demand for their "fascinating goods and . . . brandy," a demand that had fueled the trade. They asserted that the trade had undermined their traditional social relations to the point that "one brother cannot trust the other, nor one friend another. Indeed, a father hardly knows his own son!" So great was the volume of the trade from the Gold Coast, they said, that the region had become depopu-lated: "In our youth we knew of many thousands of families here and at the coast, and now not a hundred individuals can be counted." Further-more, they argued that the continual demand for slaves from inland had earned them many enemies, "and what is worse, you have remained among us as a necessary evil . . . , since if you left, the Negroes up-country would not let us live for half a year, but would come and kill us, our wives and our children. That they bear this hatred for us is your fault."[70] While these statements hardly square with the history of slavery and the slave trade in West Africa, the quote does suggest how the Fante shifted blame for the trade onto the Europeans. They saw themselves trapped in an Atlantic World not of their own making, one that had radi-cally transformed their lives, but one they intended to exploit as profit-ably and expertly as its other players. Snelgrave's speech to his rebel-lious slaves on board the *Henry* brings us as close as we are likely to get inside the mind of the European slave traders who, like their African counterparts, purchased those already enslaved. Those captives by the customs of their country were likely to suffer a worse fate than enslavement in the Americas, or so they told themselves. "Money, and not morality, is the principle of commerce and commercial nations," Thomas Jefferson claimed, and that was the British maxim. That was certainly the view of Thomas Thompson, the first English missionary on the Gold Coast, who later defended the slave trade in a published tract "as an open, public trade; encouraged and promoted by acts of parliament . . . vindicable as any species of trade whatever."[71] It also sums up the stance taken by steely-eyed and hardened traders like Snelgrave and Brew who took that view of their role in their nation's rich commercial life and their part in the long and tragic process of enslavement, a process that turned human beings into property and fueled the largest forced migration in human history.

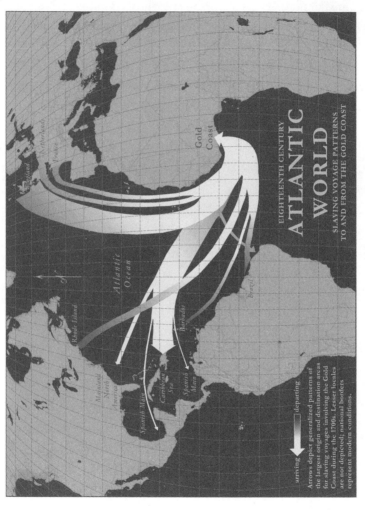

Map of the slaving-voyage patterns to and from the Gold Coast in the eighteenth century. The size of the arrows is relative to the number of voyages to and from the specified locations. Map by Richard Campanella based on campaign information from the Trans-Atlantic Slave Trade Database.

5

Tracing the Trade: Annamaboe
and the Rum Men

I N J U N E 1785 the *State Gazette of South-Carolina* carried an advertisement that read:

GOLD COAST NEGROES
Just arrived in the Brig *Gambia,*
Captain Robert Champlin,
Directly from ANAMABOO,
And to be Sold,
On THUSDAY, the 23d inst.
A Cargo of very healthy prime young Negroes,
the greatest part of them are fit to be put in-
to the field immediately. The conditions of sale:
Bonds payable the 1ˢᵗ of January, 1786, with
interest from the date; a proper discount will be
made for ready money. NATHANIEL RUSSELL[1]

South Carolina, like other southern colonies of British North America,
imported more and more slaves from the Gold Coast as the eighteenth
century progressed, a trend that continued after independence. Many of
the ships, like the brig *Gambia,* came from Rhode Island. Carolina
planters held slaves from the Gold Coast in high regard, which explains
why the prominent merchant Nathaniel Russell emphasized that his

shipment of slaves was not only from the Gold Coast, but "directly from ANAMABOO." The planters believed that slaves from the Gold Coast were less prone to suicide and running away, and were larger and physically stronger than those from other regions.[2] South Carolina's demand for slaves grew rapidly after the mid-eighteenth century, just as Annamaboe became a major exporter. Russell's advertisement indicates that South Carolina planters were familiar not only with the Gold Coast, but with Annamaboe itself. An examination of this important trade route between Annamaboe and the Americas reveals how the process of enslavement continued once the ships left Annamaboe for the Americas.

It is not always possible to trace the cargoes of slaves from Annamaboe to the Americas with much specificity beyond a port of debarkation, but a close examination of the trade activities of the Rum Men, the Rhode Island merchants who dealt primarily in that liquor, demonstrates the possibilities for mapping Annamaboe's trading partners. Following the Rum Men and exploring where and how they marketed slaves highlights just how important Annamaboe was as a supplier of slaves to the Americas. In 1764 the Rhode Island General Assembly recounted the history of the rum trade to Africa; they wrote that "formerly, the negroes upon the coast were supplied with large quantities of French brandies; but in the year 1723, some merchants in this colony first introduced the use of rum there, which, from small beginnings soon increased to the consumption of several thousand hogsheads yearly." The assembly reported that since the 1730s, about eighteen ships sailed from the little colony to Africa annually, "which have carried about eighteen hundred hogsheads of rum, together with a small quantity of provisions and some other articles, which have been sold for slaves, gold dust, and elephants' teeth, camwood, etc. The slaves have been sold in the English islands, in Carolina and Virginia." The trade in rum had created a very large distillery business in Rhode Island: "There are upwards of thirty distil houses, (erected at a vast expense . . .) constantly employed the making of rum from molasses. This distillery is the main hinge upon which the trade of the colony turns, and many hundreds of persons depend immediately upon it for subsistence." This Guinea rum, as it was called, was higher proof than other rums and most other spirits, and it was the preferred liquor on the Gold Coast.[3]

Taken together, the trade in molasses from the West Indies, rum to Africa, and slaves and other articles in return employed two-thirds of the ships in the colony. Add to that direct trade the numbers employed in building and sailing the ships, the sail and rope makers, the coopers employed in making the barrels for rum, the blacksmiths who forged the shackles, and the farmers who raised provisions for the ships, and the importance of the trade to the economic life of Rhode Island is clear. Just as the tentacles of the African slave trade extended far into the interior, the same was true of the American trade. Newport was by far the most important North American port involved in the slave trade; scholars estimate that Rhode Island merchants carried about 150,000 slaves from Africa to the Caribbean and North America and controlled up to 90 percent of the American trade in slaves.[4] The Rhode Island merchants were a fixture at Annamaboe; a 1770 list of the ships lying in Annamaboe Road counted fourteen vessels and gave a place of origin for thirteen of them—three were from Bristol, four from Liverpool, one from Barbados, one from Boston, and four from Rhode Island. As early as 1736, a Rhode Island captain reported that there were nineteen ships then at Annamaboe, "7 sail of us Rume [sic] men that we are ready to Devur [devour] one another" in their fierce competition for slaves.[5] Rum became such a popular commodity that Richard Miles, chief of Tantumquerry Fort in 1773, reported that "rum is a perfect drug on the Coast . . . there are more adventurers in trade now." Rum was so popular that it edged out its competitors like brandy, helped transform the trade on the coast after 1750, and enabled the Rum Men to gain a competitive advantage there. So prominent had they become that the New England captains were sometimes called the "Rum Gentry."[6]

Richard Brew developed close ties with the Rum Men as he sought to expand his business. Scattered references in the account books from Rhode Island slavers show transactions between them and Brew like the one from a ship called the *Active*, owned by Samuel and William Vernon, which sold twelve loaves of sugar, three barrels of flour, and sixty-four pounds of onions to Brew, while the captain, John Stockford, purchased four male and one female slave from Brew in exchange for cloth and over 650 gallons of rum. The *Active* carried sixty-four slaves from Annamaboe to Barbados after a voyage of 264 days. Records of similar accounts

with Brew and the captain of the Vernons' ship *Marigold* also include
payments to John Corrantee and William Ansah.[7]

Brew sometimes went to extraordinary lengths to win the favor of the
Rum Men. During the Seven Years' War, a French privateer, the *Count St.
Florentine,* preyed on British shipping off the African coast. The French
vessel arrived at Annamaboe in June 1758 and captured a number of
British trading ships, including the snow *Fox* from New London, Connecticut, captained by William Taylor.[8] The privateer took the ship and
cargo and released the captain and crew of the *Fox,* who were stranded
at Annamaboe. Their desperate plight gave Brew an opportunity to ex-
hibit a "singular Instance of Benevolence and Humanity." The captain
of the privateer sold the *Fox* to the commander of the Dutch fort at Cormantine, and Brew purchased the ship from him, provisioned it, and
"generously made a Present of her to Capt. Taylor, in order to bring him
Home, and the rest . . . all of which, after this Misfortune, were treated
with great Hospitality by the Gentlemen of the Coast." His act of generosity earned him favorable publicity around the Atlantic World, and no
doubt helped cement his relationship with the Rum Men.[9] In 1766 Brew
wrote an open letter to the merchants of Boston informing them that
"the Coast is very much infested with Pirates," a warning that appeared
in the Boston newspaper, in newspapers in Virginia and Georgia, and in
the *Gentleman's Magazine.*[10] Once again, he cast himself in the role of
protector of the trade and of the New England shipping interests. Brew's
relationship with the Rum Men, particularly the Vernons, was so close
that there was talk of them taking over Annamaboe as an American
station.[11]

The detailed logs of the ship *Mary* give a day-by-day account of the
activities on board a typical slave ship lying in Annamaboe Road. The
ship, commanded by Captain Nathan Henry, sailed from Providence,
Rhode Island, on November 22, 1795. The first mate opened his log with
a prayer: "May God grant success to the Ship and Crew." The ship arrived at Goree on December 24, and Henry began purchasing slaves as
the ship moved down the African coast following the typical route to
Isles De Los, Sierra Leone, Cape Mount, and Cape Coast Castle. He arrived at Annamaboe on March 28, 1796. He found three English ships
there along with four American vessels. His ship was quickly crowded

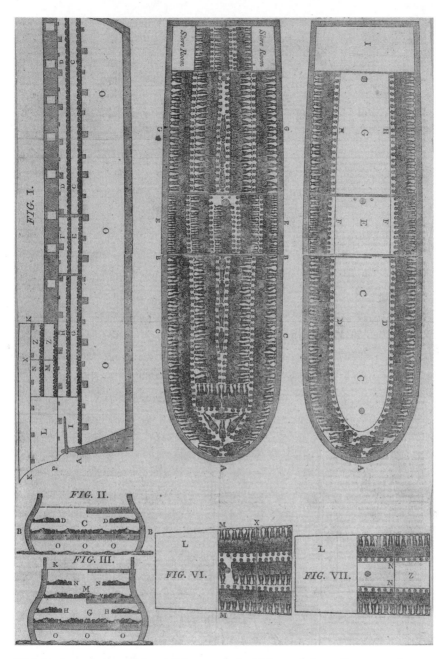

This is a later version of the well-known and widely copied set of stowage plans of the Liverpool slave ship *Brooks,* first published in 1789. British abolitionists commissioned the original drawing in 1788 to raise awareness of the inhumanity of the slave trade. The image was so effective that it was soon reproduced and distributed widely around the country and abroad. National Maritime Museum, Greenwich, London.

with a "Great Number of Blacks onboard [sic] Begging or What they Call their Ackeys to make trade for me." An ackey was a gift or payment made to the African merchants to open trade. For days afterward the Fante traders crowded his ship, sometimes buying cloth or other goods from him, sometimes selling a slave or two, giving him great "Difficulty in settling their custom." After about three weeks of this tedious business, the crew grew restless. Captain Henry left the ship to "Spend the Evening" socializing with the captain of the brig *Whim,* and when he returned, he found one of the sailors, John Burges, "Noisy and troublesome." When he tried to subdue Burges, several crew members rushed to Burges's assistance. They knocked the captain down with a hatch bar "and would have murdered him no doubt, had he not been Relieved by his Officers and some of the more Sober and Considerate part of the Crew." The captain of a nearby vessel heard the commotion, thought the slaves had rebelled, and sent assistance. Together, they managed to get the ringleaders of the near mutiny in irons. The following day, they set them on shore "to prevent them making any futer [future] Disturbance in the Ship." The next day the men demanded their wages, and they were paid and dismissed from the crew.[12] Such episodes were common; Richard Brew wrote that "ship's crews . . . are very mutinous on this Coast."[13]

The ship's troubles were hardly over. On April 23, the captain found one of the sailors, James Auburn, "beating one of the slaves with a Rope," and when the captain tried to stop him, Auburn turned on the captain, hit him four times with the rope, and bit his finger. The captain had Auburn tied up and whipped in front of the entire crew, and "also told them he would not let Auburn loose unless they would become bound by their word, for his futer [future] good behavior. And they all Unanimously Agreed too." On April 7, the first captive died on board the ship, "having Ben [been] Sick some time," and illness began to spread to the crew and the slaves. By the end of April, both the captain and the ship's doctor were "very Sick." Several slaves died of dysentery. Finally, in early June the ship left Annamaboe to trade with the Dutch at Elmina. The officers discovered that the "women Slave Appartments [sic] had been attempted to have been opened by some of the Ships [sic] crew, the locks being Spoild [sic] and sunderd [sic]." Whether or not that attempt on the part of the white crewmen to reach the enslaved women had any bearing on what followed is unclear, but it certainly could have provoked the enslaved men to action. On June 10, one of the slaves who was being employed as a sailor rather than confined below decks warned the crew that the enslaved men planned to take the ship. The captain left the ship to trade, so the first mate and others brought the enslaved men up from the hold two by two "as they were Ironed and Examined them, found all the legg Irons in good order." Almost all the men had been brought up on dcck whcn the first mate looked down the ladder and "saw a large strong Slave, with a naked legg Iron bolt in his hand." He tried to take it from the slave, but the man was too strong for him, and he was quickly surrounded by the enslaved men. The white crewmen scattered. Some made it inside the cabin and barred the door, while one of the men who could not escape was badly wounded "with their [sic] Iron about the head and would have been Murdered had it not been for our muskets." Thanks to their firepower, the crewmen were able to force the men back down below deck, and the captain of the Portuguese fort arrived with twenty armed men to help restore order. As they brought the enslaved men up again they found that about twenty had managed to free themselves of their irons. Two jumped overboard and drowned during the fighting, and one sick man was trampled to death below decks.[14]

The ship returned to Annamaboe to purchase more slaves and supplies. Several more slaves died, and many others were ill, as were members of the crew. On June 17, the ship sailed out into the Atlantic having spent about seven months on the coast, the bulk of that time at Annamaboe. The ship carried 142 enslaved men, women, and children. That same morning the captain and other crewmen saw one of the white crew, Mr. More, "sleeping in the Midle [sic] Slave Room amongst the Adult Slaves for which Capt. Henry broke him from being an Officer thinking him no longer fit Companion for the Cabin." Apparently, More was lying with the men and boy slaves, since the record indicates that men and boys were housed there. On June 25, "a Slave boy jumped overboard and drownd [sic] him self to get clear of a pain in his bowels, Occasioned by a Dysentery," and "one Meagre Man Slave" drowned himself on July 6, "having been Delirious Sometime." At least seventeen more slaves died as the ship made its way to Savannah, Georgia. The ship arrived there

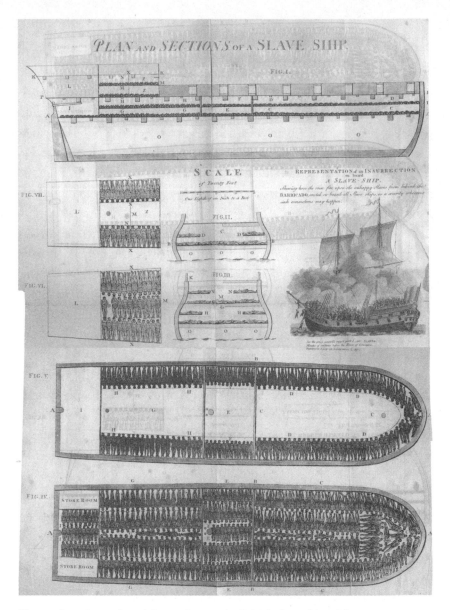

Plan and sections of an eighteenth-century British slave ship with a representa-
tion of an insurrection on board. Folded plate in Carl Bernhard Wadstrom, *An Essay
on Colonization: Particularly Applied to the Western Coast of Africa, with Some Free
Thoughts on Cultivation and Commerce; also Brief Descriptions of the Colonies already
Formed, or Attempted, in Africa, Including those of Sierra Leone and Bulama* (London:
Printed for the author, by Darton and Harvey, Gracechurch-Street. And sold by G. Nicol,
No. 58, Pall-Mall; W. Faden, corner of St. Martin's Lane, Strand; J. Stockdale, No. 191,
Piccadilly; J. Edwards, No. 78, Pall-Mall; E. [sic] & J. Egerton, No. 32, Charing-Cross;
J. Debrett, No. 179, Piccadilly; J. Johnson, No. 72, St. Paul's Church-Yard; and C. Dilly,
No. 22, Poultry, MDCCXCIV [1794–1795]).

on August 19, and the next day they took the slaves out of their irons and acquired "fresh meat for the Slaves and people." They landed the slaves on Coxburrow Island at the entrance to the harbor where they quarantined them, allowed them to exercise, and gave them "fresh provisions and Limes." The health officer inspected them on August 27, and the crew was busy "tending our Slaves and Shaving them up." The exercise, fresh food, and shaving were intended to make them look as healthy as possible before sale. At least three more slaves died during the quarantine period. On August 30, one of the ship owners from Charleston came on board with a Spanish merchant (probably from Cuba), who apparently bought the entire cargo except for fourteen slaves reserved for the owner from Charleston.[15]

It is possible to follow another of the Rhode Island vessels from Newport to Annamaboe, and then back to the Americas. In June 1774, Samuel and William Vernon, sons of a famous silversmith in Newport and the "pre-eminent" slavers in the city after the mid-eighteenth century, began outfitting the sloop *Hare* for a slaving voyage.[16] In February they contracted with seamen, and in May they signed contracts with Caleb Godfrey to serve as captain and John Arnold Hamond as first mate. By this time, the Vernons had been employing Godfrey for about ten years, and he had served as captain on at least five slave ships, the first in 1734.[17] On perhaps Godfrey's most notorious voyage, his sloop was struck by lightning and destroyed. He and the sailors on board escaped in the long boat, but the slaves on board died in the fire.[18] Along with the captain and first mate, the sloop had a second mate (who also served as cooper), eleven seamen, and a cook.[19] The ship's cargo illustrates that the cargo itself was a product of the Atlantic commercial network. The Vernons purchased 6,759 gallons of rum from seven local merchants. While the rum was locally produced, it was distilled from molasses imported from the West Indies, as was the sugar they loaded on board. When the local distillers could not keep up with demand, Rhode Island merchants had rum distilled in the West Indies to their specifications. Rum usually made up about 90 percent of the value of a ship's cargo. The other important trade article they carried was tobacco. That leaf was in high demand on the Gold Coast, but since Africans were usually supplied with high quality Brazilian tobacco, only the highest American grades would do. That product was imported to Rhode Island from the southern colonies. They bought provisions including beef, pork, bread, flour, and hams, from local supplies. They might sell or barter small amounts of these goods, as the captain of the *Active* did with Brew, but they were primarily intended to supply the needs of the crew. They also insured the vessel and its cargo through Thomlinson, Trecothick and Co., agents and merchants in London, for a voyage to the African coast, and from there to Jamaica, the Windward Islands, or South Carolina. The final destination would depend on the fluctuations in the slave market. They assured the underwriters that "Capt. Godfrey is an Experienced Commander on the Coast." The Rhode Island merchants were only now beginning to enter the South Carolina market, and William Vernon had been there himself only two years before making the necessary business contacts.[20]

The *Hare* struck out across the Atlantic in June and within a few weeks Godfrey would have been sailing down the African coast purchasing slaves. While Godfrey acquired his human cargo, the Vernons wrote Gabriel Manigault in Charleston to arrange for the sale of the slaves there. Manigault was the richest merchant in colonial Charleston and owned several plantations and nearly 500 slaves. The Vernons told him that they had received a letter from Godfrey in September, and expected that he would arrive in Charleston in March, just in time for the agricultural season. They wanted the proceeds from the sale to be paid in sterling bills of exchange, reserving sufficient funds to load the ship with rice rather than sending it home in ballast. They also asked Manigault to deliver a letter to Godfrey in which they told the captain that he could put his faith in Manigault, who they described as "a Gent'n of the utmost Generosity and Goodness." They also urged Godfrey to be frugal in his expenses in Charleston and to act with the greatest dispatch.[21]

Godfrey left Africa late in 1754, on his way to Charleston. He first made landfall at Barbados on January 29, 1755, and remained there until February 7. He stocked up on provisions for the slaves and crew, including the purchase of 650 plantains and two bushels of peas, foods favored by Africans. It was important that the slaves be well fed in preparation for their sale. Godfrey arrived in Charleston in early March 1755, and a doctor visited the ship to ensure the health of the slaves, though appar-

A group of enslaved African women are unloaded off a slave ship to be sold in the Caribbean. Plate in John Gabriel Stedman, *Narrative, of a five year's expedition, against the revolted Negroes of Surinam, in Guiana, on the wild coast of South America; from the year 1772 to 1777* (London: Printed for J. Johnson, St. Paul's Church Yard, & J. Edwards, Pall Mall, 1796), vol. 1, p. 200.

ently it was a remarkably healthy voyage. Godfrey purchased twenty-eight men, twenty-five women, twelve boys, and seven girls, and he reported that two enslaved men drowned on the coast, and "1 Negro Girl [valued at £350] lost her Life on the Passage."[22] On March 6 the following advertisement appeared in the local newspaper:

TO BE SOLD on Wednesday the 19th Instant, a choice CARGO of *Windward* and *Gold Coast* NEGROES, Just imported on the *Hare, Caleb Godfrey* Master, in a Passage of about *Five* Weeks.[23]

Manigault also hired a "post Boy" to carry copies of the advertisement "into the Country" for distribution among the planters.[24] A slave sale in colonial Charleston took on a surprisingly festive air, and Manigault spent £7 on wine and punch for the crowd. Most of the slaves sold to individuals, and the remaining twelve were sold at auction by "the Vendue Master."[25]

The men and women who bought the enslaved men, women, boys, and girls from the *Hare* were a diverse cross section of the prosperous Charleston slave-owning class. They were settlers from around the Atlantic World who had been drawn by the potential wealth generated by the Low-country plantation economy. The accounts show that twenty-nine individuals purchased fifty-four slaves. Most people purchased only one slave, seven people purchased two, two people purchased three, and one person, Henry Laurens, a prominent planter, merchant, and slave dealer, bought nine. There were two women among the purchasers—Susannah Wedderburn, who bought a boy and two men, and a Mrs. David, who bought one man. "Mrs. David" has not been identified, but Susannah Wedderburn was the widow of James Wedderburn, the younger son of Sir P. H. Wedderburn of Scotland and a prominent planter, merchant, and government official who settled in Charleston in 1733. James Wedderburn died in 1752, but her purchase of slaves indicates that Susannah Wedderburn, like many Low-country widows, continued to run the family's plantations. Among the prominent planters who bought slaves that day were Samuel Simons, of Huguenot descent,[26] and Thomas Mell.[27] Successful city merchants like Thomas Bell[28] and William Lloyd[29] also acquired slaves that day. Another of the purchasers was Lachlan

McIntosh, who was born in Scotland in 1725 and immigrated to Georgia with his father in 1736. At the age of seventeen he moved to Charleston, where he became a protégé of Henry Laurens. After a few years he returned to Georgia, became a surveyor, and acquired significant property worked by a growing number of slaves.[30] The partnership of Horry and Lessesne, composed of Elias Horry and Daniel Lessesne, both Huguenot descendants, prominent merchants, and planters, purchased seven slaves.[31] Charles Lorimer and another Thomas Bell, both Presbyterian ministers,[32] purchased two enslaved men that day. Christian Minnick, one of the German or German Swiss settlers near Orangeburg who owned "probably the largest and best cattle range in the province," came down to buy an enslaved man and a woman.[33] All told, the fifty-five men, women, and children sold for £11,144.[34]

That voyage was so profitable that the Vernons hired Godfrey to undertake the same slaving voyage the following year. The Vernons instructed him to acquire his cargo with "quick Dispatch" and to "keep a watchful Eye over 'em [the slaves], and give them no opportunity to of Making an Insurrection." Furthermore, they asked him to "let them have a Sufficiency of good Diet, as you are Sensible your voyage depends upon their Health."[35] Godfrey's records reveal that he first stopped in St. Jago, the largest island in Cape Verde, where he bought sheep and goats. Then he went to Isle May, where his purchases included grass and corn, and Isles De Los, off the coast of Sierra Leone, where he bought wood, plantains, and a turtle. From there he sailed down the coast of Guinea, the Gold Coast, and the Slave Coast, stopping at the important trading posts all along the way. Along with slaves, his purchases included rice, wood, pepper, oil, corn, beans, and fowl. The costliest expenditures were for the large quantities of rice he purchased in Sierra Leone, Cape Mount, Grand Curra, and Limpo that would be used as provisions for the slaves, and the large quantities of wood bought at Annamaboe to feed the fires necessary to cook meals during the long voyage to the Americas. At Annamaboe, Godfrey also bought two cankey stones, millstones necessary for grinding corn. He apparently purchased most of the enslaved Africans in Sierra Leone, though he would have continued to purchase slaves as he sailed farther and farther down the coast to Annamaboe, Accra, and Popo. He paid custom duties at Annamaboe, the usual prerequisite before buying slaves there, and he hired canoes and canoemen there, who would have been needed to transport slaves to the ship.[36]

As Godfrey purchased slaves in Africa, the Vernons lined up their dealers in Charleston. Manigault declined to handle this cargo; he had decided to get out of the business. The Vernons wrote, we "are sorry it is not agreable [sic] to you to continue in Business any longer, as we deem it a public Loss."[37] The brothers turned instead to George Austin, who was in partnership with Henry Laurens. Laurens warned them that the threat of war with France had hurt the price of slaves: "We may without the spirit of Prophecy pronounce that the Sales with us this Summer must become wretchedly bad and we could not wish to see your Vessell the Hare with us or one of any of our Friends on any consideration whatever."[38] Despite that dire prediction, the Vernons had heard from Godfrey that he planned to leave Sierra Leone for Charleston in June 1756, and they wrote their insurers, Thomlinson, Trecothick and Co., that they expected the premium to be lower since the risk in going to Charleston was less than to the West Indies in case of war with France.[39] That greater threat may explain in part why they chose Charleston rather than risk the ship's seizure by French privateers. Bad weather and ill winds delayed the *Hare*'s return voyage, and when the ship arrived in Charleston ten weeks later, the slaves were in poor health. Godfrey wrote the Vernons with the bad news; of the eighty-four enslaved men, women, and children he had purchased on the African coast, thirteen had died due to the "damage a Laying" becalmed in the Atlantic. Three others died in the pesthouse on Sullivan's Island, where they were quarantined according to law. "I thought by my Purchass [sic] I Should have made you a good Voyage," he wrote, "but fear the Low market and Mortality Shall miss by Expectation."[40] Though the Vernons might have preferred to continue their association with Manigault, George Austin and Henry Laurens were well on their way to becoming the largest slave dealers in North America. Between 1751 and 1761, their firm handled sixty-one slave ships with an estimated 7,800 people on board.[41]

As promised, Godfrey arrived in Charleston in June, and the following advertisement appeared in the local press:

JUST imported in the **Hare,** Capt. *Caleb* **Godfrey,** directly from
  Sierra-Leon, a Cargo of Likely and Healthy
Slaves,
To be sold upon easy Terms, on *Tuesday* the 29th Instant *June,* by
AUSTIN & LAURENS.[42]

Austin and Laurens arranged for the sale as soon as the quarantine law
would allow. To Laurens's surprise, a large crowd attended the sale,
larger than his past three or four combined, and he reported that "we
must have made a very fine Sale had the Slaves been tolerable but they
were the most shocking cargo we ever beheld."[43] Laurens reported to the
Vernons that the sale had not gone well. Even though Laurens had advertised the enslaved Africans as healthy, they were not. While the turn-
out was larger than expected, many of the prospective buyers who had
come from the country "became extremely angry that we should invite
them down from 80 or 90 Miles distance to look at a parcel of refuse
Slaves as they call'd them & were with some difficulty were prevail'd on
to wait the sale." Only ten or fifteen of the slaves brought top dollar.
They were able to sell forty-two slaves for £7,455, and two, who "seem'd
past all hopes of recovery," sold at auction for only £35. "God knows
what we shall do with those that remain," Laurens complained. "They
are a most scabby Flock all of them full of the Crocheraws. Several have
extreme Sore Eyes, three very puny children & add to this the worst in-
firmity of all others with which 6 or 8 are attended (vitz) Old Age." *Crocheraws* was another name for yaws, a bacterial infection common on
slave ships that caused painful lesions and swelling of the joints.[44]

Once again the names of the buyers read like a who's who of Charleston's merchant and planter elite, and once again two women were among
the buyers, Sarah Hext and Mary Russell. Sarah Hext was the widow of
prominent Charlestonian John Rutledge, who died in 1750, and Mary
Russell might have been the widow of Jeremiah Russell, another prominent planter. Also among the purchasers that day was Elias Ball, whose
sister, Eleanor, was Laurens's wife. Ball made the rather unusual purchase of several children, four boys and two girls.[45] Children made up
about 18 percent of the slaves on ships from the Gold Coast.[46] English
traders testified that kidnapping was common at Annamaboe, and one

trader reported having many boys and girls on board his ship who had been kidnapped there.[47] Ball's purchase and his careful record keeping and the in-depth research of his descendent Edward Ball make it possible to trace these children from West Africa to the slave sale in Charleston to a low-country plantation, and even to have some idea of their life stories. When Ball bought the children he took them to one of his adjacent rice plantations near the city, called Comingtee. His record book also shows the names and ages "as near as I can judge," he added, of his new chattel: Sancho, nine; Peter, seven; Brutus, seven; Harry, six; Belinda, ten; and Priscilla, ten. It is probable that Ball named them himself. Belinda (or Belinder, as her name appears in Ball's hand) disappears from the records and must have been sold or died. Perhaps she was one of the "puny children" that Laurens complained about. Even for those lucky enough to survive the Middle Passage, perhaps one-quarter or more died within their first year in the Americas.[48] Harry worked as a field hand in the swampy rice fields until he disappeared from Ball's record books in 1784, when he would have been about thirty-five years old, and from those records it appears that he remained single. Perhaps that hard labor and diseased environment ended his life, or he may have been sold. Peter, known as an adult as Mandingo Peter, married Monemia and raised a family. In the 1770s, they relocated from Comingtee to Ball's home plantation of Kensington. Peter's name disappeared from the slave list in 1810, by which time he would have been in his late sixties. Like Harry and Peter, Sancho worked as a field hand, and he formed a partnership with Affie. They had at least three children, named Sancho, Saby, and Belinda, and perhaps his daughter Belinda was named for the child purchased with him who disappeared from the records. Belinda and Sancho could have been related, or the bond they formed on board the *Hare* may have had a lasting significance. There are many examples from the low country of enduring bonds between shipmates.[49] Before the American Revolution, Sancho's family also relocated to Kensington, and the elder Sancho was among at least fifty-one slaves who ran away from the plantation to take refuge with the British Army. Unlike thousands of the Black Loyalists who were evacuated and freed, he was returned to Ball's ownership. In 1819, by which time he was over seventy, his wife and children were sold at auction. Separated from his family by slavery at the end of his life as at its beginning, he lived on until 1833, when he died on Christmas Day, in his late eighties.[50]

Whether or not these men and women came from Annamaboe, their experience would have reflected that of all the enslaved Africans who arrived from that port to the low country. It is virtually impossible to trace individuals whose identities are almost always lost to history once they were forced below the decks of a slave ship. When they disembarked in the Americas, their new masters often erased any trace of their former identities from the historical record by giving them new names, as Ball most likely did to the children he purchased. That did not mean, of course, that the Africans forgot their cultural heritage. It is clear that South Carolina's "new Negroes," as the arrivals from Africa were known, often banded together along ethnic lines. In 1761, for example, seven "Coromantees" (as Fante slaves shipped from Annamaboe were often called) ran away from a plantation in Prince William Parish. About 25 percent of the African runaways advertised in the colonial South Carolina newspapers ran away with someone of the same ethnic origin.[51] The isolation of the large enslaved populations on the low country's rice plantations contributed to the formation of another important marker of African Atlantic cultural survival, the Gullah language. Gullah is directly related to the trade languages along the West African coast that combined European, especially Portuguese, words and African vocabulary, and scholars have found that a significant portion of Gullah names and other features of the language, for example, can be traced back to the Gold Coast.[52]

The position the Rum Men had carved out for themselves in the Atlantic slave trade was threatened by the sweeping changes brought about by the American Revolution. The war prevented the Rum Men from engaging in the trade, and the resulting shortage of American rum brought complaints from the Africans on the Gold Coast, who were partial to it, and from traders like Brew. That demand for American rum gave the New Englanders an advantage once the war was over and trade resumed. The Second Continental Congress passed a resolution opposing the African slave trade in 1776. Virginia abolished the African slave trade in 1778. South Carolina briefly reopened the trade after the revolution, but closed it due to the state's depressed postwar economy. By 1786 the slave trade was legal only to Georgia.[53] Under the new Constitution, nothing prevented a state from abolishing the African slave trade into their state before 1808, and northern states quickly moved to do so: New Jersey and Rhode Island in 1787, Massachusetts, Connecticut, and New York in 1788. These laws did not prohibit their merchants from taking slaves elsewhere. Even the states of the Deep South followed suit. North Carolina prohibited the trade in 1794, a decision fueled by fears aroused by the bloody slave rebellion in Saint Domingue, and Georgia followed in 1798. South Carolina placed a five-year ban on slave imports in 1788, which was renewed for an additional two years and then extended every year until 1803, though that was due to a depressed economy, not opposition to the trade. For whatever reason, the trade was either illegal or banned throughout the United States until 1803.

American traders, especially the Rum Men, began smuggling slaves immediately, and everywhere enforcement was lax. In 1791 William Ellery, federal customs official in Newport, Rhode Island, alleged that "an Ethiopian could as soon change his skin as a Newport merchant could be induced to change so lucrative a trade." Smuggling was especially widespread to South Carolina and Georgia, where the trade continued so openly that merchants advertised the sale of newly imported Africans in the local newspapers, many of them supplied by the Rum Men.[54] But the Rum Men also sought new markets; they expanded their trade to Cuba, for example, and they rushed to join the trade wherever it was legal. Traders imported about 75,000 Africans into Charleston between 1804 and 1807, nearly as many as had been brought into Charleston during the seventy-five years before the revolution. The traders themselves were a mixed lot. Customs records provide background information on fifty-three of the merchants and factors involved, perhaps a third of the total number. Of those fifty-three, twenty-five were from Great Britain; eleven were from Rhode Island; seven were from Charleston; three each were from New Jersey, France, and Ireland; and one was from Massachusetts. Shipping figures reveal the same pattern; the British imported about 20,000 slaves in ninety-one ships, Rhode Islanders brought 8,000 slaves in eighty-eight ships, Charlestonians carried 2,000 slaves in thirteen ships, and the French imported over 1,000 slaves in ten ships. So great was the American involvement in the African trade that the U.S.

slaving fleet was probably about three-quarters the size of the British fleet, the primary carriers of slaves from Africa during the eighteenth and early nineteenth centuries. Efforts to introduce a constitutional amendment to allow Congress to stop the trade before 1808 failed, as did an effort to impose heavy taxes on the trade as a means of stopping it.[55]

While Congress could not abolish the trade before 1808, Congress could regulate it, and the widespread smuggling and the outbreak of the Haitian Revolution moved that body to action in 1794. On paper, the law was strict and would have stopped the Rum Men from taking slaves from Africa to any destination. Under the new law, no United States port or shipyard could be used to outfit or build a slave ship. No ship could sail from a U.S. port to deal in slaves in foreign countries, and ships sailing from the U.S. to Africa were to post a bond guaranteeing that no Africans or natives of other countries would be taken on board, transported, or sold as slaves. The law imposed fines ranging from $200 for sailors who worked on board slave ships to $200 for each slave transported to $2,000 for outfitting a slaver. Slave ships could be confiscated, and informants would receive financial rewards. The law proved to be ineffectual. It was difficult to enforce, many cases were lost on technicalities, and when ships were seized, the old owners usually bought them back at low prices with the connivance of the entire community.[56]

The success of the American Revolution transformed the relationship between the Rhode Island traders and the British on the West Coast of Africa. They went from fellow Britons to enemies, and some of the Rum Men employed the rhetoric and ideology of the revolution to inflame the Africans against the British. David Mill wrote the CMTA in May 1784 complaining about the arrival of Captain Dudley Saltonstall on the Gold Coast. Born in New London, Connecticut, in 1738, Saltonstall was descended on his father's side from a governor of the colony and on his mother's side from John Winthrop of Massachusetts. His father was a ship captain involved in the slave trade and other ventures, and Dudley followed in his father's footsteps. By 1762, at the age of twenty-four, he was a captain engaged in successful trading voyages to the West Indies and Europe. His brother-in-law was Silas Deane, a member of the Marine Committee, which supervised the Continental Navy during the American Revolution. That family connection won him an appointment as a naval captain shortly after the war began. He began his career as commander of the *Alfred* with a young Scottish immigrant, John Paul Jones, as his second in command. It quickly became clear to the capable Scot that the arrogant Saltonstall owed his position to his connections and not to his talents. The captain behaved toward his subordinates, including Jones, "as tho' they were of a lower species," and the adjectives he used to describe the captain included "rude," "ungentle," "ill-natured," "narrow minded," and "sleepy." Saltonstall's career ended in failure and controversy when he was blamed for a disaster called the Penobscot Expedition, court-martialed, and dismissed from the navy. He returned to Connecticut, turned a merchant ship into a privateer, and took a number of valuable prizes. After the war, he entered into the African slave trade but continued his fight with the British even in Africa.[57]

Mill notified his superiors in London that Saltonstall had "used every argument to inflame the Minds of the Blacks and instill into them that Spirit of Republican Freedom and Independence, which they through Rebellion have established for themselves, . . . no arguments, are so powerful with the Natives as a plentiful supply of Rum, which he has not been sparing." The British had barred the U.S. ships from Annamaboe, but Saltonstall "prevailed on them to insist on his going into Annamaboe Road," where the British fired on him from the fort, an act that enraged the Africans to "a Pitch of Insolence." Mill warned that they would only become more confrontational unless "some Measures are . . . taken by Government to curb them, and make them sensible of their Dependence." Mill seemed to have forgotten that the blacks at Annamaboe were not dependent on the British, rather the reverse, and that for at least a century the Fante had successfully resisted any attempt to control or limit their trade. Mill fumed that the Fante were "extorting from the Ships whatever they think proper," and if they refused to comply, then they "threatened them with a Stoppage of Trade." When he tried to convince them of "the allegiance they owe to the British Nation, from whom they not only receive Stipends and large annual Presents . . . they reply that the country belongs to them, and that they will admit Americans, French, Dutch or any Nation they please."[58]

Saltonstall arrived in Annamaboe on April 11, and despite the British efforts to drive him off, he was still there on April 29 when two British navy ships arrived intending to force him to depart. Mill thought that he had "reconciled the natives to it," but once the naval ships threatened the American, "it appears that so far from being reconciled to his being sent away, they threaten to stop all Trade to the Shipping if he is molested." Saltonstall did not run from the British ships, but leisurely continued his trade at Annamaboe until he was ready to sail on May 10. Even then Mill reported that "we have very good Reason to think that he will return again." Mill warned that he was "informed that one of the principal Objects of his Voyage was to treat with the Natives for an American Settlement to be built at Agah, about a mile and a half to the Eastward of Annamaboe."[59] As late as September, Saltonstall was still on the Gold Coast, and Mill found his continued presence to be "greatly detrimental" to British interests.[60] Eventually, Saltonstall carried his enslaved cargo to Charleston.[61]

The revolutionary ideas that Saltonstall introduced along the Gold Coast did not disappear with him. As late as 1788, four years after the American arrived, a British official reported that "Mulattoe, Negro, and free Traders, and we may add your black Servants [in the forts], who we can assure you, have so far imbibed the *Principles of Liberty* (so much the conversation now) as to be far above submitting to any Restrictions we may communicate to them, hinting pretty plainly, that *were* it in our Power to compel them to it by Force, they would throw off all allegiance to the English rather than comply. Indeed at Annamaboe they say their Country belongs to them, and they will trade with whom they please."[62] These tensions erupted into violence in 1803 when the governor of Cape Coast Castle imprisoned one of the "principal men for tendering base metal to him in lieu of Gold." The governor apparently intended to sell the man into slavery as punishment. The blacks who resided in town around the fort surrounded the governor's house, "armed with Muskets, knives, etc., at the same time throwing stones into the Castle, offering great insult and threatening to seize Mr. S____ by force and carry him into the interior Country." When the governor ordered the caboceers to resolve the dispute, they refused and "treated the Messengers with contempt." The following day the governor gave the townspeople one hour to pay a hefty penalty in gold, but they refused and once again treated "the message with the same contempt as yesterday." The governor

ordered "hostilities be commenced immediately against the said Natives, in order to bring them to a sense of their Duty, by firing a shot
through the principal Cabbocceer's house." The result was a riot that
entirely destroyed the town and left one Englishman and many natives
dead. The townspeople fled "into the Woods." When this news reached
London, the African Committee resolved that "the hasty adoption of
such Fatal Measures as were resorted to; was in the highest Degree improper and impolitic." They removed the governor and replaced him
with George Torrane, a seasoned veteran who had served in various capacities on the coast since 1785, who immediately set out to restore good
relations.[63]

Tracing the trade by following the Rum Men makes it possible to follow process of enslavement as it moved across the Atlantic and to the
Americas. Shipments of enslaved Africans from Annamaboe to the Americas, particularly to Charleston, where buyers placed a premium on
slaves from Annamaboe, was one of these well-traveled routes that connected Annamaboe to the wider Atlantic World. The Rum Men built
close relationships with Annamaboe's traders, especially with Richard
Brew, who carefully courted them and worked to build close relationships with them. The growing popularity of rum among Gold Coast
consumers allowed the Rum Men to gain a large share of the market
there and helped transform the economic life of Newport. Preparing for
a slaving voyage was a long process—hiring the captain and crew, outfitting the ship, buying the cargo, and insuring the voyage. The process of
enslavement had its own backstory on the American side, as it did on the
African side. The owners of vessels kept a close eye on the market and
directed their ships to American ports depending on demand. The slave
trade was a risky enterprise, and the slave ships faced dangers not only
from their enslaved cargoes but also from disaffected crewmen. Factors
in the slave-trading ports of the Americas, men of property and standing, marketed slaves for the ships' owners, and theirs, too, was a complicated business that depended on many variables including the condition
of the slaves and their ethnic origins, the availability of credit, the price
of the local commodity, and international affairs. Those sales took on a
festive air, and in places like Charleston, the town's elite men and women
turned out to purchase human property. Regular shipments of slaves

from Annamaboe to Charleston resulted in a concentration of slaves from the same cultural areas, which impacted the development of African American culture in the low country. The American Revolution disrupted some of the trade networks that had characterized the colonial slave trade from New England, but the Rum Men quickly rebounded. While many states abolished the African slave trade, smuggling kept the trade alive, and the Rum Men moved into the rapidly expanding Cuban market. The Rum Men carried the ideology of the American Revolution to the West African coast, where it found a receptive audience among the Fante and helped fuel the tensions between the Fante and the British on the Gold Coast.

6

A World in Motion: Annamaboe
in the Atlantic Community

THE ATLANTIC WORLD, as defined by John Elliott, grew out of "the movement, across and around the Atlantic basin, of people, commodities, cultural practices, and values."[1] Tens of thousands of enslaved Africans left Annamaboe in the eighteenth century, but few of these individuals were residents of Annamaboe, and once they sailed out of Annamaboe Road, their stories pass out of Annamaboe's history and into American history. But other Africans, admittedly a far smaller number, left Annamaboe, traveled the Atlantic World, and returned home again. Some of them were enslaved, others were kidnapped, others were employed on European ships, others were the children of mixed-race unions, and others were African elites engaged in diplomatic missions or sent abroad to be educated. If we are to fully understand Annamaboe's place in the Atlantic World, their stories are crucial, for they experienced the Atlantic World in ways that others did not; they brought that knowledge back home with them, and thereby altered their community's understanding of that wider world and their place in it. For them, the Atlantic World was a part of their lived experience.[2]

The importance of trade along the West African coast meant that Africans were drawn into a wide variety of relationships with Europeans; they were hired as servants by Europeans who resided on the coast, as sailors on board European ships, and as gold-takers and suppliers of food, water, and other goods, all of which brought them into direct contact with Europeans and made them potential kidnap victims. Any Africans who encountered the European traders could fall into the wrong hands, and their families and communities made every effort to retrieve them.[3] English captains often hired skilled African sailors for their voyages, and these men were easy targets for kidnapping. In 1776 Captain Benjamin Francis Hughes of a Liverpool slaver at Annamaboe hired an African sailor named Amissa to sail with him to Jamaica. Actually, he hired Amissa to navigate the ship across the Atlantic, which indicates that he was a very skilled seaman, more skilled than the Englishmen on board. When the ship reached Jamaica, the captain had Amissa and three other sailors row a group of slaves to shore after they had been sold to a local planter. When they landed on shore, the sailors broke the news to Amissa that he, too, had been sold to the planter. When the captain returned to Amissa's hometown, he informed Amissa's family that he had died during the Middle Passage. However, the surprisingly accurate web of information that circulated around the black Atlantic World worked in Amissa's favor. A year or two later, another African returned from Jamaica with the news that Amissa was alive and well. Amissa's family then complained to the AC, which commissioned the captain of another slave ship in route to Jamaica to redeem him, and they sent Coffee Abram, a gold-taker from Annamaboe who knew Amissa, to Jamaica to positively identify him. After nearly three years in slavery, Amissa traveled to London, where his case was brought before the African Committee, the successor to the Royal African Company, which ordered that the captain who enslaved Amissa be prosecuted to discourage kidnapping. The AC reported that they "have been at great Expence in obtaining Justice for him and a Suit is now depending against Captn. Hughes for Damages." Amissa was eager to return home, and the AC "provided him with Cloaths and other Necessaries" and made plans to send him back to Annamaboe. They instructed their officials at Cape Coast Castle to "deliver him in Safety to his Friends and Relations, and inform them of the pains the Committee have taken to see Justice done him."[4]

Amissa was ill, and the AC feared for his well-being; they urged the ship's captain to "take particular care of him" since "his safe arrival in Africa is of great Importance to the Trade of this Country."[5] Meanwhile, the case against Captain Hughes went to trial. The AC reported to their officials at Cape Coast Castle that they "have now at a great Expence, obtained a Verdict against Captn Hughes for a considerable Sum; when the Money is recovered, something very handsome will be remitted to Amissa."[6] England's most distinguished jurist, Chief Justice Lord Mansfield, heard the case and recommended that the jury give exemplary damages to the victim. After deliberating for only a quarter of an hour, the jury found for the plaintiff and awarded Amissa £300 in damages. In July 1779 Richard Miles wrote the AC with the good news that Amissa had arrived and was "immediately sent down to the Chief of Annamaboe who delivered him to his Friends."[7]

Captain John Wade Robinson of the *Lovely Lass* arrived in Annamaboe in April 1792 and remained on the coast until November 1793. When he prepared to sail for Jamaica he hired three African sailors from Annamaboe, Cudjoe, Joe, and Quow, to join his crew. Cudjoe was an experienced sailor who had made at least one previous voyage on a slaver, the *Mars,* from Africa to Grenada to Liverpool, where he stayed before returning to Africa on the *Jane.* Quow was hired as the ship's cook, and during the voyage the chief mate Robert Milligan gave him an order to which he answered "yes" rather than "yes, sir," which Milligan, who was drunk at the time, chose to interpret as insolence. He beat Quow, cut his head with a cutlass, and ordered another crewman, John Owen, to whip him even more severely, an order that Owen refused to carry out. Milligan then shouldered his gun and threatened to shoot Owen, who had no choice but to carry out the flogging, after which Quow was manacled to the mast. The incident apparently outraged the crew, and Owen and another white crewman, John Dixon, conspired against Milligan, who was murdered. They were charged with his murder and in 1793 sent to Newgate, London's notorious prison, to await trail. Quow died on the voyage to England, but the others "remained long in Newgate, were afterwards tried, and acquitted for want of evidence, the principal witness having died on his passage." Archibald Dalziel, governor of Cape Coast Castle, wrote the AC seeking the return of Joe and Cudjoe. He warned, "If the two surviving Blacks should not be found, and restored to their Families, we apprehend a very serious Palaver; especially as one of them belongs to Yellow Joe, a principal Caboceer at Annamaboe." The men had been taken away by Admiral Edmund Dod of the British navy, and Dalziel reported that "every succeeding Captain in the Navy, has since been questioned but all of them have given unsatisfactory Answers, and the Relations, who have heard of the acquittal of the Prisoners, are extremely importunate." When another naval vessel arrived at Annamaboe the following year, he informed the AC that the "natives have repeated to Captain Mathews the demand which they never fail to make on the arrival of every Man of War concerning the acquitted Blacks."[8] Whether or not the men were returned is unclear from the records, but officials on the coast and in London were working to have them returned, and Amissa's case indicates how diligent the AC could be in tracking down and returning Africans to avoid disruptions of the trade.

Communities rallied behind kidnapped sailors and used every means at their disposal to have their townspeople returned. Robert Stubbs, chief of Annamaboe Fort, informed the AC in 1780 of a palaver under way between the people of the town and Captain George Nelson, who arrived at Annamaboe in 1779 in the *Molly*. He hired an unidentified African sailor there, who joined his crew. The ship embarked with 450 slaves and delivered 412 for sale in Kingston, Jamaica. It was an adventurous voyage; the *Molly*, which carried fourteen guns, took a French vessel as a prize during its Atlantic crossing. The African sailor continued with Nelson to Liverpool and lived there until Nelson embarked on his next voyage for Annamaboe in March 1780. The *Molly* sailed into Annamaboe Road in June 1780, but Nelson refused to pay the sailor his wages, which amounted to about £20. In order to force him to pay, the people of Annamaboe seized a boat belonging to another English captain, John Kendall, and held it until Stubbs paid the sailor's wages, and only then did they release the boat and the people.[9]

Detailed information about the 1779 voyage is lacking, and so it is impossible to know exactly how long the sailor's entire trip lasted, but it was probably a year or so. During that time he spent many months working side by side with English sailors and he experienced the Middle Passage, which probably lasted around fifty days, not as most Africans did, as captives sweating and retching below decks, but as a sailor. He saw the terrible conditions on the ship; he witnessed the deaths of thirty-eight Africans during that passage. He saw the naval engagement that led to the capture of a French ship, and the shortage of sailors that led to his hire may have resulted in part from the American Revolution. He saw the bustling port of Kingston and the even more impressive city of Liverpool, where he lived for weeks or perhaps months before the *Molly* sailed again, probably residing in a boarding house with his fellow seamen. Amissa not only had the same experiences on board ship, but he spent years on a Jamaican plantation and months in London. Cudjoe, Joe, and Quow experienced violence and imprisonment, and for Quow the experience proved fatal, but they also won the support and camaraderie of at least some of their fellow white crewmen.

African sailors on board English ships found themselves in a complicated environment. On the one hand, they had valuable skills that were badly needed and valued on board ship. Scholars including Jeffrey Bolster and Julius Scott have emphasized that sailors were more accepting and less racist than many of their contemporaries, one reason that so many blacks became sailors to begin with.[10] While all sailors depended on one another during voyages, this was especially true of sailors on board slave ships, where the dangers were even greater than on other voyages. On the other hand, Africans from Annamaboe came from a part of the Atlantic World where they were not dominated by white men. The moment they stepped on board an English ship, however, those power dynamics changed, though the ability of Africans to get their sailors returned demonstrates that while they might not have been able to control interpersonal relationships on board, they could use their influence to have their family members returned to them.

The demand for experienced sailors along the African coast led the RAC officials there to send young Africans to England and the West Indies to be trained as sailors. For that purpose, in 1721, the RAC instructed that "two or three Negroes between 16 & 20 Years of Age" be "put on board of every one of the Company's own Ships headed to or from England or the West Indies." A short time later an official at Cape Coast Castle notified the RAC that they had "put 4 Negroes into the Guinea packet to be bred sailors."[11] The RAC was eager to send young black men and boys to England to be apprenticed for a variety of skilled occupations badly needed in their forts that were expensive and hard to fill from England like smiths, carpenters, and masons.[12] RAC officials on the coast also urged the RAC to require their skilled artisans on the coast to train "Black Boys to Learn their Trades."[13] While the RAC requested that slaves be sent for instruction, Dalby Thomas, governor of Cape Coast Castle, urged that they consider training mulatto children instead, and soon English officials were sending mixed-race children for instruction, as early as 1709: "Robert Davis, Mustee, Goes for England for Learning, & will contract with the Compy for five years, in any Station the Compy shall think fitt."[14] In 1694 the RAC sent a schoolmaster to Cape Coast Castle to teach both African and mulatto boys, but that experiment must have been short-lived since Thomas advocated the establishment of such a school. Thomas thought "it would be usefull to have at least 20 of the Comps Negroes learnt to Speak English," and he noted that a "voyage to England gives the Black Boys more English than they can learn [here] . . . it would be of great Service if I had 6 or more Slaves that could read & write English, they would be of great use . . . & the sooner its done it will be the better."[15] How many of the young men and boys who engaged in these pursuits were from Annamaboe is impossible to say, but recall that when Thomas Thompson met John Corrantee and told the old caboceer that he had set up a school for blacks and mulattoes at Cape Coast Castle, Corrantee responded by repeating "some Letters in the Alphabet, telling me that he had been a Scholar there."[16] Given Corrantee's advanced age, he probably attended the school created in 1694.

When Thomas Thompson went to Annamaboe to preach in 1752, he met a skilled artisan, Coffi, a mason working with the English builders on Annamaboe Fort who may have been educated abroad. Thompson described him as "a very Civilized Man" who "had been bred up under *John* [Corrantee], being left to him when he was a Child." Coffi's case indicates that the young men who were taught trades also learned English and other aspects of European culture. Coffi was "not entirely ignorant in Points of Christianity . . . and was desirous to be better grounded in the Knowledge of the Truth. He said he believed in *Jesus Christ,* and the Redemption he has wrought for us; and that he despised the Superstitions of his Country." During a later visit to Annamaboe Thompson met again with Coffi, who introduced him to two other men, one another mason also named Coffi and the other a gold-taker named Quow. Both expressed an interest in Christianity. How far their interest

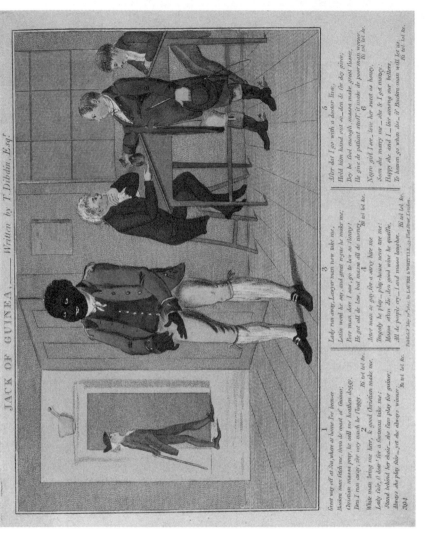

This print, and the accompanying poem by Thomas John Dibdin (1771–1841), illustrates the life story of an African servant in London named Jack of Guinea. His name suggests that he was one of the many natives of the Gold Coast who lived in Britain in the eighteenth century. The image and the poem reflect the racism that Africans faced in Britain. National Maritime Museum, Greenwich, actually went is difficult to say, but it is clear that these skilled men, whose occupations brought them into close contact with the English, had an understanding of the English language and English culture. Thompson drew up a "short Instruction for the Blacks" in the elements of his faith that he gave to Corrantee's son William Ansah, who had been given religious instruction and baptized during his stay in England. Thompson hoped that he "might use it with any of his Town's People. And it must to his Commendation be said, that he made a conscientious Point of it . . . to bring those whom he could to the Knowledge of Christianity."[17] While it is doubtful that Christianity made any real inroads in Annamaboe in this period, what is important is the circulation of ideas in this Atlantic hub, one of the hallmarks of the evolving Atlantic World. Around the English Atlantic, skilled blacks were important cultural mediators. In the contemporary English colonies of the American South, for example, a limited number of African slaves were also receiving instruction in the Anglican faith, and there a "hypothetical portrait of the slave most likely to be a church member would depict a mulatto, creole, skilled slave able to speak English well."[18]

Annamaboe's Atlantic travelers did show an interest in Christianity, as baptismal records from Anglican churches in Liverpool and London demonstrate. These were Atlantic congregations with black and white members drawn from North America, the Caribbean, and Africa, and there were Africans and African Americans in the congregation from all of these regions. The baptismal records from Our Lady and St. Nicholas with St. Anne in Liverpool show that seven Africans, African Americans, and African Britons were baptized in 1785 alone. The African Americans came from Philadelphia, Saint Kitts, and Virginia. Those from Africa included a six-year-girl born on the Windward Coast of Africa, the daughter of a sailor and an African woman named Maria; a twenty-one-year-old man from "the Coast of Guinea" (who could have been from Annamaboe); and a thirty-six-year-old man who was listed as a "native of *Annamaboe* in Africa." The baptismal records from St. James Church, Toxteth, in Liverpool reveal the names of fifteen blacks, all of them from Africa except for one man from Guadeloupe. One of them, George Butler, was identified as a "native of Annamboe in Africa," while Jonny Africa, John Christian, and John Peter were listed as natives of the Gold

Coast, and the others simply as natives of Africa. People from the Gold Coast also appear in the records of London's churches. St. George's Church in Mayfair recorded the 1743 baptism of Philip Deal "about 22 years of age, born in Golden Coast in Guinea, a Blackman." Ottobah Cugoano, the young Fante boy who was kidnapped off the coast in 1770, moved to London where in 1773 under the name John Stuart he was baptized into the congregation of St. James Piccadilly in London.[19]

Some natives of Annamaboe joined North American churches as well. The Reverend Samuel Hopkins and the Reverend Ezra Stiles sought to educate two natives of the Gold Coast and send them home as missionaries. They reported that both Bristol Yamma and John Quamine were members of the First Congregational Church in Newport, Rhode Island, who had "converted some years ago; and have from that time sustained a good character as Christians, and having made good proficiency in christian knowledge." Yamma was from the Asante nation, and he informed Hopkins and Stiles that he had been captured when he was very young by warriors from a neighboring nation, and that he had been sold several times before he was sold at Annamaboe. They wrote that Quamine "is son of a rich man at Annamaboe, and was sent by his father to this place for an education among the English, and then to return home. All this the person to whom he was committed engaged to perform, for a good reward. But instead of being faithful to his trust, he sold him a slave for life." Philip Quaque, the Anglican missionary at Cape Coast, reported that Quamine had been sent by his father with Captain Linsey of Newport in the 1750s to be educated, but that the captain had enslaved him instead. After the captain's death, Quamine won a cash prize in a lottery that enabled him to purchase his freedom. Stiles and Hopkins solicited funds to enable Yamma to purchase his freedom and to return them to Annamaboe. Both were described as about thirty years of age, "have good natural abilities; are apt, steady, and judicious, and speak their native language,—the language of a numerous, potent nation in Guinea, to which they both belong." They were eager to return as missionaries, and the two ministers wrote that "in order to do this they must be put to school, and taught to read and write better than they now can, and be instructed more fully in divinity." Their appeal brought in over £120 from around the British Atlantic World. The men's training included a year's study with John Witherspoon, president of the College of New Jersey in Princeton.[20]

As luck would have it, one of Quamine's relatives arrived in Newport from Annamaboe; he was described as "a free man, and appears to be a sensible, inquisitive person, and is recommended by the person he came with, as a man of integrity and good behavior." He was "well acquainted" with Quamine's family, and was able to corroborate his history. This Annamaboe resident also "expresses a desire to learn to read & c., and to be instructed in the Christian religion . . . He says he has heard we have a revelation among us, and he desires to know what it contains." He informed Hopkins that many young men in Annamaboe also "have a great desire to learn to read and write & c., and would come into the parts for that end, were they not afraid of being deceived and sold."[21]

Hopkins and Stiles also wrote to Philip Quaque to seek information about Quamine's family. He confirmed that Quamine was who he claimed to be. He reported that his father had died, but that his mother was still alive and eager to see "her son, once dead and lost." His entire family "desires . . . that he may be returned to them, as soon as may be; and promises that nothing shall be wanting, to make him, and all about him, comfortable and happy, amongst his own kindred." Writing in 1776, Stiles and Hopkins thought that sending these men back to Africa was a "special call" from God to "pay tribute to him," a cause that would aid the American colonies in their struggle for freedom. That very struggle for freedom interrupted their plan, and there is no evidence that the two men ever returned to their homeland.[22]

African linguisters, or translators, were essential for virtually all interactions between the English and Africans on the Gold Coast. They appear in the English records in the seventeenth century at Annamaboe. In 1698, for example, Ralph Hassell, chief of the fort, wrote that no one "can officiate the place of a linguister here better than Captain Dickall Affidoe." Hassell noted that he would be paid a salary, and in return Affidoe "promises to bring all the traders here." There are very rare examples of Englishmen who spoke one of the several Fante languages; Hassell referred to Jonas Perring "speaking Blackes," and Thomas Thompson made an effort to learn the language.[23] It was more common for the Africans and English to communicate through interpreters or though the local trade language, a variant of the creole trade languages that existed all along the West African coast and spread to the Americas. Over time, more and more residents of Annamaboe learned English. John Wilkinson sold an African sailor who had "liv'd among the English on the Coast of Guiney and can speak some English" in Maryland in 1760.[24] When an English sailor was asked in 1792 if English was "understood by the natives" at Annamaboe, he replied, "O yes, amazing well."[25] Africans took the initiative in learning European languages, rather than the other way around, and that shared language contributed to what one historian called a "climate of understanding" between African and European merchants in their zone of contact along the coast.[26]

Late in the eighteenth century, a group of Liverpool slave traders reported, "It has always been the Practice of Merchants and Commanders of Ships trading to Africa, to encourage the Natives to send their Children to England, as it not only conciliates their Friendship and softens their Manners, but adds greatly to the Security of the Trade, which answers the Purposes both of Interest and Humanity." They estimated that about two dozen Africans studied in England at any given time, a practice that helps account for the literacy and English-language skills common among the leading merchants on the Gold Coast and in other parts of West Africa.[27] Harry Brew, Richard Brew's mulatto son who was educated in England, is one example of a linguister from Annamaboe who studied in England. Mulattoes like Brew, who moved easily between their mothers' African world and their fathers' English world, enjoyed a great advantage in an occupation like linguister. He was appointed assistant linguist at Cape Coast Castle in 1792 and was praised as "the best Interpreter that can be found in the Country."[28] Every English fort, including Annamaboe's, had a linguist on its payroll, and slave ships hired linguists during their time on the coast and in some cases for their Atlantic voyages. Slave trader William Snelgrave reported in 1727 that "linguists are Natives and Freemen of the Country, whom we hire on account of their speaking good English, during the time we remain trading on the Coast; and they are likewise Brokers between us and the black Merchants."[29] They were cultural brokers as well, for a language is never learned in a cultural vacuum.

Since every slave ship that sailed into Annamaboe Road took on a gold-taker who remained on board during the ship's stay, the gold-takers were vulnerable to kidnapping, like all Africans who spent time on board English ships. In 1719, James Colier, the RAC agent in Barbados, notified the RAC that an English captain had arrived there with "a Gold taker named Quamiora" who was free and would be returned to the Gold Coast.[30] Africans viewed kidnapping as a threat to their families and their entire communities, and they used every means at their disposal to have their lost relatives returned. Africans expected to determine who could and could not be enslaved, and the European powers attempted to respect those distinctions. Among the Acts of Parliament for Regulating the Slave Trade passed in 1750 was a provision that stipulated that "no commander or master of any ship trading to Africa shall by fraud, force or violence or by any indirect practice whatsoever take on board or carry away from the coast of Africa any negro or native of the said country or commit or suffer to be committed any violence to the natives to the prejudice of the trade."[31] The AC was eager to prosecute traders who violated the law. They condemned their "wicked & foolish behavior" and notified their officers on the Gold Coast that although "it is not in our Power to call them to immediate Acct., but upon proper Proofs of the Proceedings being sent home, we shall make it our Business to get them dismissed from their Employ & if not otherwise Punished."[32]

The sons of prominent Africans along the Gold Coast also played an important part in diplomatic relations between European powers and African rulers. In many cases, sons of African rulers acted as their fathers' surrogates, and fathers were often eager to have their sons learn as much as possible about the Europeans by living in their forts, sailing on their ships, or traveling to Europe to be educated. Cases of African elites sending their children to Europe to be educated go back to the earliest arrival of the Europeans along the West African coast in the fifteenth century.[33]

Sometimes English slave traders took the sons of African merchant elites onto their ships or even to Europe and America in an effort to gain favor with their families. When Anglican missionary Thomas Thompson sailed with Captain William Williams on the *Prince George* from New York City in November 1751, he found that "Captain Williams had a Negro Youth, whom he had brought from *Africa* for Education, a

Grandson of *Peter,* King of Cape Monte. He had had him baptized, and was now carrying him Home."[34] The best example from Annamaboe is that of John Corrantee's eldest son, George Quasah, often referred to as "My Lord" in the English records. Thomas Melville reported that "this Lad went to England very early and stayed there and on Board an English ship 8 or 9 years."[35] In 1720 an English captain returned a boy to the Gold Coast "who was sent over to England in order to make him the more serviceable to the Interlopers."[36] These young men were in a very different position from hired sailors, for captains recognized their elite status and knew that treating them well could help win them favorable treatment from their fathers. As children of elite traders, these young men also must have understood that they should learn as much as they could about the broader Atlantic World given their and their families' interests in the Atlantic economy.

If captains did not return these young elites as agreed, serious problems resulted. In 1755 Thomas Melville, governor of Cape Coast Castle, wrote the RAC about a dispute involving John Corrantee's son Quasah, who complained loudly to him that Captain Henry Ellis of Bristol had taken "away a free boy from Annamaboe without leave from his family. My Lord (Quasah) says that should the boy die before he returns, he (Quasah) must be ruined." Melville pleaded with the AC "that some methods may be fallen upon to prevent such things for the future, for tho I'm willing to believe that Ellis had no design in humouring the boy by showing him England, yet his Ship & Cargo will not pay the Damages the public will Sustain should any accident befall him."[37] Ellis had taken the boy early in 1755, and it was not until April 1756 that he was back and "safe with his Friends."[38] The AC wanted to prosecute Ellis "for taking the Boy from Annamaboe without the Consent of his friends, as far as they have Power to do it."[39] Ellis, however, claimed that the boy's family approved his trip to England, so the AC sought evidence of Ellis's guilt from the Gold Coast. They were "determined to prevent all such offenses as far as it is in our power."[40] We have seen that John Corrantee sent his sons to France and to England as a part of his negotiations over the construction of a fort at Annamaboe. He intended them as his eyes and ears in Europe, and they brought back their acquired knowledge, which had a major influence over the course of those negotiations.

Another way that African elites traveled to Europe was through the system of pawning. Pawning was indigenous to Africa, and it used family members, usually the sons of the African merchant, to guarantee agreements or loans. Pawning directly connected Fante families to the larger economic, social, and political processes that arose out of the Atlantic slave trade. The complex polygamous, matrilineal families of the Gold Coast merchants baffled Europeans, who were familiar with a nuclear family structure evolving in Europe in roughly the same time period. Europeans gained some understanding of Fante family relationships, a necessary part of the Annamaboe trade, where business dealings depended on trust and reputation. They recognized that Africans valued their children and exploited those relationships in many ways. The Fante leaders may have systematically enslaved and destroyed the families of outsiders, but they went to extraordinary lengths to reunite and protect their own families. In general, Africans determined who could be enslaved, and Europeans violated those rules at their peril. Among the Fante, extended families working through their communities conducted the slave trade, not individuals. The slave trade threatened even the very individuals, families, and communities engaged in it, but Fante families and communities used every means at their disposal to protect themselves.

For Africans in Annamaboe, slave trading was a family enterprise, and the credit system known as pawning tied children to credit in a way that threatened African families.[41] If an African slave trader failed to redeem a family member he or she had pawned within the time specified, then that family member would be sold into slavery. The drastic step of selling the relatives of prominent Fante merchants off the coast into a life of enslavement in the Americas was an outcome that most everyone involved tried to avoid, though there were cases where unscrupulous British captains kidnapped pawns. Such illegal acts not only disrupted families and communities but endangered trade relations between British and African merchants and even threatened the lives of the British captains and sailors. Pawns might also die before returning to the coast, a loss that could also endanger trade relationships.[42]

Pawns were used not only to insure business deals but also as parts of diplomatic agreements. During the negotiations over the Annamaboe fort, for example, several caboceers, including John Corrantee, sent pawns to the French to guarantee an agreement allowing them to build there. Four Fante boys went to France "to be made Princes," but one of them, the son of a caboceer named Amminah, died from an illness contracted there. Amminah was inconsolable at the death of his son, and he refused a payment offered by Captain Debordieu, who brought him the news of his son's death, "and except for John [Corrantee] would have brought a Palaver against him for killing his son."[43] The boy's death undermined French interests at Annamaboe.

The British AC officials who negotiated with the Fante caboceers and principal men to exclude the French also took pawns to guarantee the agreements the two parties reached.[44] One of those pawns wanted to visit England, and as Melville wrote his London superiors, "as he is to be one of the chief priests of Fante, a little money laid out upon his Education will not be thrown away, if he is taught to read & write, it may render him more useful to us . . . besides his Father who is a man of great personal authority expects that his Son shall be taught, and in my opinion he ought to be gratified, as he has been one of the principal actors in procuring the Law [to exclude the French]."[45] Two boys, George Sackee and John Aqua, sailed from Annamaboe to Britain with Captain Cockburn, and the AC paid for their support and education. The young men's educations complete, in 1754 AC officials prepared to return "the two Young Princes" to the Gold Coast.[46] The AC dressed them like princes, and the records show that the young men dressed in the following:

12 Ruffled Shirts
1 Blue Coat and Breeches for Each lined with White, laced with
    Silver, and Silver Buttons.
1 Scarlet Cloth Waistcoat for each trimmed with Silver.
2 Frocks and Breeches.
2 Scarlet worsted Waistcoats.
2 Silver laced Hats.
2 Bay Wiggs.
8 pairs of white Stockings.
4   "   of worsted ditto.
8   "   of Pumps.
2   "   of Strong Shoes.
2   "   of Silver Buckles.[47]

The two princes made quite an impression when they met George Montagu-Dunk, second Earl of Halifax, then first lord of trade, who "being of the Opinion that they have not yet seen enough of this Country, nor rec'd sufficient Education, we have upon this authority & also at their own Request, postponed their Departure for some time with meanwhile for the Satisfaction of their Friends upon the Coast, we shall send you . . . a long Letter from each."[48] The AC paid the Reverend John Moore over £42 for a quarter's education and boarding, then sent the boys to board with William Vaughn at Shannon, Middlesex, who was to give them additional instruction "in Reading, Writing, & Accounts, & in the Christian Religion."[49]

After a year of schooling, the AC requested passage for them on board the *Humber,* a British warship under the command of Captain Samuel Scott, to return them to the Gold Coast.[50] The Fante princes traveled by coach from Middlesex to London, and the AC notified Captain Scott that his "lady does them the Favour to accompany them." The men received £50 to cover the cost of their travels and another £20 for their use at Plymouth as they waited for the ship to sail.[51] The AC notified Melville that the princes were headed home and added, "We think have made sufficient stay in England to answer every good purpose, & we believe are satisfied with their Entertainment as to remember it with gratitude, the behavior of the Gentlemen while in England has been much approved, we therefore recommend 'em to your countenance on the coast."[52]

Almost immediately, their behavior began to raise concerns. The AC approved of all the expenses incurred by the young men in Plymouth, except for the purchase of two bureaus that they had "bespoke." When Captain Scott said that the furniture would not cause any inconvenience, the AC allowed them to purchase one.[53] The AC furnished Sackee with a new sword to replace one that he lost.[54] Once the ship sailed, the princes continued to make extravagant requests. The AC apologized to Captain Scott "for the Embarrassment they have given you, that they think they have been already indulged them too far, as they make so bad usage of the Favours conferred on them, that they are absolutely against allowing them any Wines at Madeira."[55] Thoroughly exasperated with them, the AC wrote Melville complaining that the princes "cost us above £600 for their Education, maintenance, & c. since their being in England, we must therefore desire you would send us no more black gentn [gentlemen] except you find it absolutely necessary for the benefit of the trade."[56]

The AC officials were stunned by a letter from Charles Bell at Cape Coast Castle, who wrote to confirm the arrival of the "Young Princes." Bell wrote, "I shall not fail to give them proper countenance according to your Directions, but must at the same time beg leave to inform you that neither of 'em is a person of Consequence & will hardly be of any Service." This disappointing news only highlights the difficulties the British officials faced in accurately determining Fante family relationships. Bell warned the committee that "three of the Young Negroes that went to England we already rated in your Books much beyond their Deserts, & the addition of 2 more will only souse the Greediness of your Caboceers, who will be begging to send home their young Slaves, who after they have been caressed as Princes in England, will come back to Africa to be made Quills to suck through, according to the Negro Phrase, for whatever we allow to maintain them goes half to their Masters."[57]

Bell's assessment was correct; the young princes quickly ensured that the British would continue to support them. George Sackee informed Bell that Melville had sent him to Britain as a reward to his father for "the great Service" he had provided the AC, and that the AC "had given him to understand he'd be provided for upon his Return." Bell reluctantly employed him at £40 a year, and he "went away very well pleased," and Bell notified the AC that he would have no choice but to do the same for Aqua. Within a short time, both of the young men were asking for raises, which the AC denied. Bell noted that the "friends and Relations of both are crying out that we have made them white Gentlemen & must consequently support them in that character," and he warned his superiors that "this will always be the closing scene of these young Africans' Travels; if their Families are powerful they will threaten, if otherwise they will clamour pensions out of you & you well know how little your finances will bear it."[58] The AC expressed their dismay in learning that the boys were "of so little Consequence" when Melville had painted a different picture of their family connections and persuaded them to "bestow so much money on their Education."[59]

Pawning the children of Fante traders insured that contracts would be fulfilled on time, but if African traders defaulted on the contracts, then the European merchants considered them slaves and they could be sold off the coast. John Mathews, in his 1788 description of Sierra Leone, observed that pawns could "be sent off, if not redeemed in due time." He noted that if Africans failed to redeem the pawns according to contract the pawns became "the absolute property of the person to whom he was pawned . . . it is intirely [sic] at the option of the master whether he will ever after let him be redeemed . . . should he be a son of the most powerful person in the country."[60] In 1769, Gilbert Petrie, governor of Cape Coast Castle, reported to the AC that he had "never known any master of a ship to carry free Negroes off from this part of the Coast, although they often threaten to do it, and often seize & confine them on board their Ships, till they get payment of the Debts, or be ready to Sail. Some I have known to carry prisoners from Annamaboe as far as Tantumquerry, Opham & Winnebah where they were redeemed or reprisals made by the Fantees for their restitution."[61]

Despite their right to enslave unredeemed pawns, captains sometimes exchanged them for other slaves to avoid offending the Fante traders and disrupting the trade. A British trader, Robert Hume, testified to Parliament that "a Pledge [pawn] if not redeemed is a Slave," and captains had every right to sell them, but Hume explained that "I would not carry them off for fear of injuring my future Voyages, or my Interest with the Natives."[62] Trades in pawns were usually arranged by other African traders who agreed to give one of their slaves in return for a valued pawn. In 1778 Captain John Houghton wrote Richard Miles, chief of the British fort at Tantumquerry, that "Tom Coffee of Agar Desires me to pay you one Slave for a Pawn you have belonging to Qucohe Ancoboba of Annamaboe as he's afraid you'll send him off . . . please to let me know if he's to be Redeem'd and the terms."[63] Miles answered that "the Slave is due to Captain Chalmers . . . and unless redeem'd with another Slave, the Boy will certainly be sent off the Coast." As this case indicates, these transactions could become very complex. In this case, Tom Coffee in Agar, a town near Annamaboe, employed Captain Houghton to work with the chief of the fort in Tantumquerry to redeem a pawn belonging to a fellow Fante trader in Annamaboe. In 1790 James Fraser observed that an African trader "commonly borrows Slaves from a ship that is ready to depart and puts it on board the other," in order to give the family enough time to redeem him.[64] Some British traders refused to release or trade pawns unless their price was met. Such negotiations were a tricky business, for while the son of a prominent trader was more valuable than a comparable slave while on the coast of Africa, that premium disappeared across the Atlantic, so captains generally found it in their financial interest to make such deals. A British trader at Cape Coast Castle wrote, "Wm Ansah came to speak with me about redeeming a Man I had in Pawn from Class of Annamaboe for Five Ounces Gold, and who if not redeemed, I intended to send off the Coast by the Col. Joseph; we could not agree about that affair."[65] Captains who did not get their price sometimes enslaved pawns, occasionally in large numbers, but the British officials tried to avoid that potentially dangerous outcome by either encouraging captains to make trades or by paying the premium price themselves in order to prevent disruptions. In 1769 Captain James Nixon of Bristol "seized and put in Irons on board his ship at Annamaboe, two free Canoemen who had been sent to him from Mr. Drew at Commenda with two Slaves which he did not chose to accept . . . for payment of a debt due to him by Mr. Green. Mr. Grossle [chief of Annamaboe Fort] paid the Debt or I really believe the Canoemen would have been carried to the West Indies & sold as Slaves as the Captain solemnly declared he intended."[66] Other captains recognized the dangers of enslaving pawns; one captain noted that "there was always a Slave offered me for the person reclaimed, which I always accepted."[67]

Unscrupulous captains of slave ships on the Gold Coast sometimes stole pawns rather than returning them to their families even when the terms of the contract were met, a major violation of the rules governing the trade. These unlawful acts had serious consequences for the resident Europeans who operated the forts and relied on local African laws about who could and could not be enslaved. In 1786 Richard Miles, governor of Cape Coast Castle, informed his superiors in London that they had to respect African regulations governing pawnship; to do otherwise, he told them, would be "a direct Infringement of the Laws of the Country, the consequences of which among a People so tenacious of their customs is very obvious."[68] In 1719 William Williams, chief of Winnebah Fort, located ninety miles west of Cape Coast Castle, wrote that he "had a pa-laver about two Boys, which Wm [William] Welsh took as Pawns from here."[69] In this case, Williams presided over the negotiations surround-ing Welsh's actions rather than simply defending the British captain.

Kidnapping of pawns could result in an interruption of trade or in vi-olent retribution from the Fante. In order to maintain peaceful relations with their African counterparts, the British officials worked to prevent the kidnapping of pawns, and when pawns were kidnapped, they made every effort to have them returned to their families, who often rewarded such acts. In the 1750s John Newton, perhaps the most famous British slave trader of the eighteenth century, once redeemed a boy who had been illegally enslaved and sold into slavery in Rhode Island and returned him to his home in Africa in order to curry favor with the traders there.[70]

Kidnapping cases could be extremely damaging to trade and could lead to bloodshed if the Fante feared that their family members were in danger. In 1751 Thomas Melville reported from Cape Coast Castle that "affairs on the Coast [are] in as ticklish a Situation as I believe they ever were since the English first came here." Trouble began when Captain Thomas Derbyshire, captain of the *Jenny* from Liverpool, took a pawn from a Fante trader, Quaneoon Ashantee. The pawn died on board Der-byshire's ship, but rather than notifying Quaneoon Ashantee of his death and allowing him to view the body as was customary. Derbyshire threw the body into the sea, leaving no evidence of the pawn's death. Unless the Fante trader saw the body, he had no way of knowing that the captain had not simply sold the pawn and claimed that he died. Quane-oon Ashantee demanded payment for the pawn from Derbyshire, who refused and demanded repayment from Quaneoon Ashantee for the dead pawn. A palaver followed, and the Fante held Derbyshire at An-namaboe until it could be settled. A month of detention exhausted Der-byshire's patience, and he kidnapped "23 People being Free Traders & their Slaves and Canoemen" from Annamaboe in order to force a settle-ment in his favor. Despite British laws against the enslavement and sale of free people in Africa, Derbyshire said, "I will Run the Risque of the Law and Absolutely sell Them." In the face of such a violation of the laws of the country and of Britain, the people of Annamaboe resorted to their own desperate measures.[71] Melville informed his superiors that "all trade was stopp'd at Annamaboe upon Account of Captn Derbyshire's Palavar (or Quarrel) . . . The Fantees declared that if they had not their People returned they would look upon it as Declaration of War & take their revenge." Fearful AC officials on the coast tried to stop Derbyshire's rash actions, as did the Fante. In order to prevent Derbyshire from selling the members of their families and community, the Fante took British hostages and trade goods and threatened to kill their British prisoners. AC officials had no choice but to support the Fante since "this was too much in their Power as they had in hands 5 or 6 Englishmen belonging to the Ships at Annamaboe besides 2 or 3000 in Goods. Therefore we were obliged to allow all their charges against Derbyshire."[72]

During this dangerous quarrel, Derbyshire foolishly went ashore at Annamaboe, and a group of Fante attacked and beat him. Because of that assault, the British summoned the Annamaboe caboceers to Cape Coast Castle and demanded that the Fante give the injured captain ten slaves as recompense. When the Fante heard that demand, Melville reported that they stormed "out of the Castle in great rage threatening to return home saying we had only sent for them to laugh at them." Melville worked with his closest African allies in these negotiations, and ultimately the Fante conceded that the assault on Derbyshire was wrong. They agreed to pay a fine of four male slaves and one female slave for the offense, not the ten that Derbyshire wanted, and the African traders at Cape Coast Castle agreed to share the expense in order to reopen trade. Derbyshire was infuriated by the deal and he "declared he would have Satisfaction from none but the Fante themselves, and that if they did not give it him in 3 Days he would go down to Annamaboe, and Hang the most of his prisoners in sight of their friends, fire a Broadside into the Town [the *Jenny* carried ten guns], and go off the Coast." Melville went on board to *Jenny* to convince Derbyshire to accept the arrangement, and he reluctantly agreed to accept eight male slaves and one female slave. Melville and the British traders at Cape Coast agreed to pay for the extra slaves, and trade resumed at Annamaboe.[73]

Kidnapping cases might be settled by palaver or negotiation, but in cases where the kidnapper had left the coast, disputes grew into major crises with life-threatening consequences for the British as the Fante resorted to threats and violence to protect their families and communities.

James Skinner reported from Cape Coast Castle in 1754 that Africans had cut off two ships at Domeh, meaning that the Africans had attacked the ships from shore. He noted that the first ship had managed to escape once night fell, under the command of a Captain John Reffe from South Carolina and with his linguister aboard, but Reffe had left three of his sailors on shore, who had been redeemed by the French. The second ship, commanded by Captain Turnbull of London, was not so fortunate. Turnbull was being held prisoner with four of his men. Skinner reported that "the Domeh people say is on acct of Captn Bostock and another ship carrying off several of their free people. I've wrote to the Gov of Goree to redeem 'em as soon as possible."[74] After his escape, Reffe was joined by Captain Hall, a private trader in Sierra Leone, and by Captain Ellery of New England who took revenge for these attacks by sailing up and down the Domeh coast "where they've been Seizing & killing all the people they meet with; if there's not a stop put to these proceedings it will be dangerous for vessels."[75]

To avoid violence and the interruption of trade, the RAC made every effort to find stolen pawns and other kidnapped Africans and return them to their families before they were carried off the coast. James Phipps, governor of Cape Coast Castle, wrote the company in 1710 that he had returned to Sherbro Island "a free Negro boy, who was Carried off by Captn Barber, and for whom Mr. Clark at Sherbrow had some Difference with the Natives."[76] In 1722, Phipps notified the RAC that he had redeemed a woman named "Antonia a Slave belonging to S. W. de Sousa and another . . . from Captn. Ogle whom he took on board the Pirato."[77] Similarly, in 1717, Robert Plunkett told his RAC superiors about a kidnapping on the River Sherbrow and said that he would "endeavor to regain the lost . . . boy Northward." He also warned of the "mischief done by Interlopers Among the Natives by Carrying them off which puts Trade into Confusion."[78] RAC agents and merchants around the Atlantic World were on the lookout for Africans who might have been taken off the coast illegally. Samuel Tyley wrote the RAC from Boston in 1712, asking "if Thomas Barker son of a Mulatto Factor at Cape Coast who is claimed by one Mr. Barnes as a Slave be of Service to ye Comp[any]." In 1710 Charles Russell, an English merchant in Cádiz, Spain, found "two Negroes which belong to the Comp[any] on ship Leaford." Russell arranged for their transportation to England, adding that he "had no interest in the affair but . . . to Serve ye Comp and see them have Justice done."[79]

John Hippisley, governor of Cape Coast Castle in the 1760s, published a remarkable account of Anthony, whose father, a prince of Annamaboe, thought his son had been kidnapped. According to Hippisley, the father "made a great noise about his son's not being brought back to him, and threatened to seize all the English vessels and effects he could meet with." As we have seen, such threats were often put into effect. The father "took for granted his son was dead, and rejoiced at the opportunity of satisfying his avarice." But the English found Anthony and returned him to Annamaboe, much to his father's disappointment, for Anthony's return "deprived him of a pretext to put in practice his intended seizures." Hippisley wrote that

> nothing could exceed his rage at the disappointment. His son became the object of his hatred. He barely spoke to him, and this was only to tell him to provide for himself, for . . . he would never see or hear of him any more. He has kept his word; and the poor lad owes his subsistence to the charity of a Dutch gentleman, settled upon that part of the coast. He behaves very well, I am told, and wishes earnestly to go back to England. This, however, . . . can never be: no captain dare to take him home, as he would become answerable for all the damages his father might do to the English trade. Such is the state of poor Anthony, and such a dog is the father![80]

No such case appears in the records of the Company of Merchants Trading to Africa, and Hippisley's bitter story is probably a fiction, intended to play upon the British interest in the cases of royal Africans and on prejudices about African savagery and the greedy manipulations of Annamaboe's traders. It runs counter to every case where Annamaboe families did everything they could, often with the help of the entire community, to bring their children home.

Among the Fante traders, family played a central role in the slave trade since they used their own families to access credit. The children of Fante slave traders were literally and figuratively pawns in their families' slave-trading business. In the slave-trading societies along the Gold Coast, the family could not be separated from the larger social, political, and economic processes of the trade. The system of pawning directly linked elite Fante families to the economics of slave trading and put the members of slave-trading families at risk of enslavement themselves.

Kidnapping helps reveal how British and Fante slave traders reached a mutual understanding of the traffic in slaves. Coming from vastly different cultural and economic systems, over time British and Fante traders developed institutions and modes of exchange to bring order to the trade. Their early encounters were often violent, but they arrived at a regularized commerce, governed by mutually accepted rules. These rules were not imposed on Africans by Europeans, and, in fact, the terms of the trade were more often set by the Africans. Europeans came to understand that African societies "felt strongly that there were legal limits to who could be enslaved and when." The British understood the importance of following those rules to the peaceful conduct of the trade, and that explains why British officials and traders went to such extreme lengths to recover kidnap victims, especially those with royal or elite connections. The Fante's determined efforts to rescue their kidnapped relatives and the cooperation of European traders demonstrated the importance of family to the trade and "reflected the existence of a class, as well as a racial, dimension to the operation of the slave trade." British efforts to liberate members of the African slave-trading elite who kidnapped or illegally enslaved further legitimated the enslavement of other Africans and reinforced their reputations for fair dealing. African elites, who more than any other group set the terms of the trade, worked to establish "a proper order of enslavement and an orderly slave trade," a trade conducted according African to rules and customs, not by terms of the European traders.[81]

Fante merchant families enslaved tens of thousands of men, women, and children over the long course of the trade from Annaboe. Fante slave traders, like their European counterparts, believed that the enslaved men, women, and children had no family rights they were bound to respect, but when members of their own families were kidnapped or enslaved, they used every means at their disposal to have them returned. Remarkably, they often succeeded in recovering a loved one from Europe or even from the plantations of the Americas.

Historians have recognized that by 1820, about 10 million Africans had been transported to the New World, the largest forced migration in

history. The number of Africans traveling across the Atlantic to the
Americas outnumbered Europeans by four to one—in that respect, the
Atlantic was an African ocean. But that migration differed from other
migrations in another crucial respect—almost none of those African mi-
grants returned to Africa, while large numbers of Europeans moved
back and forth across the ocean. That circulation of Europeans has important implications for how they understood and experienced the Atlantic World. Partly for that reason, Africans have been portrayed as less
integrated into the Atlantic World, less aware of the contours of that
world, and more naïve than their European counterparts. While the
number of residents of Annamaboe who traveled from their homes to
Europe or America and back again was never large, and never as large as
would have been the case in an Atlantic port city in the Americas or Europe, they were there, and their experiences became a part of their community's understanding of the Atlantic World. They were significant
cultural agents—individuals ranging from the city's ruling elites, to its
skilled laborers and artisans, to its mixed-race residents—whose multi-
layered experiences added to the cultural and racial hybridity in the
zone of contact along the Gold Coast. Many aspects of Annamaboe's
economy, society, and culture changed as a result of their experiences
and their ongoing connections within the larger Atlantic community.
Annamaboe was a significant Atlantic commercial hub whose ruling
elites nurtured diplomatic and religious ties with European powers;
whose merchants built and maintained extensive commercial networks
with their European counterparts, introduced European goods, and
learned European languages and numeracy; and whose artisans and
skilled laborers brought back European skills and construction styles.
Whether the residents of Annamaboe who moved around the Atlantic
spent their time in the royal courts of London or Paris; on board English
ships; wandering through the bustling streets of Liverpool or Bristol; in
the school rooms of Kent, Rhode Island, or New York; or laboring for
years on a Caribbean plantation, they brought back vital information
and incorporated those experiences into the very fabric of Annamaboe's
society and culture.

7

Things Fall Apart: The End of the Eighteenth-Century Atlantic World

A S THE EIGHTEENTH CENTURY drew to a close, Annamaboe faced a series of challenges that dramatically altered the town and its place in the Atlantic World. Four events help illustrate the town's changing fortunes. First, Richard Brew's death removed from the scene the town's most important private trader and someone of great influence along the Gold Coast and even in London. Brew's role as a mediator between the British and the Fante, his diplomatic negotiations intended to keep peace between the Fante and the Asante, and his efforts to keep the slave trade in a flourishing condition at Annamaboe were important and sorely missed. The efforts of Horatio Smith to succeed Brew at Annamaboe showed how difficult it would be for anyone to recapture Brew's place there. Second, the disruptions to the Atlantic economy caused rising tensions in Annamaboe, tensions reflected in two episodes of violence, one among the townspeople themselves and another between the British in the fort and the townspeople that did serious damage to the town and to relations between the town and the British. Finally, England's 1807 law ending its involvement in the slave trade was revolutionary for Annamaboe. Suddenly, the town's major economic activity was virtually shut down, and the town's future hung in the balance. The career of Richard Brew's grandson, Samuel Brew, illustrates the changing nature of the slave trade on the Gold Coast in the nineteenth century. The CMAT was abolished in 1821, and with its demise a major chapter closed in what might be considered the long eighteenth century in British–West African history.

When Horatio Smith bought Castle Brew in 1776, he hoped to re-create the trading empire Brew had operated so successfully in the 1760s. Despite his experience working with Brew, his dreams ended in disaster. His problems began almost immediately when he came into conflict with the residents of Annamaboe's Fishing Town. Like many such disputes, it began over a minor affair. The Fishing Town residents complained that when they went to pay their compliments to Smith at Smith House, he treated them with disrespect. Those visits were a part of the customary relationships at Annamaboe, and when they visited, they expected to be received by Smith and given drinks. Instead of receiving them hospitably, they complained that Smith ran into his room when he saw them coming, and after keeping them waiting in the hall for half an hour, he sent out a servant boy with a dram or two for the principal men, but not enough for everyone. Private traders paid an annual rent or custom consisting of a certain amount of alcohol to the caboceers of Annamaboe, who then distributed it to the residents in return for the privilege of living and trading there. The Fishing Town men claimed that Smith paid customs to Fante Town, but not to the Fishing Town as had always been customary. When they asked for their custom, "he turned them out contemptuously calling them a pack of Fisherman that had no right to anything." Outraged, the men "resolved to make him know better."[1]

Smith soon felt their displeasure. He sent a canoe out to a schooner to pick up its captain, with whom he intended to trade, but the Fishing Town people stopped the canoe on the beach and refused to allow the captain to disembark. Smith sent his gold-taker to find out the reason, and they told him their complaints. Smith claimed not to recall any such incidents with them, and he expressed his resentment at "having his liquor case constantly open on demand." One of the town's caboceers advised him to give them a cask of liquor to settle matters before they got out of hand, but he refused to take that good advice.[2]

Smith appealed to Thomas Westgate for assistance in his capacity as commander of the fort. Westgate gave them four gallons of brandy, but he warned Smith that they were still resentful and intended to make new demands "on account of your Settling in Castle Brew." Westgate told Smith that he could not simply force the Fishing Town men to give up their demands "without involving the Publick into a troublesome expensive dispute with them." The matter was complicated by the fact that all the Fante were upset because trade had been so disrupted by the American Revolution, and "in the Present Temper of all the Fantees there is no telling what might be the consequence." They told Westgate that if Smith had sent out liquor the day before as their caboceer had asked, then they would have dropped the matter, but Smith's refusal to do so had only hardened their resolve. They said, "You have lived long enough here in Mr. Brew's time to know that all such Palavers are best made up at once with a trifling expense."[3] The price rose with every passing day.

Smith asked Westgate just how much support he could expect from the fort. He demanded that Westgate immediately settle the dispute, insisted that he must be able to rely on the fort for protection, and expressed his determination to take the matter to Westgate's superiors at Cape Coast Castle. Westgate warned Smith that if he brought every "little dispute" with the Fante to the fort, then he would have time to do nothing else, and he cautioned Smith that "it is always more pleasing to the Blacks to have a Palaver Settled by the person concerned that to refer it to another."[4]

Smith carried his complaints to Richard Miles, governor at Cape Coast Castle, but got little encouragement from that quarter. Drawing on his experience at Annamaboe as commander of the fort, Miles told Smith that he should have paid the Fishing Town residents; "it has ever been usual to include them in all Customs paid," he told Smith. "They are equally as numerous . . . and as great Traders. I . . . always found it necessary to Secure the Good will of those People as any other Quarter of the Town." He reminded Smith of the problem Brew had with the gold-takers. "You must well remember," he wrote, "the amazing Expenses your Predecessor (who carried things with as high a hand as any man who ever Settled there) was often brought into by Affairs Equally as trifling." Miles warned Smith that "the present Disposition of the Fantees, out of temper with the whole English Nation for neglecting (as they call it) their Trade without making a Grain of Allowance for our Situation in

Europe, you will perceive the impropriety of quarrelling with them for trifles." He closed by instructing Smith to "make no further stir about this."[5] Smith was clearly dissatisfied with Miles's response and maintained his innocence of the allegations of the Fishing Town people. He deeply resented that Westgate and Miles seemed to believe them and not him; "either you or he should think my word is not Testimony Sufficient to confute the assertion of a Black Man." He bitterly complained that the Fishing Town men regarded Westgate's payment of rum as a gift from him to them and not a payment from Smith, and that they continued to stop his canoes and prevent his trade. When he asked what would be required to settle the palaver, they demanded one ounce of goods and two ankers of liquor. He offered half that amount, but they refused. They did agree to reduce their demands when he dashed the mediators with liquor, tobacco, and pipes and gave liquor to the town.[6]

A few weeks later a part of Smith House collapsed due to unusually high tides and high surf. With a part of the fine Georgian mansion in ruins, Smith once again appealed to Westgate for help before the entire structure fell down around him. Westgate advised Smith to send his valuables into the fort before they were plundered and sent carpenters from the fort to stabilize the structure, but Smith expected them to actually rebuild the house. Westgate complained to Miles that he could hardly justify rebuilding a private house when the fort needed repairs, and the carpenters complained that Smith insisted that they climb high, dangerous old walls, and they feared being killed. Miles advised that Smith needed to bring workmen from Europe if he intended to rebuild the house, but given the criticism he and others in the forts had gotten for not sufficiently supporting private trades, he did allow two bricklayers and a carpenter to assist with repairs.[7]

Smith did repair the house, which still stands today, but he did not replace Brew as the greatest private merchant on the Gold Coast. Miles wrote friends in London that Smith was not faring well at Annamaboe because he was "not very open handed." He reported that Smith had talked about relocating to Cape Coast Castle, but he thought that Smith was too poorly supplied with trade goods to carry on much of a trade anywhere. Westgate told Miles that he had information that Smith was not really there to engage in trade at all, but that he had been sent out to gain information on the illegal trading activities of the governors of the forts to be used against them in London. Smith eventually joined the ranks of the African Committee and became the governor of Annamaboe Fort himself before his untimely death in 1783.[8] Smith lacked the experience Brew gained as the governor of Annamaboe Fort, and perhaps more importantly, he lacked the connections to the Fante that Brew's marriage to John Corrantee's daughter gave him.

Internal troubles appeared in Annamaboe in 1780, provoked in part by the disruptions to trade brought about by the American Revolution, which put stress on every fissure in the town's fabric. Estimates show that the number of captives exported from Annamaboe dropped by over 50 percent from 1776 to 1780, from 7,416 to 3,494. In January 1780, a long-simmering dispute between the Fishing Town and Pynin Town, also called the Upper and Lower Towns, of Annamaboe erupted in violence. When it became clear that there would be no peaceful solution, the British in the fort urged the caboceers to remain neutral and allowed the women and children from both towns to come inside the fort for safety. The dispute arose over the murder of the son of Cudjo Caboceer, the chief caboceer at Cape Coast, which the Upper Town men blamed on the Lower Town men. The Lower Town men fortified themselves inside their houses and fired on the Upper Town. The Upper Town men set fire to the Lower Town, and the two parties met in a "pitched battle" in which the Lower Town was defeated; its residents fled to neighboring towns for safety. The CMTA slaves in the fort were affiliated with the Lower Town. The British added additional soldiers to the fort to help curb "those restless turbulent People."[9] That violence, and the inability of either the leaders of the town or the fort to prevent it, was a precursor of worse violence to come.

In April 1791, a fort canoe was carrying a load of firewood to the ship *Betsy*, anchored in Annamaboe Road, when the canoe overturned and spilled its load. As the firewood washed up on the beach, boys from the town grabbed it while the canoemen picked up as much of it as they could salvage. The bomboy, whose job was to keep order on the beach, stood guard over the canoe. One of the soldiers from the fort, a Sargeant Swann, ordered the bomboy to leave the canoe and stop the boys from stealing the firewood. The bomboy refused, arguing that the canoe was more valuable than firewood and that he had been ordered to guard it. The soldier struck the bomboy and drew blood. The bomboy went to the bendefoe company to which he belonged. They consulted the priests, who put fetish on the gates of the fort, which meant that no one would be allowed to go in or out of it. Such an incident might not have amounted to much, but that day was a fetish day, a sacred day, and drawing blood on such a day was considered a great sacrilege. An angry crowd gathered and threw stones at the soldiers, driving them back into the fort.[10]

When Amoony Coomah, chief caboceer, heard of the incident, he sent his heir along with Cobea, the head captain of the bendefoe soldiers, to the fort to try to settle the matter. Thomas Miles, governor of the fort, was away, leaving a Mr. Tower in charge. The men complained to Tower that the soldier had been wrong to strike the bomboy on a fetish day and asked him to make some compensation to the town to resolve the dispute. Miles returned in the midst of these discussions and was angry to find the town in an uproar. He demanded satisfaction from the town for initiating a palaver when he was away. The representatives from the town assured him that it was not a palaver and that they were there to resolve the issue before it turned into a bigger dispute. Miles took them hostage, demanding that Amoony Coomah pay two bullocks as a fine. In an even more threatening gesture, he loaded the fort's guns and turned them toward the town. The Fishing Town pynins offered two pawns to release the hostages and settle the dispute, but Miles refused their offer, raising "the resentment of the Fantees to the highest pitch & driving them to despair."[11]

The Fante sought the protection and assistance of the nearby town of Agah, just two miles down the coast. The Agahs sheltered the men of Annamaboe and panyarred two canoes carrying twenty-two slaves owned by British ships in the Road in an attempt to force a palaver. Miles then cut off all trade between the people of Annamaboe and the ships in Annamaboe Road, and asked for assistance from the captains of British ships there. Captain John Smith of the *Jupiter* sent twenty of his seamen to help Miles defend the fort, but Miles took the unprecedented step of ordering the destruction of Agah without so much as consulting the governor or council at Cape Coast. Soldiers from the fort, assisted by sailors from the ships, marched toward Agah.[12]

Thomas Eagles, a merchant and slave-ship captain, had a factory at Agah; built on a hill in the center of the small town, the two-story white-washed building was the town's most visible structure. Thomas Owens, a mate from the ship *Mercury,* was with Eagles in his warehouse when suddenly and without any warning cannons from the ship *Betty* opened fire on Agah, and it seemed to Owens that the gunners were using Eagles's building as their mark. The men rushed to move goods from the upper floor to the lower floor when guns from Annamaboe Fort also began firing on the town. "Shot came through so hot through the upper part of the house that we were obliged to go below," Owens reported. Eagles, Owens, and their Agah workers were able to move goods into the basement storeroom, but the people of Agah would not allow them to remove their goods because "they said as long as Eagles had property in the Town" Miles "would never burn it."[13]

The people of Agah were wrong; Miles was determined to destroy the town. Firing continued on the town from the ship and the fort intermittently during the night, and the next day Miles sent an armed party of soldiers from the fort and sailors from the British ships who marched along the two-mile-long beach that separated Agah from Annamaboe. The men of Agah hid behind a pond near their approach to the town and ambushed their attackers, killing two of them and wounding others. Among the wounded Fante were the sons of Coffee Dansu, the leading caboceer of Agah, and Yellow Joe, the important gold-taker at Annamaboe. Owens and several other Englishmen were in Eagles's house when the attack began, and they fled around noon when the soldiers and sailors set fire to the entire town. They separated and headed for nearby Cormantine Fort. Captain Fraser took five slaves and a box with thirty ounces of gold dust and papers and went along the beach to the fort. Another of the men, a Mr. Drysdale, took the path through the bush to the fort, but the enraged men of Agah intercepted him; he "was very ill treated on the Road, beat in a most barbarous manner by some of the Black people . . . & confined in a black man's house." The governor of the fort heard of his plight and managed to get him into fort, though he was "naked and bruised most terribly." Eagles estimated his losses as £1,700–1,800. The men of Agah captured four sailors from the *Betty* who they held as prisoners.[14]

When the sailors and soldiers returned to Annamaboe they began looting the town. The most outrageous act they committed was to dig up the graves of the dead in search of the valuables, especially gold, that the Fante typically buried with the bodies of the dead, an act that may have been encouraged by their superiors. The Fante believed that the dead carried the wealth buried with them to the afterlife and that the soul was blessed according to the value of the property it brought with it. It was a desecration so heinous that it outraged the people of Annamaboe, to whom nothing was more sacred, and even shocked the British officials on the coast. Miles allowed four men from his garrison to venture outside the fort after the event, and they were promptly killed by the towns-people in revenge. Amoony Coomah and his townspeople "boldly assert that so long as Mr. Miles retains the Government of Annamaboe, they will listen to no kind of accommodation whatever." They promised to seize Miles if given the opportunity and take him to the Braffoe country, into the interior, where a painful death would have awaited him.[15]

The council at Cape Coast launched an investigation into the incident. One member of the council, Edgar Hickman, believed that Miles's government of the fort had been "exercised with severity," which, he warned, "will never be of any beneficial consequences when administered to so Powerful, Political and Free a People as the Fantee's, indeed it's well known it is what they never have been accustomed to."[16] In fact, almost exactly the same incident occurred at Annamaboe in 1769 when a white soldier cut a Fante man's head almost down to his skull "upon one of their holy days when it is unlawful for any Black to Strike another much less to draw blood as this Soldier did from the Fantee man." Governor Bell acknowledged that his soldier was in the wrong and paid £23 in cloth and twenty-three and a half gallons of rum to the town to settle the palaver, a precedent that Miles should have followed.[17]

Hickman condemned Miles for refusing the offer of the Fishing Town people to settle the dispute "with honor and credit to his constituents and himself" and his "rash and precipitous" decision to destroy Agah. He criticized Miles's use of seamen from the ships and particularly bemoaned "the circumstance of their Graves (which they look upon as sacred) being disturbed and plundered." He warned that the desecration of the Fante graves was still "fresh in their recollection, and stimulates them to actions too horrid to relate." Since they could trade freely with British and American ships at Cormantine, he concluded that they could continue the palavar and their attacks on any Englishmen who fell into their hands for an indefinite period. William Roberts, governor of Cape Coast Castle, agreed with Hickman's grim assessment. He, too, condemned the incident with the graves, saying that "unfortunate affair of the Graves being dug up for the sake of Plundering the Dead is in its nature so horrid a crime that it convinces me there was a want of order and Discipline (at that time) in Mr. Miles' government. The Seamen were spared from the ships to assist the Fort, and not to plunder the buried bodies of the Fantees, as a reward for any service they did the publick, such transactions so horrid and Dreadful in their nature how can any man truly in his senses and possessed of an ordinate share of Human feelings attempt to Palliate or justify." The council agreed with their harsh assessments, concluded that Miles acted with "Manifest impropriety," and immediately dismissed him from his post. Miles was yet one more in a long line of chiefs who lost his position in the face of determined Fante opposition.[18]

Even though Miles left in disgrace, that did not settle the palaver, and the Fante expected to be compensated for all the damage done to the town. Negotiations dragged on for four years as trade stood at a standstill. In July 1792 the British sent additional troops and guns to the fort. That alarmed Amoony Coomah, who "called together the Fantee Pynins & Caboceers, who seem inclined to take off the Interdict that had been laid on the Fort." The Council ordered "a Quantity of Liquor" to be sent to them to encourage a favorable outcome, and they sent a message assuring the Fante that they had no hostile intentions (some of those messages were carried by Harry Brew), but still they reached no agreement. In June 1793 eleven mulatto soldiers deserted from Annamaboe Fort, a very substantial part of the garrison and an indication of where their loyalties lay in any dispute between the town and the British. Only in 1794 did the British redeem the four British sailors who were taken at Agah. The palaver was not settled until September 1795, when fifteen caboceers from Annamaboe and Agah met with the Cape Coast Council, with Harry Brew acting as linguist, and agreed to end the dispute. The British paid hefty sums and agreed to resume all customary payments, expenditures that brought complaints from London but were necessary to bring the matter to an end. It had been a century since a dispute between the Fante and the chief of the fort had led to such violence and destruction. In the view of Henry Meredith, an AC official on the coast, the people of Annamaboe "conceived the chief's dismissal was in consequence of his having destroyed the town: and, influenced by this supposition, instead of relinquishing their ill practices, they gave the reins to their licentiousness, to the frequent interruption of the trade; and committed acts of violence to the prejudice both of the Service and the publick," a negative assessment that hints at the poisoned relations that the event left in its wake.[19]

Along with internal troubles and a bitter conflict with the British, the Fante also faced a challenge from the Asante. Ever since the tense negotiations of 1765, relations between the Asante and the Fante had been peaceful, sometimes strained, but without the major conflict that had been feared. In part that extended period of peace was due to internal troubles within the Asante kingdom, and to the long life of Osei Kwadwo, the Asantehene who agreed to keep the peace and who lived until 1781. A long period of instability followed his death, during which no major wars were undertaken. He was succeeded by a minor, which, according to the British at Cape Coast, had "thrown this once populous and powerfull Country into great Disorder, so as to weaken it very much." It was not until 1800, when Osei Bonsu was enstooled as Asantehene, that the Asante found another capable leader. During their time of troubles, the Asante made efforts to open trade paths to the coast by peaceful means. In 1775 the Asante contacted David Mill, governor at Cape Coast Castle, and asked for his assistance in their goal of opening "a Market nearer the Waterside." Eager to see the flow of slaves increased, Mill wanted to encourage their efforts by sending "the best presents." He requested "a large Umbrella of crimson Damask, with gold Fringe, and Gilt Elephant as top, to spread 15 feet—a large white satin cloth to be lined, and a double row of scalloped gold lace, with large Tassels—a very large silver basket-hilted sword, and a gold-headed cane with the arms of the company engraved, with a Hat and feathers or rather an Elegant coronet." He ordered the same lavish gifts for Amoony Coomah to help gain his support for the opening of an Asante market, but the Fante maintained their long-standing opposition to such a scheme that would cut them out of their profitable position as intermediaries. They resolutely kept the paths blocked. They allowed the Asante to come no farther than their northern market towns where traders from a number of nations, including the Asante, supplied Annamaboe and other Gold Coast ports. William Mutter, writing in 1765, had quite rightly doubted that the Fante would ever willingly allow the Asante to have a "free & open communication with the Forts." The British feared the Asante and their "despotic tyrannical Prince," and expressed their support for the Fante, "a people long used to the manner of the Europeans and pretty much civilized." They pledged to support the Fante, to supply them with gunpowder and guns, and to give them the protection of their forts. The Asante looked for other paths around the Fante, and they opened a path to Cape Appolonia to the west, but that did not satisfy their long-held desire for direct trade with the major European forts.[20]

Against this backdrop occurred a relatively minor dispute between the Asante and one of their dependent states, the Assin. In 1806, after repeated insults from the rulers of Assin, Osei Bonsu invaded Assin, determined to punish the offenders at any cost. Two of those rulers, Kwadwo Tsibu and Apute, fled to the Fante for protection. The Asantehene prepared to follow them into Fante territory, and he assured the Fante that he had no hostile intentions toward them. The Fante joined forces with Kwadwo Tsibu and Apute and fought the Asante when they entered Fante territory. The Fante were badly defeated, and Kwadwo Tsibu and Apute escaped and headed for the coast, where the leaders of Annamaboe unwisely agreed to protect them against the counsel of their leading oracle. Even at this stage the Asantehene was willing to discuss peace terms with the Fante if they would only surrender the men he sought, but again, the Fante refused. The Asante marched in pursuit, defeating every Fante army that attempted to stop them, and by May 1806 they were within fifteen or twenty miles of the coast. The British grew increasingly alarmed, and Governor George Torrane at Cape Coast offered to mediate, but the Fante refused their assistance since "the Annamaboes, who placed a vain dependence on their name and strength, fully expected that the king and his army would be conquered; and that if not the whole, the greater part of the army, would fall into their hands;

and hence were not disposed to pacific measures, nor would they permit the governor's messenger to proceed inland."[21]

After a spectacular defeat of the main Fante army at Abora in May 1806, the Asante were within four miles of Cape Coast Castle. One branch of their army attacked the Dutch fort at Cormantine, destroyed the town surrounding it, and took possession of the fort, which the Dutch quickly surrendered to them. The Asante commander dipped his sword three times into the sea to symbolize his victories over the coast, and he sent seawater back to the Asantehene as proof of his success. Edward William White, chief of Annamaboe Fort, was now genuinely alarmed and sent messengers to Cormantine to determine the Asante's aims. The victorious commander sent back a message saying that he would discuss matters with the British only after they delivered twenty barrels of gunpowder and one hundred muskets, a demand that White refused. He offered to mediate, but warned that if the Asante approached the fort with hostile intent they would be fired upon. He then fired two or three of the fort's heaviest guns as the messengers prepared to leave to demonstrate their power. The people of Annamaboe also grew more fearful and asked for the fort's protection, and White assured them that if the Asante attacked they would have "all the assistance and protection in his power." He also advised them to station strong lookout forces on every path leading into the town, and if the Asante approached, to send the elderly, women, and children into the fort or under its walls for safety.[22]

A week passed with no movement from the Asante, but then to better assess the strength of Annamaboe, the commander at Cormantine captured the nearby town of Agah from which he could observe the goings-on at Annamaboe. The men of Annamaboe decided to challenge the Asante there, and on June 14 almost the entire military force of the town attacked the Asante at Agah and forced them out of the main town and into its hinterland. But while they were engaged at Agah, the Asante moved into the paths that the Annamaboe militia had unwisely left unguarded and arrived within three miles of the town. Early on the morning of June 15 the sentries reported that the Asante army was on the move toward Annamaboe. Every able man was armed and marched out to meet the enemy. Soon the British in the fort saw smoke rising from the countryside and heard heavy gunfire. The elderly, women, and children fled into the fort and the gates were slammed shut behind them. The fighting grew closer and closer, and it was soon apparent that the Fante were in full retreat; the British fired the great guns of the fort at the approaching Asante army in hopes of frightening them off, "but they were too much elated with hopes of conquest, and too resolute to be affrightened." About 11:00 that morning the musket balls began to fly through the fort, and the Asante troops poured into the town from every direction; they pursued the desperate Fante men down to the beach "where the slaughter was great." The Fante men had hoped to be able to reach their canoes or swim to out sea, but the Asante were too close behind them. A few managed to reach the sacred Bird Rocks, where they clung for safety, but thousands died in a terrible slaughter.[23]

As the attack intensified, the English turned the guns of the fort on the Asante army and fired "grape-shot among them, whereby vast numbers must have fallen," but "fresh parties came on much quicker than they could be repelled: and at length they came under the walls, for the purpose of carrying away the women who could not be received into the fort." There were about thirty men in the fort, including soldiers (white and mulatto), slaves, and others, to face an army of thousands. White, chief of the fort, was seriously wounded when a ball passed through his mouth and knocked out four of his teeth, and another went through his left arm. Others were wounded, and one man died. The Asante seemed determined to take the fort, which they thought would be filled with loot. As the number of wounded grew, only eight men remained who could continue the defense of the fort. They fired round after round; one man fired three hundred rounds and was so bruised by his musket's recoil that he could barely use his arm for days afterward. The Asante tried to break down the gates but were twice pushed back; they attempted to set fire to the massive wooden gates, but the man carrying the fire was shot and extinguished the flames when he fell dead onto them. The fighting stopped only with nightfall.[24]

When the sun rose the following morning, the British looked out on a scene of horrible devastation. Bodies of the dead surrounded the fort in heaps and lay for a mile along the beach, the dead bodies mingled with the wounded who cried out in pain, and their cries mingled with the

The Asantehene and his court celebrate the first day of the yam custom, a harvest festival. Note the rich umbrellas, gifts from the European powers on the coast. The Asantehene sits under a crimson umbrella topped with a gilt elephant, the symbol of the Royal African Company. Folded plate in T. Edward Bowdich, *Mission from Cape Coast Castle to Ashantee: with a Statistical Account of that Kingdom, and Geographical Notices of Other Parts of the Interior of Africa* (London: J. Murray, Albemarle-Street: printed by W. Pulmer and Co., Cleveland-Row, St. James's, 1819), p. 274.

tears of the women and children inside the fort. Of the town's 15,000 inhabitants, two-thirds lay dead, about two thousand crowded inside the fort, another two hundred clung for life on the Bird Rocks, and another two or three thousand escaped into the surrounding countryside. Fortunately for the handful of exhausted men in the fort, the Asante did not resume the attack, but the situation remained desperate. The Asante had the fort completely surrounded by land, and provisions were short. The corpses began to putrefy quickly in the tropical sun, and the stench filled the air. Governor George Torrane of Cape Coast Castle, himself fearful of an Asante attack, sent what reinforcements he could spare, and on the afternoon of June 16, twelve men and four officers made their way from their canoes into the fort under cover of smoke from the fort's heavy guns. Torrane ordered that a flag of truce be sent to the Asante with messengers to sue for peace. The Asantehene responded that "it was not his intention to commence hostilities with the Whites; his enemies were the Assins and Fantees." The king agreed to send deputies to Cape Coast to negotiate, but he added that "he must have those who sought the protection of the fort," meaning the Fante elderly, women, and children who were under British protection. Henry Meredith, now in command at the fort given White's wounds, added that if they did give the people up, they "ought to be assured of their being used kindly." He added that supplies in the fort were running out and he feared that disease might break out among them.[25]

Torrane tried to lure the Asantehene to Cape Coast Castle, but the Asante were in the position of strength, and he insisted that Torrane come to him. It was the first time an Englishmen had met any Asantehene, and they tried to put on as much ceremony as they could muster under the circumstances. They began by sending gifts to the king, but the most important thing they sent him was Kwadwo Tsibu, one of the men the Asante sought who had been given protection at Cape Coast Castle. Kwadwo Tsibu was old and blind, and some of the AC officials on the coast protested that Torrane should not surrender someone he had vowed to protect, but Torrane was eager to gain the Asantehene's goodwill. Kwadwo Tsibu was tortured and executed by the Asante. At the appointed time about twenty of the castle's artificers marched in front, followed by a guard of forty soldiers and a band, followed by the governor, ten officers, and a few British traders bringing up the rear. They walked through thousands of curious Asante soldiers, many of whom had never seen a white man. The governor first met the men of rank surrounding the king who were gathered under huge umbrellas. He then approached the Asantehene himself, "who was surrounded by a number of attendants, whose appearance bore evident signs of riches and authority: chains, stools, axes, swords, flutes, message-canes, & c. were either of solid gold or richly adorned with that metal: those dazzling appearances, added to damask, taffety, and other rich dresses, gave a splendour to the scene." The Asantehene was not the ogre the British had expected; instead, he was described as being "of the middle size, well formed, and perfectly black, with regular features and an open and pleasing countenance. His manner indicated understanding and was adorned with gracefulness; and in all respects he exceeded the expectations of every person."[26] He was someone Torrane could work with.

Before the Asantehene left the area, Torrane was eager to settle the question of what would become of the Fante that the British had protected inside their fort during the battle for Annamaboe. The Asantehene demanded that they be turned over to him; he told the British that "as he destroyed the town, he had a claim to every person, and to every thing belonging to it." He now regarded all the Fante as his slaves to be disposed of as he wished, but Torrane negotiated a deal whereby the Asantehene would take half of those residents of Annamaboe. Torrane "begged him for half," which the Asantehene allowed. Torrane took them, approximately a thousand people, and sold them into slavery. It was a shocking move, even by the lax moral standards of the Gold Coast. John Swanzy, the chief of the British fort at Accra, was dangerously ill at the time, but he made the arduous journey to Cape Coast to protest the sale; his threats to expose the underhanded dealings in London persuaded Torrane to try to stop the sale and redeem the people of Annamaboe, but it was too late—they had already been shipped off the coast. The Asante soon left Annamaboe in pursuit of Apute and his followers, who were quickly defeated, and the Asantehene marched most of his army back toward home, where other conflicts occupied his attention, leaving a trail of destruction and famine in his wake.[27]

The Asante had achieved their long-held objective of reaching the coast and the coastal forts, but just at the moment that the British abolished the slave trade. Their defeat of the Fante and other smaller nations that had served as buffer between them and the Europeans on the Gold Coast completely altered the political realities on the Gold Coast. Among the claims the Asantehene took from his coastal conquests were the notes or leases that the Europeans had negotiated with the coastal nations. From that time forward, they would pay their ground rents for their forts not to the Fante Braffo, for example, but to the Asantehene, who now expected to be recognized as their landlord. He also expected that opening paths to the coast would provide a ready market for the large numbers of slaves his conquests had won him. Since the Asante were distracted with other conflicts, the Fante continued to brood and plot, even claiming that the Asante had been forced to retreat from Fante territory, and in 1809 they launched attacks on Elmina and Accra, which they blamed for giving support to the Asante in the 1807 war. The Asante sent two armies back into the coastal region, and their 1811 invasion failed, but they sent a large force in 1814 and reoccupied the Gold Coast, including Annamaboe and Cape Coast, where they remained until 1816. Any doubts about the Asante conquest of the coast was removed, and the entire region was incorporated into the Asante state and placed under Asante governors.[28]

The British abolition of the slave trade did not by any means end the traffic, but it did end the system as it existed in the eighteenth century and particularly at its forts on the Gold Coast.[29] Built to protect the slave trade, the forts now became enforcers of the ban against it, and the economies of Cape Coast, Annamaboe, and the other towns surrounding those forts simply collapsed. Henry Meredith, who was serving in Annamaboe Fort at the time of the Asante attack, published a history of the Gold Coast intended in part to encourage British trade to the region in the wake of the abolition of the African slave trade by the British in 1807. Writing in 1812, he observed that "at present, the Gold-coast is almost neglected by the British merchants." British travelers through Annamaboe's once rich hinterland described it even a decade later as depopulated and impoverished. The once extensive plantations were overgrown, and once thriving towns and villages were destroyed and

This highly stylized print depicts an African warrior or chief in robes, carrying a spear and wearing a feathered headdress. In his right hand he holds a paper inscribed "slave trade abolish'd 1806," referring to the Foreign Slave Trade Bill enacted in 1806, which restricted the British slave trade prior to its abolition the following year. National Maritime Museum, Greenwich, London.

inhabited by a handful of poor people in wretched huts. In places the ground was bleached white with ash and littered with the skulls and bones of the slain. It was a momentous change from the previous century, when British ships crowded Annamaboe Road. The British had outlawed the slave trade, prohibited its conduct from their forts, and sent a naval squadron to the African coast to patrol it, but the slave trade continued to be legal for other European powers for years to come. Even though the United States outlawed the importation of slaves after 1808, it did not prohibit its citizens from taking slaves elsewhere. The immediate result of the British ban was a sharp decline in the trade, but the number rebounded quickly and the trade resumed under new arrangements. The slave trade moved away from the forts and into the hands of private traders, many of them the mixed-race descendants of European men and African or mixed-race women who were already established traders.

Understandably, none of this made much sense to the Africans engaged in the slave trade, who were baffled at the sudden about-face. The slave trade might have been outlawed by the British, but not in Africa. When Joseph Dupuis visited the Asantehene on a diplomatic mission in 1818, the king wanted to discuss the closing of the slave trade with him. The Asantehene said, "A long time ago the great king liked plenty of trade, more than now; then many ships came, and they bought ivory, gold and slaves; but now he will not let the ships come as before, and the people buy gold and ivory only . . . so now, tell me truly, like a friend, why does the king do so?" Dupuis tried to explain and acknowledged that he was "at a loss for an argument that might pass as a satisfactory reason." Rightly so, for the Asantehene "did not deem it plausible, that this obnoxious practice should have been abolished from motives of humanity alone; neither would he admit that it lessened the number either of domestic or foreign wars." The king sensibly asked, "If they think it bad now, why did they think it good before?" He explained to Dupuis that he did not catch slaves in the bush, nor did he make war to capture slaves, but that his was a warrior nation, and when he defeated his enemies, he took them as his slaves. He explained that his recent victory against the northern province of Gyaman had brought him 20,000 captives. He gave many of them to his captains, but he reported, "Unless I sell or kill them, they will grow strong and kill my people." He asked Dupuis to tell the British monarch that "these slaves can work for him, and if he wants 10,000 he can have them. And if he wants fine handsome girls and women to give his captains, I can send him great numbers."[30]

John Hope Smith, an opponent of the trade and governor of Cape Coast Castle, reported to the AC that only the British navy could stop the slave trade. He called it an activity "from which the natives can never be weaned." He reported that "this traffic is the only object of Commerce congenial to the Natives, or to which they are actively disposed; they will cling to it to the last moment; they may be deprived of it, but they cannot be alienated from it, they will never quit it but from necessity."[31] How could it be otherwise? The European powers had spent centuries engaged in and fostering the trade, and its tentacles had spread as deeply in Africa as they had around the Atlantic World. To simply cut off the economic activity that had been the basis of the coastal economy for centuries was no simple matter. Smith was about to learn just how committed the Asante were to the trade.

The most important merchant engaged in the slave trade at Cape Coast at the time of the abolition of the trade was Samuel Brew, Richard Brew's grandson and linguist Harry Brew's son. He was very much like his grandfather in the scale of his ambitions and in his skills. In the British abolition of the slave trade, he saw opportunity. He was regarded as "the most notorious slave-dealer in Fantee." His audacious goal was to make himself the conduit for the Asante slave trade, just as his grandfather had hoped to do, and like Richard Brew, he planned to accomplish that feat by inserting himself into the diplomatic negotiations between the two powers. The British were eager to stop Brew's trading activities at Cape Coast, and in 1817 they found reasons to expel him from Cape Coast. Brew simply moved his base of operations to a deserted fort near Winnebah, raised a Spanish flag, and continued to openly conduct a thriving trade selling slaves he acquired from the Asante to any and all comers. The British reported that the "grand focus of the Slave trade on the Gold Coast lies within 20 leagues perhaps to leeward of Accra, and as near to Annamaboe as vessels dare anchor . . . to prevent this, it would be necessary to disable Sam Brew from carrying on his nefarious trade, as he has ever a supply of Slaves ready to ship them, where the vessel stands out to sea for fear of Capture."[32]

The nineteenth-century slave trade was taking shape in these years. No longer could ships simply sail openly to the British forts, purchase slaves from either the fort or local traders, advance their goods, take on pawns, and spend weeks or even months negotiating these deals along the coast. The threat of seizure meant that ships had to avoid the forts and towns, and traders like Brew moved their operations to more hidden or isolated areas. In addition, slavers now wanted to sail in and out quickly, because they were in greatest danger of capture when loading slaves or lying at anchor off the coast. To speed up the loading of slaves, traders like Brew operated barracoons, compounds that included holding areas for hundreds of slaves. Rather than extending credit to traders and allowing them to take trade goods to interior markets, slavers now insisted on buying slaves immediately, loading a full cargo in one night, and sailing back across the Atlantic as quickly as possible. The economy of the trade changed entirely. Slavers no longer carried only trade goods—they carried barrels of specie. Traders either had to have sufficient capital to operate, or the sellers of the slaves had to extend the credit. If the coastal traders still used trade goods, they now acquired those from independent traders, so British merchants began to carry their cargoes of goods for the slave trade for sale directly to traders like Brew, which was perfectly legal. But the entire trade became based more on currency rather than barter. Over time, these networks would be better established; firms in Havana, for example, dealt with specific traders on the coast, arranged in advance for shipments on specific dates, and might even have supply ships from New York or Baltimore rendezvous with them off the coast of Africa.[33]

When the British sent their first official delegation to the Asantehene in 1817, they were shocked that one of the most important issues on his mind was their treatment of Sam Brew. The situation was eerily reminiscent of Richard Brew's role in the 1762 negotiations. In October 1817 the Asantehene summoned William Hutchinson, the principal British negotiator, to appear before him in his palace. He asked him to explain why Brew had been driven out of Cape Coast, and he informed Hutchinson that Brew had alleged that there was a plot to kill him and that they had even sent armed men against him at his new headquarters. Hutchinson was fuming that this "insolent Mulatto man, by presents to the King and his principal men, and being the chief support of the Slave trade between this nation and the coast, has made the King interest himself in his favour, in an improper degree." Brew had cleverly sent samples of guns, powder and other goods from a Spanish slaver to the Asantehene to encourage him to send slaves down to him. When the Asantehene asked Brew's messenger why his master did not live at Cape Coast, the messenger "made a long harangue, stated he owed some white man money to the Amount of 8 ounces, which caused the guard to be turned out to take him, and that he made his escape; since which the chief men at Cape town have desired his death." The king ordered his governor at Cape Coast to call Brew there to hear from both parties and said that the guilty party should pay a fine to him. Hutchinson told the Asantehene and his chiefs that Brew could not return until he "made proper submission to the Castle, and behaved in a peaceable manner, he would not be allowed to Cape Coast."[34]

This issue raised much larger ones regarding sovereignty over Cape Coast that remained a source of disagreement. Were the British simply tenants of the fort with no power beyond its walls, and no authority to say who could or could not reside at Cape Coast? Or were they in a position of responsibility over the town and, by extension, over the Fante? The Asantehene made Hutchinson wait twelve days to see him again, and when they met, he called him in to dictate a letter to him regarding Brew. The king wrote, "Sam Brew who now lives at Winnebah has been made war upon by the Cape Coast people and some of the Soldiers belonging to the Fort, which is not a good palaver on your part." He wanted Brew along with the "authorities of the town" to appear before his captain

that the palaver may be talked, and that I may know whether it is the white men or Black man who have done wrong . . . If Sam Brew has done wrong he has broke my laws—if the Cape Coast people they have broke it . . . Sam Brew made me a present of several articles which made the Cape Coast people think he dashed them to me—but they as well as the Fantees over all the Country are my Slaves—Mr. Hutchinson has informed me that Brew got bad gold from the Slave Ships and went to Ships in Cape Coast roads at night and exchanged it for Guns and powder and refused to answer your Complain when called on and treated your messenger with insults—I wish to know if your Officer speaks truth ... It is for Cape Coast people going to kill Sam Brew that I am sorry and not for your palaver, which I hope you will settle soon.[35]

Smith responded that the king had been encouraged to intervene in the Brew affair by "evil advisors" and advised him not to interfere with matters involving the town under the fort's protection. He told the king that the proceedings against Brew did not involve the town, that he had personally given the orders to have Brew arrested and sent to Cape Coast, and he assured the king that Brew's death had not been "decreed by any person." His attempt to have Brew captured by a party of Africans failed, and he escaped on a Spanish schooner with the help of his African allies and brazenly returned a few weeks later in a Spanish ship. Clearly exasperated with Brew, who he described as an "old offender" who had "too often escaped with impunity," Smith was eager to take him. Brew must have been delighted that the seeds of discord he had sown between the British and the Asantehene had grown to such a height. Smith stressed to the king that "the Cape Coast people are not his slaves, nor have they ever been acknowledged as such; neither can they nor any of the natives residing under British protection be included in that most degrading title."[36] If Smith intended to insult the king, he could not have done better.

As the linguist Smith sent from Cape Coast to read his letter to the king began his recitation, the king grew more and more furious. He gave orders to put the linguist "in irons as a prelude to his execution for daring to bring such an account." Hutchinson pleaded for the man's life and protested that the king would "lay hands on a Servant of the Company, under your protection, and with a Cane in his hand." But as the letter was read before a public audience, "the uproar was violent and general." The king responded that the Cape Coast people took every opportunity to defy him. He added that he thought that the banners and flags he had received as gifts from the king of England indicated that that monarch "was his great Captain," and while he recognized that the British king was the "greatest monarch in Europe," they did not seem to recognize that "he was the same among the black nations here."[37]

The king spent five hours complaining to Hutchinson about Smith's letter. In his response, he reminded Smith that the Cape Coast people claimed that they had not be conquered by him, but it was only British intervention that prevented him from having "every one of them brought before me and put to death." He reported that he was about to go to war, and he asked for as many guns and as much powder as the British could get, adding, "I shall see who is my best friend among the Governors on the Coast." Smith asked the king if he had given orders for his men to help Brew escape capture. The Asantehene reported that he knew nothing about the matter, but he continued to press Smith on Brew's behalf. Hutchinson threatened that if the king persisted in his support of Brew and the slave trade that he would ask to be recalled. Day after day, Brew continued to be the main topic of discussion. The king offered to give Smith a present in order to settle his dispute with Brew and leave him unmolested. Outraged, Hutchinson told the king that he clearly did not "appreciate the English character. Glowing with indignant feelings, I told the King it was the first time I had received an insult from him, and stated my wish to retire." The king asked if Hutchinson thought that Smith "would listen to any more solicitations about Brew. I replied that I thought I had informed him of your ultimatum, and declined talking any further about such an outlaw." Still, the king insisted that his chief at Cape Coast make one more request to Smith about Brew, and if he still declined, then he would insist no further on Brew's return to Cape Coast.[38]

Smith informed his superiors in London that the Asantehene had an "eager desire" for the slave trade to continue, a desire that had interfered with negotiations between the parties. It was that commitment to the trade, he wrote, that explained "how warmly he has been induced to insert himself in the cause of a Mulattoe Man named Brew." Brew had convinced the king that he could attract Spanish slavers and keep the trade flowing, and furthermore, "Brew has also represented to the King that he has been persecuted by the English solely from his zealous attachment to the Slave Trade, and has therefore solicited his protection and assistance to enable him to establish so regular a System of it as cannot be easily obstructed—This man who is a great Slave Trade Merchant, was banished from the town some time ago for improper behaviour, he has also been a troublesome and refractory character, and his late treacherous conduct to the people of this town has proved him to be so very dangerous a person, that the Governor intends if he succeeds in securing him, to transport him from the Colony."[39]

Hutchinson was not able to capture Brew, who continued his operations and maintained his close ties with the Asante. The Company of Merchants Trading to Africa was abolished in 1821, and its holding passed to the Crown. In 1822 Sir Charles Maccarthy arrived at Cape Coast to assume the new governorship, and at the time of his arrival many of the questions surrounding British-Asante relations—the slave trade, exercise of authority on the coast, oversight of the populations surrounding the forts—remained unsettled. These matters resurfaced when in August 1818 the Fante insulted and abused messengers from the Asantehene. What should have been a minor issue snowballed into a major crisis in the relations between Cape Coast and the Asante, and Smith seemed intent on breaking off relations with the Asantehene. The Asante representative at Cape Coast, who was a young and vigorous man, died suddenly, and the chief caboceer was rumored to have poisoned him. Tensions grew higher and higher until an incident at Annamaboe sparked conflict. An Asante trader visited Annamaboe, and he and a native-born sergeant of the newly created Royal African Colonial Light Infantry quarreled and traded insults—the Asante trader insulted the governor of the fort, and the sergeant made disparaging remarks about the Asantehene. The affair was reported to the king, who demanded that the sergeant be turned over to him for punishment. The British refused to turn over one of their officers, but the Asantehene sent word throughout the region that he wanted the man taken prisoner if possible. A few months later the sergeant was sent on a mission to Abora Dunkwa, a few miles from Annamaboe, where he was captured by Fante caboceers who turned him over to the Asante officials in the town in an effort to curry favor with the Asantehene. After four or five months he was executed, and his hands and head were sent to the Asantehene as evidence of his fate.[40]

Once Charles Maccarthy heard about the execution of the British officer, he made plans to avenge his death. Brew had managed to ingratiate himself with Maccarthy, who "consulted him on various occasions," and refused to listen to Smith and others who tried to convince him "that the real character of this man was decidedly of the worst kind." He informed his superiors in London that he tried to guide Brew toward "lawful commerce, agriculture and every species of honest industry," which did not show a very good understanding of Brew's ambitions. Maccarthy did not believe that the Asante were prepared for war given the losses they had suffered in recent conflicts. He informed his superiors that they had been threatening the fort since the previous August without any cause, and that they were trying to extort money from the town and from the fort. The Fante had promised to support him in any action against their old enemy. He saw only two choices; to try to make peace with the Asantehene, who he considered "a Ruffian who had committed an atrocious act, or to show to him, and all the other African Chiefs, that we would not leave such a deed unpunished." He raised a small force of about 200 men intending to make a quick raid on Abora Dunkwa and surprise the small group of Asante there.[41]

Samuel Brew offered to join the expedition. The troops left Cape Coast at about 7:00 p.m., and one of the party stayed behind with Brew, who had requested arms and ammunition for himself and about twenty of his men. After Brew had the men drink fetish and swear loyalty to him, his party left about an hour after the others. He caught up with the expedition the following day, and at one point he led the group toward a source of water. As the small force traveled along a narrow, rugged path through a thickly wooded area, they were ambushed by a combined force of Asante and Fante soldiers who massacred the British force. Six men died, thirty-eight were wounded, and four were missing. The British were convinced that Brew had actually led them into a trap. In addition, they alleged that Brew had sent a messenger to a Fante caboceer allied with the Asante informing him that the British force was on the march, and that he had sent false messages to several caboceers and towns around Cape Coast, all intended to thwart the mission. After an investigation and testimony from a number of the men involved, including Africans, Maccarthy was convinced of Brew's guilt, and he informed

Annamaboe and its fort as it appeared later in the nineteenth century. From the
Illustrated London News (1873).

his superiors in London that "the misconduct of S. Brew on that occasion, when he had made a tender of Services, was consonant to the tenor
of his life—he carried on the traffic in Slaves in the view of the Castle (at
Mouree, four miles distant) within a few months before the transfer of
the Forts to his Majesty in 1821—he had taken 'Fetish' with the Ashantees." He also charged him with cruelty to his slaves. Maccarthy believed
that there was "ample evidence to establish the guilt of Brew before a tri-
bunal," but given Brew was "allied to some of the principal families of
Cape Coast," he decided to exile him to Sierra Leone. He thought that
this solution would "best provide against difficulties, and at the same
time act with greater leniency towards him," though why he deserved
leniency if he was indeed guilty of the ambush is unclear. He even suggested that he could be "left at liberty without any danger or inconvenience, and he may acquire principles of Loyalty."[42]

The captain of the HMS *Cyrene* agreed to take him to Sierra Leone;
"he was not placed under any control or restraint and appeared perfectly
satisfied." In the early morning hours of May 24, Brew was found dead,
his throat slashed with a razor belonging to William Mitchison, the carpenter with whom he shared his cabin. Mitchison saw no signs that indicated that Brew had any intention of taking his own life, but he reported

that Brew awakened him in the middle of the night and whispered "that there was some person wanting to cut his throat." The carpenter told him that was impossible, but Brew said he heard them coming below deck. Mitchison said he heard crewmen coming down out of the rain, but Brew said that it was not raining. Mitchison offered to get up and check; Brew said that "he would thank me if I would." When he returned to the cabin Brew was gone. At about the same time, a sailor saw blood on the deck and on the ladder leading down into the main hold. He and others followed the trail and found Brew's body lying facedown on the water tanks with a great deal of blood all around him. The ship's surgeon examined the body and found a cut of about four and a half inches on the left side of Brew's neck. He had "no doubt it was inflicted by himself." Maccarthy believed that he was driven to the act by his belief in fetish. He wrote that Brew "united to the outer appearance as to dress and language (not color, as he was a dark mulatto) of an European, the very grossest superstition, idolatry and *fetish*. I am convinced that he acted under a momentary impression of his belief in the latter." The official verdict read, "Sam. Brew—accused to Treason has destroyed himself." Suspicions lingered about Brew's suicide, especially among his family and the African residents of the Gold Coast, and given the fact that he had alleged for years that the British intended to kill him, those suspicions are understandable. Since he was accused of treasonably causing death and injury to scores of British soldiers, his murder on board a naval ship would hardly be surprising.[43]

Brew's death brought an end to the slave-trading dynasty established by Richard Brew in the previous century, though Sam Brew's descendants were prominent and influential on the Gold Coast.[44] The literal collapse of Castle Brew and the failure of Horatio Smith's dreams of recreating the trading network Brew had built in Annamaboe signaled an end to the conduct of the slave trade in Annamaboe by a powerful independent British merchant. The conflict at Annamaboe between Miles and the people of the town, culminating in bloodshed and the destruction of Agah, was the last in a long series of such controversies between the governors of the fort and the town's wealthy and independent caboceers, but it was the most serious incident of the eighteenth century and it interrupted trade at Annamaboe for several years. That event was followed a few years later by the British abolition of the slave trade, a blow to the economic foundations of Annamaboe, and combined with the devastating defeat of Annamaboe by the Asante, 1807 was truly an "annus horribilis" for the town, double blows from which it never fully recovered. Even the British who were critical of what they perceived as the Annamaboe's many failings could not help but sympathize with their changed circumstances. Henry Meredith, a CMTA official at Annamaboe, heaped criticism on them, but wrote in 1812, "The late changes which have taken place; the destruction of their town, with the greater part of its inhabitants; and the abolition of the Slave-trade; may probably be considered as too great a punishment for all their transgressions and offenses."[45]

Conclusion

Annamaboe grew into one of the hubs of Atlantic commerce, comparable in size to its Atlantic sister ports Charleston, South Carolina, and Newport, Rhode Island. Its capable and crafty merchants relied on the exportation of maize and slaves and the importation of European goods to build a wealthy, independent, and powerful commercial center. The first stage of Annamaboe's place in the Atlantic World, the era of the gold trade, began with European contact in the 1430s and continued until the trade shifted to the traffic in human beings around 1700. Of the changes and innovations that the contact with Europeans and Annamaboe's first tentative links to the Atlantic World introduced, three stand out: the introduction of maize, the fort system, and the development of trade languages. The cultivation of maize ushered in a constellation of economic, social, and political changes that reshaped life on the Gold Coast. Maize fostered population growth, territorial expansion, state formation, military conquest, and enslavement, and all those developments fed on one another through the eighteenth century. The Portuguese quickly discovered that they could not conquer West Africa and sought relationships with rulers on the Gold Coast that fostered trade. They innovated the system whereby European powers paid rent to the local state for the privilege of building a fort as a base for trade. This system endured until the early nineteenth century and shaped the relations between Africans and Europeans on the Gold Coast. That system recognized African sovereignty and power, and the Fante jealously guarded their independence and consistently reminded Europeans of those realities. The emergence of a trade language enabled Europeans and Africans to communicate more effectively—an essential component of trade at a time when trust and face-to-face relationships were an important part of commerce and credit. The emergence of a shared language also points to the cultural changes underway in that narrow band of contact along the West African coast.

The second stage in Annamaboe's Atlantic history began with the shift from gold to the slave trade. So long as the primary article of trade was gold, then the interior states enjoyed the economic advantage, but the balance of economic power shifted toward the coastal states with the rise of the slave trade. Annamaboe grew from a small, dependent town to an independent polity. It controlled a rich interior hinterland where its productive maize plantations, worked by enslaved laborers, contributed to its economic growth and made it an essential stop for slave ships before they embarked on the Middle Passage. Annamaboe and its wealthy and capable caboceers played an increasingly important role in the growing Fante confederacy. Annamaboe's chief caboceer at the height of its power, John Corrantee, acted as a major merchant, a military commander, a local ruler, a magistrate, and one of the leaders of the state. He helped guide the town as it expanded its economic and military power and played the rival European nations off one another. He was a leader of the confederacy when it conquered its neighbors, integrated them into the confederacy, and successfully countered the rising power of the Asante state.

A close examination of the conduct of the trade at Annamaboe also reveals the inner workings of the Royal African Company and its successor, the Company of Merchants Trading to Africa. As one of the primary engines driving the movement of goods, people, and ideas around the Atlantic World, it is vital that its functioning be well understood. Because Annamaboe was the primary market on the Gold Coast, its relationship with the RAC and the CMTA is especially significant. Initially envisioned as a trading company with a strict monopoly on the African trade, the RAC evolved into an organization intended to foster and protect an open trade, but the RAC and CMTA officials on the coast often exploited the system for their own personal advantage. Their distance from the metropole enabled them to construct a trade network extending around the Atlantic World that worked more to their advantage than to anyone else's benefit. Annamaboe's leaders refused to accept the restrictions of a monopoly and maintained their right to trade with all comers. While they allowed the RAC to build a fort at Annamaboe, they maintained their superiority over it, forced the RAC to change personnel and practices to suit them, and maintained their political and economic independence. In 1753 Thomas Melville, governor of Cape Coast Castle, recognized that reality when he referred to Annamaboe as a place "where the Negroes are Masters."

The end of the RAC's monopoly and the often troubled relationship between the town and the RAC resulted in the fort's closing, but Corrantee recognized the advantages of having a fort in Annamaboe for himself, for his family, and for the growth of the trade there. The existence of the forts brought significant changes into the town, none more important than the personal relationships between the men in the forts and the women of the town that resulted in a mixed-race population that played an important role in the social, cultural, and economic life of the town. While many RAC and CMTA officials spent only a few years on the coast with the intention of getting out as quickly as possible, Richard Brew put down deep roots in the town and played an important role in it. He manipulated his position as chief of Annamaboe Fort to his own personal advantage, and when forced out of the organization, he settled permanently in the town, allied himself through marriage to John Corrantee, and used his deep understanding of the RAC, the CMTA, the slave trade, and Fante culture to build a major slave-trading empire on the Gold Coast. His trade networks spread around the Atlantic World, and his political intrigues helped shape the relationship between the British and the Fante, the relationship between the Fante and the Asante, and British policy toward the RAC and the CMTA.

Annamaboe's role as the chief market on the Gold Coast comes into sharper focus by tracing the conduct of the trade with New England's Rum Men, who played an increasingly important role in the economic life of the town as the eighteenth century progressed. Their trade was emblematic of Atlantic commerce and its long reach. They carried molasses from the Caribbean to their distilleries, where it was used to produce rum, which became the liquor of choice on the Gold Coast and enabled them to gain a larger and larger share of the market there. From the fitting of a ship, to the hiring of a captain and crew, to the acquisition of an enslaved cargo, to the management of that cargo and crew, to the Middle Passage, to the determination of the most profitable point of sale, these voyages were extremely complex, risky, and dangerous. Ever attuned to changes in the market, Brew capitalized on the Rum Men's growing clout and nurtured relationships with them. The slave trade became a vital part of the New England economy, and the Rum Men helped supply the hungry markets of the southern colonies where cargos of Annamaboe slaves were highly valued. That trade connected the nodes of the Atlantic World—Annamaboe, Newport, Kingston, Charleston—and defined an Atlantic economy and culture.

While it is extremely difficult to trace individuals caught up in the slave trade from their homes in Africa to new homes in the Americas, following individual ships from New England to the Gold Coast to Charleston does provide some very specific indications of what that journey meant for the multitude of its victims. Far more Africans crossed the Atlantic in the eighteenth century than those from Europe or the Americas, and their degradation, enslavement, and brutal deaths continue to haunt the world they built and the world they left behind.

For the overwhelming majority of Africans, the voyage across the Atlantic was one of no return, but some Africans from Annamaboe escaped enslavement with the help of their families and community and returned home again. Other residents of Annamaboe traveled the Atlantic as sailors, others were sent to Europe to learn trades, some members of the elite traveled to America and to Britain to be educated, and other elites traveled to the capitals of Europe on diplomatic missions. While historians have characterized Africans as the least knowledgeable of the Atlantic World's citizens, that view must be revised to take into account the efforts Africans made to understand that world and their firsthand experience of it. Those former slaves, travelers, sailors, students, and diplomats were cultural brokers whose experiences shaped their town's collective understanding of the Atlantic World. They learned trades; they learned to read and write in English; they joined churches; they walked the streets of Liverpool, London, and Paris; and they met princes and kings. In doing so, they also impacted the cultures of those faraway places. In some cases powerful ideas ricocheted around the Atlantic basin; the ideals of liberty growing out of the American Revolution fired minds from Philadelphia to London, from Port-au-Prince to Annamaboe. Religious ideas, too, moved from Africa to the Americas, and from Europe to Africa. Most pieces of legislation enacted in the capitals of Europe did not reverberate around the Atlantic World, but in some cases, a string plucked in London sounded everywhere the Atlantic touched. The abolition of the slave trade was one act that revolutionized the Atlantic World in ways no one anticipated. All of these currents, and more besides, found their way to Annamaboe Road.

By the late eighteenth century there were signs of stress in Annamaboe as the era of the slave trade came to an end. Some of those stresses resulted from the economic troubles brought about by the American Revolution, which had a negative impact on the slave trade. Those hard economic times affected traders like Richard Brew, who faced serious economic problems and whose death marked the end of his empire despite the efforts of Horatio Smith to revive it. Tensions flared in Annamaboe between the townspeople and between the town and the fort, tensions that resulted in violence and deaths. The abolition of the slave trade by Great Britain and the United States in 1807 and 1808 marked a major turning point in the town's history. Combined with the devastating Asante invasion of 1807, Annamaboe faced body blows from which it never fully recovered. The town lost two-thirds of its inhabitants in the war, and its rich hinterlands were depopulated and devastated. With the loss of the slave trade, Annamaboe had no means of recovery, and its economic life ground to a halt. Without the slave ships and their need for slaves and provisions, the town's role as an important Atlantic port vanished. The fort that had once been used to promote the trade was now used to suppress it, and the townspeople were too broken to resist.

Individuals like Sam Brew did resist, and Brew played a remarkable game as he engaged in the illegal slave trade, ingratiated himself with the Asante, acted as their connection to European and American slave traders, and became a major player in the diplomatic negotiations between the British and the Asante. He lost his life in that game, but through him the contours of the next phase in the history of slave trade and the history of the British and the Fante can be discerned, though that story lies beyond the scope of this book.

Annamaboe lost its place as one of the hubs of the Atlantic economy after 1807, and today the town is far removed from the busy eighteenth-century port it once was. Much of that history remains, though much has been forgotten. The impressive fort still stands. Until recently it served as a prison, but today the town hopes to make it the centerpiece of a tourist economy. That effort has moved slowly. In 2011 only fifty-four people signed the fort's guest book, compared to the 64,000 who visited the better-known Cape Coast Castle just a few miles away. The Dutch Lodge, or Omanhen's Palace, once occupied by John Corrantee, still stands, and it is still occupied by the current holder of that office, who claims descent from Corrantee. Even Castle Brew still stands, though today it is known as aban kakraba, or Little Fort, and its builder is largely forgotten in Annamaboe today.

Important Terms, Names, and Places

Abra (also Abora, Abrah, Abura) Town located in the interior on the main trade route from Annamaboe to Kumase and regarded as the Fante political capital. Fante caboceers often met here to conduct the business of the confederation.

Accra Located in modern Ghana. First settled by the Ga in the fifteenth century. The English established Fort James there in the 1670s; also home to Fort Crevecour, a Dutch fort, and to Fort Christiansborg, a Danish fort. Conquered by the Akwamu in 1680, it remained an important slave-trading port.

Agah (also Agya, Egya, Aga, Agga, Aja) Village located one mile east of Annamaboe where the English first opened a factory in the 1670s.

Aggery beads Beads made of natural stones highly prized on the Gold Coast and considered to have sacred properties.

Agona Coastal kingdom on the Gold Coast. Defeated by the Akwamu in 1689. Winnebah Fort was located there.

Akans Ethnoliguistic group in modern southern Ghana, the western Volta region, Togo, and the Côte d'Ivoire. Includes the Fante, Asante, Denkyira, Assin, Wasa, and Abrons, among others.

Anker Liquid measure, ten and a half gallons.

Akim (also Akyem) Akan forest kingdom located on the lower Guinea coast between Akwamu and Denkyira and pressured by its larger rivals. Known as traders of gold, salt, and slaves. Led a coalition that defeated Akwamu in 1730. Defeated by Asante in 1742. Divided between eastern or Akyem Abuakwa and western or Akyem Bosume.

Akwamu Akan forest kingdom located on the lower Guinea coast competing to control the gold trade. A major power in the region, it expanded over the eastern Gold Coast and western Slave Coast. Exported gold, ivory, and, after the 1690s, slaves. Weakened by internal rebellion, it fell to a coalition led by Akyem in 1730.

Amanahia   Gold Coastal Akan kingdom. Site of the British Fort Apollonia. Conquered by the Asante in a war lasting from 1715 to 1721.

Amissa   Kidnapped from Annamaboe in 1776 by a Liverpool slave captain who hired him as a sailor. Sold into slavery in Jamaica, freed thanks to his family's efforts in a case heard by Lord Mansfield. Returned to Annamaboe in 1779.

Amoony Coomah   Succeeded John Corrantee as chief caboceer of Annamaboe, and almost certainly related to Corrantee along the female line. Later took the title of king of Fante.

Ando   Old Etsi kingdom incorporated into Fante early in the eighteenth century.

Aowin (Awomweye)   Gold Coast Akan kingdom. Conquered by Denkyira between 1686 and 1690 and a few years later by Asante. Important gold producer.

Apollonia (also Cape Apollonia)   Considered the western boundary of the Gold Coast, located near the modern boundary between the Côte d'Ivoire and Ghana. The British fought with the Dutch over it several times in the eighteenth century and built a fort here in 1768.

Apperley, John   Built the Plymouth Dockyards in England. Employed as an engineer in Madras, India, in 1749. Chief engineer overseeing the construction of Annamaboe Fort, he died of an illness there in 1753.

Aquamboo   See Akwamu.

Asantehene   Title of the Asante king.

Assin   Gold Coast Akan nation bounded on the north by Asante, on the south by Fante, on the west by Denkyira, and on the east by Akim. Conquered by Denkyira in the late seventeenth century and incorporated into the Asante Empire in the early eighteenth century.

Ball, Elias   Owner of several plantations along the Cooper River in South Carolina and nephew of Henry Laurens.

Bassi   Son of John Corrantee taken to France in the 1740s and celebrated as "Louis Bassi, Prince de Corrantryn." Later resided with Ludewig Ferdinand Rømer.

Bell, Charles   Began his career as captain of slave ships. Appointed interim governor of Cape Coast Castle from 1756 to 1757 and governor from 1761 to 1763. Chief of Commenda Fort in 1769 and of Annamaboe Fort in 1769. Died in England in 1785.

Bendefoe companies (also asafo companies)   Local militia companies in Fante towns. Command of these companies could be handed down from father to son, and membership in a specific company followed the patrilineal line, unusual in this matrilineal society.

Bloome, John   Chief of the RAC factory at Anashan in 1687 and chief at Annamaboe in 1691.

Bomboy   An African employed to supervise the loading and unloading of canoes and to maintain good order on the beaches at the Gold Coast forts. Occasionally a European filled this role. Also a foreman overseeing slaves.

Bonnishee   Influential caboceer in Annamaboe in the late seventeenth century.

Bosman, William   Born in Holland in 1672, he went to Africa at the age of sixteen in the service of the Dutch West India Company and spent fourteen years on the Gold Coast serving at various Dutch forts. His letters describing the region were first published in English in 1705.

Braffo   See Obrafo.

Brew, Henry (Harry)   Richard Brew's son from a country marriage with an unidentified African woman. Educated in England, he worked as a clerk in his father's business after his return to Annamaboe in 1768. He married Abba Kaybah, who was related to Philip Quaque along the female line. After his father's death, he moved to Cape Coast, where he became a successful linguist in the fort. He died of smallpox in 1796.

Brew, Richard, Sr.   Native of Ireland, arrived on the Gold Coast in 1745, became chief of Tantumquerry (Tantumkweri) Fort in 1750, served as chief of Dixcove Fort in 1750–1751, then resumed command at Tantumquerry from 1751 to 1754. Suspended in 1753 for illegal trading, he was reinstated with command at Annamaboe in 1756. He served in that capacity until 1760, when he resigned. He was reappointed in 1761 and served until 1764, when he left the CMTA to engage in private trade. He became the largest private slave dealer on the Gold Coast. He entered into a country marriage with John Corrantee's daughter Effua Ansah, who bore him two daughters. He had two sons from a previous country marriage. He died in Annamaboe in 1776.

Brew, Richard, Jr.   Richard Brew's son from a country marriage with an unidentified African woman. Educated in England, he worked as a clerk in his father's business after his return to Annamaboe in 1768. He fell out of favor with his father and was employed at Annamboe Fort as a gunner and at Cape Coast Castle in several capacities including as a writer, accountant, and personal secretary to the governor. Unable to hold onto his position there, he died having taken refuge with the Dutch at Elmina in 1782.

Brew, Samuel   Son of Henry Brew. Became an important trader at Cape Coast and continued to engage in the slave trade after the British abolished it. He was accused of leading British soldiers into an ambush during a campaign against the Asante. British authorities arrested him and sent him to Sierra Leone for trial, but he died under mysterious circumstances on board the ship, allegedly a suicide.

Caboceer (also **Cabushier)**   Derived from the Portuguese word *caboceiro* meaning captain. Fante official or chief who served as a political leader, magistrate, and military leader.

Camplin, Richard   Prominent London merchant and secretary of the African Committee in the 1770s.

Canoemen   Since ships could not dock at the Gold Coast ports but rather lay at anchor off the coast, highly skilled African canoemen ferried goods and people from the ships to the shore and back in canoes they carved from the silk-cotton tree *(Ceiba pentandra)*. They monopolized this business, and their position was inherited. They were indispensable to trade.

Cape Coast Castle   The largest British fort on the Gold Coast and the seat of operations for the RAC and the CMTA. Originally founded by the Swedes in 1655, it belonged to the Dutch and the Danes before the English captured it in 1664.

Cape Lopez   Forms the southern boundary of the Gulf of Biafra in modern-day Gabon, located at the mouth of the Ogowe River. An important slave-trading port in the late eighteenth and nineteenth centuries.

Chaignoan, Mr.   Chief of Annamaboe Fort in 1704.

Chamba (also **Duncos**)   The northeastern district of the Asante Empire and a source of slaves sold on the coast. Described as a peaceful agricultural people, the Fante called them Duncos, a derogatory term meaning an ignorant country person or stupid person.

Champlin, Christopher and Robert   Owners of a prominent family firm Champlin and Champlin in Newport, Rhode Island, engaged in the African trade. Robert began his career as a captain on slavers owned by his father and uncle.

Charles Fort   First English fort constructed at Annamaboe in 1679 and abandoned in 1730.

Chichee (also **Chicko**)   A messenger or public crier.

Clarke, Peleg   Began his career as a captain of ships owned by others, but became a merchant in his own right and formed a successful partnership with his brother, Audley Clarke. Their business including insuring slave voyages.

Coffee Aboe   Linguist at Annamaboe Fort in the 1760s.

Commenda (Comenda, Komenda)   Located east of Sekondi in the kingdom of Eguafo (Aguaffo), it was occupied off and on by the English from 1683. John Cabess was its most important trader-chief before his death in 1722. Most important for the trade in gold and provisions. The Dutch maintained a factory here.

Company of Merchants Trading to Africa   The African Trade Act of 1750 abolished the Royal African Company and replaced it with a new corporation carrying this name. The new law opened the trade to all British subjects, and those merchants who traded on the African coast between Cape Blanco and the Cape of Good Hope paid token dues to form this corporation.

Cormantine (Coramantine, Cormantyne, Kormantin)   Location of the first English fort built on the Gold Coast in 1624, captured by the Dutch in 1662. Three miles from Annamaboe.

Coromantees (Koromanti)   Name given to Fante slaves from the Gold Coast in high demand in the Americas.

Corrantee, John   (ca. 1670–1764). His Fante name was Eno Baisee (Ano Bassi) Kurentsi. Noted warrior, diplomat, magistrate, and merchant. Annamaboe's powerful chief caboceer from about 1740 until his death.

Country marriages   Formal relationships between British men and African or mixed-race women on the Gold Coast.

Cracra money   Small bits of adulterated gold, widely circulated on the Gold Coast as a medium of exchange.

Croom   Sometimes described as the center of a number of planation hamlets, a village where the plantation owners maintained their residences. Elite Fantes who lived in Annamaboe also owned plantations and maintained residences in their croom.

Cross, William   Chief of Annamaboe Fort in 1691.

Cugoano, Ottobah   A Fante native of the Gold Coast, captured as a boy and sold into slavery in 1770. He became an important African abolitionist in late eighteenth-century Britain and a friend of Olaudah Equiano. Author of an important antislavery tract called *Thoughts and Sentiments on the Evil and Wicked Traffic of the Slavery and Commerce of the Human Species, Humbly Submitted to the Inhabitants of Great Britain* (London, 1787).

Curranteer (Corrantier, Quarranter)   Fante title for the ruler of an individual town, more commonly used in the seventeenth century.

Dagomba   Kingdom in the middle Volta region with a strong Muslim influence. Conquered by the Asante in 1744–1745.

Dalziel, Archibald   A native of Scotland. Slave ship captain and owner, active in the trade for over forty years. Trained as a surgeon. Employed by the CMTA from 1763 to 1770 and 1791 to 1802. Chief of Whydah and governor of Cape Coast Castle in 1762, from 1762 to 1798, and from 1800 to 1802. Author of *A History of Dahomey* (London, 1762). His brother Andrew was a professor of Greek and literature at the University of Edinburgh.

Dancing custom   A payment made by the chief of Annamaboe Fort to the town to honor the Dancing Time, a festival of commemoration for the dead that took place in June or July.

Dashes (also **dashee**)   Gifts.

Del Rey   River at the eastern edge of the Niger River system. Merchants based along its banks were linked to the Efik slave-trading networks.

Denkyira (Dankera)   Akan forest kingdom located on the lower Guinea Coast competing to control the gold trade. Expanded rapidly in the seventeenth century when it conquered Aowin, Sefwi, and Wasa to the southwest and the coastal kingdoms of Adom and Fetu. Dominated much of the southwestern Gold Coast and part of what is today the Côte d'Ivoire. Fell to the Asante in a series of wars between 1699 and 1701.

Dixcove   One of the smallest British forts on the Gold Coast, built in 1691. Located fifty miles southwest of Cape Coast Castle in the Ahanta country.

Domeh   One of three small islands in Ambas Bay, Cameroons. Located where the West African coast meets the southern African coast.

Duncos   See Chamba.

Effua Ansah   Daughter of John Corrantee and country wife to Richard Brew. She bore him two daughters, Eleanor and Amba.

Eggin   A prominent caboceer in Annamaboe in the late sixteenth and early seventeenth centuries.

Elmina (El Mina)   The common name used for the famous fort called the Castle of S. Jorge da Mina, built by the Portuguese in 1482, the first European fort on the Guinea coast. Captured by the Dutch in 1637. It was the prototype for the European forts along the Gold Coast, most of which copied its medieval style long after it was abandoned in Europe.

Eukobah (also **Ekua)**   One of John Corrantee's principal wives. The daughter of Ansah Sessarakoo (Ansa Sasraku), king of Aquamboo (Akwamu), and niece of the king of Akron.

Factories   Trade outposts located in smaller towns and villages. These establishments often included only one European, who acted as factor and employed several Africans to assist him.

Fetish   From the Portuguese *feitiço,* or agent, the term embraced a complex set of religious beliefs and practices. To make fetish was to perform worship or cast a spell, to take fetish was to swear an oath, to drink or eat fetish was to drink water or swallow a substance made sacred by a priest that was believed to bring death to anyone who swore a falsehood during the ritual, and anything made in honor of a god was a fetish. Disputes were often resolved by eating or drinking fetish, and the method was used to judge guilt or innocence in trials.

Fetu   Coastal Akan Gold Coast state. Conquered by Denkyira in the late seventeenth century and by the Fante by 1730.

George Banishee   Son of John Corrantee and a trader at Annamaboe.

Gold-takers   Brokers in the slave trade on the Gold Coast. They weighed and deter-mined the purity of gold. They acted as middlemen between the African and European slave traders for any articles that changed hands between those parties including not only slaves but ivory, gold, or European trade goods. They took a percentage of the trade from both parties as a brokerage fee. They were numerous and influential.

Gonja   Kingdom on the middle Volta established in the late seventeenth century by the Mande. Influenced by the Muslims, but maintained a cultural mix. Conquered by the Asante between the 1730s and the 1750s.

Gore, Gerrard   Agent general at Cape Coast Castle in 1701, reappointed in 1714 and served until 1717, when he died on the coast.

Goree   Located on an island in modern Senegal, it became an important slave-trading post and changed hands among the Portuguese, Dutch, French, and British seventeen times from 1588 to 1814. France controlled it for much of the eighteenth century, and it was the primary port for the French slave trade.

Gregory, John   Chief at Annamaboe in 1691.

Grosle, John (also **Grossle)**   Chief of Annamaboe Fort in 1767–1768 and governor of Cape Coast Castle from 1769 to 1770. He died in office in 1770.

Ground rent   Sums that the Europeans paid to their African landlords to lease the land where their forts were located.

Hassell, Ralph   Factor at Accra in 1681. Chief of Annamaboe Fort forced out by the Fantes in 1787 and transferred to Fort Fredericksburg, located east of Cape Coast that same year.

Hippisley, John, (also **Hippersley)**   Governor of Cape Coast Castle from 1763 to 1766, he died in 1767. Son of a famous actor and comedian by the same name who spent much of his career at Covent Garden. He briefly followed his father on the stage, where he appeared as Tom Thumb in 1740. Author of *Essays. I. On the Populousness of*

Africa: II. On the Trade at the Forts on the Gold Coast. III. On the Necessity of Erecting a Fort at Cape Appolonia (London, 1764).

Hutchinson, William   First employed by the CMTA as a writer at Cape Coast Castle. He was a member of the first British embassy to the Asante in 1817, and spent months as the British consul in Kumasi. Chief of Annamaboe Fort in 1830. He later became a private trader on the coast. He died in his native Scotland in 1834 at the age of 41.

Huydecoper, Jan Pieter Theodoor (1728–1767)   Member of a prominent Amsterdam family, educated in Geneva, he was said to have come to Africa after being disappointed in love. Arrived in 1756, served as president of the Dutch fort of Elmina, but he was not successful there and was transferred to Axim in 1760. Director general and president of the Second West India Company from 1758 to 1760 and again from 1764 to 1767.

Interloper   English traders who violated the Royal African Company's monopoly on the African trade, which ended in 1698.

Isles De Los   Five islands located near the Rokel River at the northern border of Sierra Leone where the British maintained a factory. An important embarkation site for slaves and a frequent stop for ships sailing down the West Coast of Africa.

James Fort   Located in Accra on an island in the River Gambia, originally built by the Portuguese in the mid-1600s and occupied by the RAC and rebuilt in 1673.

Johnston, Robert   A former CMTA official in Senegal and on the Gold Coast who turned private trader at Winnebah. Left the coast after a 1770 fire destroyed his property.

Kumasi (Coomassie, Kumase)   Capital of the Asante Empire.

Lagoe   (Lagoo) Trading town located about two miles from Tantumquerry Fort and twenty-three miles east of Annamaboe.

Linguister, linguists   Translators employed in the forts and by the captains of ships on the Gold Coast.

Logoe (Port Loko)   First established by the Portuguese. Location of a British factory in the eighteenth century. North of Freetown in modern-day Sierra Leone.

Maccarthy, Sir Charles (1768–1824)   Native of Ireland. Joined the British army in 1794. Appointed to the Royal African Corps in 1811. Appointed governor of Sierra Leone in 1812 and first crown governor of the Gold Coast in 1822. Knighted in 1820, he died in a battle with the Asante, who took his head as a trophy.

Manigault, Gabriel   Vied with Nathaniel Russell for the title of Charleston's richest merchant. Invested his profits from trade, including the slave trade, into plantation agriculture. Owned almost 500 slaves and over 50,000 acres of land.

Mankessim   See Murram.

Melville, Thomas (also Melvil, Melvill)   Native of Dumfriesshire, Scotland, and distant relative of prominent London merchant Richard Oswald. Governor of Cape Coast Castle from 1750 to his death in 1756.

Meredith, Henry   Author of *An Account of the Gold Coast of Africa with a Brief History of the African Company* (London, 1812). Governor of Winnebah Fort. He was murdered by the Africans there in 1812 after a dispute over a box of gold dust. As a result, both the town and the fort were destroyed by the British.

Miles, Richard   Served with the CMTA on the Gold Coast for over eighteen years. Appointed a writer in 1765, he became Chief of several forts including Whydah, Tantumquerry, Apollonia, and Annamaboe before becoming governor of Cape Coast Castle from 1777 to 1780. He was suspended for carrying on illegal trade but was reinstated in 1782. While in London in the 1780s, he entered into a partnership to engage in the African trade with Jerome Bernard Weuves. Contemplated taking his country wife, Sal, back to England with him. Left the CMTA in 1792. Afterward a successful slave trader based in London, where he fought efforts to close the trade in the 1790s. One of few Europeans on the coast who learned the native language.

Miles, Thomas   Brother of Richard Miles. Began as a writer with the CMTA in the 1780s, governor of Annamaboe Fort (1789–1792). Suspended after the burning of Agah. Employed by the firm of Miles and Weuves, and operated a private factory at Little Popo from 1793 to 1796. He died there in 1796.

Mill, David   He spent sixteen years on the Gold Coast before becoming governor of Cape Coast Castle from 1770 to 1777. From a family with deep roots in the slave trade. His cousin was a partner of Richard Oswald, a prominent London merchant who contracted with the CMTA to supply its forts and who did business with CMTA officials on the coast. His brother was James Mill of the prominent London-based slave-trading firm of Ross & Mill, and another brother was Hercules Mill, the captain of slavers bound for the Gold Coast. He resigned his post and prepared to return to England but died en route on the island of Antigua.

Mitchell, Jeremiah   English soldier at Annamaboe in 1686–1687.

Mouree (Mouri, Moure)   Location of the first Dutch fort (called Fort Nassau) on the Gold Coast established in 1612. Four miles from Cape Coast. The most important center of Dutch trade on the Gold Coast.

Mulatto   The child of a European and an African.

Mumford (Montfort, Mountfort)   Located between Tantumquerry and Winnebah. The early Fante territory ended here. The Dutch built a fort here in 1725, but it fell into disuse. The British maintained a factory here in the eighteenth century.

Murram (also **Mankessim)**   Located in the interior about ten miles from the coast, the Fante regarded this town as their original settlement and their ancestral home, and they often gathered there to conduct important deliberations.

Mustafee   The child of a mustee and a European.

Mustee   The child of a mulatto and a European.

Mutter, William   Began his career as a surgeon's mate in 1752. Governor of Cape Coast Castle from 1763 to 1766. Dismissed for exporting slaves from the coast in violation of the CMTA's regulations.

Nananom Mpow   A sacred grove in the hills behind Annamaboe where the town's chief oracle resided.

Nightingale, James   Chief of Charles Fort in the 1690s.

Obrafo (Braffo)   The highest-ranking person in the Fante confederacy.

Old Calabar   Composed of several Efik towns located on the Cross River system in modern-day Nigeria. Major exporters of slaves in the eighteenth century.

Osei Bonsu (1799-1823)   Seventh Asantehene, enstooled in 1800. Under his capable leadership, the Asante expanded northward and then turned south in 1806-1807 after two rulers of Assin defied him. The Asante quickly overran the Fante state. The Asante achieved their long-held goal of reaching the sea, but those conquests brought them into conflict with the British.

Osei Kwadwo (1735-1777)   Fourth Asantehene. Reformer and capable military leader. Expanded the kingdom and helped strengthen the central government.

Ounce (oz.)   Used to measure units of exchange on the coast equivalent to the value of an ounce of gold, or about four pounds sterling.

Palaver   Formal means of settling disputes. Brought together all the parties involved, such as members of a household or extended family, individuals engaged in disputes over trade, and rival towns or nations. Most towns had a Palaver House where cases were heard and judged by the town's elders, or pynins. Trade often stopped during palavers, which could last for days, months, or even years.

Panyarring   A widespread practice on the Gold Coast whereby persons seized goods or people and held them until a dispute was resolved or payment was made. It could be used as a means of forcing a palaver. It differed from pawning in that this was not a mutual agreement but a seizure of goods by a creditor or by the aggrieved party in a dispute, and it was employed by both Africans and Europeans.

Pawning   An indigenous credit system adapted to the slave trade. African traders gave European merchants collateral, which could take the form of gold or other valuables or their own children, which European merchants held for a specified time to insure that a contract was fulfilled. If it was not, then the valuables were forfeited.

Pawns   Usually the sons of African traders who were held as collateral by European traders to insure the satisfaction of a contract. If the terms of the contract were not met, pawns were considered slaves.

Petrie, Gilbert   Spent sixteen years employed by the CMTA on the Gold Coast. Chief of Seccunde before becoming governor of Cape Coast Castle from 1766 to 1769. Alleged to have embezzled £7,000 from the company . After leaving the Gold Coast he became a planter in Tobago, where he became a prominent member of the Assembly. His brother John was among the strongest defenders of slavery in the House of Commons in the 1790s.

Phipps, James   From a family with longtime connections with the African trade. His cousin, Seth Grosvenor, served in Africa, and his father was engaged in the African trade. His older brother William served with the East India Company and became governor of Bombay. His younger brother Peter served as factor at Commenda and in other posts. He began his career in 1703 as a writer at Cape Coast and later as chief at Accra. Governor of Cape Coast Castle from 1711 to 1722. Prosecuted over seventy pirates, most of whom were executed at Cape Coast. He died on the coast in 1723.

Popo   A small state located around the Mono River on the Slave Coast. Its principal slave-trading ports were Great and Little Popo. There was a short-lived Dutch lodge at

Great Popo in 1680. Little Popo was said to have been established by emigrants from the Gold Coast.

Pynins (also **panyin**)   Elders or senior members of Fante society.

Quaque, Philip   Born about 1741 at Cape Coast into the extended family of Cudjoe Caboceer, he was one of three boys sent to London by Thomas Thompson in 1754 to be trained as missionaries. Appointed by the Society for the Propagation of the Gospel as missionary to the Gold Coast in 1765, he returned to Cape Coast in 1766. He held his position as missionary there until shortly before his death in 1816.

Quasah, George   Also known as My Lord or My Lord Augustus FitzRoy. Another of Corrantee's sons and his heir. Also an important merchant at Annamaboe.

Redwood, Jonas and William   Brothers, business partners, and prominent merchants in Newport, Rhode Island. Active in the slave trade in the second half of the eighteenth century. Their ship the *Cassada Garden* was named for the sugar plantation their father, Abraham, owned in Antigua before his move to New England in 1715.

Roberts, John   Chief of the British factory at Dixcove in 1750.

Rømer, Ludewig Ferdinand   Employed on the Gold Coast at Christiansborg Castle by the Danish West India and Guinea Company from 1739 to 1749. He published two accounts of his stay.

Ronan, William   Chief of Charles Fort in 1695.

Royal African Company.   A joint-stock company created in 1672 after the failure of the Royal Adventurers into Africa. Its charter gave it a license for trade lasting a thousand years. Among its provisions was one requiring the company to provide the English monarch with two elephants should he or she visit Africa. The first governor and largest shareholder was James, Duke of York. Its shareholders included royals, noblemen, merchants, and even the philosopher John Locke. It exported over 750,000 Africans to the Americas, and sent about 150,000 firearms to Africa every year. It lost its monopoly in 1698, and it was dissolved in 1750 when it was replaced by the Company of Merchants Trading to Africa.

Russell, Nathaniel   A native of Bristol, Rhode Island, he moved to Charleston, South Carolina, as a young man in 1765. Began as an agent for merchants in his native Rhode Island. He became one of the wealthiest, most prominent, and most successful merchants in the city, and slave trading was among his interests. His lavish mansion at 51 Meeting Street, built at a cost of $80,000, is regarded as the city's finest example of Federal architecture. He was a noted philanthropist and member of the Congregational Church.

Senior, Nassau   A prominent West Indian sugar planter and slave trader who become governor of Cape Coast Castle from 1767 to 1771.

Sessarakoo, William Ansah   The son of John Corrantee who was kidnapped and enslaved on the island of Granada before being taken to England and celebrated as the prince of Annamaboe. He worked as a writer at Cape Coast Castle before becoming an independent trader at Annamaboe.

Settling custom   A payment made to the town of Annamaboe at the appointment of a new chief of the fort.

Shaddo   British factory near Winnebah.

Smith, Horatio   Young cousin of Samuel Smith who Brew employed until a financial dispute drove them apart. He purchased Castle Brew after Brew's death but failed in his attempt to establish himself as a private trader. Employed by the CMTA, became governor of Annamaboe Fort, died in 1783.

Smith, John Hope   Became a writer at Cape Coast Castle at the age of fourteen. After winning commendation for his service during the Asante attack in 1806, he became chief of a fort. Governor of Cape Coast Castle from 1817 to 1822. He supported sending the first embassy to the Asante. He died in London in 1831.

Smith, Samuel   London merchant, partner in the firm Barton and Smith, and member of the Committee of the African Merchants Trading to Africa. He was elected to represent London and Bristol on that committee from 1756 to 1767. Formed partnership with Richard Brew sometime around 1764. Barton and Smith contracted with the CMTA to supply the committee's forts in Africa. Smith's financial troubles came to light in 1768 and ended in bankruptcy proceedings beginning in 1774, which almost ruined Brew's fortunes.

Snelgrave, William   Slave ship captain active in the trade from 1704 to 1734. Author of *A New Account of Some Parts of Guinea, and the Slave Trade* (London, 1734).

Stockwell, Richard   Governor of Cape Coast Castle 1749–1750.

Stubbs, Robert   Began his career as a slave ship captain in the 1750s. Appointed chief of Annamaboe Fort in 1780. With no previous experience on the coast, his tenure was a disaster. Suspended after his conflict with the Fante, he left the coast on board the notorious slave ship *Zong* in 1781. When the captain died, Stubbs took command of the ship and is implicated in the deaths of over 200 Africans who were thrown overboard during that voyage.

Swanzy, John   A native of Ireland. Appointed chief of Accra in 1804. Protested the sale of the Annamaboe people following the Asante invasion in 1806 and died a short time later of malaria.

Tantumquerry (Tantumkweri)   Small British fort located seventeen miles east of Cormantine on the Gold Coast near the Fante border with Agona.

Ten Percent Men   Changes to the RAC regulations in 1698 allowed any Englishman to trade in Africa upon payment of a ten percent duty on imports and exports, which gave these traders the name Ten Percent Men.

Thelwall, Richard   Chief of Annamaboe factory from 1681 to 1685.

Thomas, Sir Dalby   Governor of Cape Coast Castle from 1703 until his death in 1711. Previously in Barbados, where he made a fortune as a sugar planter. Author of *An Historical Account of the Rise and Growth of the West Indian Colonies* (London, 1690). Daniel Defoe dedicated his *Essay on Projects* (1697) to him.

Thomlinson, Trecothick and Co.   London firm involved in insuring slave voyages. Thomlinson was a native of Antigua; Trecothick was a British merchant who organized opposition to the Stamp Act. In 1762 the company became Trecothick, Apthorp and Thomlinson.

Thompson, Thomas   Dean at Oxford before becoming a missionary with the Society for the Propagation of the Gospel in Foreign Parts. Served in New Jersey from 1745 to 1751, then on the Gold Coast from 1751 or 1752 until 1756 as the first British missionary there.

Tom Coffee   Successful gold-taker in Annamaboe in the late eighteenth century who lost his fortune in an expensive palaver.

Torrane, George   Began his career in 1785 as a clerk for the CMTA and member of the Council from 1790 to 1792. Governor of Cape Coast Castle from 1805 to 1807. Promoted an alliance with the Asante. Sold Assin and Annamaboe captives off the coast. Died in office in 1807.

Trade languages   Languages spoken along the West African coast that combined European, especially Portuguese, words and African vocabulary. Spread across the Atlantic, where they are related to languages like Gullah, spoken in the South Carolina low country, and similar languages in the Caribbean.

Trinder, Thomas   Began his career as with the CMTA as overseer of works in the 1750s. Chief of several forts including Fort Appolonia in 1769, of Winnebah in 1770, and subsequently of Annamaboe and Accra. He died there in 1775, leaving an estate valued at over £7000.

Twifo (Twifu, Cuffero)   Inland Gold Coast Akan kingdom. Skilled traders who sold the best gold on the Gold Coast. Conquered by the Asante between 1713 and 1715.

Vernon, Samuel and William   Brothers, business partners, and prominent merchants in Newport, Rhode Island, active in the slave trade in the second half of the eighteenth century. Trading partners of Richard Brew.

Wasa (Warsaw, Wassa)   Gold Coast Akan kingdom. Expanded between 1630 and 1670, largely through peaceful means. Conquered by Denkyira between 1686 and 1690 then by Asante in the early eighteenth century.

Westgate, Thomas   Entered the CMTA's employ in 1751 with the backing of Samuel Smith. Chief of Dixcove in the 1750s, resigned as chief of Commenda Fort in 1760. After a stay in London, returned to the coast as an employee of Richard Brew's until poor health forced him to return to London. Reentered the CMTA's service in 1770. Forced to resign as chief of Annamaboe Fort in 1779.

Weuves, Jerome Bernard   Began his career as a writer at Cape Coast Castle and remained on the coast for fourteen years. May have come from one of the Dutch forts; identified in some sources as Swiss. One of the executors of Richard Brew's estate. Chief of Annamaboe Fort from 1773 to 1780. Governor of Cape Coast Castle from 1781 to 1782. Returned as chief of Annamaboe in 1782–1784 when he left for London. He married in that city in 1789 and opposed ending the slave trade in a petition signed that same year. Entered into a partnership with Richard Miles to engage in the African trade. He died in 1794.

White, Edward William   Began his employment with the CMTA on the coast in 1790, and was chief of Annamaboe Fort during the Asante invasion. Appointed governor of Cape Coast Castle upon the death of Governor Torrane in 1807. Advocated British annexation. Died in 1815 the day after he returned to his native Scotland from Africa.

Whydah Located in the Bight of Benin and called Ouidah by the French. Many nations maintained factories there, but the French were in a predominant position. Conquered by Dahomey in the 1720s.

Winnebah (Winneba) Location of a British fort on the Gold Coast about twelve miles east of Tantumquerry. A factory was established there in the 1670s but abandoned. Due to fears of a French effort to settle there, a fort was established in 1693. It was a part of the kingdom of Agona and a trade depot for the Akyem, located inland.

Yellow Joe Successful and influential gold-taker in Annamaboe in the late eighteenth century.

Notes

Introduction

1. J. Spencer Ewart, "Colonel Edward Hamilton of the Honourable East India Company's Service," *Blackwood's Magazine* 208 (December 1920), 773–774; Elizabeth Donnan, *Documents Illustrative of the History of the Slave Trade to America: Vol. II; The Eighteenth Century* (Washington, DC, 1931), 490–491.

2. Throughout the book I have used the names for people and places most common in the early modern British Atlantic World rather than the contemporary usage.

3. Ruth Fisher, "Extracts from the Records of the African Companies," pt. 4, *Journal of Negro History* 13 (July 1928): 372 (first quotation); Richard Miles to James Boyle French, n.d. [February 1773], Public Records Office (PRO), National Archives, Kew, United Kingdom, T70/1482 (second quotation).

4. Fernand Braudel, *The Mediterranean and the Mediterranean World in the Age of Philip II* (New York, 1972), 662.

5. Paul Gilroy, *The Black Atlantic: Modernity and Double Consciousness* (Cambridge, MA, 1993).

1. Annamaboe Joins the Atlantic World

1. George D. Winius, "The Enterprise Focused on India: The Work of D. Joao II," in *Portugal, the Pathfinder: Journeys from the Medieval toward the Modern World, 1300– ca. 1600,* ed. George D. Winius (Madison, WI, 1995), 89–120 (first quotation, p. 92); John Vogt, *Portuguese Rule on the Gold Coast, 1469–1682* (Athens, GA, 1979), 21–59, 89.

2. W. E. F. Ward, *A History of the Gold Coast* (London, 1948), 72–87; John Thornton, *Africa and Africans in the Making of the Atlantic World, 1400–1680* (Cambridge, 1992), 64–71. See also Ray A. Kea, *Settlements, Trade, and Polities in the Seventeenth Century Gold Coast* (Baltimore, MD, 1982); Harvey M. Feinberg, "Africans and Europeans in West Africa: Elminians and Dutchmen on the Gold Coast during

the Eighteenth Century," *Transactions of the American Philosophical Society,* n.s., vol. 79 (1989): 1–155.

3. David P. Henige, *The Chronology of Oral Tradition: Quest for a Chimera* (1974; repr., Westport, CT, 1987), 147–149 (first and second quotations on p. 147); Vogt, *Portuguese Rule,* 178–179; Ray A. Kea, "City-State Culture on the Gold Coast: The Fante City-State Federation in the Seventeenth and Eighteenth Centuries," in *A Comparative Study of Thirty City-State Cultures: An Investigation,* ed. Mogens Herman Hansen (Kgl., 2000), 519–529 (quotation on p. 524); Kea, *Settlements, Trade, and Polities,* 38, 133; Rebecca Shumway, *The Fante and the Transatlantic Slave Trade* (Rochester, NY, 2011), 72; Robin Law, ed., *The English in West Africa, 1691–1699: The Local Correspondence of the Royal African Company of England, 1681–1699,* pt. 3 (Oxford, 2006), 277 (quotation).

4. Feinberg, "Africans and Europeans," 53, 55–58, 63; Law, *English in West Africa,* 3:277; Herbert S. Klein, *Atlantic Slave Trade* (Cambridge, MA, 2010), 59; Richard Miles to William Bourke, 31 January 1773, Public Records Office (PRO), National Archives, Kew, United Kingdom, T70/1482 (quotation).

5. Alfred W. Crosby Jr., *The Columbian Exchange: Biological and Cultural Consequences of 1492* (Westport, CT, 1972), 64; Law, *English in West Africa,* 3:277 (first quotation); James McCann, "Maize and Grace: History, Corn, and Africa's New Landscapes, 1500–1999," *Comparative Studies in Society and History* 43 (April 2001): 248–254; Henry Meredith, *An Account of the Gold Coast of Africa with a Brief History of the African Company* (London, 1812), 213 (second quotaton).

6. Law, *English in West Africa,* 3:284, 285 (first quotation), 287, 313, 354; Stanley B. Alpern, "What Africans Got for Their Slaves: A Master List of European Trade Goods," *History in Africa* 22 (1995): 12–13, 16–17.

7. Kea, *Settlements, Trade, and Polities,* 97–205; Robin Law, ed., *The English in West Africa, 1685–1688: The Local Correspondence of the Royal African Company of England, 1681–1699,* pt. 2 (Oxford, 2001), 192 (first quotation), 193 (second quotation), 195, 198, 199; Ludewig Ferdinand Rømer, *A Reliable Account of the Coast of Guinea (1760),* trans. Selena Axelrod Winsnes (Oxford, 2000), 140. Asante soldiers carried small bags of meal by their sides and mixed it with water with their hands to avoid building cooking fires that might expose them to the enemy.

8. Some scholars have argued that the Fante were weak and disunited, but I follow James Sanders, who sees the Fante in this period as "undergoing a constructive process of political evolution." See James Sanders, "The Expansion of the Fante and the Emergence of Asante in the Eighteenth Century," *Journal of African History* 20 (1979): 349–364 (quotation on p. 350); William Bosman, *Description of the Coast of Guinea: Divided into the Gold, the Slave and the Ivory Coasts* (London, 1967), 35, 56–57; Law, *English in West Africa,* 2:154n5, 181 (quotation); 3:357–59; Shumway, *Fante,* 183n105; Henige, *Chronology of Oral Tradition,* 149–151.

9. Law, *English in West Africa,* 2:xiv, 154 (first quotation), 156, 176, 177 (second and third quotations), 184 (fourth quotation); 3:342, 367, n. 232; Henige, *Chronology of Oral Tradition,* 149–151.

10. Law, *English in West Africa,* 2:154 (first quotation), 155 (second and third quotations), 156 (fourth quotation), 160.

11. Ibid., 161 (first quotation), 162 (second quotation), 163, 164 (fourth, fifth, and sixth quotations). On palavers see Philip M. Peek and Kwesi Yankah, *African Folklore: An Encyclopedia* (New York and London, 2004), 663 (third quotation); Joseph Corry, *Observations upon the Windward Coast of Africa: The Religion, Character, Customs &c., of the Natives; with a System Upon Which They May Be Civilized, and a Knowledge Attained of the Interior of this Extraordinary Quarter of the Globe; and Upon the Natural and Commercial Resources of the Country: Made in the Years 1805 and 1806* (London, 1807), 42, 43, 48, 58, 59, 67, 70, 127; Robert Smith, "Peace and Palaver: International Relations in Pre-Colonial West Africa," *Journal of African History* 14, (1973): 599–621; Rømer, *Reliable Account,* 165.

12. Rømer, *Reliable Account,* 185–187 (quotation on p. 185).

13. Thomas Phillips, "A Journal of a Voyage Made in the Hannibal of London, Ann. 1664, 1664," in *Collection of Voyages and Travels: Some Now First Printed from Original Manuscripts, Others Translated Out of Foreign Languages, and Now First Published in English,* ed. Awnsham Churchill (London, 1745), 208; Bosman, *Description,* 211 (third quotation); John Adams, *Remarks on the Country Extending from Cape Palmas to the River Congo* (London, 1823), 42; Meredith, *Account of the Gold Coast,* 107 (first quotation), 109 (second quotation). Bosman agreed that the bride charge usually included "a little Gold, Wine, Brandy, and Sheep for the Relations, and new Cloaths for the Bride," along with the expenses of the wedding celebration. Bosman, *Description,* 198; Rømer, *Reliable Account,* 183, 185.

14. Meredith, *Account of the Gold Coast,* 233 (first quotation); Mrs. R. Lee, *Stories of Strange Lands* (London, 1895), 194–195 (second quotation on p. 195). Thomas Thompson baptized many mulatto children and made most of his converts among mulattoes during his stay on the Gold Coast. See Thomas Thompson, *An Account of Two Missionary Voyages By the Appointment of the Society for the Propagation of the Gospel in Foreign Parts* (London, 1758), 30, 32, 34, 53–54, 62, 74. For information on mixed-race marriages in other areas along the West Coast of Africa, see George Brooks, *EurAfricans in Western Africa: Commerce, Social Status, Gender and Religious Observance from the Sixteenth to the Eighteenth Century* (Athens, OH, 2003); Peter Mark, *"Portuguese" Style and Luso-African Identity: Precolonial Senegambia, Sixteenth–Nineteenth Centuries* (Bloomington, IN, 2002); Michael Marcson, "European and African Interaction in the Pre-Colonial Period: Saint Louis du Senegal, 1758–1854" (PhD. diss., Princeton University, 1976); Hilary Jones, "From Mariage a la Mode to Weddings at Town Hall: Marriage, Colonialism, and Mixed-Race Society in Nineteenth-Century Senegal," *International Journal of African Historical Studies* 38 (2005): 27–48. On African Creoles, see Ira Berlin, "From Creole to African: Atlantic Creoles and the Origins of African-American Society in Mainland North America," *William and Mary Quarterly,* 3rd ser., 53 (1996): 254.

15. Law, *English in West Africa,* 2:197 (first and second quotations), 217 (third and fourth quotations), 377; 3:377 (fifth quotation).

16. Phillips, "A Journal of a Voyage," 205 (first quotation); Rømer, *Reliable Account,* 232–234. Nightingale complained that a Doctor Wolber, who was trading with the blacks at Annamaboe, "puts more confidence in a Black man then in a White." Law, *English in West Africa,* 2:233. Gerrard Gore, chief of Annamaboe fort, faced a mutiny when he tried to interfere with the soldiers trading in town. Law, *English in West Africa* 3:377–378.

17. Law, *English in West Africa,* 3:174 (first and second quotations), 175 (third quotation), 176 (fourth quotation), 177.

18. Ibid., 189 (first quotation), 190 (second quotation), 192–193, 195, 196 (third quotation); Rømer, *Reliable Account,* 16, 89–109; William Pietz, "The Problem of the Fetish," *RES: Anthropology and Aesthetics* (1985): 5–17; Acts of Council, 12 October, 1780, PRO T70/152.

19. Thompson, *An Account,* 51 (first quotation), 60–63; William Bosman, *A New and Accurate Description of the Coast of Guinea* (1705; repr., London., 1967), 147–60; Shumway, *Fante,* 134–144; Rømer, *Reliable Account,* 16, 89–109; Pietz, "Fetish," 5–17; Ruth Fisher, "Abstract from the Minutes Kept by W. Charlest on Bence Island from April, 1727, May 20, 1727," in "Extracts from the Records of the African Companies," pt. 2, *Journal of Negro History* 13 (July 1928): 336.

20. Law, *English in West Africa,* 2:196 (first quotation), 203 (second quotation), 204 (third quotation), 205, 207 (fourth quotation), 212, (fifth quotation).

21. Ibid., 212.

22. James Arnold, "Some Particulars of a Voyage to Guinea," in *House of Commons Sessional Papers of the Eighteenth Century,* ed. Shelia Lambert (Wilmington, DE, 1975), 69:52.

23. On pawning see Paul E. Lovejoy, "Pawnship and Seizure for Debt in the Process of Enslavement in West Africa," in Gwyn Campbell and Alessandro Stanziani, eds., *Debt and Slavery in the Mediterranean and Atlantic Worlds* (London, 2013), 63–91; Paul E. Lovejoy and David Richardson, "The Business of Slaving: Pawnship in Western Africa, c. 1600–1810," *Journal of African History* 42 (2001): 67–89; Toyin Falola and Paul E. Lovejoy, eds., *Pawnship in Africa: Debt Bondage in Historical Perspective* (Boulder, CO, 1994); Paul E. Lovejoy, *Transformations in Slavery: A History of Slavery in Africa* (Cambridge, 2000), 109–110, 117–118, 176–182; Thomas Clarkson, *An Essay on the Slavery and Commerce of the Human Species, & Particularly the African* (London, 1788), 27–28; Randy J. Sparks, "Gold Coast Merchant Families, Pawning, and the Eighteenth-Century English Slave Trade," *William and Mary Quarterly,* 3rd ser., 70 (April 2013): 317–340.

24. Law, *English in West Africa,* 2:212 (first quotation); Fisher, "Extracts," 2:326.

25. Law, *English in West Africa,* 2:212 (quotations).

26. Law, *English in West Africa,* 2:210 (quotation), 260–261. The bendefoes blocked John Gregory from the Annamaboe fort in 1691 under similar circumstances, and he feared the same treatment that Nightingale had received. Law, *English in West Africa,* 3:285–286 See also 365, 468, 474. Even some Englishmen blamed their countrymen inside the fort for the problems. Independent traders reported in 1709 to the RAC that "the Company have had Differences with the Natives inhabiting near their owne Factorys, and that some of their Factorys particularly

Anambo [Annamabo] and Commenda have been insulted by the Natives, but
they say these difference were occasioned by the Company's usage and bad
Treatment of them in Trade, and sometimes by joining with one Prince to depose
others (which last mentioned Fact the Company have admitted)." Elizabeth Donnan, *Documents Illustrative of the History of the Slave Trade to America: Vol. II;
The Eighteenth Century* (Washington, DC, 1931), 57.

27. Law, *English in West Africa*, 2:213 (first quotation), 214 (second, third, fourth, and
fifth quotations), 213 (sixth quotation), 216 (seventh quotation).

28. Ibid., 176.

29. Law, *English in West Africa*, 3:278–290, 293, 295, 339.

30. Ibid., 278–290, 293, 295, 339 (first quotation on p. 285, second quotation on p. 286,
third quotation on p. 290, fourth and fifth quotations on p. 289). On panyarring,
see Shumway, *Fante*, 59–60; Lovejoy, "Pawnship and Seizure."

31. Law, *English in West Africa*, 3:290–293 (first, second, third, fourth, and fifth quotations on p. 290; sixth quotation on p. 293; seventh quotation on p. 290; eighth and
ninth quotations on p. 291).

32. Ibid., 303 (first quotation), 351 (second quotation); Fisher, "Extracts," 1:310–311.

33. Rømer, *Reliable Account*, 67; Shumway, *Fante*, 74, 183–184n109; Gomer Williams,
*History of the Liverpool Privateers and Letters of Marque with an Account of the
Liverpool Slave Trade* (London, 1897), 466–470; David Eltis, "The Volume and
Structure of the Transatlantic Slave Trade: A Reassessment," *William and Mary
Quarterly*, 3rd ser., LVIII (January 2001): 33, 34 (third quotation).

2. John Corrantee and Slave-Trade Diplomacy at Annamaboe

1. David P. Henige, *The Chronology of Oral Tradition: Quest for a Chimera* (Oxford,
1974), 150–151. On the Fante in this period see James Sanders, "The Expansion of
the Fante and the Emergence of Asante in the Eighteenth Century," *Journal of African History* 20 (1979): 349–364.

2. *The Royal African: or, Memoirs of the Young Prince of Annamaboe. Comprehending
a Distinct Account of His Country and Family; His Elder Brother's Voyage to France,
and Reception There; the Manner in Which Himself Was Confided by His Father to
the Captain Who Sold Him; His Condition While a Slave in Barbadoes; the True
Cause of His Being Redeemed; His Voyage from Thence; and Reception Here in England. Interspers'd throughout with Several Historical Remarks on the Commerce of
the European Nations, whose Subjects Frequent the Coast of Guinea. To which Is
Prefixed a Letter from the Author to a Person of Distinction, in Reference to Some
Natural Curiosities in Africa; As Well As Explaining the Motives which Induced Him
to Compose These Memoirs* (London, 1750). 25. Corrantee's years in power marked
the high point of the slave trade from the Gold Coast. See David Eltis, "The Volume
and Structure of the Transatlantic Slave Trade: A Reassessment," *The William and
Mary Quarterly*, 3rd ser., 58 (January, 2001): 44.

3. Melville to AC, 11 July 1751, Public Records Office (PRO), National Archives, Kew,
United Kingdom, T70/29.

4. Stockwell to Board of Trade, 23 July 1751, PRO CO 388/45.

5. *Royal African*, 24.

6. On the Gold Coast slave trade see John Vogt, *Portuguese Rule on the Gold Coast, 1469–1682* (Athens, GA, 1979); Ray A. Kea, *Settlements, Trade, and Polities in the Seventeenth Century Gold Coast* (Baltimore, MD, 1982); Stephen D. Behrendt, "'The Journal of an African Slaver,'1789–1792, and the Gold Coast Slave Trade of William Collow," *History in Africa* 22 (1995): 61–71; William St. Clair, *The Door of No Return: The History of Cape Coast Castle and the Atlantic Slave Trade* (New York, 2006); Robin Law, ed., *The English in West Africa, 1685–1688: The Local Correspondence of the Royal African Company of England, 1681–1699*, pt. 2 (Oxford, 2001); Ty M. Reese, "Eating Luxury: Fante Middlemen, British Goods, and Changing Dependencies on the Gold Coast, 1750–1821," *William and Mary Quarterly*, 3rd ser., LXVI (October 2009): 853–872; Kwame Yeboa Daaku, *Trade and Politics on the Gold Coast, 1600–1720: A Study of the African Reaction to European Trade* (Oxford, 1970).

7. David Northrup, *Africa's Discovery of Europe, 1450–1850* (Oxford, 2009), 55, 57.

8. Since inheritance among the Fante was matrilineal, it is also possible that the man Corrantee refers to as his father may have been his uncle. Corrantee lived until 1764, and the 1670s date for his birth is probably too early since it is unlikely that he lived to be over 90 years old. Still, a birth date somewhere in the late seventeenth century seems appropriate. Thomas Thompson, *An Account of Two Missionary Voyages By the Appointment of the Society for the Propagation of the Gospel in Foreign Parts* (London, 1758), 47. See Robin Law, ed., *The English in West Africa, 1691–1699. The Local Correspondence of the Royal African Company of England, 1681–1699*, pt. 3 (Oxford, 2001), 290, 291, 297, 333, 341, 354.

9. Ruth Fisher, "Abstract of M. Roulles' Letter to Mr. Ruysieulx—July 24, 1751—Gold Coast," in "Extracts from the Records of the African Companies," pt. 3, *Journal of Negro History* 13 (July 1928): 361; Melville to AC, 14 March 1753, PRO T70/30. Law, *English in West Africa*, 3:372n256.

10. Dalby Thomas to RAC, 20 & 21 September 1705, PRO T70/5.

11. Fisher, "Extracts," 3:353.

12. Thompson, *An Account*, 48.

13. Ibid., 198–199, 211.

14. Ludewig Ferdinand Rømer, *A Reliable Account of the Coast of Guinea (1760)*, trans. Selena Axelrod Winsnes, (Oxford, 2000), 164 (first quotation), 176 (second quotation).

15. Margaret Priestley, *West African Trade and Coast Society: A Family Study* (London, 1969), 12. Priestley notes that Corrantee's position as military captain generally went to the eldest son and probably was tied to the patrilineal military companies she called *asafu*, referred to in other sources as *asafo* or *bendefoes*. These companies continue to play an important role in the cultural and social life in Annamaboe. See Ibid., 15; Law, *English in West Africa*, 2:xiv, 210; Rebecca Shumway, *The Fante and Transatlantic Trade* (Rochester, NY, 2011), 125–127, 144–145.

16. Law, *English in West Africa*, 2:267, 373; Rømer, *Reliable Account*, 118–124; Mark R. Lipschutz and R. Kent Rasmussen, *Dictionary of African Historical Biography*

(Berkeley, CA, 1989), 5, 12, 16; Priestley, *West African Trade,* 14; Henige, *Chronology of Oral Tradition,* 152–153.

17. Thompson, *An Account,* 46.
18. John Joseph Crooks, *Records Relating to the Gold Coast Settlements from 1750 to 1874* (London, 1973), 19. On Europeans employing Africans against their enemies see Robin Law, "The Komenda Wars, 1694–1700: A Revised Narrative," *History in Africa* 34 (2007): 138–141, 145–147, 152–157; Sanders, "Expansion of the Fante," 350.
19. Sanders, "Expansion of the Fante," 350, 352.
20. Quoted in ibid., 356.
21. Ibid., 356.
22. Elizabeth Donnan, *Documents Illustrative of the History of the Slave Trade to America: Vol. II; The Eighteenth Century* (Washington, DC, Carnegie Institute of Washington, 1931), 489 (quotation); Board of Trade, *Journal of the Commissioners for Trade and Plantations from January 1749–1750 to December 1753* (London, 1932), 272 (quotation); Sanders, "Expansion of the Fante," 358.
23. William Bosman, *A New and Accurate Description of the Coast of Guinea* (1705; repr., London, 1967), 132.
24. Thompson, *An Account,* 47–48.
25. Donnan, *History of the Slave Trade,* 2:237; Law, *English in West Africa,* 2:174–175; Fisher, "Extracts," 3:362.
26. M. Bwhe (?) to CCC, 24 March 1750, PRO T70/68.
27. Melville's letter reproduced in Vincent Caretta and Ty M. Reese, eds., *The Life and Letters of Philip Quaque: The First African Anglican Missionary* (Athens, GA, and London, 2010), 189.
28. Thomas Tinder to AC, 17 July 1767, PRO T70/31.
29. Rømer, *Reliable Account,* 179; Great Britain. Parliament. House of Commons. Select Committee Appointed to Take the Examination of Witnesses Respecting the African Slave Trade, *An Abstract of the Evidence Delivered Before a Select Committee of the House of Commons, in the Years 1790 and 1791, on the Part of the Petitioners for the Abolition of the Slave Trade* (New York, 1855), 27.
30. Rømer, *Reliable Account,* 178–179.
31. Ibid., 178.
32. Tobias Lesle to AC, 16 September 1756, PRO T70/30.
33. Sheila Lambert, ed., *House of Commons Sessional Papers of the Eighteenth Century* (Wilmington, DE, 1975), 73:206.
34. Bell to AC, 16 June 1762, PRO T70/31.
35. Charles Bell to AC, 12 May 1762, PRO T70/31.
36. Thomas Buckeridge to AC, 27 February 1693/4; Law, *English in West Africa,* 3:24–25.
37. In the 1780s the chief linguist at Cape Coast Castle received a salary of £100 per annum. Priestley, *West African Trade,* 16–17, 19.
38. Buckeridge to RAC, 27 February 1693/4.
39. On the French in Senegal see James F. Searing, *West African Slavery and Atlantic Commerce: The Senegal River Valley, 1700–1860* (Cambridge, 1993).

40. Fisher, "Abstract of M. Roules' Letter to Mr. Ruysieulx—July 24, 1751—Gold Coast," in "Extracts," 3:361.

41. Fisher, "Messrs. Roberts & Co to the Commanding Officers of the French Vessels off Cormantine & Amissa Dated Cape Coast Castle 22 febry 1750," in "Extracts," 3:346.

42. Fisher, "Abstract of M. Roules' Letter to Mr. Ruysieulx—July 24, 1751—Gold Coast," in "Extracts," 3:361.

43. Rømer, *Reliable Account,* 65–69.

44. Elizabeth Donnan, *Documents Illustrative of the History of the Slave Trade to America: Vol. I; 1441–1700* (Washington, DC, 1931), 28.

45. Ibid., 28–29.

46. Rømer, *Reliable Account,* 68.

47. Quoted in Madge Dresser, *Slavery Obscured: The Social History of the Slave Trade in an English Provincial Port* (London and New York, 2001), 63.

48. He "was received with all the Honours due to a Prince; he was not only cloathed [sic], lodged, maintained, and attended, but educated in all Respects in a Manner suitable to one of that Dignity; and as such was received and treated at Court, where he appeared on all Occasions in a splendid Dress, and was allowed to wear a Knot upon his right Shoulder. . . . He was . . . highly pleased to see his Son safe returned to *Africa,* and to hear what mighty Honours had been paid him in *Europe*." *Royal African,* 30–31.

49. Rømer, *Reliable Account,* 69.

50. Ibid., 37, 68. See the *Gentleman's Magazine* 19 (1749), 89, 3a2. Corrantee reportedly had thirty to forty sons living with him at this time.

51. *Royal African,* 42–45.

52. Danby Pickering, *The Statutes at Large from the 23d to the 26th Year of George II,* vol. XX (Cambridge, 1765), 120. Slave traders knew that they could be prosecuted for kidnapping. When James Fraser, a British slave trader, encountered a French captain and crew who planned to kidnap pawns and sell them in the West Indies, he "remonstrated against the impropriety and injustice of it . . . [and] assured them that the Chamber of Commerce in France, and the African Company in England, would prosecute him and his Officers for so doing." Lambert, *House of Commons Sessional Papers,* 71:15. The AC was eager to prosecute traders who violated the law. They condemned the "wicked & foolish behavior of separate Traders in the River [Gambia], who are often ye Cause of these Differences," and notified their officers on the Gold Coast that although "it is not in our Power to call them to immediate Acct., but upon proper Proofs of the Proceedings being sent home, we shall make it our Business to get them dismissed from their Employ & if not otherwise Punished." Poirier to Tobias Lesle, 26 November 1757, PRO T70/29. For very early examples of Europeans kidnapping African elites see Northrup, *Africa's Discovery,* 3–11; Linda Heywood, "Slavery and its Transformation in the Kingdom of Kongo, 1491–1800," *Journal of African History* 50 (2009), 6. For examples from the Gold Coast in this period see Fisher, "Extracts," 3:355, 356, 358; Randy J. Sparks, "Gold Coast Merchant Families, Pawning, and the Eighteenth-Century English Slave Trade," *William and Mary Quarterly,* 3rd. ser., 70 (April 2013): 317–340.

53. Fisher, "Roberts, 4 Dec. 1749," in "Extracts" 3:347 (quotation). Voyage 27205, Voyages Database, The Trans-Atlantic Slave Trade Database. http://www.slavevoyages .org (accessed December 30, 2011).

54. *Royal African,* 47–51.

55. On the press coverage of the emotional scene see the *Gentleman's Magazine* 19(1749), 89–90. On the history of the play see Jane Spencer, *Aphra Behn's Afterlife* (Oxford, 2000).

56. *The Scots Magazine* 11 (June 1749) 299.

57. Helen Wrigley Toynbee and Paget Jackson Toynbee, *The Letters of Horace Walpole: Fourth Earl of Orford,* vol. 2 (London, 1903), 367.

58. Walpole quoted in George F. E. Rude, *Hanoverian London, 1714–1808* (Berkeley, CA, 1971), 44–45.

59. *Gentleman's Magazine,* vol. xx (1750).

60. John Nichols and Samuel Bentley, *Literary Anecdotes of the Eighteenth Century,* vol. 1 (London, 1812), 658.

61. *Gentleman's Magazine* 19 (1749), 522.

62. Willie Sypher, "The African Prince in London," *Journal of the History of Ideas* 2 (April 1941): 237–247 (quotation on p. 244). See also Gretchen Garzina, *Black London: Life Before Emancipation* (New Brunswick, NJ, 1995), 11–14; Willie Sypher, *Guinea's Captive Kings: British Anti-Slavery Literature of the XVIIth Century* (New York, 1969), 59, 166–167; David Brion Davis, *The Problem of Slavery in Western Culture* (Oxford, 1988), 472–482; Randy J. Sparks, *The Two Princes of Calabar: An Eighteenth-Century Atlantic Odyssey* (Cambridge, MA, and London, 2004), 119–120. Barry Weller, "The Royal Slave and the Prestige of Origins," *The Kenyon Review,* n.s., 14 (Summer, 1992): 65–78; Laura Brown, *Fables of Modernity: Literature and Culture in the English Eighteenth Century* (Ithaca, NY, and London, 2001), 177–220.

63. David Brion Davis, *The Problem of Slavery in the Age of Revolution, 1770–1823* (Ithaca, NY, 1975), 47.

64. Fisher, "John Roberts to Henry LaSalles, 23 March 1750," in "Extracts," 3:347–349.

65. Fisher, "Copy of a Letter from Messrs. Robert, Husbands and Boteler to Mr. Clifton at Annamaboe, 22 Feb. 1749," in "Extracts," 3:344–45.

66. John Newton, *The Journal of a Slave Trader (John Newton), 1750–1754* (London, 1962), 19.

67. J. Spencer Ewart, "Colonel Edward Hamilton of the Honourable East India Company's Service," *Blackwood's Magazine* 208 (December 1920), 773–774. In 1753 Governor Engman, at the Danish Fort Christiansborg requested that "6 hats with *point d'Espange* and beautiful white feathers in them" be sent as gifts for the "King *of Assiante, Aquamboe* and *Ackim* Caboceers." All these were in the same region as Annamaboe. Ole Justesen, *Danish Sources for the History of Ghana, 1657–1754,* vol. 30(1), (Kgl., 2005), 892. Archibald Dalziel, who served as governor of British forts at Whydah and Cape Coast Castle, noted the importance of dress as a signifier of status in his discussion of the kingdom of Dahomey. "The head is usually covered with a beaver or felt hat," Dalziel wrote, "according to the quality of the wearer. The

king, as well as some of his ministers, often wears a gold or silver laced hat, and feather." Archibald Dalziel, "Religion, Government, Manners and Character of the Dahomans," *The New Annual Register or General Repository of History, Politics, and Literature* (1795), 89. I am grateful to Sarah Purcell for her insights into how the stripping of William Ansah might be interpreted as a ceremony of reintegration.

68. Bosman, *New and Accurate Description,* 119–120. The clothes William Ansah wore on this occasion are similar to those worn by "a man of fashion going into society in town in the early years of George III's reign." On clothing see Lady Alice Frances Lindsay Archer Houblon, *The Houblon Family: Its Story and Times,* vol. 2 (1907), 83–84. See also Aileen Ribeiro, *Dress in Eighteenth-Century Europe, 1715–1789* (New Haven, 2002).

69. *The British Chronologist: Comprehending Every Material Occurrence, Ecclesiastical, Civil, or Military, Relative to England and Wales, from the Invasion of the Romans to the Present Time,* vol. 3 (1775), 100; William Ansah Sessarakoo to Lord Halifax, 20 February 1752, PRO CO 388/45.

70. Melville to AC, 11 July 1751, PRO T70/29.

71. He wrote, Corrantee "takes great Notice of him, and his Behaviour & the Countenance of the People here get him the respect from the Blacks." Crooks, *Records Relating to the Gold Coast,* 20.

72. Melville to AC, 14 March 1752, PRO T70/29.

73. Ibid.

74. Shumway, *The Fante and the Transatlantic Slave Trade,* 78–81. Melville to AC, 30 October 1752, PRO T70/29. In 1753 the House of Commons allocated £6,000 to rebuild the fort at Annamaboe. When the HMS *Glory* arrived at Cape Coast Castle in 1752, Melville thought a display of power might be in order, so he sent the ship to Annamaboe where its captain, George Cockburn, attended by Quasah and William Ansah, raised the British flag over the site of the old fort. *The Universal Magazine,* vol. 12–13 (October 1753), 168.

75. David Hancock, *Citizens of the World: London Merchants and the Integration of the British Atlantic Community, 1735–1785* (Cambridge, 1995), 182–185.

76. Board of Trade, *Journal of the Commissioners, January 1749–1750 to December 1753,* 1–35.

77. Hancock, *Citizens of the World,* 183–185.

78. Board of Trade, *Journal of the Commissioners, January 1749–1750 to December 1753,* 94, 217, 259–260, 262–263, 264, 272, (quotations on p. 259).

79. Ibid., 272.

80. William Ansah Sessarakoo to Lord Halifax, 20 February 1752, PRO CO 388/45.

81. Ibid.; Board of Trade to Melville, n.d. 1752 (?), PRO CO 388/45.

82. William Ansah Sessarakoo to Lord Halifax, 20 February 1752, PRO CO 388/45.

83. Fisher, "Abstract of M. Roulles' Letter to Mr. Ruysieulx—July 24, 1751—Gold Coast" in "Extracts," 3:361.

84. Ibid. (second quotation); Melville to AC, 14 March 1752, PRO T70/29 (remaining quotations).

85. Melville to AC, 14 March 1752, PRO T70/29.

86. Owen's journal extracted in "The 18th century slave trade," accessed March 12, 2012, http://englishdemocrat.blogspot.com/2007/03/18th-century-slave-trade.html.

87. Melville to AC, 11 June 1752, PRO T70/29.

88. Melville to AC, undated [June 1752?], PRO T70/29, p. 45; Rømer, *Reliable Account,* 179.

89. Melville to AC, 14 March 1752, PRO T70/29; Fisher, "Extracts," 4:365.

90. Board of Trade, *Journal of the Commissioners, January 1749–1750 to December 1753,* 318–319.

91. Ibid., 321–322.

92. Ibid., 326–327 (quotations), 328–329, 407.

93. Crooks, *Records Relating to the Gold Coast,* 25–26; Fisher, "John Apperley to the Committee, 9 Sept. 1753," in "Extracts," 4:374.

94. Melville to AC, 25 January 1753, PRO T70/29. See also Melville to George Cockburn, 21 February 1753, PRO T70/30.

95. Melville to AC, 14 March 1753, PRO T70/30.

96. Fisher, "Extracts" 4:367.

97. Melville to AC, 26 December 1753, PRO T70/30.

98. Ibid.

99. Fisher, "Melville to AC, 24 Feb. 1753," in "Extracts," 4:373.

100. Melville to AC, 25 January 1753, PRO T70/29.

101. Thompson, *An Account,* 57–58; Fisher, "Melville to the Committee, 23 June 1753," in "Extracts," 4:374. On Corrantee's palace see Courtnay Micots, "African Coastal Elite Architecture: Cultural Authentification During the Colonial Period in Anomabo, Ghana" (PhD diss., University of Florida, 2010), 137–143.

102. Melville to the Committee, 25 January 1753, PRO T70/29; Melville to the Committee, 22 September 1753, PRO T70/1520; Apperley to the Committee, 8 September 1753, PRO T70/1520; Priestley, *West African Trade,* 42.

103. *A Letter from a Merchant of the City of London, to the R——t H——ble W——P—— Esq; upon the Affairs and Commerce of North America, and the West-Indies; our African trade; the Destinations of our Squadrons and Convoys; New Taxes, and the Schemes Proposed for raising the extraordinary Supplies for the Current Year* (London, 1757), 54–56 (quotation on p. 56).

104. Ibid., 31–33. Brew married one of Corrantee's daughters and established a prominent mixed-race family on the coast. Northrup, *Africa's Discovery,* 72–73. See Chapter 3.

105. Board of Trade, *Journal of the Commissioners, January 1754–December 1758,* 257.

106. Fisher, "Melville to the Committee, 30 May 1753," in "Extracts," 4:374 (quotation); Board of Trade, *Journal of the Commissioners, January 1754–December 1758,* 311.

107. Thomas Melville to the Royal African Committee, April 24, 1753, "A Narrative Relative to the Building the Fort at Annamaboe," in "A Narrative of the Proceedings of the Committee of the Company of Merchants Trading to Africa, Relative to the Building the Fort at Annamaboe, April 1755," in Adm. 1/3810 (first, second, third, and fourth quotations); Thomas Westgate and Richard Brew to the Committee, 12 January 1759, PRO T70/30 (fifth quotation); Crooks, *Records Relating to the Gold Coast,* 14.

108. Annamaboe Day Books, September–October 1753; November–December 1754 (third quotation); July–August 1754 (first and fourth quotations); May 1754 (fifth and sixth quotations); March–April 1754 (second quotation); May–June 1755, PRO T70/985.

109. Annamaboe Day Books, July–August, September–October (first quotation), November–December 1758; May–June 1759 (second and third quotations), November–December 1795 (fourth and fifth quotation), PRO T70/986; July–August, 1768, PRO T70/988.

110. Annamaboe Day Book, 24 January 1756, PRO T70/986.

111. Ibid., January–February, March–April 1763, July–August 1762 (first and second quotations), November–December, 1760, PRO T70/987; January–February 1756 (third quotation), PRO T70/986.

112. William Mutter to Charles Bell, 2 October 1761, PRO T70/30.

113. Mutter to Bell, 10 October 1761, PRO T70/30.

114. Gilbert Petrie to Bell, 4 December 1761, PRO T70/30. Melville to AC, 8 April 1755, 28 April 1756, PRO T70/30; Poirier to John Cleveland, 15 August 1755, Poirier to Melville, 15 September 1755, PRO T70/29.

115. Melville to CCC, 11 June 1752, PRO T70/29.

116. Henige, *Chronology of Oral Tradition,* 150. Succession for positions like caboceer on the Gold Coast was usually matrilineal, which the British often seem to ignore. The heir apparent would not normally be the eldest son but rather the caboceer's nephew, his sister's son. See Law, *English in West Africa,* 3:372n256.

117. Melville to AC, 11 June 1752, PRO T70/29.

118. Elizabeth Donnan, *Documents Illustrative of the History of the Slave Trade to America: Vol. III; New England and the Middle Colonies* (Washington, DC: Carnegie Institute of Washington, 1931), 223.

119. Board of Trade, *Journal of the Commissioners,* 9, 259. See also Fisher, "Roberts to Lord ?" in "Extracts," 4:368.

120. Brew to Capt. T. Eagles, 10 Nov. 1764/74, PRO T70/1532. William Mutter, Governor of Cape Coast Castle, reported Corrantee's death to the AC in June 1764. William Mutter to AC, 20 July 1764, PRO T70/331.

121. Henige, *Chronology of Oral Tradition,* 150–152.

122. Fisher, "Melville to Committee, 14 March 1752," in "Extracts," 3:364.

123. Henige, *Chronology of Oral Tradition,* 150–152. Amoony Coomah appears frequently in the Annamaboe records. See Fisher, "Extracts," 4: *passim.*

124. Hancock, *Citizens of the World.* David Northrup also reminds us that while "Europeans dominated the long sea routes . . . Africans dominated over the land and resources of their continent." Northrup, *Africa's Discovery,* 55, 57.

3. Richard Brew and the World of an African-Atlantic Merchant

1. John Newton, *The Journal of a Slave Trader (John Newton), 1750–1754* (London, 1962), 81.

2. "The Three Brew Royal Descents," *Isle of Man Family History Society Journal* 12 (November 1990): 132–137. Accessed March 13, 2011. http://www.isle-of-man.com/manxnotebook/famhist/v12n4.htm#132-137; Margaret Priestley, *West African Trade*

and Coast Society: A Family Study (London, 1969), 29–32. No captain by that name appears in the Trans-Atlantic Slave Trade Database. http://www.slavevoyages.org (accessed December 10, 2011).

3. Hugh Archibald Wyndham, *The Atlantic and Slavery* (Oxford, 1935), 26; "A New Check List of the Forts and Castles of Ghana," *Transactions of the Historical Society of Ghana* 4, 1(1959): 57–67; William Walton Claridge, *A History of the Gold Coast and Ashanti* (London, 1964), 171; Elizabeth Donnan, *Documents Illustrative of the History of the Slave Trade to America: Vol. II; The Eighteenth Century* (Washington, DC, 1931), 433–453.

4. Priestley, *West African Trade*, 36–37.

5. John Roberts, *Considerations on the Present Peace, As Far as it is Relative to the Colonies, and the African Trade* (London, 1763), 47–49.

6. Donnan, *History of the Slave Trade*, 2:501–502; Rebecca Shumway, *The Fante and the Transatlantic Slave Trade* (Rochester, NY, 2011), 55.

7. Donnan, *History of the Slave Trade*, 2:502–503.

8. Ibid., 506; Charges Against Governor Melville, 27 April 1753, Public Records Office (PRO), National Archives, Kew, United Kingdom, T70/1521; Melville to AC, 4 April 1754, PRO T70/1522; AC to Melville, PRO T70/29; AC to Melville, PRO T70/143 (quotation).

9. Elizabeth Donnan, *Documents Illustrative of the History of the Slave Trade to America: Vol. III; New England and the Middle Colonies* (Washington, DC, 1931):165–166.

10. John Hippisley, *Essays. I. On the Populousness of Africa: II. On the Trade at the Forts on the Gold Coast. III. On the Necessity of Erecting a Fort at Cape Appolonia.*(London, 1764), 19–32, 57–65 (first quotation, p. 23; second quotation, p. 57; third and fourth quotations, p. 58).

11. New York *Mercury*, 14 January 1760; Boston *Evening Post*, 28 January 1760; *The Boston News-Letter*, 21 May 1761.

12. Donnan, *History of the Slave Trade*, 3:526. The Newport *Mercury*, 6 May 1765; *The New-York Mercury*, 11 November 1765.

13. Donnan, *History of the Slave Trade*, 3:526.

14. Bell to AC, 1 September 1756, Colonial Office Board of Trade, PRO CO 388/47.

15. Priestley, *West African Trade*, 43–45.

16. Annamaboe Day Books, 1752, 1753, 1754, PRO T70/986; Priestley, *West African Trade*, 45–46.

17. John Joseph Crooks, *Records Relating to the Gold Coast Settlements from 1750 to 1874* (1923; London, 1973), 4, 32–33.

18. Bell quoted in Priestley, *West African Trade*, 46–47.

19. Ibid., 47–48.

20. Priestley, *West African Trade*, 48–49.

21. Roberts, *Considerations*, 53.

22. Donnan, *History of the Slave Trade*, 2:482 (quotation).

23. Ibid., 148–151; Petrie to AC, 31 March 1768, PRO T70/31 (first quotation); Mutter to AC 20 July 1765, PRO T70/31 (second quotation).

24. James Bramston, *The Man of Taste: Occasion'd by an Epistle of Mr. Pope's on that Subject* (London, 1733), 15.

25. Jennifer L. Anderson, *Mahogany: The Costs of Luxury in Early America* (Cambridge, MA, 2012), 16, 32, 37, 51, 38, 93, 134, 138, 147, 150, 200; Kenneth Morgan, *Slavery and the British Empire: From Africa to America* (Oxford, 2007), 45; Madeleine Dobie, *Trading Places: Colonization and Slavery in Eighteenth-century French Culture* (Ithaca, NY, 2010), 68 (quotation); Jeffrey R. Young, *Domesticating Slavery: The Master Class in Georgia and South Carolina, 1607–1837* (Chapel Hill, NC, 1999), 42.

26. "Inventory of the Effects of Rich. Brew, Esq. deceased as taken this 5th day of August 1776 at his House at Annamaboe," PRO T70/1534; Priestley, *West African Trade,* 100. Nicholas Owen, *Journal of a Slave-Dealer,* ed. Eveline Martin (London and New York, 2009), 38 (quotation).

27. "Inventory of the Effects of Rich. Brew," PRO T70/1534; David Hancock, *Citizens of the World: London Merchants and the Integration of the British Atlantic Community, 1735–1785* (Cambridge, 1995), 90–102; Maxine Berg, *Luxury and Pleasure in Eighteenth-Century Britain* (Oxford, 2007), 115, 117, 144.

28. "Inventory of the Effects of Rich. Brew," RPO T70/1534; Westgate to Brew, 14 October 1773, 20 February 1770, PRO T70/1536; Brew to Eagles, 10 November 1774, PRO T70/1532; Brew to Richard Miles, 7 November 1775, PRO T70/1534; David Hall, "Introduction," in *The Colonial Book in the Atlantic World,* eds. Hugh Amory and David D. Hall (Chapel Hill, NC, 2007), 6 (second quotation), 29, 480, 484.

29. Hancock, *Citizens of the World,* 110–111; Priestley, *West African Trade,* 34; Westgate to Brew, 24 September 1770, PRO T70/152 (quotation).

30. Donnan, *History of the Slave Trade,* 3:186–87.

31. Bell to AC, 14 April 1763, PRO T70/31; Cape Coast Castle Council Minutes, 21 April 1769, PRO T70/31.

32. Vincent Caretta and Ty M. Reese, eds., *The Life and Letters of Philip Quaque: The First African Anglican Missionary* (Athens, GA, and London, 2010), 41–42, 46, 47, 56, 58, 70, 75–77, 79, 80–81, 91–92, 106, 107, 120, 121, 127, 130, 133, 141, 146, 153, 174, 177, 184, 201 (first quotation on p. 56); Thomas Phillips, "A Journal of a Voyage Made in the Hannibal of London, Ann 1693, 1694, From England, to Cape's Monseradoe, in Africa, And Thence Along the Coast of Guiney to Whidaw, the Island of St. Thomas, An So Forward to Barbadoes: With a Cursory Account of the County, the People, Their Manners, Forts, Trade, &c," reprinted in *Collection of Voyages and Travels: Some Now First Printed from Original Manuscripts, Others Translated Out of Foreign Languages, and Now First Published in English,* ed. Awnsham Churchill (London, 1745), 209–210 (remaining quotations); David Northrup, *Africa's Discovery of Europe, 1450–1850* (Oxford, 2009), 71.

33. John Mensah Sarbah, *Fanti Customary Laws: A Brief Introduction to the Principles of the Native Laws and Customs of the Fanti and Akan Districts of the Gold Coast* (London, 1904), 41–56; Roger Gocking, *Facing Two Ways: Ghana's Coastal Communities Under Colonial Rule* (Lanham, MD, 1999), 89; R. Porter, "English Chief Factors on the Gold Coast, 1632–1753," African Historical Studies 1 (1968): 203; Toyin Falola, *Globalization and Urbanization in Africa* (Trenton, NJ, 2004), 278; Northrup, *Africa's Discovery,* 71.

34. Brew to Gwyther, 17 May 1767, PRO T70/1534. Philip Quaque commented on the common usage of the term *wenches* on the Gold Coast; see Caretta and Reese, *Life and Letters*, 81–82.

35. Mark Morton, *The Lover's Tongue: A Merry Romp Through the Language of Love and Sex* (Toronto, 2000), 65; Gordon Williams, *A Dictionary of Sexual Language and Imagery in Shakespearean and Stuart Literature*, (Atlantic Highlands, NJ, 2001), vol 1; *Gentleman's Magazine*, (June 1752), 271; (October 1829), 316 (third quotation); Michael A. Gomez, *Exchanging our Country Marks: The Transformation of African Identities in the Colonial and Antebellum South* (Chapel Hill, NC, 1998), 70, 103, 122, 140, 238; Elmer T. Hutchinson, *Documents Relating to the Colonial History of the State of New Jersey, Calendar of New Jersey Wills,* Vol. IX, 1796–1800 (Westminister, MD, 2009), 8, 14, 18, 36, 79, 93, 105, 130, 161, 185, 190, 197, 220, 243, 251, 266, 284, 305, 312, 313, 314, 356, 366, 378, 385, 387, 407, 428; Margaret Peckham Motes, *Blacks Found in the Deeds of Laurens & Newberry Counties, SC, 1785 to 1827* (Baltimore, MD, 2002), 1, 4, 10, 11, 14, 16, 23–27, 31–33, 36, 49, 74, 109, 111–112, 121, 124, 126; Noah Webster and John Walker, *An American Dictionary of the English Language* (New York: N. and J. White, 1834), 922 (fourth quotation); Maureen Elgersman, *Unyielding Spirits: Black Women and Slavery in Early Canada and Jamaica* (New York, 1999), 25, 30, 33, 107; *The Sailor's Opera: or, A Trip to Jamaica* (1745, fifth quotation), 9; Douglas Hall, *In Miserable Slavery: Thomas Thistlewood in Jamaica, 1750–86* (Kingston, Jamaica, 1999), 133, 137, 224, 258. The term was used to describe African women in similar relationships in the American colonies. In 1771, for example, a Dr. Collins in Jamaica "kept a wench . . . named Catherine" with whom he had three sons who carried their father's surname. See B. W. Higman, *Plantation Jamaica, 1750–1850: Capital and Control in a Colonial Economy* (Kingston, Jamaica, 2005), 144, 172. An eighteenth-century New York farmer left the use of his farm to "my wench Rose" and left money to their "negro children." See Graham Russell Hodges, *Root and Branch: African Americans in New York and East Jersey, 1613–1863* (Chapel Hill, NC, 1999), 71; J. B. Moreton, *West India Customs and Manners: Containing Strictures on the Soil, Cultivation, Produce, Trade, Officers, and Inhabitants: With the Method of Establishing, and Conducting a Sugar Plantation. To Which is Added, the Practice of Training New Slaves* (London, 1793), 89, 97, 105, 129. Jane Schaw, who traveled to Jamaica with her brother and other relatives in the 1770s, criticized "young black wenches" who "lay themselves out for white lovers." Londa L. Schiebinger, *Plants and Empire: Colonial Bioprospecting in the Atlantic World* (Cambridge, 2007), 140; Barbara Bush, "White 'Ladies,' Coloured 'Favourites' and Black 'Wenches': Some Considerations on Sex, Race, and Class Factors in Social Relations in White Creole Society in the British Caribbean," *Slavery and Abolition* 2 (December 1981): 245–262.

36. Westgate to Brew, 18 July 1770, PRO T70/1536.

37. Richard Miles to Unidentified Correspondent, 10 November 1780, PRO T 70/1483. There is no evidence that he did take Sal to England.

38. David Henige, "'Companies Are Always Ungrateful': James Phipps of Cape Coast, a Victim of the African Trade," *African Economic History* 9 (1980): 27–47;

John Atkins, *A Voyage to Guinea, Brazil, and the West Indies; In His Majesty's Ships, the Swallow and Weymouth* (London, 1735), 94–95 (quotations).

39. Westgate to Brew, 28 October 1768, PRO T70/152. On African Creoles see Ira Berlin, "From Creole to African: Atlantic Creoles and the Origins of African-American Society in Mainland North America," *William and Mary Quarterly*, 3rd ser., 53 (1996): 254.

40. Priestley, *West African Trade*, 108.

41. Caretta and Reese, *Life and Letters*, 46–47, 51–52, 91–92, 125 (first, second and fourth quotations on p. 46, third quotation on p. 47, fifth quotation on p. 52).

42. Ty M. Reese, "'Sheep in the Jaws of So Many Ravenous Wolves': The Slave Trade and Anglican Missionary Activity at Cape Coast Castle, 1752–1816," *Journal of Religion in Africa* 34 (August 2004): 357, 362, 367.

43. Priestley, *West African Trade*, 121.

44. Travis Glasson, "Missionaries, Methodists, and a Ghost: Philip Quaque in London and Cape Coast, 1756–1816", *Journal of British Studies* 48 (January 2009): 29–50.

45. Priestley, *West African Trade*, 122–123 (quotation on p. 123); Cape Coast Castle Day Books, 2 August 1795, PRO T70/1067.

46. African Committee to Robert Collins, 31 January 1794 (quotation); 7 May 1794; 25 June 1794, PRO T70/71.

47. Priestley, *West African Trade*, 122 (first and fourth quotations); Richard Miles, who settled the estate, gave rum and powder to the townspeople for Spooner's funeral custom and bast to "his Wench" for a winding sheet. Miles to Mill, 11 and 15 August 1773, PRO T70/1479 (second quotation); Miles to John Shoolbred, 1 December 1780, PRO T70/1479 (third quotation).

48. William Bosman, *A New and Accurate Description of the Coast of Guinea, Divided Into the Gold, the Slave, and the Ivory Coasts* (London, 1967), 141–142.

49. Shumway, *Fante*, 115; Jane Fletcher Fiske, *Gleanings from Newport Court Files, 1659–1783* (Boxford, MA, 1998), 6; Donnan, *History of the Slave Trade*, 3:248n2.

50. Priestley, *West African Trade*, 64–65, 72–78; Charles Bell to AC, 14 April 1763, PRO T70/31 (first and second quotations); Brew to Thomas Eagles, 21 June 1770, PRO T70/1582; John McLeod, *A Voyage to Africa with Some Account of the Manners and Customs of the Dahomian People* (London, 1820), 12.

51. Brew to "Gentlemen," 20 February 1776, PRO T70/1534; Priestley, *West African Trade,* 72–73. Brew maintained a factory at Cape Lopez and employed an African named John Congo who ran a cutter between Cape Lopez and Annamaboe. See G. A. Robertson, *Notes on Africa; Particularly Those Parts Which Are Situated Between Cape Verd and the River Congo* (London, 1819), 335.

52. Petrie to AC, 20 October 1766, PRO T70/31; Mutter to AC, 25 October 1765 (third quotation), PRO T70/31; Priestley, *West African* Trade, 75–77.

53. William Lacy to AC, 31 January 1767, PRO T70/31.

54. Petrie to AC, 7 June 1767, PRO T70/31.

55. Petrie to AC, 15 May 1768, PRO T70/31.

56. Mutter to AC, 10 January 1764, PRO T70/31.

57. Mutter to AC, 25 October 1765, PRO CO 388/53.

58. Brew and Webster to Mutter, 16 August 1765, PRO CO 388/53.

59. Brew and Webster to Mutter, 26 August 1765, PRO CO 388/33.

60. Mutter to Brew and Webster, 27 August 1765; Brew and Webster to Mutter, 28 August 1765; Mutter to Brew and Webster, 29 August 1765; PRO CO 338/33.

61. Hippisley and Petrie to Mutter, 13 August, 10 October 1765; Governor and Council to Brew and Webster, 24 August 1765; Brew and Webster to Francis Cahuac, n.d.(quotation); PRO CO 388/33.

62. Mutter to AC, 15 September 1765, PRO CO 388/33.

63. Huydecoper to Mutter, 28 August 1766; Mutter to AC, 14 December 1765; PRO CO 388/33.

64. Petrie to AC, 21 October 1768, PRO T70/31.

65. Hippisley and Petrie to Mutter, 1 October 1765.

66. Mutter to AC, 14 December 1765, PRO CO 388/33.

67. Petrie to AC, 21 October 1768, PRO T70/31.

68. Mill to AC, 7 May 1776, PRO T70/1482.

69. David Mill to AC, 27 June 1774, 15 April 1775, 7 May 1776, PRO T70/32.

70. Lord's Commissioners of His Majesty's Treasury, *Journal of the Commissioners for Trade and Plantations from January 1776 to May 1782* (London, 1938), 182; John Peter Demarin, *A Treatise Upon the Trade from Great-Britain to Africa Humbly Recommended to the Attention of Government* (London, 1772), 66–114.

71. Demarin, *Treatise Upon the Trade*, 64.

72. Brew to Bell, 23 January 1771, PRO T70/1586.

73. Bell to Brew, n.d. [January 1771?], PRO T70/1586.

74. Bell to Brew, 24 January 1771, PRO T70/1586.

75. Brew to Bell, 19 December 1774, PRO T70/1586.

76. Brew to David Mill, 20 December 1774, PRO T70/1586.

77. Demarin, *Treatise Upon the Trade*, 108–109, 20.

78. Donnan, *History of the Slave Trade*, 3:261–262, 264, 175–176, 64–65, 272, 293, 304 (quotation).

79. Ibid., 307–308.

80. Ibid., 314.

81. Dalziel to AC, 25 April 1769, PRO T70/1532.

82. Donnan, *History of the Slave Trade*, 2:538; Demarin, *Treatise Upon the Trade*, 91. For Mill's voyage see the Trans-Atlantic Slave Trade Database, Voyage 788532.

83. Demarin, *Treatise Upon the Trade*, 91–92, 114–115. For more information on fetish see Bosman, *New and Accurate Description*, 148–153.

84. Demarin, *Treatise Upon the Trade*, 114–15.

85. As early as 1709 Sir Dalby Thomas advised the company that one of their officials was guilty of conducting private trading at Shadoe. See Donnan, *History of the Slave Trade*, 2:101.

86. Ibid., 87, 91, 104, 108, 122.

87. Ibid., 105 (quotation), 106.

88. Ibid., 111 (quotation), 120.

89. Westgate to Brew, "Sunday night," n.d. [1770], PRO T70/1536 (first quotation); Westgate to Miles, 10 April 1777, PRO T70/32 (second and third quotations); CCC

Council Minutes, 21 April 1769, PRO T70/31; Acts of Council, 3 July 1779, PRO T70/152 (fourth quotation).

90. Richard Camplin to Barber, 25 February 1771, PRO T70/1531 (first quotation); Brew to M. Coghlan, 28 August 1775, PRO T70/1533 (second and third quotations).

91. Barber to Brew, 28 December 1769; Barber to Brew, 27 January 1771, PRO T70/1531 (quotation).

92. Arthur Heyward, John Dobson, Gilbert Slater, William James, and Miles Barber to AC, 25 January 1771, PRO T70/1531.

93. Petrie to Miles, 3 December 1770, PRO T70/1531.

94. Petrie to Miles, 14 March 1772, PRO T70/1531.

95. Mill to Miles, 21 October 1771; Miles to Ross & Mill, 15 March 1771; Ross & Mill to Miles, 22 March 1771; PRO T70/1536, Pt. 2.

96. Mill to Miles, 10 December 1770, PRO T70/1536.

97. Mill to Miles, 12 October 1771, PRO T70/1536.

98. Camplin to Miles, 5 February 1778, PRO T70/1536. See also Miles to Petrie, n.d., and Miles to Ross & Mill, 21 February 1771, PRO T70/1536.

99. *South Carolina Gazette,* 5 February 1732. On the importance of reputation for merchants in this period see T. H. Breen, *The Marketplace of Revolution: How Consumer Politics Shaped American Independence* (Oxford, 2004), 137–138.

100. Westgate to Brew, 8 October 1770, PRO T70/1536 (first quotation); "Mr. Bell's Answer," 24 January 1771, PRO T70/1531 (second quotation); Bell to Brew, 5 January 1775, PRO T70/1533; Brew to Bell, 5 January 1775 (third, fourth, and fifth quotations), PRO T70/1533; Bell to Brew, 6 January 1775 PRO T70/1533 (sixth quotation); Priestley, *West African Trade,* 90.

101. Donnan, *History of the Slave Trade,* 3:307.

102. Grosle to AC, 19 February 1770, PRO T70/31.

103. Priestley, *West African Trade,* 63, 68–69, 80–84; "An Annual Register of the Number of Slaves exported from the Gold Coast of Africa from 1755 to December 1768," PRO T70/1531; David Eltis, "The Volume and Structure of the Transatlantic Slave Trade: A Reassessment," *William and Mary Quarterly,* 3rd ser., LVIII (January 2001): 19–46; Westgate to Brew, 24 August 1767, PRO T70/152 (quotation).

104. Brew to the Assignees, 30 March 1776, PRO T70/1482.

105. Brew to M. Coghlan, 28 August 1775, PRO T70/1533 (second quotation); Priestley, *West African Trade,* 97.

106. Donnan, *History of the Slave Trade,* 3:313–314; Priestley, *West African Trade,* 90.

107. Lord's Commissioners of His Majesty's Treasury, *Journal of the Commissioners,* 14:84–85.

108. Ibid., 127.

109. Ibid., 129–131 (quotation on p. 130). For Dunn's voyages see the Trans-Atlantic Slave Trade Database, Voyages 24612, 25251, 25376, 26037.

110. Lord's Commissioners of His Majesty's Treasury, *Journal of the Commissioners,* 14:131–134.

111. For more on mercantilism and economic thought in this period, see "Forum: Rethinking Mercantilism," *William and Mary Quarterly,* 3rd ser., 69 (January 2012), 3–70.

112. Lord's Commissioners of His Majesty's Treasury, *Journal of the Commissioners,* 14:131–134, 140–142. There were twelve pence in a shilling. On the volume of the slave trade from the Gold Coast, see Eltis, "The Volume and Structure," 17–46. The Trans-Atlantic Slave Trade Database shows 172 British voyages from the Gold Coast from 1760 to 1765 and 120 from 1770 to 1775 at a time when the British trade was increasing rapidly in other regions.

113. Lord's Commissioners of His Majesty's Treasury, *Journal of the Commissioners,* 14:132–134.

114. Ibid., 137.

115. Ibid., 137–138, 142.

116. Ibid., 139, 143–146 (quotations); Priestley, *West African Trade,* 90.

117. William Cobbett, *Cobbett's Parliamentary History of England: From the Norman Conquest, in 1066 to the year 1803. Comprising the Period from the Twenty-ninth of January 1777, to the Fourth of December 1778,* vol. 19 (London, 1814), 291–316; Donnan, *History of the Slave Trade,* 2:552–554 (first quotation on p. 553n3; Miles to John Caezeneau, 15 January 1778 (second quotation), PRO T70/1483; Miles to James John Shoolbred, 20 January 1778 (third quotation), PRO T70/1483.

118. Governor and Council to AC, 5 May 1780, PRO T70/32.

119. Westgate to Brew, 10 August 1773, PRO T70/1536 (first quotation); Brew to Miles, 7 November 1775, PRO T70/1534.

120. Brew to Miles, 28 May 1776, PRO T70/1534.

121. Mill to Miles, 3 August 1776, PRO T70/1534.

122. Richard Brew Estate Inventory, August 1776, PRO T70/1504; Lord's Commissioners of His Majesty's Treasury, *Journal of the Commissioners,* 14:139–146, 182, 348, 357, 359, 362, 375, 384, 439, 441–442, 443, 450.

123. Donnan, *History of the Slave Trade,* 3:320.

124. Miles to Petrie, 10 November 1776, PRO T70/1482.

125. Brew to Peregrine Cust, 5 April 1776, PRO T70/1534.

126. Miles to "Dear Father," 15 February 1776, PRO T70/1482 (quotation); Miles to Dalziel, 22 September 1776, PRO T70/1482.

127. Miles to Shoolbred, 19 October 1776, PRO T70/1482.

128. Mill to Miles, 3 August 1776, PRO T70/31; Miles and Weuves to ?, 10 August 1776, PRO T70/31. Similarly, the Dutch at Elmina had asked officials in Holland to issue "Standing Orders [to] forbid . . . any White in the service of the Noble Company to marry a Mulatta or native woman, since they thus become related to our Negroes, and it is dangerous for the government to punish a subordinate as the offence merits if he had such extensive family ties." Ole Justesen, ed., *Danish Sources for the History of Ghana, 1657–1754,* 2:1735–1754 (Copenhagen, ?), 724; Priestley, *West African Trade,* 86.

129. Richard Brew Estate Inventory, August 1776, PRO T70/1504.

130. Bosman, *New and Accurate Description,* 229–230.

131. Richard Brew Estate Inventory, August 1776, PRO T70/1504.

132. The ships were the *St. George,* Captain Moore, and the *Fox,* Captain Farley. Joseph Mill to Miles and Weuves, n.d., PRO T70/1534; Ross & Mill to Miles and Weuves, n.d., PRO T70/1534; Miles to James Mill, 31 January 1778, PRO T70/1483.

133. Miles to Petrie, 10 November 1776, PRO T70/1482 (quotation); Miles to AC, 26 July 1779, PRO T70/32.

134. Brew to William Devaynes, 21 May 1770, PRO T70/1531.

4. The Process of Enslavement at Annamaboe

1. House of Commons, *Abridgement of the Minutes of the Evidence Taken Before a Committee of the Whole House: To Whom it was Referred to Consider of the Slave-Trade* (London, 1789), 9.

2. Great Britain, Parliament, House of Commons, Select Committee Appointed to Take the Examination of Witnesses Respecting the African Slave Trade, Great Britain, Privy Council, Committee on the Slave-trade, *Observations on the Evidence Given Before the Committees of the Privy Council and House of Commons in Support of the Bill for Abolishing the Slave Trade* (London, 1791), 71 (second quotation); House of Commons, *Abridgement*, 1:9 (first quotation), 34 (third quotation); Charles Royster, *Fabulous History of the Dismal Swamp Company: A Story of George Washington's Times* (New York, 1999), 169; Board of Trade, *Journal of the Commissioners for Trade and Plantations from January 1749–1750 to December 1753* (London, 1932), vol. 58, 9 (third quotation), 16 (fourth quotation).

3. Ruth Fisher, "Extracts from the Records of the African Companies," pt. 2, *Journal of Negro History* 13 (July 1928): 322. The best study of warfare on the Gold Coast in this period is John K. Thornton, *Warfare in Atlantic Africa, 1500–1800* (London, 1999), chap. 3.

4. Ludewig Ferdinand Rømer, *A Reliable Account of the Coast of Guinea (1760)*, trans. Selena Axelrod Winsnes, (Oxford, 2000), 154–159, 201 (quotation); Harvey M. Feinberg, "Africans and Europeans in West Africa: Elminians and Dutchmen on the Gold Coast During the Eighteenth Century," *Transactions of the American Philosophical Society*, n.s., 79 (1989): 15, Thornton, *Warfare*, 70–71 (quotation on p. 70).

5. Feinberg, "Africans and Europeans," 10–11, 13–16; Ivor Wilks, *Asante in the Nineteenth Century: The Structure and Evolution of a Political* Order (Cambridge, 1975), 18–29, Thornton, *Warfare*, 71.

6. Rebecca Shumway, *The Fante and the Transatlantic Slave Trade* (Rochester, NY, 2011), 57; Kwame Arhin, "Asante Military Institutions," *Journal of African Studies* 7 (1980): 22–30; Donna J. E. Maier, "Military Acquisition of Slaves in Asante," in *West African Economic and Social History: Studies in Memory of Marion Johnson*, eds. David Henige and T. C. McCaskle (Madison, WI, 1990), 119–132; Thornton, *Warfare*, 5–6, 56–57, 61–64 (quotation on p. 57). In 1816 Thomas Edward Bowdich, who led a British diplomatic mission to the Asante, reported that the British would not provide the Asante with guns and powder, but the Dutch at Elmina did. As a result the Asante "trade visits to Cape Coast consequently almost suspended" while the Dutch had "engrossed almost the whole of this . . . valuable commerce." Bowdich to Simon Cock, 20 August 1816, Public Records Office (PRO), National Archives, Kew, United Kingdom, T70/36. S. Tenkorang, "The Importance of Firearms in the Struggle between Ashanti and the Coastal States," *Transactions of the Historical Society of Ghana* 9 (1968): 1–16.

7. Wilks, *Asante*, 21–22, 26–29, 35, 55 (quotation), 66–71, 144.

8. Elizabeth Donnan, *Documents Illustrative of the History of the Slave Trade to America: Vol. II; The Eighteenth Century* (Washington, DC, 1931), 526–527; Thornton, *Warfare*, 72.

9. Wilks, *Asante*, 21–22, 26–29, 35, 55, 66–71, 144; Donnan, *History of the Slave Trade*, 2:526–527 (first, second and third quotations); House of Commons, *Abridgement*, 2:152 (fourth quotation); Mutter to AC, 20 July 1765, PRO CO 388/53; Trans-Atlantic Slave Trade Database. http://www.slavevoyages.org (accessed December 30, 2011).

10. Annamaboe Day Books, July–August, November–December, 1768, PRO T70/988.

11. Grosle to AC, 24 April 1769 (first quotation), PRO T70/31; House of Commons, *Abridgement*, 1:39, 43, 48; 2:152; Feinberg, "African and Europeans," 15; the Trans-Atlantic Slave Trade Database.

12. David Mill to AC, 27 June 1774 (first quotation), 15 April 1775, PRO T70/32; Elizabeth Donnan, *Documents Illustrative of the History of the Slave Trade to America: Vol. III; New England and the Middle Colonies* (Washington, DC, 1931), 318. Estimates on trade from the Trans-Atlantic Slave Trade Database.

13. Wilks, *Asante*, 21–22, 26–29, 35, 55 (quotation), 66–71, 144. Demand for enslaved labor rebounded in the Asante Empire in the nineteenth century, whether to meet the internal needs of the Asante or for the slave trade is unclear, but tribute payments in slaves were once again commonplace in the nineteenth century and amounted to thousands of slaves annually. See Wilks, *Asante*, 66–67.

14. William Smith, *A New Voyage to Guinea* (1744; London, 1968), 158. Richard Miles reported that he "saw 3 or 4 Arabian horses" in the years he spent on the coast, and added that he "imported horses, but they did not live." Brew also apparently kept horses at Castle Brew, though it is doubtful that he succeeded any better than anyone else in keeping them alive. Thomas Edward Bowdich, *Mission from Cape Coast Castle to Ashantee* (London, 1873), 13–14; House of Commons, *Abridgement*, 16, 46 (second quotation), 60 (first quotation), 55 (third quotation). In 1769 Miles Barber wrote Brew from London saying that he had sent him oats, hay, a saddle, a whip, a bridle, and six sets of horse shoes and nails. Barber to Brew, 28 December 1769, PRO T70/1536.

15. Henry Meredith, *An Account of the Gold Coast of Africa; With a Brief History of the African Company* (London, 1812), 59–61.

16. Wilks, *Asante*, 8–9, 55 (quotation), 66–71, 144.

17. Rømer, *Reliable Account*, 172 (first quotation); Mutter to AC, 10 January 1764, 27 May 1764 (second quotation), PRO T70/31. The Asante road system played a major role in its military successes. See Thornton, *Warfare*, 73.

18. House of Commons, *Abridgement*, 1:14, 15, 34–35.

19. Mutter to AC, 10 January 1764, 27 May 1764 (first, second, and third quotations), PRO T70/31; Feinberg, "African and Europeans," 15–16; Ole Justesen, ed., *Danish Sources for the History of Ghana, 1657–1754.* 2 vols. (Copenhagen, 2005), 2:551, 578, 699, 711, 713, 724, 792.

20. Mill to AC, 30 December 1775, PRO T30/32; Annamaboe Fort Day Book, November 10, November–December 1775, PRO T70/990; Donnan, *History of the Slave Trade*, 2:554n2.

21. Fisher, "Extracts," 4:371.

22. House of Commons, *Abridgement,* 16, 46, 60, 55.

23. House of Commons, *Minutes Of The Evidence Taken Before A Committee of the House of Commons, Being A Select Committee, Appointed on the 29th Day of January 1790, For the Purpose of taking the Examination of such Witnesses as shall be produced on the Part of the several Petitioners who have petitioned the House of Commons against the Abolition of the Slave Trade,* 147.

24. Fisher, Commenda Fort Diary, August 4, 1715, in "Extracts," 2:335 (second quotation).

25. House of Commons, *Abridgement,* 1:53.

26. Thomas Thompson, *The African Trade for Negro Slaves, Shewn to be Consistent with Principles of Humanity, and with the Laws of Revealed Religion* (Canterbury, 1772?), 25 (first quotation); John Adams, *Sketches Taken During Ten Voyages to Africa Between the Years 1786 and 1800: Including Observations on the Country Between Cape Palmas and the River Congo, and Cursory Remarks on the Physical and Moral Character of the Inhabitants, with an Appendix Containing an Account of the European Trade with the West Coast of Africa* (London, 1822), 9–10 (third quotation); Wilks, *Asante,* 58.

27. House of Commons, *Observations on the Evidence,* 82–83, 100 (second quotation), 241 (first quotation).

28. Ottobah Cugoano, "Thoughts and Sentiments on the Evil and Wicked Traffic of the Slavery and Commerce of the Human Species, Humbly Submitted to the Inhabitants of Great Britain," in *Pioneers of the Black Atlantic: Five Slave Narratives from the Enlightenment, 1772–1815,* eds. Henry Louis Gates Jr. and William L. Alexander (Washington, DC, 1998), 92–95.

29. House of Commons, *Observations on the Evidence,* 36.

30. Ibid., 52 (first quotation), 69 (second quotation), 10 (third quotation).

31. Ibid., 36, 40. Shumway, *Fante,* 119 (second quotation).

32. John Atkins, *A Voyage to Guinea, Brazil, and the West Indies: In His Majesty's Ships, the Swallow and Weymouth* (London, 1735), 188; Shumway, *Fante,* 59–61; Getz, "Mechanisms of Slave Acquisition and Exchange in Late Eighteenth-Century Anomabu: Reconsidering a Cross-Section of the Atlantic Slave Trade," *African Economic History* 31 (2003): 85.

33. House of Commons, *Observations on the Evidence,* 10 (first, second, and third quotations), 12 (fourth quotation), 14–15, 33; John Adams, *Remarks on the Country Extending from Cape Palmas to the River Congo* (London, 1823), 21.

34. Captain Robert Champlin told his brother Christopher in 1775 that "I believe Capt Dunkin Dont Entend to Come Down Here . . . the Customs is so Hie that I Dont think He will Pay them." Donnan, *History of the Slave Trade,* 3:307. Thomas Phillips, "A Journal of a Voyage Made in the Hannibal of London, Ann 1693, 1694, From England, to Cape's Monseradoe, in Africa, And Thence Along the Coast of Guiney to Whidaw, the Island of St. Thomas, An So Forward to Barbadoes: With a Cursory Account of the County, the People, Their Manners, Forts, Trade, &c," reprinted in *Collection of Voyages and Travels: Some Now First Printed from Original Manuscripts, Others Translated Out of Foreign Languages, and Now First Published in English,* ed. Awnsham Churchill (London,

1745), 209; Royster, *Fabulous History,* 171–172 (second quotation); J. Heblethwaite to Richard Miles, 31 March 1778, PRO T70/1536; Roberts to AC, 17 April 1781, PRO T70/32. RAC and CMTA ships and forts flew the "Guinea Jack" as their ensign, a St. George's Cross within a double border of red-and-white checks.

35. Donnan, *History of the Slave Trade,* 3:257–258 (second and third quotations), 260n2 (fourth quotation), 261–262, 293–294 (first quotation on p. 294). Captain Peleg Clarke complained in 1776 that "all the Slaves is at 12 oz for Men and 10 oz for Women that's purchased from the Whites, and from my Unhappy Situation, and the Excessive dull trade I have made very little other trade than with the Whites, So that I labour under every disadvantage in point of profits to the Voyage." Donnan, *History of the Slave Trade,* 3:317.

36. Captain John Bell reported in 1776 that "C't Noble has keep't his goods, in order to lower the price [of slaves], but 'am, affraid will not succeed." Donnan, *History of the Slave Trade,* 3:49, 325 (Bell), 306, 322 (first, second, and third quotations). Clarke got a slave to replace the runaway pawn by panyarring a woman of the town. Ibid., 326.

37. Ibid., 325.

38. Donnan, *History of the Slave Trade,* 3:78–79.

39. Rømer, *Reliable Account,* 192 (first quotation); Mrs. R. Lee, *Stories of Strange Lands; And Fragments from the Notes of a Traveller* (London, 1895), 125 (second and third quotations); Meredith, *Account of the Gold Coast,* 58–59. For an example of the accounts of a slave ship showing payments to Annamaboe canoemen see Donnan, *History of the Slave Trade,* 3:179, 235; House of Commons, *Abridgement,* 1:41, 42; Adams, *Sketches Taken During Ten Voyages,* 107.

40. Adams, *Remarks on the Country,* 10–11; House of Commons, *Abridgement,* 1:34, 44. For slave ship accounts showing payments to gold-takers at Annamaboe see Donnan, *History of the Slave Trade,* 3:127, 223, 237.

41. Brew to [Miles?], 20 February 1776, PRO T70/1534. Abra or Abora was the northernmost state of the Fante confederacy.

42. Ibid.

43. Ibid.

44. Miles's postscript added to Brew to [Miles?], 20 February 1776, PRO T70/1534.

45. Atkins, *Voyage to Guinea,* 185; Thomas Edward Bowdich, *The African Committee* (London, 1819), 59–61; *The State of the Trade to Africa, Between 1680 and 1707, As Well Under the Management of an Exclusive Company, as Under that of Separate Traders, Impartially Considered, with Regard to Matter of Fact and Demonstration* (London, 1708?), 3.

46. Mrs. R. Lee, *The African Crusoes or the Adventures of Carlos and Antonio* (Boston, 1873), 99–101; Lee, *Stories of Strange Lands,* 21–22. Mrs. Lee was the widow of Thomas Edward Bowdich and lived on the Gold Coast with her husband in 1817. Those gold ornaments in various shapes may have been gold weights.

47. Meredith, *Account of the Gold Coast,* 104–105.

48. Fisher, "Extracts," 88.

49. *Gentleman's Magazine,* July 1763, 330.

50. Phillips, "A Journal of a Voyage," 206 (quotations); Petrie to AC, 10 March 1769, PRO T70/31.

51. Donnan, *History of the Slave Trade*, 3:223.

52. Lee, *Stories of Strange Lands,* 195–196.

53. William Fielde to AC, 30 June 1790 (first and second quotations); 3 January 1791; 20 June 1791; Dalziel to AC, 27 July 1792, PRO T70/33.

54. Thomas Morris to AC, 20 November 1788, PRO T70/33.

55. Thomas Morris to AC, 31 March 1789, PRO T70/33.

56. Lead bars were the least valuable item of trade on the Gold Coast, so someone not involved in manufacturing even that lowly commodity was of little account. Adams, *Remarks on the Country*, 11–12. For other examples of this naming practice see Lee, *Stories of Strange Lands,* 69–70.

57. Adams, *Remarks on the Country,* 17–20. Yellow Joe and Fat Sam appear in the accounts of the Annamaboe Fort, where they were paid a custom, an indication of their prominence. Annamaboe Day Book, January 1780, PRO T70/1237; Shumway, *Fante,* 119. Mrs. Lee reported that a palaver was "often an excuse for entirely stripping a wealthy person of his riches," as it was in Coffee's case. Lee, *Stories of Strange Lands,* 151.

58. House of Commons, *Abridgement,* 17–18; Robin Law, *Ouidah: The Social History of a West African Slaving Port, 1727–1892* (Athens, OH, 2004), 141.

59. House of Commons, *Abridgement,* 18 (first quotation), 46 (second quotation); House of Commons, *Minutes Of The Evidence,* 13–14.

60. House of Commons, *Minutes Of The Evidence,* 206; Law, *Ouidah,* 141. For other examples of adult and infant captives who could not be sold being put to death see House of Commons Papers, Commons Committee, Reports of Committees, *Report Of The Lords of the Committee of Council appointed for the Consideration of all Matters relating to Trade and Foreign Plantations; Submitting To His Majesty's Consideration The Evidence and Information they have collected in consequence of his Majesty's Order in Council, dated the 11th of February 1788, concerning the present State of the Trade to Africa, and particularly the Trade in Slaves; and concerning the Effects and Consequences of this Trade, as well in Africa and the West Indies, as to the general Commerce of this Kingdom* (London, 25 April 1789), Pt. 1, 44, 45.

61. Ibid., 37.

62. Ibid., 76.

63. Ibid., 76 (quotations), 22.

64. Ibid., 54.

65. Donnan, *History of the Slave Trade,* 3:321 (second quotation), 323 (first quotation).

66. Donnan, *History of the Slave Trade,* 2:323 (first quotation), 324, 354–355 (second and third quotations). A 1731 letter in the *Boston News-Letter* complained that several slavers from Annamaboe had faced rebellions on board. See Ibid., 431n1. House of Commons, *Minutes Of The Evidence,* 193.

67. Snelgrave quoted in Donnan, *History of the Slave Trade,* 2:358–359. Sandglasses that measured the hour, half hour, or minute were commonly used on ships to set watches and to measure the ships' speed. See Edward G. Hinkelman and Sibylla

Putzi, *Dictionary Of International Trade: Handbook Of The Global Trade Community* (Petaluma, CA, 2005), 250; Paul Glennie and Nigel Thrift, *Shaping the Day: A History of Timekeeping in England and Wales, 1300–1800* (Oxford, 2009).

68. House of Commons, *Abridgement,* 1:36, 46 (quotations), 69; 2:37; William Chambers to Richard Miles, 16 March 1777, 21 January 1778, PRO T70/1536.
69. Donnan, *History of the Slave Trade,* 3:317.
70. Rømer, *Reliable Account,* 35.
71. Thompson, *The African Trade for Negro Slaves,* 11–12. Rhode Island trader John Brown made the same arguments when he spoke against efforts to ban the trade from there in 1800. See Donnan, *History of the Slave Trade,* 3:383n2.

5. Tracing the Trade

1. *State Gazette of South-Carolina,* 23 June 1785.
2. Philip D. Morgan, *Slave Counterpoint: Black Culture in the Eighteenth-Century Chesapeake and Lowcountry* (Chapel Hill, NC, and London, 1998), 63, 65–67.
3. "Remonstrance of the Colony of Rhode Island to the Board of Trad, 1764," reproduced in Elizabeth Donnan, *Documents Illustrative of the History of the Slave Trade to America: Vol. III; New England and the Middle Colonies* (Washington, DC, 1931), 203–204; Jay Coughtry, *The Notorious Triangle: Rhode Island and the African Slave Trade, 1700–1807* (Philadelphia, 1981), 13, 15–16, 81–88.
4. Coughtry, *Notorious Triangle,* 25–42; Hugh Thomas, *The Slave Trade: The Story of the Atlantic Slave Trade, 1440–1870* (New York and other cities, 1997), 260–261, 270–271.
5. Elizabeth Donnan, *Documents Illustrative of the History of the Slave Trade to America: Vol. II; The Eighteenth Century* (Washington, DC, 1931), 543n4, 131 (quotation). Henry Livingston reported a similar crowd of Rum Men at Annamaboe in 1754. See p. 144n1.
6. Miles to William Bourke, 31 January 1773, Public Records Office (PRO), National Archives, Kew, United Kingdom, T70/1482 (first quotation); Thomas Westgate to Richard Brew, 1 August 1774, PRO T70/152; David Richardson, "West African Consumption Patterns and Their Influence on the Eighteenth-Century Slave Trade," in *The Uncommon Market: Essays in the Economic History of the Atlantic Slave Trade,* eds. Henry A. Gemery and Jan S. Hogendorn (New York, 1979), 324–327; Coughtry, *Notorious Triangle,* 80–90.
7. The "Blew Bast" mentioned in the account is an Indian coarse cloth from India. Donnan, *History of the Slave Trade,* 3:177, 244, 249. On the *Active* see Voyage 36370, Voyages Database, The Trans-Atlantic Slave Trade Database. http://www.slavevoyages.org (accessed December 20, 2011). Bristol, Rhode Island, was famous for its onions, which often appear in the cargoes of ships from that port. Coughtry, *Notorious Triangle,* 87.
8. On the voyage of the *Fox* see the Trans-Atlantic Slave Trade Database, Voyage 25058; Anne Farrow, Joel Manfred Lang, and Jenifer Frank, *Complicity: How The North Promoted, Prolonged, and Profited From Slavery* (New York, 2005), 119. A snow is a type of ship similar to a brig.
9. *The Pennsylvania Gazette,* 26 October 1758. See also Donnan, *History of the Slave Trade,* 3:184.

10. Donnan, *History of the Slave Trade,* 2:528.

11. Thomas, *Slave Trade,* 351.

12. Donnan, *History of the Slave Trade,* 3:365–370.

13. Brew quoted in John Peter Demarin, *A Treatise Upon the Trade from Great-Britain to Africa Humbly Recommended to the Attention of Government* (London, 1772), 78.

14. Donnan, *History of the Slave Trade,* 3:373–375.

15. Ibid., 375–378.

16. Thomas, *Slave Trade,* 261.

17. The Trans-Atlantic Slave Trade Database, see Voyages 36025, 36030, 36035, 36062, 36026, 36075.

18. Donnan, *History of the Slave Trade,* 3:131.

19. Donnan, *History of the Slave Trade,* 2:146–147. Not all the seamen served the entire voyage. Their terms ranged from twenty-two days to ten months. Even the cook was discharged in Barbados after serving only about six weeks, which would indicate that he was hired on the African coast.

20. Donnan, *History of the Slave Trade,* 2:146–147, 156; Coughtry, *Notorious Triangle,* 85–102.

21. Donnan, *History of the Slave Trade,* 2:150; Maurice Crouse, "Gabriel Manigault: Charleston Merchant," *South Carolina Historical Magazine* 68 (1967): 221–228; William Dusinberre, *Them Dark Days: Slavery in the American Rice Swamps* (Athens, GA, and London, 2000), 4.

22. Donnan, *History of the Slave Trade,* 2:152, 154, 156 (quotation). There is a discrepancy between the list of slaves purchased and the list of slaves sold. The list of slaves sold shows twenty-nine men, twenty-one women, four boys, and one girl.

23. *The South-Carolina Gazette,* 6 March 1755.

24. Donnan, *History of the Slave Trade,* 2:157.

25. Ibid., 154.

26. *South Carolina Gazette; and Country Journal,* 13 February 1770.

27. Patrick Hues Mell and Annie R. Mell, *The Genealogy of the Mell Family in the Southern States* (Auburn, AL, 1897), vi–x.

28. Bell was a prominent merchant and political leader, and a member of a group whose influence was increasing in this period. See Walter J. Fraser, *Charleston! Charleston!: The History of a Southern City* (Columbia, SC, 1991), 75.

29. Lloyd was a dry goods merchant in Charleston and an officer of the South Carolina Society. He left his business in 1756 and died in 1761. See Henry Laurens, *Papers of Henry Laurens, Volume 2: November 1, 1755–December 31, 1758,* eds. Philip May Hamer and George C. Rogers (Columbia, SC, 1970), 212, 214.

30. Charles Colcock Jones, *Biographical Sketches of the Delegates from Georgia to the Continental Congress* (Boston and New York, 1891), 139–154.

31. *South Carolina Gazette; and Country Journal,* 6 January 1767; *South Carolina and American General Gazette,* 3 October 1770.

32. George Howe, *History of the Presbyterian Church in South Carolina,* vol. 1 (Columbia, SC, 1870), 271; Frederick Lewis Weis, *The Colonial Clergy of Virginia, North Carolina, and South Carolina,* vol. 7 of Publications, Society of the Descendants of the Colonial Clergy (Baltimore, MD, 1976), 72.

33. South Carolina Historical Association, *The Proceedings of the South Carolina Historical Association* (Columbia, SC, 1935), 24.

34. Donnan, *History of the Slave Trade*, 3:154.

35. See Joseph T. Campbell, epilogue to *Middle Passages: African American Journeys to Africa, 1787–2005* (New York, 2007).

36. Ibid., 151, 158.

37. Ibid., 167.

38. Ibid., 168–170 (quotation on p 169).

39. Ibid., 170.

40. Godfrey quoted in Campbell, epilogue to *Middle Passages*.

41. Edward Ball, *Slaves in the Family* (New York, 1998), 190–191.

42. *South-Carolina Gazette*, 17 June 1756.

43. Laurens to Gidney Clarke, 30 June 1756, in Philip May Hamer, *Papers of Henry Laurens*, (Columbia, SC, 1970), 2:235–36.

44. Laurens to Samuel and William Vernon, Ibid., 238–239. On yaws see Campbell, *Middle Passages*, 475.

45. There is a discrepancy in the records. Laurens's accounts show that Ball purchased three boys and two girls for £460, paid in cash. Ball's own accounts record the purchase of four boys and two girls at a cost of £600. Perhaps one of the boys was purchased separately. See Donnan, *History of the Slave Trade*, 3:161 and Ball, *Slaves*, 193.

46. Morgan, *Slave Counterpoint*, 72.

47. American Reform Tract and Book Society, *An Abstract of the Evidence Delivered Before a Select Committee of the House of Commons, in the Years 1790 and 1791, on the Part of the Petitioners for the Abolition of the Slave Trade* (Cincinnati, OH, 1855), 27.

48. Morgan, *Slave Counterpoint*, 444–445.

49. Ibid., 448–449.

50. Ball, *Slaves*, 193–194.

51. Morgan, *Slave Counterpoint*, 447.

52. One study found that 44 percent of names in Gullah originated in the Gold Coast and the Bight of Benin, while significant syntactic features of the language can be traced to Twi, the language of the Akans, who were frequent victims of the Annamaboe slave trade. See Kwasi Konadu, *The Akan Diaspora in the Americas* (Oxford, 2010), 182–186.

53. John Chester Miller, *The Wolf by the Ears: Thomas Jefferson and Slavery* (New York, 1977), 8–9, 17, 22; Dumas Malone, *Jefferson the Virginian* (Boston, 1948), 264; Christa Dierksheide, "'The great improvement and civilization of that race': Jefferson and the 'Amelioration' of Slavery, ca. 1770—1826," *Early American Studies* 6 (Spring 2008), 177; Winthrop Jordan, *White Over Black: American Attitudes Toward the Negro, 1550–1812* (Chapel Hill, 1968), 519–521; Hugh Thomas, *The Slave Trade: The Story of the Atlantic Slave Trade, 1440–1770* (New York, 1997), 329, 481 (quotations), 482; Paul Finkelman, "Regulating the African Slave Trade," *Civil War History* 54 (2008): 383; Jay Coughtry, *The Notorious Triangle: Rhode Island and the African Slave Trade, 1700–1807* (Philadelphia, 1981), 114–115.

54. Thomas, *Slave Trade,* 501–502, 544; Jordan, *White Over Black,* 318; Paul Finkelman, *An Imperfect Union: Slavery, Federalism and Comity* (Union, NJ, 1981), 41–45;
James McMillin, *The Final Victims: Foreign Slave Trade to North America, 1783–
1810* (Columbia, SC, 2004), 72–86; James A. Rawley, *The Transatlantic Slave
Trade: A History* (Lincoln, NE, and London, 2005), 307 (quotation).

55. William Edward Burghardt Du Bois, *The Suppression of the African Slave-trade to
the United States of America, 1638–1870* (New York, 1904), 85–87, 91–93; McMillin,
Final Victims, 86–91; Thomas, *Slave Trade,* 545–546.

56. Du Bois, *Suppression,* 80–81 (quotation, p. 81); Thomas, *Slave Trade,* 544; Rawley,
Transatlantic Slave Trade, 307–309.

57. Louis Arthur Norton, *Captains Contentious: The Dysfunctional Sons of the Brine*
(Columbia, SC, 2009), 64–86.

58. Mill to AC, 8–10 May 1784, PRO T70/33. Saltonstall's efforts to arouse Africans
against the British through the rhetoric of the American Revolution was part of an
ongoing ideological battle between the two rivals. See Matthew Mason, "The Battle
of the Slaveholding Liberators: Great Britain, the United States, and Slavery in the
Early Nineteenth-Century," *William and Mary Quarterly,* 3rd ser., LIX (July 2001):
665–696.

59. Mill to AC, 8–10 May 1784, PRO T70/33.

60. Mill to AC, 11 September 1784, PRO T70/33.

61. The Trans-Atlantic Slave Trade Database, Voyage 25502.

62. Mill to AC, 20 November 1788, PRO T70/33.

63. John Joseph Crooks, *Records Relating to the Gold Coast Settlements from 1750 to
1874* (1923; London, 1973), 99–103.

6. A World in Motion

1. J. H. Elliott, "Afterword, Atlantic History: a Circumnavigation," in *The British Atlantic World, 1500–1800,* eds. David Armitage and Michael J. Braddick (New York,
2002), 239. On Africans in the Atlantic community, see Robin Law and Kristan
Mann, "West Africa and the Atlantic Community: The Case of the Slave Coast,"
William and Mary Quarterly, 3rd ser., 56 (1999): 307–334.

2. Historians have examined Africans who moved around the Atlantic World and back
to Africa from the Slave Coast and the connections that grew up between the Slave
Coast and Brazil. See Law and Mann, "West Africa," 307–334; Robin Law, "Ethnic-
ity and the Slave Trade: 'Lucumi' and 'Nago' as Ethmonyms in West Africa," *His-
tory of Africa* 24 (1997): 205–219; J. Lorand Matory, "The English Professors of Brazil:
On the Diasporic Roots of the Yoruba Nation," *Comparative Studies in Society and
History* 41 (1999): 72–103; J. Lorand Matory, *Black Atlantic Religion: Tradition,
Transnationalism, and Matriarchy in the Afro-Brazilian Candomble* (Princeton,
NJ, 2005), 1–72, 267–300; David Northrup, *Africa's Discovery of Europe, 1450–1850*
(Oxford, 2009), 1–23.

3. Linda Heywood in her study of Kongo made the point that "ultimately every Kongo
was a potential slave." Linda Heywood, "Slavery and Its Transformation in the
Kingdom of Kongo, 1491–1800," *Journal of African History* 50 (2009): 22.

4. For Hughes see Voyages 92491 and 92518, Voyages Database, the Trans-Atlantic Slave Trade Database. http://www.slavevoyages.org (accessed November 30, 2012). AC to Captain Eagles, 11 November 1778, Public Records Office (PRO), National Archives, Kew, United Kingdom, T70/69; AC to Captain Hughes, 27 August 1777, PRO T70/69; Amissa & Benjamin Francis Hughes, 20 February 1779, Hilary Term, 19 Geo. 3rd, KB 18/29.

5. AC to Captain Thompson (?) of HMS *Lord George Germaine,* 5 March 1779, PRO T70/69.

6. RAC to Governor and Council, Cape Coast Castle, 11 March 1779, PRO T70/69.

7. AC to Governor and Council, Cape Coast Castle, 30 December 1778, PRO T70/69; AC to Guion, Forbes and Co., 3 March 1778, PRO T70/69; AC to Joseph Roberts Wood, 13 March 1779, PRO T70/69; AC to Governor and Council, Cape Coast Castle, 11 March 1779, PRO T70/69; Miles to AC, 26 July 1779, PRO T70/31; *Gentleman's Magazine* (March 1779); London *Chronicle* (March 1779); James Oldham, "New Light on Mansfield and Slavery," *Journal of British Studies* 27 (January 1988): 65; Emma Christopher, *Slave Ship Sailors and Their Captive Cargoes, 1730–1807* (Cambridge, 2006), 61.

8. Archibald Dalziel and Council to AC, 27 July 1792, PRO T70/33 (quotations); AC to Admiral Edmund Dod, 8 April 1797, PRO T70/71; Race to Evan Nepean, 15 April 1797, PRO T70/71; Christopher, *Slave Ship Sailors,* 66–68. On the *Lovely Lass* see Voyage 18149, on the *Mars,* Voyage 82483, and on the *Jane,* Voyage 81993 and 81994, the Trans-Atlantic Slave Trade Database.

9. Nelson had been trading on the Gold Coast regularly since 1773. See Voyages 91169, 91170, 91171, 91172, 92456, 82846, 82847; on Kendall's 1780 voyage see Voyage 82767, the Trans-Atlantic Slave Trade Database. The Annamaboe accounts show a payment to an Annamaboe linguister for "going to get Capt. Kendall's Boat and People released they having been panyared on account of Capt Nelson's not paying a man his wages to and from England." October–November 1780, Annamaboe Day Books, PRO T70/990. In 1720 "Jaggee a black Sailor took up by Annamaboes & recovered for about £12 expence, he has £25 wages due to him." Phipps to RAC, 6 April 1720, PRO T70/4. Captain Webster stopped at Annamaboe in 1775 "for Black Sailors." Mill to Miles, 16 May 1774, PRO T70/1533. Probably John Webster, see Voyage 91985, the Trans-Atlantic Slave Trade Database.

10. Jeffrey Bolster, *Black Jacks: African American Seamen in the Age of Sail* (Cambridge, MA, 1998), 70; Julius S. Scott III, "The Common Wind: Currents of Afro-American Communication in the Era of the Haitian Revolution," (unpublished PhD diss., Duke University, 1986), 64–65.

11. RAC to Robert Plunkett and Abraham Knox, 16 May 1721 (first quotation) PRO T70/60; RAC to Alexander Archibald, 27 November 1723, PRO T70/60; Phipps, Dodson and Boyd to RAC, 28 June 1721 (second quotation), PRO T70/7. In September 1721 officials at Cape Coast Castle sent "three Boy Slaves to be bred up Sailors . . . names Peter, Paul & Andrew." Their English names could indicate that they were, in fact, mulattoes. Phipps, Dodson and Boyd to RAC, 30 September 1721, PRO T70/7.

12. John Clark to RAC, 30 June 1707, PRO T70/5; Phipps, Dodson and Boyd to RAC, 2 November 1720, 24 June 1721, PRO T70/7.

13. John Clark to RAC, 3 May 1712, PRO T70/5.

14. John Clark to RAC, 24 October 1709, PRO T70/5.

15. Dalby Thomas to RAC, 20 & 21 September, 23 & 27 November 1705 (quotation), PRO T70/5. Northrup, *Africa's Discovery*, 67–68, 120.

16. Thomas Thompson, *An Account of Two Missionary Voyages By the Appointment of the Society for the Propagation of the Gospel in Foreign Parts* (London, 1758), 48.

17. Ibid., 48–49 (quotations), 58–59.

18. Robert Olwell, *Masters, Slaves and Subjects: The Culture of Power in the South Carolina Lowcountry, 1740–1790* (Ithaca, NY, and London, 1998), 125.

19. For the records of Our Lady and St. Nicholas see http://www.lan-opc.org.uk/Liver pool/Liverpool-Central/stnicholas/baptisms.html (accessed on August 20, 2012). For the records of St. James see http://freepages.genealogy.rootsweb.ancestry.com /~hibernia/baptisms/black_baptisms.html (accessed on August 20, 2012). For a copy of Cugoano's and Deal's baptisms see http://www.culture24.org.uk/places %20to%20go/london/art47250 (accessed on November 10, 2012).

20. John Ferguson, *Memoir of the Life and Character of Rev. Samuel Hopkins, D.D.: Formerly Pastor of the First Congregational Church in Newport, Rhode Island* (Boston, 1830), 175–178; Samuel Hopkins to Philip Quaque, 10 December 1773 in Vincent Caretta and Ty M. Reese, eds., *The Life and Letters of Philip Quaque: The First African Anglican Missionary* (Athens, GA, and London, 2010), 114–115. Probably David Lindsay, captain of the *Sanderson*, who purchased slaves in Annamaboe in 1753. See Voyage 36159, the Trans-Atlantic Slave Trade Database.

21. Ferguson, *Memoir*, 182.

22. Ferguson, *Memoir*, 183–184 (quotations). In 1773 Quaque baptized an African man at Cape Coast Castle who had been kidnapped and sold to Rhode Island. He was owned by a Quaker ship captain named Samuel Collins, and after over forty years in America, he returned to Cape Coast. Caretta and Reese, *Life and Letters*, 110–120. Collins, identified as a Quaker in his obituary, died in Newport in 1772 at age 86. *The Providence Gazette and Country Journal* (7 March 1772).

23. Affidoe's title of captain probably refers to his position in one of the Annamaboe military organizations called bendefoes, a local militia. Robin Law, ed., *The English in West Africa, 1685–1688: The Local Correspondence of the Royal African Company of England, 1681–1699*, pt. 2 (Oxford, 2001), 178 (first quotation), 182 (second quotation), 58; Thompson noted that while the "language of the Coast is very various, each nation having that which is peculiarly its own . . . *Fantee* is the most extensive . . . and is occasionally spoken, as far as betwixt *Cape Appollonia* to the River *Volta*, that is, about a hundred Leagues." Thompson, *An Account*, 69–73.

24. Lathan A. Windley, comp., *Runaway Slave Advertisements: A Documentary History from the 1730s to 1790, vol. 2, Maryland* (Westport, CT, 1983), 39.

25. Examination of Mr. Cleveland, 1792, PRO T70/161.

26. A. G. Hopkins, *An Economic History of West Africa* (New York, 1973), 109.

27. Sheila Lambert, ed., *House of Commons Sessional Papers of the Eighteenth Century* (Wilmington, DE, 1975), vol. 71, 543. Paul Lovejoy and David Richardson, "Trust, Pawnship and Atlantic History: The Institutional Foundations of the Old Calabar Slave Trade," *American Historical Review* 104 (1999): 342–344. In 1720, an English captain returned a boy to the Gold Coast "who was sent over to England in order to

make him the more serviceable to the Interlopers." James Phipps to RAC, 25 January 1720, PRO T70/4. Dalby Thomas at Cape Coast Castle wrote in 1710 that "John Williams the Mulatto who comes from England by Captain Bates is a very useful person and it will be for the Compys Interest that he return to Cape Coast." Thomas to RAC, PRO T70/5. John Clark to RAC, 24 October 1711, PRO T70/5.

28. Brew's sons arrived in London in 1768. See Westgate to Brew, 28 October 1768, PRO T70/162. Cape Coast Castle Council Minutes, 12 June 1792, PRO T70/153 (quotation); "List of the Principal Kings, Caboceers and others in the Pay of the Committee, as they stood 1st Dec. 1776," PRO T70/1534.

29. Snelgrave quoted in Elizabeth Donnan, *Documents Illustrative of the History of the Slave Trade to America: Vol. II; The Eighteenth Century* (Washington, DC, 1931), 355 (quotation), 593–594; Christopher, *Slave Ship Sailors*, 16, 57, 143, 145–147. Hugh Thomas, *The Slave Trade: The Story of the Atlantic Slave Trade: 1440–1870* (New York, 1999), 404; Bolster, *Black Jacks*, 52.

30. Colier to RAC, 30 April, 1 May, 25 May 1719; PRO T70/8. Barry Ayrest delivered over 200 slaves to Barbados on the *Dorothy* in 1717. Voyage 76498, the Trans-Atlantic Slave Trade Database. Bergeson made many voyages from Africa to Barbados in this period. See Voyages 20418, 20452, 20477, 20531, 25131, the Trans-Atlantic Slave Trade Database.

31. Danby Pickering, *The Statutes at Large from the 23d to the 26th Year of George II,* vol. XX (Cambridge, 1765), 120.

32. Samuel Poirier to Tobias Lesle, 26 November 1757, PRO T70/29. Poirier was the secretary to the Royal African Committee.

33. See for examples Heywood, "Slavery and Its Transformation," *Journal of African History* 50 (2009): 6.

34. Thompson, *An Account*, 23 (first quotation), 24 (second quotation). For Williams see Voyage 37050, the Trans-Atlantic Slave Trade Database.

35. Melville to AC, 11 June 1752, PRO T70/29.

36. James Phipps and Council to RAC, 25 January 1720, PRO T70/4.

37. For Ellis see Voyage 17365, the Trans-Atlantic Slave Trade Database. Melville to AC, 8 April 1755, PRO T70/30.

38. Melville to AC, 28 April 1756, PRO T70/30.

39. Poirier to John Cleveland, 15 August 1755, PRO T70/29.

40. Poirier to Melville, 15 September 1755, PRO T70/29.

41. On the Gold Coast slave trade see Rebecca Shumway, *The Fante and the Transatlantic Slave Trade* (Rochester, NY, 2011); John Vogt, *Portuguese Rule on the Gold Coast, 1469–1682* (Athens, GA, 1979); Ray A. Kea, *Settlements, Trade, and Polities in the Seventeenth Century Gold Coast* (Baltimore, MD 1982); Stephen D. Behrendt, "'The Journal of an African Slaver,' 1789–1792, and the Gold Coast Slave Trade of William Collow," *History in Africa* 22 (1995): 61–71; William St. Clair, *The Door of No Return: The History of Cape Coast Castle and the Atlantic Slave Trade* (New York, 2006); Law, *English in West Africa*, pt. 2.

42. Randy J. Sparks, "Gold Coast Merchant Families, Pawning, and the Eighteenth-Century English Slave Trade," *William and Mary Quarterly,* 3rd ser., 70 (April 2013) 317–340.

43. John Apperley to Melville, 21 September 1755, PRO T70/30.

44. The English often held the sons of local kings as hostages to insure the trade. On the Gold Coast, "we always looked upon it as a Surety for Traders to have a King's Son by way of Hostage." Joseph Debat to AC 26 June 1762, PRO T70/30. Africans sometimes held Englishmen as hostages as well. See Randall Logan to Joseph Blaney, 2 March 1714/1715; Blaney to Martin Harderett, 27 February 1715, Robert Mason to The Chiefs at Cape Coast Castle, 13 September 1715, PRO T70/3. When CMTA agent Joseph Debat at James Fort retained as a "slave a young Black Man named Bram, Son of the King of Cassika," Captain Joseph Stoddart, who planned to trade there, had "Apprehensions of Danger from the Said King & his People." Debat to AC, 11 September 1761, PRO T70/29. The AC considered the matter, but determined that holding Bram "as a Hostage . . . has been so far from a Prejudice to the Trade to Cassika, that it has rather been an advantage thereto." AC to Debat, 10 November 1763, PRO T70/29.

45. Melville to AC, 11 March 1753, PRO T70/30.

46. Poirier to George Cockburn, 8 August 1754; 26 September 1754; Benjamin Read to Cockburn, 16 October 1754, Poirier to John Cleveland, 23 October 1754; PRO T70/29.

47. John Joseph Crooks, *Records Relating to the Gold Coast Settlements from 1750 to 1874* (1923; London, 1973), 29.

48. Poirier to Melville, 31 October 1754, PRO T70/29; Crooks, *Records Relating to the Gold Coast,* 29.

49. Poirier to Vaughan, 2 November 1754, PRO T70/29; Crooks, *Records Relating to the Gold Coast,* 30.

50. Poirier to George Cockburn, 11 January 1755; Poirier to John Cleveland, 2 June 1755; Poirier to Samuel Scott, 17 July 1755; PRO T70/29.

51. Poirier to Samuel Scott, 17 July 1755, PRO T70/29.

52. Poirier to Melville, 28 June 1755, PRO T70/29.

53. Poirier to Joseph Debat, 31 July 1755; 30 August 1755; PRO T70/29.

54. Crooks, *Records Relating to the Gold Coast,* 30.

55. Poirier to Scott, 15 September 1755, PRO T70/29.

56. Poirier to Melville, 17 December 1755, PRO T70/29.

57. Bell to AC, 20 March 1756, PRO T70/30.

58. Bell to AC, 3 April 1756, PRO T70/30.

59. Poirier to Bell, 4 November 1756, PRO T70/29.

60. John Mathews, *A Voyage to the River Sierra Leone* (London, 1788), 155–156; Paul E. Lovejoy and David Richardson, "The Business of Slaving: Pawnship in Western Africa, c. 1600–1810," *Journal of African History* 42 (2001): 12.

61. Gilbert Petrie to AC, 10 March 1769, PRO T70/68.

62. F. William Torrington, ed., *House of Lords Sessional Papers, 1789–1799* (Dobbs Ferry, NY, 1974), 3:112; Lovejoy and Richardson, "Business of Slaving," 78.

63. Houghton to Miles, March 1778, PRO T70/1536. Houghton made many voyages to Africa in the 1770s and 1780s. Voyages 92438, 91928, 91926, 91647, 91646, 91599, 91598, 83722, 83721, the Trans-Atlantic Slave Trade Database.

64. Lambert, ed., *House of Commons Sessional Papers,* 71:15; Lovejoy and Richardson, "Business of Slaving," 83–84.

65. John Grant to William Mutter, 30 October 1761, PRO T70/30.
66. Voyage 17675, the Trans-Atlantic Slave Trade Database; Petrie to AC, 10 March 1769, PRO T70/68. RAC officials reported in 1711 that "two Negro sailors were taken aboard the French ship Casar which Cpatn Legg would not part with." Grosevnor to Phipps, 16 May 1711, PRO T70/5. For another example of canoemen kidnapped from Annamaboe see William Mutter to AC 25 April 1765, PRO T70/68. On Gold Coast canoemen see Bolster, *Black Jacks,* 54–56.
67. Lambert, *House of Commons Sessional Papers,* vol. 71, pt. 2, 44.
68. Miles and Council to AC, 19 August 1786, PRO T70/33.
69. William Williams to General Deane, 4 April 1719, PRO T70/6.
70. Bernard Martin and Mark Spurrell, eds., *The Journal of a Slave Trader: John Newton, 1750–1754* (London, 1962), 39, 42.
71. Thomas Melville to AC, 11 July 1751, PRO T70/29 (first and second quotations); "Captain Derbyshires Palaver, CCC Sunday 23 June 1753 according to the Fanteen Relation," PRO T70/68 (third and fourth quotations). For the details of this voyage, see Voyage 90148, the Trans-Atlantic Slave Trade Database. He made several voyages between 1741 and 1754. See Voyages 90147, 90476, 94754, 94783, and 94817, the Trans-Atlantic Slave Trade Database.
72. Thomas Melville to AC, 11 July 1751, PRO T70/29 (quotations); Thomas Malvern to Derbyshire, 25 June 1757; John Roberts to ?, 7 July 1753, PRO T70/68.
73. Thomas Melville to AC, 11 July 1751, PRO T70/29. In 1789, the people of Annamaboe captured and beat the supercargo of a French ship who threatened to take off two of their people. Morris and Council to AC, 31 March 1789, PRO T70/33. In 1804, the people of Chamah seized Thomas Perry, the chief of Succandee Fort, carried him "into the bush," and severely beat him after Charles Graves sold some Chamah people off the coast. John Fountain and Council to AC, 31 December 1804, PRO T70/34.
74. On Reffe see Voyage 37248, on Turnbull see Voyage 76998, on Peter Bostock's voyage see Voyage 77622, the Trans-Atlantic Slave Trade Database. James Skinner to AC, 9 May 1754, PRO T70/30. Reffe is misidentified in the documents and in the database; see *South-Carolina Gazette,* 16–21 October 1755. For other examples of English traders being cut off by Africans see Thomas Burnett to RAC, 3 January 1716, Anthony Rodgers to RAC, 20 June 1732, PRO T70/6; William Fields and Council to AC, 30 April 1795, PRO T70/33. See Joan M. Fayer, "African Interpreters in the Atlantic Slave Trade," *Anthropological Linguistics* 45 (Fall 2003): 281–295.
75. Possibly James Birchall. See Voyages 24945, 77604, the Trans-Atlantic Slave Trade Database; Captain Ellery of Boston. See Voyage 25022, the Trans-Atlantic Slave Trade Database; Robert Lowrie to AC, 5 June 1754, PRO T70/30. For a similar dispute between Captain William Atkinson after he kidnapped a caboceer from St. Andrews see RAC to John Brathwaite, 9 July 1730. For a case between the king of Barra and an English trader see David Mill to AC, 6 April 1751, PRO T70/68, and for a case between Prince Davie of Badagry and Captain Joshua Johnson of the *Patty* see AC to Governor and Council, Cape Coast Castle, 4 December 1776, 21 December 1776, 25 December 1776, 2 January 1777, 6 February 1777, PRO T70/69; Voyage 25155 (Atkinson), Voyage 92599 (Johnson), the Trans-Atlantic Slave Trade

Database. The king of Sesto captured an English ship and killed crewmen after Captain Joseph Yowart of the *Hardman* took "one of the Kings Sons away with him." "Translation of Captain Wickman's Certificate of his son's death being killed at River Sesto on acct of Captn Yowart of the Hardman," May 1750, PRO T70/68. See Voyage 90510, the Trans-Atlantic Slave Trade Database.

76. Probably Isaac Barber's 1709 voyage. Voyage 24051, the Trans-Atlantic Slave Trade Database. John Phipps to RAC, 8 March 1710, PRO T70/5.

77. Phipps, Dodson and Boyd to RAC, 2 July 1722, PRO T70/7.

78. Plunkett to William Johnson, 16 September 1717, PRO T70/6; Plunkett to RAC, 16 June, 1718, PRO T70/6. Interlopers were slave traders who smuggled slaves outside the RAC's monopoly. They often cheated Africans, kidnapped free people, and endangered the trade, leaving the company to deal with the consequences. See George E. Brooks, *Eurafricans in Western Africa: Commerce, Social Status, Gender and Religious Observance from the Sixteenth to the Eighteenth Century* (Athens, OH, 2003), 105, 145, 174.

79. Charles Russell to RAC, 7 April 1710, PRO T70/9. The men reached Bristol, where Captain John Yeamens sent them to the Africa House in London (headquarters of the RAC), found "them victuals & lodging," and "gave them 2 each for their pocket." John Yeamans to RAC, 1 May, 3 June, 10 June 1710, PRO T70/9.

80. "Part of Letter from Mr. J. Hippisley, dated at Cape Coast Castle, relative to a young Black, that was a servant in London about two Years ago, and proved to be the son of the Prince of Annamaboe," *The British Magazine or Monthly Repository for Gentlemen and Ladies,* October 1761, 528. Hippisley may be referring to Corrantee's son Bassi, though Bassi went to France, not England, and his case occurred decades before Hippisley's arrival on the coast.

81. John Thornton, "African Political Ethics and the Slave Trade," in *Abolitionism and Imperialism in Britain, Africa, and the Atlantic,* ed. Derek R. Peterson (Athens, OH, 2010), 38–62 (quotation on p. 39).

7. Things Fall Apart

1. Westgate to Miles, 13 September 1778, Public Records Office (PRO), National Archives, Kew, United Kingdom, T70/1536.

2. Smith to Westgate, 11 September 1778, PRO T70/1536.

3. Westgate to Smith, 12 September 1778, PRO T70/1536.

4. Smith to Westgate, 12 September 1778; Smith to Westgate, 12 and 13 September 1778); Westgate to Smith, 13 September 1778 (quotations); PRO T70/1536.

5. Miles to Smith, 15 September 1778, PRO T70/1536.

6. Westgate to Miles, 19 September 1778, PRO T70/1536.

7. Miles to Westgate, 5, 9, 14 November 1778; Westgate to Miles, 6, 8, 10, 15 November 1778; Smith to Westgate, 6 November 1778; Smith to Miles, 12 November 1778; PRO T70/1536.

8. Thomas Miles to Charles Bell, 10 January 1779, PRO T70/1483.

9. Thomas Miles to AC, 22 January 1780 (quotation); Governor and Council to AC, 26 October 1780, PRO T70/32. Estimates from the Trans-Atlantic Slave Trade Database. http://www.slavevoyages.org (accessed January 13, 2013).

10. Cape Coast Castle Council Minutes, 11 May 1791, PRO T70/153.

11. Ibid.

12. Cape Coast Castle Council Minutes, 11 May 1791, PRO T70/153; Examinations of George Cleveland, Peter W. Brancker, Jonothan Hibblethwaite, John Mark Cleland, 1791, PRO T70/161; Examination of Captain Fraser, 28 December 1791, PRO T70/160.

13. Examination of Thomas Owens, 28 December 1791, PRO T70/160. On the *Mercury* see Voyage 82695, the Trans-Atlantic Slave Trade Database.

14. Examinations of Captain Fraser and Thomas Owens, 28 December 1791, PRO T70/160.

15. Examinations of Captain Fraser and Thomas Owens, 28 December 1791, PRO T70/160; Cape Coast Council Minutes, 5 June 1793; 12 September 1795, PRO T70/153; AC to Robert Collins, 5 November 1794, 1 June 1796, PRO T70/71; Mrs. R. Lee, *Stories of Strange Lands* (London, 1895), 29, 30.

16. Cape Coast Castle Minute Books, 11 May 1791, PRO T70/153.

17. Annamaboe Day Books, September–October 1769, PRO T70/989.

18. Cape Coast Castle Minute Books, 11 May 1791, PRO T70/153.

19. Ibid.; Governor and Council, Cape Coast Castle to AC, 8 October 1780, PRO T70/32 (first quotation); Cape Coast Castle Council Minutes, 11 May 1791, 15 August 1795, PRO T70/153 (third and fourth quotations); Payment to Brew recorded in Cape Coast Castle Day Books, 2 August 1795; Henry Meredith, *An Account of the Gold Coast of Africa with a Brief History of the African Company* (London, 1812), 131. The Fante would not allow gunpowder to be traded to the Asante and sent parties of armed men to guard the paths to prevent it. Gilbert Petrie to AC, 9 October 1767, PRO T70/31.

20. David Mill to AC, 30 December 1775, PRO T70/32 (first and second quotations); Mutter to AC, 25 October 1765, PRO T70/31; Cape Coast Council Resolution, 11 August 1772, PRO T70/152, (third and fourth quotations).

21. Meredith, *Account of the Gold Coast,* 136–138 (quotation on p. 136).

22. Ibid., 138–139, (first quotation on p. 138).

23. Ibid., 140–141, (first quotation on p. 141).

24. Ibid., 143 (first and second quotations), 144 (third quotation), 145.

25. Ibid., 144–152 (first quotation on p. 151, second quotation on p. 152).

26. Ibid., 155–158 (first quotation on p. 158, second on p. 159); W. E. F. Ward, *A History of the Gold Coast* (London, 1948), 147–149. For a critical view of Torrane's activities see Joseph Dupuis, *Journal of a Residence in Ashantee* (London, 1824), 250–264.

27. Meredith, *Account of the Gold Coast,* 161 (first quotation); Ward, *History of the Gold Coast,* 148–149 (second quotation on p. 149). Torrane also sold forty members of the Assin nation who were captured along with Kwadwo Tsibu. John Joseph Crooks, *Records Relating to the Gold Coast Settlements from 1750 to 1874* (1923; London, 1973), 107; Lee, *Stories of Strange Lands,* 66.

28. Ward, *History of Gold Coast,* 150–158; Ivor Wilks, *Asante in the Nineteenth Century: The Structure and Evolution of a Political Order* (Cambridge, 1975), 144–51; William Hutchinson to J. H. Smith, 26 May 1817, PRO T70/41.

29. Meredith, *Account of the Gold Coast,* ii (first quotation); Dupuis, *Journal of a Residence in Ashantee,* 2–35.

30. Dupuis, *Journal of a Residence in Ashantee,* 162–163.

31. John Hope Smith and Council to AC, 5 March 1817, PRO T70/36.

32. Lee, *Stories of Strange Lands,* 190 (first quotation); William Hutchinson to John Hope Smith, 11 October 1817, PRO T70/41 (second quotation).

33. For an overview of the slave trade in this era see Hugh Thomas, *The Slave Trade: The Story of the Atlantic Slave Trade, 1440–1870* (New York, 1997), 561–590.

34. William Hutchinson to John Hope Smith, 11 October 1817, PRO T70/41 (first and second quotations); Fey Footoo Quamina to John Hope Smith, 25 October 1817, PRO T70/41 (third quotation).

35. Fey Footoo Quamina to John Hope Smith, 25 October 1817, PRO T70/41.

36. Smith to Hutchinson, 21 November 1817, PRO T70/41.

37. Ibid. Messengers carried messenger sticks, canes engraved with the name or insignia of the sender to indicate that the messenger was on official business or acting with a person's authority. One resident of the coast observed that a cane served as a badge of office for messengers, and the person carrying a cane was considered sacred, so much so that even slave stealers avoided taking them. To seize such a person was considered justification for war. See Lee, *Stories of Strange Lands,* 73.

38. Hutchinson to Smith, 17 November 1817 (first quotation), Hutchinson to Smith, 23 November 1817 (second quotation), 20 December 1817, PRO T70/36.

39. Smith and Council to AC, 21 February 1818, PRO T70/36.

40. For details of the history leading up to the Annamaboe event see Carl Christian Reindorf, *History of the Gold Coast and Asante, based on traditions and historical facts: comprising a period of more than three centuries from about 1500 to 1860* (Basel, Switzerland, 1895), chap. 1–14. Margaret Priestley, *West African Trade and Coast Society: A Family Study* (London, 1969), 138–139; Dupuis, *Journal of a Residence in Ashantee,* 201–216.

41. Lee, *Stories of Strange Lands,* 191 (first and second quotations); Maccarthy to Earl Bathurst, 7 April 1823, (third quotation), Maccarthy to Bathurst, 4 August 1823 (second quotation); PRO CO 267/58; Ward, *History of the Gold Coast,* 168–169.

42. H. I. Ricketts to Bathurst, 7 April 1823, Maccarthy to Bathurst, 17 May 1823 (quotations), PRO CO 267/58; H. I. Ricketts, *Narrative of the Ashantee War with a View of the Present State of the Colony of Sierra Leone* (London, 1833), 19–21, Priestley, *West African Trade,* 139–141; "Proceedings relative to Sam Brew taken at Cape Coast Castle," PRO CO 267/58; Reindorf, *History of the Gold Coast and Asante,* 181.

43. Maccarthy to Bathurst, 17 May 1823, PRO CO 267/58 (first and fourth quotations); Testimony of William Mitchison (second quotation), Jonas Heath, John Dunsmore, Patrick Hayes, John Hall, and Joseph Steret (third quotation), 24 May 1823, PRO CO 267/58; Chief Justice Record, 4 August 1823, PRO CO 267/58; Priestley, *West African Trade,* 141.

44. Brew's son Samuel Collins Brew (c. 1810–1881) was a prominent Gold Coast trader in legal African goods who also relied heavily on connections with the Asante. His son, James Hutton Brew (1844–1915) was one of West Africa's earliest nationalists and journalists. After 1915 he lived in Britain and lobbied against British imperial-

ism in Africa. J. E. Casely Hayford, founder of the National Congress of British West Africa, was a Brew descendant on his mother's side. See Priestley, *West African Trade,* pt. 3.

45. Meredith, *Account of the Gold Coast,* 131.

Acknowledgments

I presented aspects of this work at the "Centering Families in Atlantic Worlds, 1500–1800" conference, cosponsored by the Omohundro Institute of Early American History and Culture and the Institute for Historical Studies, University of Texas at Austin, and I would like to thank the conference organizers and the conference participants for their useful input. I also presented portions of the work at the American Historical Association, and I profited from remarks from the commenters and the audiences. I would also like to thank Ira Berlin, Evelyn Thomas Nolen, Pernile Ibsen, David Northrup, Sylvia Frey, E. Stanly Godbold, Thomas Adams, and Elizabeth McMahon for their helpful suggestions and comments, and Rosemary Brana-Shute, Gordon Innes, and Andrew Brana for research assistance and for their hospitality during my research stays in Kew. Research for this project was supported by the Tulane University Department of History, by Tulane University's Research Enhancement Fund, and by a Monroe Fellowship from Tulane's New Orleans Center for the Gulf South.

Index